BLeSSiNGs of the DaiLY

BLeSSiNGs of the DaiLY

A Monastic Book of Days

Brother Victor-Antoine
d'Avila-Latourrette

Liguori/Triumph
LIGUORI, MISSOURI

Imprimi Potest:
Richard Thibodeau, C.Ss.R.
Provincial, Denver Province
The Redemptorists

Published by Liguori/Triumph
An imprint of Liguori Publications
Liguori, Missouri
www.liguori.org
www.catholicbooksonline.com

Compilation copyright 2002 by Brother Victor-Antoine d'Avila-Latourrette

Excerpts used for February 2, February 10, and April 2 adapted from *The Monastic Year* by Brother Victor-Antoine d'Avila-Latourrette and reprinted by permission of Taylor Publishing.

Library of Congress Catalog Card Number: 2002108763

Printed in the United States of America
06 05 04 03 02   5 4 3 2 1
First edition

*Holy Mary,
our most gracious Theotokos,
Our Lady of the Resurrection,
Mater et Regina Monachorum
Pray for us,
that we may be worthy
of the promises of Christ.*

Contents

January

February

March

April

May

June

July

August

November

Introduction

*The light of Christ is an endless day
that knows no night.*

SAINT MAXIMUS OF TURIN

Since writing several of my monastic-themed cookbooks (*Twelve Months of Monastery Soups, From a Monastery Kitchen,* and *In Celebration of the Seasons*), I have occasionally received requests and suggestions from various readers to amplify some of the monastic themes expressed in these books. These requests gave birth to the idea of putting into writing the daily moments of monastic living, as experienced here at Our Lady of the Resurrection. I do not find it easy to write in a purely conceptual way, and this book is not intended to be read as a theoretical work. Rather, I attempt to describe simple, lived experiences in concrete language.

The content of this book follows closely the secular and liturgical calendar of the years 2000 through 2001, when these short essays were composed on the days indicated. It all started with the first day of Advent, 1999, and then the rest followed. There were occasional month-long lapses which made it necessary to wait until 2001 to relive these months, so as to write from *within* them rather than *about them.*

Readers may adapt the meditations in this book to the changing dates of various liturgical observances by use of the Table of Contents—for example, Advent reflections begin in this book on page 1 with December and Lenten reflections on page 109.

The book concentrates on the mystery of the ordinary daily, as shaped by the seasonal rhythms of both Mother Nature and Mother Church. These two sources deeply influence the day-by-day unfolding of the monk's life as he continues his inner monastic journey towards God, his only Absolute. The pages in this book are plain, modest, and, hopefully, humble. What a travesty and odious thing it would be for a monk to try and exalt himself, instead of glorifying God, to Whom alone all praise belongs. If there is any meaning in the monk's life, it consists in the daily decreasing of his self, so that Christ may increase, grow, and dwell fully in him. Then, and then only, can the monk speak the words of Saint Paul: "I live, but no longer I, for Christ lives in me."

The message of this book is to convey to all of good will the joys of finding God in the simple and ordinary of daily life. To truly seek God as Saint Benedict counsels is to walk with him through every step, every occasion, and every event each individual day brings us.

This book has found a good home with Liguori/Triumph, who has successfully published some of my previous books. I am particularly happy for this, for I think that the Lord, in his mysterious Providence, had planned the book all along for Liguori. I am grateful to my editor Judy Bauer and to Father Harry Grile, C.Ss.R., for choosing and encouraging the publication of the book. It is always a joy to collaborate with Judy, for she is a finely attuned editor, both to the work and to the author. I am also grateful to friends in the monastic family in France, whose support and prayers during the writing meant a great deal to me. Finally, and not least, my warmest gratitude to Michael Centore, who closely collaborated with the shaping of most of the manuscript, and who has participated in and experienced the monastic daily life here during these past two years. His contribution to the book is unique and thus, to me, precious.

May through these simple pages the light of Christ continue to shine and to illuminate our darkness, filling us with hope and fortitude as we continue to walk in the steps of the Gospel.

Br. Victor-Antoine d'Avila-Latourrette
1 May 2002
Feast of Saint Joseph the Worker

BLeSSiNGs of the DaiLY

DECEMBER

Charles de Foucauld

Jesus, our only model.

PERE CHARLES DE FOUCAULD

Today, all around the world, the spiritual family of Charles de Foucauld holds a quiet vigil of silence and prayer in remembrance of the anniversary of his martyrdom in the Sahara Desert on December 1, 1916.

Charles de Foucauld's only desire, after undergoing what was a famous conversion, was to imitate the life of Jesus whom he called the "unique and only model." He explains how he sought to bear witness: "The servant is not greater than his Master; he becomes perfect only if he resembles his Master." It is only in the context of his great desire to imitate Jesus that his life and death can be understood.

One night, as dark shadows enveloped his desert hermitage, a group of robbers arrived with evil plans in mind. They destroyed the religious objects in the chapel, tied Father Charles's hands behind his back, and, after much insult and cruelty, demanded that he accept the Koran and reject his Christian faith. Father Charles, kneeling on the sands of the desert, realized that his hour had come. Following the example of Jesus, he prayed: "Father, forgive them, for they do not know what they do." Then, one of the bandits beheaded him with an axe. His death occurred on a First Friday of the month, consecrated to the Sacred Heart, to whom Charles de Foucauld was entirely devoted.

During these initial days of Advent, how rightfully appropriate it is to reflect on Charles de Foucauld's words on the mystery of the Incarnation—words written on November 6, 1897, during a retreat he made in Jesus' hometown of Nazareth:

> The Incarnation sprang from the goodness of God. The humility contained in this mystery is amazing, marvelous, astonishing. It shines forth with a dazzling brilliance. God, the Essence, the Infinite, Perfection, Creator, All-powerful, the great Sovereign and Lord of all, becomes a man and takes on himself the body and soul of a man. He appears on earth as a man and, at that, the humblest of men....
>
> He was born, lived, and died in deepest abjection, in the lowest humiliation, for He took once for all the lowest place so completely that no one has ever humbled himself lower that he did.

— DECEMBER 2 —

Salvation Is Near

On that day sweet wine will flow from the mountains, milk and honey from the hills, alleluia.

VESPERS ANTIPHON, ADVENT

Advent is a time for thankfulness. We give thanks to God for all that He has done. In particular, we thank God for the gift of salvation accomplished by the coming of His eternal Son into our world. The name Jesus means "He Who Saves"—a name given to him by the angel—and it was meant to signify the specific role the Father assigned to His only-begotten Son as He entered into our world.

During Advent, as we listen to the Scriptures read at church or at home, we are filled with a profound sense of hope at the eventuality of our redemption. The salvation promised by God is now near; the glad tidings of the Gospel tell us that our salvation is close at hand. We hear these consoling words from Scripture: "Your salvation is coming quickly, Jerusalem, why are you then wasted with sorrow?" In another Scripture passage, we are reminded: "People of Sion, behold the Lord will come to save the nations!" Advent reminds us that we await a Savior, who will come to take us on the last day into the heavenly Jerusalem where the kingdom of God will be fully realized.

A responsory from the Vigils Office of Advent's first week sums up our hopes perfectly during the incipient days of this blessed season: *We are looking for our Savior, the Lord Jesus Christ. He will take our poor bodies and make them like His glorified body. Therefore, we must live soberly, virtuously, and temperately in this world, awaiting with peaceful hope the glorious appearance of our great God.*

— DECEMBER 3 —

The Advent Journey

Come, let us go to the mountain of the LORD, to the house of the God of Jacob. He will teach us his ways, and we will walk in his paths.

ISAIAH 2:3

The Advent journey is an invitation to climb the mountain of the Lord. The journey consists of a slow, gradual ascending up the mountain path. As with all uphill climbing, there are certain dangers along the way, but also the joyful expectation of one day reaching the mountaintop that is the house of the Lord.

The Advent journey is also the remembrance of another journey: that of our earthly pilgrimage toward God, toward the fullness of life with Him. The very nature of Advent is to restore in us the sense of our Christian life as a constant pilgrimage, as a dynamic ongoing movement towards a final encounter, and ultimate destination where we enter into the possession of the One for whom our hearts are longing.

Advent is a journey from the forces of darkness and sin into the light of hope and grace. At its inception, we may undertake the journey with feelings of fear and insecurity. Yet as we continue traveling, and grow into the realization that He who is the object of our destination is also our Companion on the road, the landscape of this inner journey begins to change. We discover the joy found in expectancy and patient waiting. We "rejoice with great joy," for we discover, as once did the disciples on the road to Emmaus, that He has been by our side all along. Jesus is waiting for us at the final moment of the journey, but He is also with us now as we walk through the whole of it.

To learn the art of the journey we must never loose sight of this Divine Presence who facilitates the journey by driving away those negative elements in our lives: despair, fear, insecurity, sinfulness. During the long nights of our Advent journey, we can find comfort in the prayer of the Eastern Church: *To those who are caught in the night straying into the works of darkness, grant, O Christ, your light and your blessing.*

— DECEMBER 4 —

Fostering the Spirit of Advent

The King is coming; Jerusalem prepares herself for His coming; behold, He stands in your midst.

ADVENT LITURGY

We are pressing forward with our Advent journey in the hope of reaching our goal. The difficulties of winter begin to be felt all around us. We seek comfort and relief from the bleak, frosty days. We must be careful not to try to seek relief from our winter blues by jumping quickly into early Christmas celebrations. Instead of escaping into banal, superficial early festivities, we must make every effort to keep the true spirit of Advent in the monastery, in the parish, at home, and, if possible, in the workplace. We can foster the true spirit of Advent by cultivating practices that enhance the spirit of the season. Here are some suggestions:

1.   Cultivate an attitude of stillness, of silence, an atmosphere of peace and calm within. This, in turn, fosters inner prayer and recollection.

2.   Let us think of Our Lady, the expectant mother, and reflect on her attitude of mind and heart with which she prepared herself to welcome Jesus on that first Christmas day. Let Our Lady and Saint Joseph be our models during these weeks of Advent. Place an ikon of the Annunciation in a relevant spot at home to remind yourself of Mary's presence.

3.   Make time for Bible reading. God speaks to us through the Prophets who announced the coming Messiah. From them, we learn the joyful message of the arrival of the Messianic Kingdom. The Scriptures proclaimed in Church and during the monastic offices are rich in symbolism and full of the power of the Holy Spirit. During our long winter evenings, we can read the book of Isaiah and other parts of the Scripture in the quiet intimacy of our homes. Such a reading feeds our inner journey and is a source of great joy to our souls.

4.   Advent has its own music of rare, haunting beauty. We could listen to, or sing, the Gregorian chant melodies for Advent: the hymns, the antiphons, the O Antiphons. Bach's Advent Cantatas are an inspiration to prayer, fostering a quiet, contemplative mood very appropriate for the season. There is also Handel's *Messiah*, especially in the last days of Advent. Other popular hymns can also nurture the Advent spirit of joyful expectancy.

5.   Participation in the liturgy, in the sacramental life and the divine mysteries, are sources of grace that serve to increase Christ's presence in all of us.

6.   Advent, though quiet and contemplative, is not a season of gloom and sadness. Rather, it is full of expectant joy. We may delay putting up the Christmas tree and the decorations, but we can replace them with a beautiful and simple Advent wreath with its four candles, each lighted progressively during the four weeks

of the celebration. We can pray, read, sing, and eat by the Advent wreath. Lighting one of its candles is a moment filled with promise, peace, and longing, for we know that hour of our liberation is at hand. In the words of the liturgy, we pray: "Come, and deliver us, O Lord. Come, do not delay."

7.   In our refectory, a small creche is placed in a prominent place at the start of Advent, but without the statue of the Infant Jesus. A candle next to it is lit during the evening meal. The empty crib in the creche is a constant reminder in the words of the Christmas antiphon that "the Eternal Word emptied himself for our sake and became man." It also increases our yearnings to see his face on Christmas eve when after the singing of the first Vespers of the Solemnity the infant is placed in the creche and the Christmas tree is lit.

8.   We must be particularly faithful to the daily Angelus— the great prayer of the mystery of the Incarnation.

— DECEMBER 5 —

Light From the East

People, look East, the time is near
Of the crowning of the year.
Make your house fair as you are able,
Trim the hearth and set the table.
People, look East and sing today,
Christ, the Lord, is on the way.

ANCIENT FRENCH CAROL

From ancient times, monks and nuns have kept the venerable custom of praying with their eyes turned towards the East. This was not based on simple, personal preference, but on sound biblical grounds. As we read in the Gospel of Matthew: "For as the lightening comes from the east and flashes as far as the west, so will be the coming of the Son of Man (Mt 24:27).

Our monastic chapel is built towards the East, and during these early days of Advent, I am struck at how apt it is that we continue to preserve our timeless custom of praying towards the

East. A life-size ikon of the Christ Pantokrator, enrobed in majesty, presides in the apse of our chapel, surrounded on each side by the ikons of the Mother of God and John the Baptist. Both of them, with their hands pointing to the Lord, make silent intercession for all of us. In Greek, the triptych ikons together are called "The Deësis," that is, "The Intercession." The Lord, clothed in glory, looks with gravity at us, while Mary and John quietly plead for our cause.

During our Advent journey, I hold on to the vision expressed in the Deësis ikon. The mystery of Advent tells me that Christ became incarnate in time, became part of our human history, and revealed to us what lays beyond time, awaiting all of us. The vision holds a promise that, at the end of time, when the glorious Christ appears from the East, as Savior and Judge, we, his disciples, shall hear the glad tidings from his mouth: "Come, you that are blessed by my Father, inherit the kingdom prepared for you from the foundation of the world" (Mt 25:34–35).

These words from the Gospel are particularly consoling to hear during our Advent days, filled as they are with earthly cares and busy Christmas preparations. They bespeak of the *beata pacis visio*, the blissful vision of peace promised to all of us in the new Jerusalem, where the kingdom of God will be fully realized.

— DECEMBER 6 —

Saint Nicholas

Saint Nicholas, the most human of saints, was always ready to help where need existed. By his very humanity, the Saint reflected popular hopes and fears. He changed because human needs changed.

MARTIN EBEN, *SAINT NICHOLAS: LIFE AND LEGEND*

The feast of Saint Nicholas is a welcome pause during Advent. We can take leave along the path, gather our thoughts and probe into the meaning of the journey. Saint Nicholas is very much an Advent saint. Like John the Baptist, he points to Christ, who is surely coming and for whom we wait with eager expectation.

The Gospel teachings were very real to Saint Nicholas and he preached the Word of God powerfully, not only in speech, but with the convincing example of his own life. In all things, he tried to adhere to the example of his Divine Master. Like Jesus, Saint Nicholas showed a particular zeal for helping the poor, the outcasts, and the oppressed. We read in his life that one day a nobleman who lived in the same city as Saint Nicholas had three daughters of marriage age whom he wished to sell into slavery, for he could not find a suitor who could afford the formidable dowry expected by the nobleman. When Saint Nicholas became aware of the nobleman's malicious intent, he went one night to his house with a bag of gold, sufficient for the dowry of a daughter, and threw the bag into the house through an open window. He did this again on the next night, and the night after that, until he obtained the freedom of the three young maidens. This story reminds us that Saint Nicholas was a good shepherd of his flock who was always ready to give his life for the sake of his sheep. Saint Nicholas's gentle goodness reached well beyond the boundaries of his own metropolis, thus attracting many nonbelievers to the Christian faith.

It was said of Saint Nicholas that he gave away everything he had, and continued to give, until he had no more. In our age, where greed, consumerism, and selfishness seem to be the order of the day, perhaps Christians could try to emulate the humble Saint Nicholas and learn to give of what they have. We all, rich and poor, have something to give. The rich can provide material assistance to those in dire need, and the rest of us can give what those who come to us expect: help, compassion, understanding, patience, tolerance, time, a listening ear, and wholehearted affection. God has made it possible for all of us to be capable of giving something, and ample opportunities for doing good are presented to us daily. Giving, after the example of Saint Nicholas, is putting the Gospels into practice. I think this is the lesson he would wish us to learn as we go about preparing to receive God's unique gift of Himself to us on Christmas day.

— DECEMBER 7 —

Saint Ambrose of Milan

O Splendor of the Father's Light and glory of eternal Day. True Light begotten of True Light. Its very source and fountainhead.

SAINT AMBROSE (340–397 A.D.), *SPLENDOR PATERNAE GLORIAE*

Years ago I was attending the Office of Vespers in an Orthodox Church. After completion of the Office, I walked to the side toward a tall ikon that had attracted my attention. To my surprise, I discovered it was an ikon of Saint Ambrose. I say I was surprised because I was expecting the ikon to represent an Eastern saint, not a Western one. Finding Saint Ambrose present in an Orthodox Church brought to mind the lost sense of what the One Undivided Church of Christ must have been like during the first thousand years of Christianity, and what it could be again when the much desired unity of the Church is one day achieved.

Discovering this ikon also brought back memories of my childhood. I vividly remember the small collection of books on the lives of the saints given to me by my mother. The books were very small in size and they were written for children. Among them was the life of Saint Ambrose. I tried then to remember the few facts that I could recall from reading his life at such an early age. Perhaps the one historical fact that I retained was the unusual way he was chosen bishop of Milan. Saint Ambrose, I recalled, was only a catechumen when he was assigned to settle a dispute between two factions over the choice of a bishop for the church of Milan. In the middle of the dispute, a voice was heard crying out: "Ambrose, bishop!" after which the multitudes assembled there repeated the same cry, bringing the two factions together in their unanimous choice of Ambrose as bishop.

Later, I learned to appreciate Saint Ambrose's commentary on the psalms and especially his hymns, which enrich us as we continue to sing them here in this small monastery in their original Gregorian melodies, either in Latin or in English. His hymns, marvelous jewels of religious poetry, vibrate with the authentic tradition of the One Undivided Church. As we keep the memory of this Father of the Church on his feast day, we hope his example will rekindle the Advent spirit in us. During these Advent days, Saint Ambrose's words seem especially appropriate: *In Christ you have everything you need: If you are burning with fever, He is the fountain that will refresh you; If you feel down, oppressed by your faults, He is the deliverance. If you feel weak and in need of help, He is the strength. If you are afraid of death, He is the Life. If you desire heaven, He is the Way. If you wish to escape the darkness, He is the Light. If you are hungry, in need of nourishment, He is Food* (author's translation from the French).

— DECEMBER 8 —

Immaculate Conception of the Theotokos

Draw us, O Immaculate Virgin; we will run after the perfume of your ointments.

VESPERS ANTIPHON OF THE FEAST

The sun sets quietly in the rural surroundings of our small monastery. One special winter joy is to gaze upon the transfigured splendor of those last extraordinarily luminous sunbeams. They paint the whole sky pink and bright red before they recede, allowing the falling darkness to take its rightful place. These quiet moments before Vespers seem naturally conducive to recollection, prayer, and preparing oneself to praise the Lord. These moments are as natural as the cool, crisp air we breathe on these winter days.

Today we celebrate the solemnity of the Immaculate Conception of the Mother of God. The hymn at Vespers is the *Ave Maris Stella* in its solemn form. The hymn, written in the first Gregorian mode, has a beautiful melody whose cadences are full of majesty and gravity. We always kneel at the first verse of the hymn to show our reverence to Mary, just as we bow at the last doxology, to show our adoration of the Divine Trinity. The antiphons and psalms of Vespers are of tender serenity. They portray the fullness of grace granted to Mary at the moment of her conception, for in the divine plan, Mary, the humble maiden is to become the spotless Mother of God, the abode of the Most High.

The Scripture reading at Vespers is taken from Romans 5:20. It stresses the great mystery of grace that, like Mary, we all receive, thanks to God's salvation offered to us in Jesus Christ, His Son.

Vespers concludes with the Magnificat and its very appropriate antiphon: "Hail Mary, full of grace, the Lord is with you; blessed are you among women and blessed is the fruit of your womb." Today's celebration presents us with the arrival of Mary as the dawn of our salvation. Christ is near because Mary, who is to be His mother, is already here. Our solemn feast comes to a close and we commend our Advent journey to the unfailing protection of the Mother of God. We greet her with the words of today's first antiphon: *You are all beautiful, O Mary; in you there is no trace of original sin.*

— DECEMBER 9 —

He Who Comes

See how glorious He is, coming forth, as Savior of all peoples.

VESPERS ANTIPHON, FOURTH SUNDAY OF ADVENT

Advent is all about the coming of God in our midst. This sense of Christ's approaching as the Savior of all is what gives Advent its distinct and special character.

Of course, we know indeed that Christ already came some two thousand years ago, but what Advent does is to renew the awareness of His presence among us. The grace of Advent also intensifies our longing for the Lord, for our full communion with Him.

Advent helps us relive anew, each year, the mystery of the Incarnation, of Christ coming in the flesh on that first Christmas. Just as he came long ago into the womb of Mary, his mother, and later, on Christmas day, to the world at large, so now He comes again to be reborn in our hearts. Through the grace of the sacraments, especially the Eucharist, he penetrates our innermost selves. Advent also brings to mind that other coming of the Lord, His final coming in glory, reminding us that we must become like the vigilant servant of the Gospel, always ready for Christ's return. We anticipate this second coming in joy, praying as the first Christians did: *Come, Lord Jesus, come.*

— DECEMBER 10 —

Advent Longing

Our hearts are restless until they rest in You.

SAINT AUGUSTINE

During Advent's shorter days and longer nights, we intensify our waiting and hope. We work to purify our desire through active faith. We wish to be well prepared for the inestimable gift of God's coming into our midst and of His much expected and wondrous visitation to us.

Advent is the season par excellence for cultivating and listening to the deepest and most intense longings of our hearts. These longings that inhabit each one of us express the deepest cravings of our innermost selves. Advent allows us the time to be attentive to these powerful yearnings within and provides us the opportunity for redirecting them towards the Only One who can appease them. In the O Antiphon assigned to December 22, we cry out as we sing, "O King and Desired of all nations, the only joy of every human heart, come and save the creature you fashioned from the dust!" This piercing cry of the human heart expresses our deep hunger for God, for the Messiah who comes to save us. It is the complete acknowledgment that He alone can quench the thirst and yearning of the human heart.

— DECEMBER 11 —

Prepare the Way of the Lord

He [John] went into all the region around the Jordan, proclaiming a baptism of repentance for the remission of sins, as it is written in the book of the words of Isaiah the Prophet, "The voice of one crying out in the wilderness: / 'Prepare the way of the Lord, / make His paths straight.'"

LUKE 3:3–4

In the second week of Advent, we are plunged deep in the middle of our "Advent-desert experience." We hear through the words of the Precursor a clear message of what is to be our Advent undertaking for the remaining weeks: "Prepare the way of the Lord, / make His paths straight." This is our task.

Advent is a special time of interaction between God and us. It is a time given by God to strengthen our relationship with Him. God pours his grace into our hearts through His Holy Spirit, but he wants our cooperation. John the Baptist's message to us is clear. We must prepare the way for the Lord to come into our hearts. In the Baptizer's words and in those of the prophet Isaiah: "We must level out the hills and the valleys," that is, we are to remove obstacles and impediments to smooth out His path, so He may take possession of us in complete freedom.

The message of John the Baptist resounded with unusual clarity in the Judean desert. As such, it is also important for us to make an interior journey into our own desert, into the innermost recesses of our hearts. It is there that God is waiting and where He wishes to speak with us, in the intimacy of our hearts. There He wishes to reveal Himself and interact with us in that loving relationship to which we are continuously invited.

— DECEMBER 12 —

Our Lady of Guadalupe

Blessed are you, Holy Virgin Mary, deserving of all praise;
from you rose the sun of justice, Christ our God.

GOSPEL ACCLAMATION OF THE FEAST

Whenever I think of Our Lady of Guadalupe, I remember our dear friend, Dorothy Day, who loved Our Lady with that tender love that only the saints seem to possess. One day, Dorothy told me of her particular devotion to Our Lady of Guadalupe. She mentioned how much she loved making her pilgrimage to Our Lady's shrine in Mexico City. I asked her why she was particularly drawn to Our Lady of Guadalupe, and she replied, "She is the Mother of the poor. Whenever I visit the shrine, I am moved to tears to see the throngs of poor people who come to Mary with such trust and confidence. She is truly their Mother."

For me, this began a new appreciation for Our Lady under the special title of Guadalupe. I reflected on how Mary fulfilled perfectly the role of the "anawim," the poor of God. If she was chosen by God to be the Mother of His eternal Son, if He fell in love with her, it is because He admired the lowliness, the humbleness, the poverty of His servant Mary. And if the Almighty One chose Mary to be the Theotokos, the Mother of God, He also chose her to be the "Mother of the poor": the Mother of all of us. For we are all, in one way or another, poor before God.

Nothing expresses so well Our Lady's spirit during the time of the Incarnation as her own Magnificat. And although we sing the Magnificat at Vespers daily, today's feast gives us the opportunity to reflect slowly, profoundly, prayerfully upon it. As we taste the words of the Magnificat, with new insight, we understand better why Mary, God's Mother and our own, is for us the perfect role model during our Advent-Christmas journey. She is there, close by, to guide us, protect us, and lead us directly to her Son, Jesus. We can surely count on her.

— DECEMBER 13 —

The Prophets:
Our Advent Companions

The preaching of the prophets, foretelling the manifesta-
tion of Christ, today receives its saving fulfillment: for
the Lord comes in the flesh to enlighten those in dangerous
darkness.

BYZANTINE MATINS OF THE FORFEAST OF THE NATIVITY

During Advent the readings proclaimed in the Church's liturgy are in large part taken from the books of the prophets,
especially Isaiah. The prophets and their messages also play a prominent role in our daily *lectio divina* and thus become our guides and
teachers during this blessed period, during which their prophetic
voice rings out: "Hear, O heavens, and give ear, O earth, for the
Lord speaks."

Through the prophets, God slowly prepared the chosen moment of history when He would send His only Son, the Savior,
into the world. There is a progression in God's revelation of the
Messiah in the Old Testament, and the prophets adapted themselves, sometimes with a bit of pain, to this aspect of God's plan.

During these Advent weeks, we are likewise invited to listen
to the prophetic word attentively and courageously, letting the
prophets gradually unfold before our eyes God's plan of salvation. We are invited not only to listen to them, but more importantly, to make their sentiments our own. Humanity's longing
for the Messiah, the Redeemer, so beautifully expressed in Isaiah
as well as in the other prophets, must become our own: *Shower,*
O heavens, from above, and let the skies rain down righteous-
ness; let the earth open, that salvation may spring up, and let it
cause righteousness to sprout up also (Isaiah 45:8).

Accompanied by Isaiah and our other sure guides, we are
inspired to walk our Advent journey along the path from prophecy to prophecy until we reach the culminating point on Christmas Day, when the awaited vision opens forth gloriously before
our very eyes.

— DECEMBER 14 —
Saint John the Baptist

One who is more powerful than I is coming after me;
I am not worthy to carry his sandals.

MATTHEW 3:11

An essential figure of the Advent drama is the Precursor, John the Baptist. Throughout the season, either in the Gospels or Office of Vigils, we feel his presence and hear his words, urging us to prepare the way of the Lord. We also hear the words of Jesus: "What then did you go out to the wilderness to look at?...A prophet?...I am sending my messenger ahead of you, / who will prepare your way before you." The spirit of John the Baptist remains with us through the culmination of the Christmas season with the feast of the Theophany, which commemorates the baptism of Jesus by John as well as the first time the entire Trinity is revealed in the New Testament.

God sends John, his messenger, to underscore the words of the prophet Isaiah: "All the ends of the earth shall see the salvation of our God!" John the Baptist heralds the good news. He is Christ's Precursor, and he is also the "friend of the Bridegroom." During the course of the year, the liturgy provides us several occasions to return to the person, message, and ministry of John the Baptist, for example, his birth date in June and his decapitation in August. However, during these last days of Advent, what matters most to us is to pay close attention to his message: a message of conversion and repentance. It is through true conversion and humble repentance that we can "level out the hills and the valleys" in our hearts and prepare the way for the Lord. If we do this, following the words and example of the Precursor, we too may be given the extraordinary grace accorded to him on that first Theophany day and hear the words of the Father bearing witness to His eternal Son: *This is my beloved Son. Listen to him.*

— DECEMBER 15 —

The Lord Is Near

I, the Lord, am coming to save you; already I am near; soon I will free you from your sins.

VESPERS ANTIPHON, THIRD SUNDAY OF ADVENT

A s we move midway into our Advent-Christmas journey, an extremely cold period usually descends on those of us who live in the northern hemisphere. The words of John Nathan Hutchins, an eighteenth-century poet, come to mind: "Now days are short, nights long, with pinching frost, and slabby rain and snow."

In the midst of this winter gloom, a message of joy and hope is proclaimed by the Church who adopts the words of Saint Paul, telling us: "Rejoice in the Lord always; again I will say, Rejoice! Let your gentleness be known to everyone. The Lord is near" (Phil 4:4–5). The only reason for this spiritual rejoicing is the fact that the Lord is near. This "nearness" tells us that the Messiah, our Savior, is close at hand and coming to free us from the captivity caused by sin. God's approach is full of the promises of grace and redemption. Our Advent longing for liberation and for salvation will soon be fulfilled. Indeed, we can now rejoice with true joy, for the hour of our salvation is imminent.

— DECEMBER 16 —

The Annunciation

The angel Gabriel said to Mary in greeting: Hail, full of grace, the Lord is with you; blessed are you among women.

ADVENT ANTIPHON

D uring this blessed season, the Church never ceases to remind us that Advent and Christmas are all about the mystery of the Incarnation—a mystery that begins when Mary, after being greeted by Gabriel and left dumbfounded by his message, utters her fiat in complete submission to the plan of God.

Mary, of course, already knew the words of the prophet Isaiah: "For a child has been born for us, a son given to us; authority rests on his shoulders; and he is named Wonderful Counselor, Mighty God." What she never knew, until that point in history, is that she was eternally destined to bear Emmanuel, the Father's only Son. As one of the lovely antiphons of Advent tells us, "This is the good news the prophets foretold: The Savior will be born of the Virgin Mary."

Throughout the whole of Advent, the ikon of the Annunciation lays next to the lectionary in our chapel. Several times a day, as we enter or leave the oratory, we offer it a profound homage and kiss it reverently. During the liturgy, candles are lit next to the ikon and incense is offered. As we gaze upon the ikon, we see Mary in deep prayer. Suddenly, she is visited by Gabriel, and in her profound humility she seems bewildered by his greeting.

If Mary is startled by the vision of the angel, she is even more startled by his message: "Do not be afraid, Mary, for you have found favor with God. And now, you will conceive in your womb and bear a son, and you will name him Jesus."

"How can this be, since I am a virgin?" we can hear Mary asking the angel. She had promised God to remain a virgin; was God asking her to do otherwise? Gabriel answered Mary quickly, reassuring her that the gift of her virginity would remain untarnished: "The Holy Spirit will come upon you, and the power of the Most High will overshadow you; therefore, the child to be born will be holy; he will be called the Son of God."

Overwhelmed, Mary, a woman of deep faith, utters her fiat: "Here am I, the servant of the Lord; let it be with me according to your word." Her "yes," spoken softly in a humble home in the village of Nazareth, changed the course of history. Through her simple utterance, God's plans for the world begin to unfold, and the Son of God descends into the womb of Mary, uniting heaven and earth. At that precise moment, the Word is made flesh and dwells among us. In the words of the Akathist hymn:

Rejoice, O Mary, the Restoration of the fallen Adam;
Rejoice, O Virgin, the Redemption of the tears of Eve.
Rejoice, O Mary, height hard to climb for human minds;
Rejoice, O Mary, you are the throne of the King;
Rejoice, O Virgin, for you sustain the sustainer of all.
Rejoice, O Mary, the star that causes the sun to appear;
Rejoice, O Virgin, womb of the divine Incarnation.
Rejoice, O Mary, through whom creation is renewed;
Rejoice, O Virgin, through whom the Creator became a babe.

— DECEMBER 17 —

O Sapientia

O Wisdom, O holy Word of God's mouth, you govern all creation with your strong yet tender care. Come, and teach us all the ways that lead to life.

GREAT ANTIPHON OF ADVENT

A December chill permeates the quiet of the monastery, sometimes seeping into our very bones. We long for the warmth and comfort of a cozy fireplace. Starting today, the monasteries around the world make their solemn entrance into the last week of preparation before Christmas. The text of the first of the great O Antiphons, "*O Sapienta,*" begins to be sung. These beautiful antiphons, pregnant with meaning, are bearers of Advent hope and joy. In them, the liturgy of Advent finds its fullness and plenitude. This O Antiphon of the day opens with these words: *O Wisdom, O holy Word of God's mouth.*

The wisdom called forth is the Word of God. The Word, according to Saint John, has existed from the beginning in God's bosom. "In the beginning was the Word, and the Word was with God, and the word was God," he writes. The antiphon takes us to that moment before time began, to the Father's eternal engendering of the Son, of He who has "gone forth from the mouth of the Most High." Here, at our evening celebration, we sing of that first night before the world was created, when the Word came forth from the mouth of the Father, full of splendor and majesty.

The antiphon continues: *You govern all creation with your*

strong yet tender care. Saint Paul tells us in his letter to the Colossians that "In Him were all things created in heaven and on earth, visible and invisible." God is the Creator, and Jesus, his eternal Son, is the Lord of this created universe. The universe was created for Him, who in turn would come one day to redeem it. This universe, and all of us within it, he tends to with loving care." In the words of the Scriptures, "He orders all things mightily and sweetly."

The antiphon continues with these words: *Come; and teach us all the ways that lead to life.* This *veni* of the antiphon is the pleading of our Advent journey. Up until this point, we have been praying for our Lord Jesus to come. Now, in these solemn final days, we intensify our plea for redemption. Once more we beg Him to come and teach us the ways that lead to life eternal.

— DECEMBER 18 —

O Adonai

O Lord and Giver of the Law on Sinai, the Leader of your chosen people Israel, appearing in the burning bush, revealed to Moses face to face, O come, stretch out your mighty arms to set us free.

GREAT ANTIPHON OF ADVENT

During these last Advent days, the majestic O Antiphons, full of poetic richness, nurture our expectation. They are our daily food, as we continue to climb the mountain of the Lord.

The antiphon calls forth: *O Lord and Giver of the Law on Sinai.* We call forth the Savior with the invocation O Adonai, which in Hebrew translates to *"El Shaddai,"* the God who reveals himself to Moses on the mountain of Sinai. He is the God of the covenant and the Ruler of the House of Israel. The Church stands firm on its belief in the divinity of Christ by calling the Savior with the name applied only to God in the Old Testament. In the words of the Creed, Jesus, the Messiah, is "the only Son of God, eternally begotten from the Father, God from God, Light from Light, true God from true God." Today, as in ages past, there will be those who contest this belief. There is no point in arguing with them, for their minds are already made up. As Jesus said to the Samaritan woman, "If you only knew the gift from God." Our faith is this gift from God, the faith preserved in the Church that reveals Jesus as the Son of God.

The O Antiphon then recalls the Passover when the Lord leads His chosen people through the desert for forty days and forty nights. In the words of the antiphon: *Appearing in the burning bush, revealed to Moses face to face.* After that arduous journey, God reveals Himself to Moses in the burning bush—he not only reveals Himself, but He also reveals His name. We too are called to traverse the desert during our Advent journey, attempting to reach the mountain of the Lord where he will reveal his name to us. The difference now is a new name: Emmanuel, that signifies the forging of a new covenant with His people.

The antiphon pleads, *O Come, stretch out your mighty arms to set us free.* In the old covenant, God's love for his people was made visible in their deliverance from Egypt and His guiding them into the promised land. In the new covenant, His great love for us is not only manifested in His Incarnation and birth, but even more so during later years in Calvary when he "stretches out his mighty arms" on a wooden cross to save us. It is then that our true deliverance takes place, our eternal freedom is gained.

— DECEMBER 19 —

O Radix Jesse

O Root of Jesse, sign of peace, before whom all nations stand in awe; kings stand silent in your presence; the nations bow down in worship before You. O come, and set us free; delay no longer in your love.

GREAT ANTIPHON OF ADVENT

The days grow shorter at this time of the year, and a great darkness descends and unfolds upon our universe. Today's evening prayer presents us with another beautiful image of He-who-is-to-come: O Radix Jesse, O Root of Jesse, or, in another

translation, O *Flower of Jesse's stem*. The prophet Isaiah once
foresaw the destruction of Judah and the Kingdom of David.
The only remnant, Isaiah asserts, would be a humble root, a root
from Jesse's stem: David's father. It is this humble root that would
salvage the lineage of David. From the stem of this root the Savior will bud and flower. The words of one of our Christmas car-
ols expresses this tenderly:

> Behold, a rose of Judah,
> From tender branch has sprung!
> A rose from root of Jesse,
> As prophets long had sung.
> It bore a flower bright
> That blossomed in the winter
> When half-spent was the night.
> This rose of royal beauty
> Of which Isaiah sings
> Is Mary, maiden Mother,
> And Christ the flower she brings.

The root of Jesse, in the words of the antiphon, is a sign of
peace for all peoples. Jesus, our Emmanuel, is sent by the Father
to seal this new alliance of peace and reconciliation between the
world and God. Colossians 1:20 expresses this precisely: "God
was pleased to reconcile to himself all things, whether on earth
or in heaven, by making peace through the blood of his cross."
Jesus is the Prince of Peace, "whose face the whole world longs to
see," prays the very first antiphon of Christmas Vespers. As he arrives on Christmas day, small and humble, yet clothed in eternal
splendor, all nations and kings stand in awe: *Kings stand silent in
your presence; the nations bow down in worship before You.*

This part of the antiphon not only anticipates Christmas, but
already gives us a glimpse into the Solemnity of the Epiphany,
when God's glory will be manifested to the Gentiles. The Magi
kings, seeing this glory shining in a little child, stand dumbstruck in
his presence. Just as the Magi are awestruck, we too can only be
silent before the great mystery and offer Him our humble worship.

The final words of the antiphon: O *come, and set us free; delay no longer in your love* has been the cry of our hearts throughout Advent. Now that we see salvation arriving, so close at hand, we add, *Hurry, Lord, do not tarry in your love for us, delay no longer in your coming.*

— DECEMBER 20 —

O Clavis David

O Key of David and Power of the house of Israel, what you unlock, no man can close, for you alone can bind fast. O come, break down the prison walls of death for those who dwell in darkness and the shadow of death.

GREAT ANTIPHON OF ADVENT

Tomorrow is officially the first day of winter. Our gloomy evening is tempered by the activities in our chapel. The solemnity of these last days of Advent is expressed by the many candles burning at Vespers, including the oil lamps in front of our many ikons, the incense used at the *Lucernarium* and the Magnificat, and the bells ringing joyously during the singing of the great O Antiphons and the Magnificat. The beauty of the chant, the sweet scent of the incense, the lovely sound of the bells change an ordinary winter evening into a festive moment.

The antiphon begins with the words: *O Key of David and Power of the House of Israel.* These are the ancient messianic titles used by the prophets to foretell the coming of the Messiah and designate his role. When Christ, the Key of David, arrives, he will unlock all the mysteries of the old covenant. In Him shall all the prophecies be fulfilled. In the new dispensation and covenant, He is head of a new Israel, the Church, to which we all belong. Therefore, He has power and dominion over us all.

The antiphon proceeds: *What you unlock, no man can close, for you alone can bind fast.* Christ, the Messiah, the Key of David, comes to unlock for all, Jews and Gentiles alike, the doors of the kingdom of God. He alone possesses the keys and it will be He who invites all, be they just or sinners, into His eternal banquet. This is precisely the good news of the Gospel.

Finally, the antiphon proclaims: *O come, break down the prison walls of death for those who dwell in darkness and the shadow of death.* This is the fervent prayer of the expectant house of Israel, the cry for its liberation.

— DECEMBER 21 —

O Oriens

O Daystar, splendor of eternal light and Sun of Justice,
O come, shine on those who dwell in darkness and the
shadow of death.

GREAT ANTIPHON OF ADVENT

Today, in our hemisphere, the calendar marks the winter solstice—the shortest day of the year. Beginning on December 22, daylight slowly begins to lengthen. Similarly, we are at the point of our Advent journey in which we see the Light approaching, the true Light who will shine on Christmas day—the Light that will finally dispel all darkness from our hearts.

The antiphon begins: *O Daystar, splendor of eternal light and Sun of Justice.* The Latin beginning "*O Oriens*" is translated in several different ways: O Daystar; O Dayspring; O Radiant Dawn. Each of these is rich in meaning and symbolism. In the early days of the Church, the first Christian temples were constructed looking towards the east, the Orient, from where Christ came and was expected to return. The sun, a symbol of Christ, rises daily from the east. And from the sun comes light and life. Similarly, it is from Christ, the Sun of Justice, that we Christians receive light and life. Christ, the *Oriens* from on high, is the light of the world, and it is ultimately in his light that we shall one day see the radiance and splendor of the Father. "He who sees me sees the Father," proclaims Jesus. As we sing daily at Vespers, "O gladsome light of the holy glory of the Immortal Father; heavenly, holy, blessed Jesus Christ."

The antiphon next refers to this darkness: *O come, shine on those who dwell in darkness and the shadow of death.* Because we are in darkness, the darkness of our confusion and helplessness, we recognize our instinctual need for light and salvation. Sinners that we all are, we recognize the deadly effects of sin in our lives. We know ourselves sitting in a desperate state, under the "shadows of darkness and death." Christ alone can liberate us from these shadows. Fortunately for us, we know of His great love, His unbroken promise to come to us as our Savior.

— DECEMBER 22 —

O Rex Gentium

O King of all nations, the desired One of their hearts, the cornerstone that joins in one the peoples sin had kept apart. O come, and save the creature you once formed from earth and dust.

GREAT ANTIPHON OF ADVENT

I hold to the view that to benefit spiritually, at least at a deeper level, from the great O Antiphons, one has to learn to sing them in their original melody, either in Latin or in English. Fortunately there are wonderful adaptations of English texts to the Gregorian melody. In the chanting of the O Antiphons, the music is so tied together with the words that we must sing them in order to distill, syllable by syllable, the meaning of the words. The exquisite Gregorian melody, used for all the seven O Antiphons, is written in the second mode, the "D mode," expressing beautifully the richness of the texts in all their evocative complexity. This soul-stirring melody creates a soothing and serene effect in all those who sing or listen to it. The sung antiphons become semi-sacramental, flowing like rivers through the body and mind, carrying us away in their currents.

Those who cannot sing the antiphons in their original Gregorian melody can still use the text and sing them to the tune of "O Come, O Come, Emmanuel"—a very practical solution for home use. Those who cannot sing at all can listen to a recorded rendition of the antiphons while praying them.

In the preceding O Antiphons, our point of reference was the Jewish Old Testament, using the messianic titles the Israelites

applied to the expected Messiah. Starting today, the horizon of
the O Antiphons enlarges to encompass all peoples: *O King of
all nations, the desired One of their hearts.* The Messiah, the
Savior sent by God, comes to be King not only of the chosen
people, but of all peoples, including the Gentile nations. As a
matter of fact, a literal translation of *O Rex Gentium* would
read "O King of the Gentiles." God, in his great love, calls all his
children of the earth to salvation. He offers them, Jews and Gentiles alike, a Savior who will unite all peoples and be King of all.
In the words of Saint Paul, "There is no longer Jew or Greek,
there is no longer slave or free, there is no longer male and female; for all of you are one in Christ Jesus" (Gal 3:28). The people's
great longing for his coming, therefore, is not surprising. He is the
"Desired One" of their hearts, come to free them from their previous captivity, the cornerstone that joins into one the peoples sin
had kept apart.

The antiphon next reminds us: *The cornerstone that joins in
one the peoples sin had kept apart.* Jesus, in Matthew 21:42,
calls himself the cornerstone upon which His Church will be built.
It is in this Church, His body, that He will gather all people into
one.

*O come, and save the creature you once formed from earth
and dust.* Our Advent cry for help is again heard at the completion of the antiphon. It is our plea to God's pity and love. We
pray, and never cease praying. As a great saint once said, "Prayer
is the one thing that touches the heart of God." In these last days
of Advent we keep vigil in constant prayer, that we may worthily
receive the gift from on High: Christ, our Savior.

— DECEMBER 23 —

O Emmanuel

O Emmanuel, our King and Lawgiver, the long awaited
hope of the nations, Savior of all people; O come, our
Lord and God, set free the people whom you love.

GREAT ANTIPHON OF ADVENT

As Advent draws to a close, our thoughts turn to Bethlehem. In spirit, we travel to that faraway place, where the great mystery is to be unveiled in a humble babe. A poignant Byzantine liturgical text tells us: "Now that the time of our salvation draws near...prepare yourself, O Bethlehem, for the birth. Receive the Mother of God: for she comes to you to give birth to the Light that never sets."

Tonight we praise the Lord with the last of our Advent O Antiphons. Already at Lauds, our morning prayer, the liturgy tells us to ready ourselves: *"Ecce completa sunt"* is proclaimed, or "Behold, all things are accomplished which were spoken by the angel concerning the Virgin Mary." As the bells ring during the singing of the last great O Antiphon and the Magnificat, we draw deeply into ourselves, knowing now that the prophecies of long ago are soon to be fulfilled. The promised One is at the door, ready to knock.

The antiphon begins: *O Emmanuel, our King and Lawgiver, the long awaited hope of nations.* For the first time today we call upon He-who-is-coming with the name given to Him by the angel: Emmanuel, meaning "God is with us." We recall also the words of the prophet Isaiah: "Behold, the virgin shall be with child and bear a Son, and shall name him Emmanuel." The name Emmanuel reveals to us the great depth of God's love for us. True lover that He is, He waits eagerly to be with us. He wants to be one of us, to dwell and remain with us always. He desires to share our human nature, and He wants us to share His divine life. Indeed, He is the "lover of humankind," as the Eastern liturgy frequently calls Him. The long awaited hope of all nations is soon to be fulfilled.

The final "O come" of the antiphon summarizes all of our Advent yearning for salvation: *O come, our Lord and God, set free the people whom you love.* These last words give us the necessary incentive for the last miles of our journey. A little bit longer, and then tomorrow His glory shall be revealed to us.

— DECEMBER 24 —

Christmas Eve

Today you will know that the Lord is coming, and in the morning you will see his glory.

MATINS FOR DECEMBER 24

Christmas Eve holds a unique place in the monastic calendar. In days of old, December 24 was a day of strict fasting—a fast that could not be broken until after the completion of Solemn Vespers. Not even a piece of candy could be eaten. Later, when the fast was dispensed, we could enjoy a small supper as a prelude to tomorrow's feast.

On the morning of Christmas eve, during the hour of Prime, the Abbot, vested in the appropriate ornaments, with two candle bearers and a monk carrying incense, sings the solemn announcement of the Nativity. It is an incomparable moment. The proclamation begins with the fixation of the date according to ancient counting. Then the announcement continues with these words:

> In this era of the world's history,
> Jesus Christ, eternal God and Son of the eternal Father,
> desires to save the world by his gracious coming.
> He was conceived by the Holy Spirit,
> and now after nine months...
> *(At this point, the monks kneel)*
> He is born at Bethlehem in the Tribe of Judah
> as Man from the Virgin Mary...
> *(The monks lay prostrate and touch their foreheads to the ground)*
> This is how it took place,
> the birth of our Lord Jesus Christ in the flesh.

The profound prostration of the monks at that precise moment expresses the totality of their humble adoration before God's great mystery. After the solemn proclamation of the feast of the Incarnation is made, the Martyrology is read until its usual conclusion. Then the Abbot gives a brief homily and offers his first Christmas greeting to the monastic community. One by one, the monks offer the Abbot and each other the kiss of peace and their warmest Christmas wishes. The whole monastery, though immersed in stillness, begins to show signs of joyful anticipation.

The rest of the monastic day, until Vespers, is spent as in every other Christian household. We make final preparations for the arrival of Jesus: decorating the tree, placing the last touches on the different creches around the monastery, final cleaning, choir practice, preparing of the food for the *réveillon* (Christmas postmidnight celebration) and for Christmas day itself. It is a busy series of moments in an otherwise quiet and ordinary monastic day. As much as possible, one tries to temper the business by holding on to the silence and meditative spirit of Advent. After all, the great event we are about to celebrate, the birth of Jesus, must occur—before anyplace else—within the innermost spaces of our hearts.

The danger we all face, especially in the last days before Christmas, is to allow ourselves to be taken up with the bustling activities of the season. The gifts, parties, and other such things reduce our attention from the focal point of our celebration, the arrival of Christ on the Holy Night. It may be almost impossible to avoid the so-called "Christmas rush" altogether; however, with a bit of creativity and a sense of priorities, we can limit its influence by making room for deeper silence in our lives, and by taking time for quiet prayer.

The first two antiphons of today's Vespers, the first Vespers of the Solemnity, address the Savior as the King of Peace. He comes to each of us personally and to the whole world at large, as our King bearing His gift of peace. He makes his face shine upon us, and with His shimmering radiance, He saves us.

— DECEMBER 25 —

Christmas: The Holy Night

Today true peace came down to us from heaven. Today the heavens drip honey upon the whole earth. Today a new day dawns, the day of our redemption, prepared by God from ages past, the beginning of our deliverance and of our never-ending gladness.

RESPONSORY, CHRISTMAS MATINS

The birth of Jesus renews all creation. Earlier last evening, during the first Vespers of the Nativity, while we sang the beautifully poetic hymn of the feast, *Jesu Redemptor Omnium*, we were transported during the first verse to that first birth—to the eternal begetting of the Word in the bosom of the Father. It was a reminder that today's celebration has its origin in that eternal beginning. Later, during the fourth and fifth verses, we were brought back to the event that gives reason to our celebration today: the birth in the flesh of Jesus, the eternal Son of God. These verses are so lovely, so full of hidden meaning, that they are worth quoting here:

> This is the great day of the year
> When Christians join to celebrate
> Your coming down to save mankind,
> The Father's glory laid aside.
>
> The earth, the sky, the very sea,
> And all that live in them, rejoice,
> And praise the Father who decreed
> That you should come to us in human form.

Christmas celebrates this *admirabile commercium*, this marriage of Divinity and humanity in the person of Jesus, humble infant of Bethlehem. This very infant is the admirable bridge that unites heaven and earth. He is the center of our history. Everything on heaven and earth was created by him and for him; everything looks to him for renewal, life, and redemption. He comes forth tonight, from the womb of the Virgin Mother, to an empty cave of Bethlehem, precisely to accomplish all of these things.

During this event, great things spring forth from small, humble elements. A cave, a small village, a demure maiden, are each chosen by God to accomplish his great mystery in our midst. Simple country shepherds have the first privilege of gazing upon the human face of God. Humble animals, like the shepherds' sheep, are the first to pay homage to the Lord of all creation. Tonight, a truly blessed night, is a night of contrasts and unfathomable depths. The Son of God assumes our lowly humanity, and through the mystery of his human birth, He gives us the living example of the incomprehensible humility of God. As Saint Paul says: "For our sake He emptied Himself, and took our human form."

The peak moment of our Christmas celebration is the traditional midnight Mass, when the Lord of Lords, the small infant of Bethlehem, comes to be born in us sacramentally through the Eucharist. There is a great symbolism in this liturgy, celebrated in the darkest hours. The magnificent antiphon *Dum Medium Silentium* describes it in a beautiful way: *While all things were in deep silence, and the night was in the midst of her course, your almighty Word lept down from heaven, from your royal throne, O Lord.*

Our midnight celebration is a symbol, both of that eternal night before time began when the Word came forth from the Father, and of that night in time in Bethlehem, when the same Word becomes flesh: *Et Verbum caro factum est.*

There is another reason, however, why Jesus comes to us at night. He comes as Light to our hearts plunged in the darkness of night and in dire need of Him. He is Light from Light, the "Light of the world." In the obscurity of our own personal night, the mystery of Christmas is renewed again and again. Jesus comes to console us, to be near us, to save us. And when He comes, He brings for us the gifts of light and peace, so that all may be well within us and around us. With Mary and Joseph, with the angels in heaven and humble shepherds on earth, let us thank God the Father for His great gift on this holiest of nights: Jesus Christ, His eternal Son and our Savior.

— DECEMBER 26 —

Legend of the Lamb

Tell us shepherds, what have you seen? Who has appeared on earth? We have seen a newborn infant and a choir of angels praising the Lord, Alleluia.

CHRISTMAS ANTIPHON

Early Christmas morning, during the singing of Lauds, we are transported to the manger in Bethlehem, to the story of the angels, to the shepherds and their flocks of sheep. With them, we are awestruck by the wonder before our eyes.

Here in our monastery, we easily relate to this part of the Christmas story. Like the shepherds of Bethlehem, we keep a small flock of sheep, which we tend lovingly all year round. Christmas is thus special to us and to our flock, for then the small monastery becomes, indeed, a small Bethlehem. The fact that we are small and frugal is very appropriate in claiming this resemblance. In the barn, where the sheep are sheltered from the cold of winter, and where they usually deliver their lambs, we arrange a small crèche, complete with a terra-cotta figure of the Infant Jesus in the center. All throughout the Christmas season, the sheep pay homage to their little Lord and maker. When children come to visit at Christmas time, I take them to the barn to see the crèche and the sheep. They are usually full of questions. When they finally stop, I read to them from a charming old story someone sent us long, long ago, and which we have adopted as our own. It is the legend of the Lamb:

> It was Christmas night, and the little lamb had nothing to give the tiny Christ Child who shared his stable. Suddenly, the lamb noticed that the Baby's blankets were thin and poor and the straw upon which he lay offered little warmth. So the lamb very quietly snuggled close to the Baby Jesus and sheltered Him from the cold. The Christ Child smiled and touched the lamb's shaggy coat, whereupon it was transformed into soft, curly wool. From that day to this, all sheep wear the warm symbol of Christ's gratitude for the selfless action of the one small lamb on that first Christmas night.

Beloved Disciple

John gave testimony to the Word of God; he gave witness to Jesus Christ whom he had seen.

ANTIPHON OF THE FEAST

Yesterday we celebrated Saint Stephen, the first martyr of the Christian community; today we celebrate the feast of Saint John, the disciple for whom Jesus had a special preference. We may ask: Why do we celebrate these early saints during the Christmas season, the Christmas octave to be precise? What have they to do with the mystery of Christmas? What have they to tell us?

Both Stephen and John were witnesses to Christ. Stephen, a martyr, gave up his life. John, an apostle, gave testimony to the Word made flesh, whom he had seen, heard, and touched. In his own words, this is what he passed on to us:

> We declare to you what was from the beginning, what we have heard, what we have seen with our eyes, what we have looked at and touched with our hands, concerning the Word of life— this life was revealed, and we have seen it and testify to it, and declare to you the eternal life that was with the Father and was revealed to us—we declare to you what we have seen and heard so that you also may have fellowship with us; and truly our fellowship is with the Father and with his Son Jesus Christ. We are writing these things so that our joy may be complete (1 John 1:1–4).

Both Stephen and John, like the star that guided the Magi to a small infant in a cave of Bethlehem, also point us to Christ. Stephen, with his martyrdom, and John, with his apostolic teachings, point to Jesus and tell us: Behold, the Lamb of God. The role of the saints is to efface themselves in the act of pointing to Him, the only One that matters. During these grace-filled days of the Christmas season, we can follow the worthy example of Saint Stephen and Saint John by making the resolution to lead our lives as acts of continual witness to Christ, the Incarnate Word made flesh, who dwelt among us.

— DECEMBER 28 —

The Holy Innocents

All praise to you, infant martyr flowers
Cut off in life's first dawning hours.
As rosebuds snapped in tempest strife
When Herod sought your Savior's life.

LAUDS HYMN OF THE FEAST

The dramatic story of the Holy Innocents continues on to our day. Not too long ago, almost by chance, I watched a television documentary on the violence perpetuated against children around the world. The documentary concentrated on three specific groups of children. In the first part of the documentary, a reporter interviewed children from both Israel and Palestine. He showed vividly how each side, in its fierce hate for the other, would go so far as to kill and destroy children of the opposing nationality. This killing is done without any remorse; to them, these children are simply disposable.

In the second part of the documentary children on both sides of the conflict in Northern Ireland were interviewed. The two sides in conflict, Catholics and Protestants, again inflicted violence on children of the opposite side, letting their innocent blood be spilled throughout the countryside without the slightest bit of remorse. Though a peace agreement has been signed, the memory of it, as shown in the documentary, remains in the minds of many.

The third and worst part of the documentary covered the harm inflicted on the African children of Burundi. A case of real genocide, children were slaughtered right and left by their own people. In one scene, a reporter showed the mass grave of three hundred children. It was a holocaust that affected me deeply. Besides the sight of the mass grave and the armed slaughterers, the documentary showed how these same adult slaughterers trained older children to kill younger ones. How could this perpetuated violence be permitted?

The viewer is so affected by this portrait of violence that the mind and the heart linger with all-consuming pain and sorrow at the seeming hopelessness of the case. I thought of the Holy Innocents and how their story is often repeated in this world of ours. I know I pray for these children, but that is not enough. I believe that society as a whole must take a fresh look at how we treat and tolerate the abuse and violence of these little, less fortunate ones.

Of course, this indifference is a symptom of something much deeper. We are a society obsessed by violent movies and television. Our newspapers carry daily stories of violence and hate. We have become numb to such a degree that we no longer react profoundly when we see children killing other children. In a few days, we forget the story. Worst of all, we worship guns and arms of destruction, as if they were sacred gifts from God.

The "culture of death" of which the present Holy Father speaks, is pervasive. Violence is presented to us so graphically, so profusely that we seem to have become so accustomed to it, so accepting of it, so immunized against it that we do nothing about it. Today's feast of the Holy Innocents is a good day to meditate upon this tragedy and declare with our actions that all life is a sacred gift from God and that, as disciples of Jesus, we reject violence in all its forms.

— DECEMBER 29 —

Come, Lord, Without Delay

Today, Jesus wishes to be born in the inner life of every human being. He wishes to be born in the history of our towns and villages, in the very history of humanity. This birth, therefore, shall become the most important event of our lives.

CARDINAL CARLO MARIA MARTINI, *VOICI NOEL*

In our monastery today, we experience both the joy of Christmas and the darkness of a cold winter day. I find inspiration for this day in the emotive words of the Italian poet, David Turoldo. His poem "Come, Lord, Without Delay" was written expressly for Christmas. I translate it from a French version:

> You come during the night,
> As in our hearts, it is always night.
> Come without delay, Lord!
>
> You come in silence,
> As we no longer know what to tell ourselves.
> Come without delay, Lord!
>
> You come in profound solitude,
> As each of us feels more and more alone.
> Come without delay, Lord!
>
> You come as a Prince of peace,
> As we no longer know what peace is.
> Come without delay, Lord!
>
> You come to console us,
> As more and more these days we are sad, disheartened.
> Come without delay, Lord!
>
> We are stranded, lost,
> We no longer know who we are, or what we want.
> Come, Lord,
> Come without delay, Lord.

— DECEMBER 30 —

The Holy Family

Mary, the mother of Jesus, and Joseph were filled with wonder at all that was said of the child.

LUKE 2:33

One of the lovely customs of the season, in homes or monasteries, is to prepare the crèche just before Christmas day itself. In the monastery, we set up the Nativity scene in several places: the Church, the refectory, the library, and the common room.

The Nativity set used in the Church is stark in its simplicity. Many years ago, at the beginnings of our monastery, someone made us the beautiful gift of the set. It comes from the Philippines, and the figures are made of a dark, handsome wood proper to that place. Unlike other Nativity sets, which sometimes are elaborate this one has only three figures: the Baby Jesus, Mary, and Joseph. The Infant Jesus, small as he is, is the center of the crèche. Mary and Joseph turn toward Him. All things look to the small, silent Infant, and find in his smile an expression of God's tenderness for his people. The grace of God that brings salvation appears in his little person, and radiates from Him for all people to see.

Through this humble crèche, Jesus is present in our midst, telling each one of us, "See how much I love you." In the crèche, he awaits our visit. He wishes to see us, so that we can share with Him everything that is happening in our lives. As we draw close to him, we hear his welcome to each of us: "Peace be to you."

In the humble crèche, Jesus introduces us to the two persons he loves the most on earth, and the ones who also love Him the most: Mary, his mother, and Joseph, his stepfather. Now that we are accepted into such a privileged company, we make ourselves at home in the crèche and, like the ancient shepherds, keep company with the tiny Infant. We are stunned at the great mystery before our eyes, and we plunge ourselves into silent adoration of the Word-Made-Flesh. As we stand in silence before the humble crèche of Bethlehem, we can all learn to discover Christ and find out who He really is. Here we begin to learn the first lessons of the Gospel.

— DECEMBER 31 —

Year's End

Ring out, wild bells, to the wild, wild sky;
The flying cloud, the frosty light;
The year is dying in the night.
Ring out, wild bells, and let him die.

Ring out the old, ring in the new,
Ring, happy bells, across the snow:
The year is going, let him go;
Ring out the false, ring in the true.

ALFRED, LORD TENNYSON

The year draws to a close. December, the final month, is complete. For us Christians, all time is sacred, either in its beginning or at its end. All time is God's time.

We can only begin to fathom the mystery of time when we look at it from God's perspective. For Him, time and eternity are intertwined. Today, we find ourselves firmly rooted in time but already looking ahead to eternity. With the passing of another year, our time on earth gets shorter, and eternity is much closer.

Christians do not cling to time, but learn to use it wisely. The reason for our life on earth, for our earthly pilgrimage, lies elsewhere. As a saint once put it, "We are given our time on earth for only one purpose, to gain eternal life." We look forward to the promised land, to our eternal home with God. We learn to live as Saint Paul told us at the beginning of our Advent journey: soberly, virtuously, and temperately in this world, awaiting eagerly the appearance of our great God. All things earthly, including ourselves, pass away. God alone remains the same.

As we get ready to begin a new calendar year, we scrutinize our goals. We become re-energized by our firm desire to make use of our time wisely, to learn to live hidden with Christ in God, in his mystery, until the seasons come to a final end.

JANUARY

Holy Mother of God

How blessed are you, Virgin Mary, for you carried within
you the Lord, the Creator of the world.

RESPONSORY OF THE FEAST

Today, the Octave of Christmas, the Church invites us to honor
Mary, the Mother of Jesus. This honor is fitting, for Mary is
central to the mystery of the Incarnation. Without her consent,
the Incarnation would not have taken place. The beautiful antiphons of today's Vespers, very ancient liturgically, make constant
reference to this fact: "By your miraculous birth of the Virgin,
you have fulfilled the Scriptures: like a gentle rain falling upon
the earth, you have come down to save your people. O God, we
praise you."

As we contemplate the mystery of Christmas, our eyes are
turned toward the humble creature chosen to be God's Mother.
In God's masterful plan, Mary is the link between divinity and

humanity. We render homage to that supreme role assigned to her by God the Father and mysteriously accomplished in her by the Holy Spirit.

The first antiphon of today's Vespers, O *Admirabile Commercium*, expresses this great mystery precisely: "O marvelous exchange! Man's Creator has become man, born of a Virgin. We have been made sharers in the divinity of Christ who humbled himself to share in our humanity."

Mary was a humble maiden, an ordinary creature. Everything in her life was pre-ordained by God to prepare her for the great mystery that was to be accomplished in her. And Mary, humble and obedient to all that God was doing for her, surrendered every inch of her being to Him, uttering her fiat daily: "Behold the handmaid of the Lord, be it done in me according to your Word." Time and again, she had to surrender to God and live by those words, including that most difficult of moments when she stood at the foot of the Cross and saw her son die a most cruel death.

From ancient times, Christians honored Mary as the Theotokos, that is, as the Mother of God. That title is the highest honor that God ascribed to Mary and should be our title of choice when we pray to her. Note how the final words of Saint Bernadette, who was privileged to see the Mother of God many times during her life, were, "Holy Mary, Mother of God, pray for me, a sinner."

The mystery of the Mother of God is embedded deeply within mystery of Christ. It is a mystery that we cannot explain or touch or decipher. All we can do is to assent to it in wonder and awe. If we do this, and approach Mary humbly and reverently, we shall perceive her presence as very real within our everyday lives. For Mary is not only the Mother of God; she is the Mother of us all and we all are her children.

— January 2 —

Saint Basil the Great and Saint Gregory Nazianzen

The man...who acts as a steward of the goods received from God and does not amass wealth for his own private enjoyment is justly accorded praise and affection because of his charity to his brethren and the benevolence of his character. He should, however, administer these possessions rightly. He will be generous in giving of his abundance to the needy and he will offer physical assistance to the infirm and regard that part of his wealth which is superfluous as belonging to any destitute persons as much as it does to himself.

Saint Basil, *Concerning Envy*

On the second day of the New Year we commemorate two great pillars of the Church: Saint Basil of Caesaria and his friend and collaborator, Saint Gregory Nazianzen. The two started their religious life as ordinary hermits, were ordained priests, and later were elected bishops by their own people.

Saint Basil, who Saint Benedict lovingly calls "our father," is considered one of the founders of monasticism. The rules that he wrote had great impact on the early monastic movement; these rules are still in use in many monasteries of the Eastern rite. Greatly admired for his learning, wisdom, and virtue, Saint Basil was raised in a devout Christian family. He made every effort, through the example of his life, his preaching, and his writings, to preserve the authenticity of the Christian faith as received from the apostles.

The Christian community of the time of Saints Basil and Gregory was very much divided by contentious factions that argued about the two natures of Christ, the idea of the Trinity, and various other customs and beliefs. The conflict was deep and tumultuous. Even in our own time, we continue to see a polarization between members of the Body of Christ who hold opposing views about the faith. At times, pride and individualism seem to triumph. It would seem that many would like to reject the faith handed over by the Apostles, solidified by the teachings of the Fathers, and sealed by the blood of the martyrs, and would like to change the deposits of faith to suit their personal views.

As we enter a new year, we can take comfort in knowing that Basil and Gregory confronted similar situations in the Church of their time. Gregory's beautiful letter in praise of his friend Basil is a clear testimony to the mutual support and affection they gave each other during those turbulent years. Anchored in Christ and in their close friendship, they undertook together the difficult task of reforming the Lord's vineyard. In these passages, one marvels at the work of God in his two servants:

> Basil and I were both in Athens. We had come, like streams of a river, from the same source in our native land, had separated from each other in pursuit of learning, and were now united again as if by plan, for God so arranged it. I was not alone at that time in my regard for my friend, the great Basil. I knew his irreproachable conduct, and the maturity and wisdom of his conversion. I sought to persuade others, to whom he was less well known, to have the same deference for him. Many fell immediately under his spell, for they had already heard of him by reputation....Our single object and ambition was virtue, and a life of hope in the blessings that are to come; we wanted to withdraw from this world before we departed from it. With this end in view we ordered our lives and all our actions. We followed the guidance of God's law and spurred each other on to virtue.

— JANUARY 3 —

A Season of Joy

Joy to the world! The Lord is come.
Let earth receive her King.

CHRISTMAS CAROL

During this blessed Christmas season, we ponder anew the mystery of the Incarnation and affirm once more that Christ, the Son of God, was made human for our sake and came to dwell among us. In the person of Christ, the gifts of God's forgiveness, love, and mercy have embraced the whole earth and have become visible to all.

The Advent liturgy steadfastly has prepared us for the experience of joy at the arrival of the Savior. The Advent and Christmas Scripture readings contain many quotes about joy and gladness, reminding us that our God is the author of joy, and that He made us all for the supreme joy of possessing Him.

We are also reminded that Bethlehem, though poor and lowly, was a place of joy. This joy continued through the long years in Nazareth where Mary, Joseph, and their neighbors and friends must have rejoiced in Jesus' company. Jesus knew how to bring joy into people's lives. The Gospels recount how frequently He was invited to celebrations such as the Cana wedding and the table at Bethany. Would He have been invited so often if He were a joyless person? Would His disciples have so eagerly followed Him if He didn't bring joy into their hearts? Even after his Resurrection, Christ made their joy complete by appearing to them and sharing their meal; and after his departure to the Father He showered his disciples with the gift of the Holy Spirit, who fills the hearts of those in whom He abides with joy.

The saints certainly knew how to rejoice in the Lord. During the days following Christmas, Saint Teresa of Ávila would often dance and play her musical instruments during the community recreations. She was deliriously happy at the presence of her Lord, at seeing his tiny face shining with the Father's splendor. She wanted her sisters to experience the same joy. Teresa didn't hesitate to spread this joy to every corner of her monastery.

The apostle Paul urges us to "rejoice in the Lord always!" The more we grow in the love of God and the more we assimilate the message of the Gospels into our lives, the more natural it seems for us to live in joy. Abbot Marmion used to repeat to his monks: "Joy is the echo of God's presence in us." The joy of the Christmas season is, in a way, an anticipation of the eternal rejoicing to which one day we shall be summoned by the invitation to "enter into the joy of the Lord."

— JANUARY 4 —

A Mystery Ever New

Blessed is he who possesses Bethlehem in his heart,
And in whose heart Christ is born daily.

SAINT JEROME

During these past few days we have contemplated the mystery of God-Made-Flesh for our sake. In his infinite love for humankind, God assumes our nature and shows us his human face.

Though this birth is the focal point of our Christmas celebration, there is another birth, more intimate and personal, of which the Fathers of the Church often spoke. It is the spiritual birth of the Son of God in the hearts of those who desire and welcome Him. "In them," according to Saint Maximus the Confessor, "he is born as an infant as he fashions Himself in them by means of their virtues. He reveals Himself to the extent that He knows someone is capable of receiving Him."

The mystery of Bethlehem is renewed each year, each Christmas, each day, in the innermost parcels of our hearts where Jesus seeks comfort and shelter. It is in our hearts that He wishes to make a permanent dwelling, revealing to us the meaning of His words in the Gospel. There, He teaches us how to pray and call upon his name. It is also in our innermost hearts that He shows us the Father's face, for "he who sees me, sees the Father." Finally, He comes to this innermost part of ourselves, this most intimate of sanctuaries, when we receive Him in the Eucharist. It is there that He remains, as he did in the crib of Bethlehem and in the arms of His Mother, waiting for our silent love and adoration.

— JANUARY 5 —

Vigil of the Epiphany

The Magi knew with certainty that You, the Heavenly King, were born on earth. Led by the light of a star they came to Bethlehem and offered their precious gifts: gold, frankincense, and myrrh. Falling before You they worshiped You: for they saw You, the Timeless One, lying as a babe in the cave.

JOHN THE MONK

The entire landscape around our monastery is covered with an austere and rugged winter beauty. We are in the very dead of winter; no one can escape its dark and somber pall. Yet a bright star shines in the sky, pointing to a humble cave, and the brightness of that star fills our chilly dark night with hope. All we must do is follow the star to that small and simple cave of Bethlehem.

At our arrival, we find the cave inundated with light. Inside, we discover a young child and a peaceful light that emanates from his tiny face. This light is the full measure of God shining forth, for the little child is himself the uncreated light who tomorrow will be manifested to us as the "Light of the World."

On that first Epiphany, the Magi obediently followed the star and arrived safely at their ultimate destination: the Christ child. We, too, if we are obedient to God's word and follow faithfully our inner star, the light of the Holy Spirit within, shall one day arrive at our own meeting with Christ the Lord. As we step into His holy presence, we shall, like the Magi, find ourselves enveloped by the divine light, the light that dispels all shadows hidden even in the deepest recesses of our lives. In that light, we shall see the true Light, for we shall see Him in whom we have placed all our hope and trust. As we get ready to greet our Savior on the day of the Epiphany, what better salutation can we find than to utter these words, taken from the beautiful Byzantine Liturgy:

What shall we offer You, O Christ, who for our sakes has appeared on earth as man? Every creature made by You offers You thanks. The angels offer you a hymn; the heavens a star; the Magi, gifts; the shepherds, their wonder; the earth, its cave; the wilderness, the manger: And we, we offer You a Virgin Mother. O ever-eternal God, have mercy upon us.

— JANUARY 6 —

Epiphany of the Lord

Arise, shine; for your light has come,
and the glory of the LORD has risen upon you.

ISAIAH 60:1

Rise up in splendor, O Jerusalem!
For although we see darkness covering the earth,
Our Savior, the Dayspring from the East,
Comes to visit us from on high
And we who are seated in the shadows of darkness
Perceive the light of truth:
For the Lord is truly born of a Virgin.

Rise up in splendor, O Jerusalem!
Celebrate with gladness, people of the earth!
Rejoice, O heavens! And you mountains, dance for joy!
For Christ is manifested to the world
From a Virgin who carried Him in her bosom as on a throne,
The shepherds glorify the new-born child,
And the Magi offer gifts to their Lord and Master.

Rise up in splendor, O Jerusalem!
Be radiant and shout for joy!
For it pleased the Eternal Father
That his only begotten Son, the Word,
Takes flesh from a Virgin Mother
And thus enters into our world,
A star above proclaiming the glad tidings
And leading the Magi to worship
The only true God and Lord.

Rise up in splendor, O Jerusalem!
The glory of the Lord dawns upon you.
For the God who does wonders,
Eternally begotten before the morning star,
Today is seen in a humble cave.
All of creation is made new
For God has become man:
That which He was, He has remained,
And that which He was not,
He has taken on Himself.

Rise up in splendor, O Jerusalem!
From now on, people of every race and nation
Shall walk in the splendor of your light.
For today the great mystery is revealed to you:
God who is without flesh becomes incarnate;
The Word takes up a body.
The wholly Invisible is today seen;
He whom no hand can touch is handled;
And He who knows no beginning now begins to be.
The Son of God becomes the Son of Mary:
And He, Jesus Christ, the Holy One
Is the same yesterday, today, and forever.

Rise up in splendor, O Jerusalem!
Today in you a star glitters from the East.
It leads wise men to the cave where the Incarnate Word lies,
To the Child long foretold by the Prophets.
Let us all, therefore, glorify the Word of God
Manifested today in the flesh,
Appearing to angels, shepherds, and Magi,
And proclaiming salvation to all the nations.
Let us all, at the sight of this little Child,
Fall down before Him in humble adoration.

— JANUARY 7 —

Manifestation of God

Begotten before the daystar, and before all ages, the Lord our Savior is this day made manifest to the world.

VESPERS ANTIPHON: FEAST OF THE EPIPHANY

The feast of the Epiphany, one of the most beautiful of the liturgical year, is rich in content and meaning. We let its glow shine forth to penetrate our hearts, as we continue to contemplate the mystery of Emmanuel, who came to dwell among us.

Early in the Christmas season, we celebrate the revelation of the Word made flesh to the Jews, the chosen people. On the feast of the Epiphany, we go further and celebrate the manifestation of God to the world at large, Jews and pagans alike. Jesus came as Savior for all who are delighted to behold his face.

In the cave of Bethlehem, along with the angels and shepherds, relatives and neighbors, are other witnesses: three foreign travelers, the Magi, arrive from the Orient expressly to contemplate this mysterious and divine manifestation, and pay homage to the King of kings.

In manifesting Himself to the world at large, God shows us that He loves all his children and wishes to save them all. He makes it clear that He comes for all and wishes to be seen by all. He reveals himself to those who wish to receive Him: Jews and pagans, men and women, rich and poor, children and adults, just and sinners, young and old, sick and healthy. All peoples of the earth are invited to the banquet of life prepared by God who is Love, and who loves every one of us without exception.

Today, we feel very small, very humble, filled with wonder and gratitude as we witness the glorious appearance of God in our midst. With the Magi, we render homage and offer Him the gifts of our lives. As we go forward with these lives, we promise to live our days in the Light that shines forth from his face, from his gentle and loving manifestation to the world.

— JANUARY 8 —
Fullness of Time

When the fullness of the time had come, God sent his
Son, born of a woman, born under the law, in order to
redeem those who were under the law.

GAL 4:4–5

Christmas, Epiphany, and the Theophany gently remind us that a transcendent event, the Incarnation, has changed the history of the world, and consequently nothing is the same as before.

We are now living in the fullness of time, in the "Kairos of God," the time of plenitude, the time of the Word-Made-Flesh, the time that was created by Him, solely for Him. God became incarnate at a precise moment in history to share his divine life with us all.

The fullness of time has arrived when the creatures of the earth can gaze on the human face of God; it has arrived when a newborn Infant smiles and offers love, mercy, and salvation to all; it has arrived when, through the tiny body of that newborn, God makes manifest his presence to the whole world; it has arrived when his Mother calls Him by his first name, Jesus; it has arrived when he makes his earthly appearance as the long-awaited Savior foretold by the prophets; it has arrived when his glory is sung by the angels across the surrounding countryside; and it has most certainly arrived when, in the words of 1 Timothy 3:16, the world saw: *He [Christ] revealed in flesh, vindicated in spirit, seen by angels, proclaimed among Gentiles, believed in throughout the world, taken up in glory.*

— JANUARY 9 —
Winter: A Contemplative Season

The aim of the contemplative life is to teach the monk to live in God.

THOMAS MERTON

Winter in upstate New York, like that of the whole northeast, tends to be intense. The blanket of snow covering the countryside lingers for weeks and sometimes even months. After the arrival of the first snowstorm, we take things slowly, and spend more time indoors. In turn, we enter into a greater sort of solitude, taking time to rest, reflect, write, read, meditate, and pray.

These wintry indoor activities blend perfectly with our contemplative style of living. Monastic life, after all, is an inner life that grows in silence and solitude and is nourished daily by reading, meditation, and much prayer. Thus, winter is a cherished time. No other season seems so attuned to a recollective spirit. Nature seems asleep all around us and, as we progress into the season, our solitude grows deeper and becomes more complete.

Our small guest house is usually closed after Christmas for the remaining winter months. Often days will pass before I see a single human being. This is especially true when we are shut in by a snowstorm: all roads to the outside world seem to disappear. The only thing visible at those times are the deer tracks and the trails between the monastery and the barn created by our flock of sheep. Very early in the morning, these always-hungry sheep approximate the monastery, looking for crusts of the old, stale bread which one of the local food stores saves for them.

Monastery life is naturally contemplative, and the harshness of winter enhances this bent. The supreme state of stillness found in the winter months is a gift from God. Sometimes when I question what monastic life is all about, all I have to do is to look at our lovely, snow-covered hills, or at the beautiful winter trees glistening with icicles, or breathe deeply the crisp, cold air. And with that, I find a quiet response to all of my inquiries.

— JANUARY 10 —

Nazareth

Nazareth is a kind of school where we may begin to discover what Christ's life was like, and even to understand His gospel.

POPE PAUL VI

With the celebration of Epiphany, our Advent journey is drawing to a close. Bethlehem time has almost ended, and we now look forward to the feast of the Theophany of the Lord which concludes the Christmas cycle. However, before we witness the Lord's glorious baptism on the banks of the river Jordan, we have a short time between Epiphany and the Theophany to make a stop at Nazareth. The Lord spent thirty quiet years there in the company of Mary, Joseph, and other relatives and neighbors.

The Gospels record little about this time in Nazareth, but it is extremely important to Jesus' subsequent ministry. Those quiet years in the company of his parents and friends who so deeply loved him were the best preparation for his announcement of the Kingdom of God and the redemptive sacrifice that followed. Jesus even choose to begin his public ministry in Nazareth (Lk 4:21).

Jesus' life in Nazareth was one of silence, study, prayer, friendship, work, and obedience to his parents. He concentrated on his spiritual growth, becoming more and more attuned to the Father's plan for Him, forever growing "in wisdom and stature and in grace with God and men." He knew that he needed this time of preparation, so as to later accomplish the Father's mission. From the quiet silence of Nazareth, Jesus reminds us to cultivate our own spiritual life, for without a spiritual life we remain deaf to God's voice and to his plans for our lives.

In Nazareth Jesus led a ordinary existence of work and filial piety. At times, we are tempted by the idea that in order to please God we must do great things for his glory. We forget the value of the small things which make up the reality of our daily lives. The call to do extraordinary things for God is really the exception rather than the rule. God only asks that we perform the small, insignificant actions of everyday life in a well-ordered fashion in order to please Him. This is precisely what Jesus did in Nazareth and, thus, this is the mystery and lesson of Nazareth.

— JANUARY 11 —

Jesus' Hidden Life in Nazareth

Then He went down with them and came to Nazareth, and was obedient to them....And Jesus increased in wisdom and in years, and in divine and human favor.

LUKE 2:51–52

One of the most remarkable men of the twentieth century, Charles de Foucauld, in his tender love for his "beloved Lord Jesus," tried not only to imitate the life of the Savior in Nazareth, but went to live in Nazareth for three years, so as to understand better the Savior's hidden years. While at Nazareth, he wrote about his new understanding of the Lord's early years:

My God, you appear in the likeness of man, and becoming man you make yourself the lowest of men. Yours was a life of abjection. You took the lowest of the low places. You went down with them, to live their life, the life of the poor working people, living by their labor. Your life, like theirs, was poor, laborious, hard-working. They were humble and obscure. You lived in the shade of their obscurity. You went to Nazareth, a little village, lost, hidden in the mountains whence, it was said, "no good came forth...."

You were subject to them under their authority, as a son is to his father or his brother. It was a life of submission, of filial submission. You were a good obedient son. If your parents' wishes were not in perfect accord with your divine vocation you would not carry them out. You would rather "obey God than man," as when you stayed those three days in Jerusalem. But except in such a case when your vocation would claim you rather than the fulfilling of their wishes, you would fulfill them like the best of sons, not only obeying their smallest wish, but forestalling them, doing all that could give them pleasure, consoling them, making life sweet and pleasant for them, trying, with all your heart, to make them happy, being a model for all sons, having great thought for your parents, that is to say, in the measure allowed you by your vocation....

Thus during those thirty years you were, as a Son, always tender, compassionate, sympathetic, kind. You gave all the happiness you could to your parents, helping, supporting, encouraging them in their daily labor, taking the greater part on yourself to save them fatigue, never crossing them except when the Son of God required it, and then what sweetness and gentleness you would show, so that your nonacquiescence would be sweeter to them than obedience; it would be like a heavenly dew, full of that grace and delicacy and consideration with which a beautiful soul makes life sweet to others. Nothing was left out that could make your parents' life happy and make their little home a heaven.

CHARLES DE FOUCALD, *MEDITATIONS OF A HERMIT*, 1930

— JANUARY 12 —

More of Jesus' Hidden Life

They returned to Galilee, to their own town of Nazareth. The child grew and became strong, filled with wisdom; and the favor of God was upon him.

LUKE 2:39–40

We uncover many treasures of grace when we meditate on Jesus' life in Nazareth. Here is more of Charles de Foucald's words:

Yours was the life of a model Son with your humble working parents. It made up half of your life, that half that was of the earth though it spread a heavenly perfume through heaven. This was the visible half. The other invisible half was your life in God which was perpetual contemplation. You worked and helped your parents and had holy tender exchange with them and prayed with them during the day, but in the solitude and shadow of the night your soul poured itself out in silence.

Always, continually, you prayed, for praying is to be with

God, and you are God. But your human soul continued this contemplation though the night as, all through the day, it was united to your divinity. Your life was a constant outpouring before God, your soul looked always upon God, always contemplating him. What then was this prayer that was the half of your life at Nazareth? Before and above all things, it was adoration, contemplation, silent adoration which is the most eloquent of all praise—a silence that expresss the most passionate declaration of love.

CHARLES DE FOUCALD, MEDITATIONS OF A HERMIT, 1930

— JANUARY 13 —

The Theophany of the Lord

When in the Jordan, You were baptized, O Lord, the mystery of the Trinity was made manifest. For the voice of the Father bore witness to You, calling You his "Beloved Son." And the Spirit in the form of a dove confirmed the truth of these words. O Christ, our God, who has appeared in the Jordan to enlighten the world, glory to you.

TROPARION OF THE FEAST OF THE THEOPHANY

The week after the Epiphany, we are presented with the feast of the Theophany of the Lord, the manifestation of the Holy Trinity to the world at Christ's baptism in the Jordan.

In the Eastern Church, the Theophany is a major feast celebrated on January the sixth, whereas the Western Church celebrates the Solemnity of the Epiphany on that day. Originally, these two feasts were celebrated on the same day. However, through the centuries, the Western Church came to separate these two celebrations, prescribing that the Theophany of the Lord be celebrated on the octave of the Epiphany. I prefer this latter arrangement so that each aspect of mystery in the life of Christ receives our undivided attention. This arrangement also prolongs the Christmas season for one more week.

The word *theophany* comes from a Greek word meaning "the manifestation of God." While the Lord manifests himself to a chosen few on the occasion of the Epiphany, on the day of the Theophany, he goes to the banks of the Jordan and manifests himself to John the Baptist, to John's disciples, and to the large crowd present. We, like John the Baptist, are moved by the Lord's utmost humility in presenting himself for baptism, as if he ever had need for it. He did this, however, to give us an example of conversion and repentance signified by the rite of baptism.

Jesus' humility so baffles John the Baptist that he tells Jesus: "I need to be baptized by you, and do you come to me?" But Jesus had anticipated that his baptism would begin his public life, his initial announcement of the good news of the Gospel. He wanted the beginning of his ministry marked with humility. This, in turn, shows us that whenever we are called to assist the spreading of God's kingdom, we must always do so with humility.

When the waters of the Jordan touch the Lord during his baptism, the voice of the Father is heard proclaiming Jesus as his beloved Son, and telling us: "Listen to Him." At that moment, the Holy Spirit, in the form of a dove, descends over Jesus and anoints him in his mission. This moment is the first time in the New Testament that the three divine Persons appear together. It is also the first time that the dazzling mystery of the Trinity is revealed to the world.

In this glorious manifestation of the Holy Trinity, the Father gives witness to the Son: "This is my beloved Son, in Whom I am well pleased." And the Holy Spirit gives testimony to the Son by descending like a dove over Him and anointing Him. Jesus is witness to the Father and the Holy Spirit by being the receptor of this intimate, loving relationship that unites the three of them.

As part of His divine plan, the Father chooses the humble moment of Jesus' baptism to bestow his good pleasure on Him. It is a lesson for all of us. If, like Jesus, we wish to please the Father, we must follow his example and embrace willingly the ways of humility in our own lives.

— JANUARY 14 —

Baptismal Grace

Today the nature of the waters is sanctified, and the Jordan is parted in two: it holds back the stream of its own waters, seeing the Master being baptized.

SOPHRONIUS, PATRIARCH OF JERUSALEM

The celebration of Christ's baptism in the Jordan is significant for every Christian. Many of us were probably tiny babes at our own baptism and perhaps have not reflected enough on all of its implications. We know, for example, that baptism has washed original sin from us and has made us new creatures in Christ. But do we also realize that by our baptismal grace we are made temples of God and that the same Trinity manifested at Jesus' baptism now dwells in us, in an ineffable but ever so real way?

The same divine Trinity that revealed itself over the waters of the Jordan is the same Trinity present when each one of us is baptized, as our heads are signed with the name of the Father, the Son, and the Holy Spirit. Our baptism into Christ incorporates us into the bosom of the Trinity. It seals forever the mystery of the Trinitarian life into our souls. It makes us partakers of the divine life.

During these lovely days of the Theophany, the ikon of the feast is prominently placed for veneration in our Chapel. It is an ikon of rare beauty that speaks volumes to us each time we venerate it. As I contemplate this ikon, I cannot help but think what a treasure we have in our baptismal grace which brings us into and makes us share in the eternal communion of the Father, the Son, and the Holy Spirit. *Glory to You, O Lord, glory to You!*

— JANUARY 15 —

A Theophany Homily

When the waters saw you, O God,
*   when the waters saw you, they were afraid;*
the very deep trembled.

PSALM 77:16

Sophronius, Patriarch of Jerusalem and author of biographies, sermons, and poems, meditates on the Theophany in the excerpt from this prayer said at the Byzantine Divine Liturgy for the feast of the Theophany:

> In the preceding feast [the Epiphany] we saw You as a child, while in the present we behold You as full-grown, our God made manifest, perfect God from perfect God. For today the time of the feast is at hand for us: the choir of saints assembles with us and angels join with men in keeping festival.
>
> Today the grace of the Holy Spirit in the form of a dove has descended upon the waters. Today the Sun that never sets has risen and the world is filled with splendor by the light of the Lord. Today the moon shines upon the world with the brightness of its rays. Today the glittering stars make the inhabited earth fair with the radiance of their shining. Today the clouds drop down upon mankind the dew of righteousness from on high. Today the Uncreated of his own will accepts the laying on of hands from his own creature.
>
> Today the Prophet and Forerunner approaches the Master, but stands trembling before Him, seeing the condescension of God towards us. Today the waters of the Jordan are transformed into healing by the coming of the Lord. Today the transgressions of men are washed away by the waters of the Jordan. Today Paradise has been opened to men and the Sun of Righteousness shines down upon us.

— JANUARY 16 —

More Praise in Honor of the Theophany

The sea looked and fled;
Jordan turned back.
The mountains skipped like rams,
the hills like lambs.
Why is it, O sea, that you flee?

PSALM 114:3–5

S ophronius continues his sermon of praise on the feast of the
Theophany:

Today the bitter water, as once with Moses and the people of
Israel, is changed to sweetness by the coming of the Lord. Today
we have been released from our ancient lamentation, and as
the new Israel we have found salvation. Today we have been
delivered from darkness and illuminated with the light of the
knowledge of God. Today the blinding mist of the world is
dispersed by the Epiphany of our God. Today the whole of
creation shines with light from on high. Today error is laid low
and the coming of the Master has made for us a way of
salvation. Today things above keep feast with things below,
and things below commune with things above. Today the
triumphant assembly of the Christian keeps this holy festival
with great joy. Today the Master hastens towards baptism that
He may lift man up to the heights. Today He that bows not,
bows down to His own servant so that He may set us free from
bondage. Today we have purchased the Kingdom of Heaven,
for the Lord's Kingdom shall have no end. Today earth and sea
share the joy of the world, and the world is filled with gladness.
The waters saw You, O God, the waters saw You and were
afraid. The Jordan turned back, seeing the fire of the Godhead
descending bodily and entering its stream. The Jordan turned
back, beholding the Holy Spirit coming down in the form of a
dove. The Jordan turned back, seeing the Invisible made visible,
the Creator made flesh, the Master in the form of a servant.
The Jordan turned back and the mountains skipped, looking
upon God in the flesh; and the clouds gave voice, marveling at
He who had come, the Light of Light, true God of true God.

— JANUARY 17 —

Saint Antony: The Father of Monks

I am a servant of Christ.

SAINT ATHANASIUS, *LIFE OF SAINT ANTONY*, CHAPTER 53

A statue of Saint Antony sits in our rock garden—a symbol of how much the father of monks is present in our daily monastic life. I feel particularly drawn to Saint Antony, my patron saint. I often think of how much my own monastic life is directly related to his intercession on my behalf. Through his ikon, he is present in our small monastery, not only in the chapel, workrooms, and cells, but even in the kitchen. The chapel ikon representing Saint Antony is rather striking. His noble face portrays a rare, austere beauty. During prayers, an oil lamp remains lit in front of his image, and a radiance seems to pulsate from his face, providing a soothing glow that envelops the entire ikon.

As a young man, Antony decided to leave the world in order to follow Christ, having heard the Gospel text: "If you wish to be perfect, go and sell all that you have, give it to the poor, and then follow me." At that moment, he decided to leave wealth and riches behind and retire to the solitude of the desert.

There he strove to center his whole life on God, and follow in the footsteps of the Gospels, after the example of Jesus. Saint Antony was deeply attached to the person of Christ. Saint Paul's words can aptly be applied to Saint Anthony: "For me, to live is Christ." Day and night he spent meditating upon the Word of God, especially the Holy Gospels. Before he died, his last admonition to his disciples was: "Always breathe Christ and trust him."

Antony's love for Jesus was shown in the frequent invocation of his name. He not only prayed the Jesus prayer constantly, but also healed the sick, expelled demons, and imparted wisdom, all in the name of Christ. For Antony, the essence of the monastic life consisted not in extraordinary penances and austerity, but in believing in Christ and loving him. Like Saint Benedict, who came two centuries later, he counseled his disciples "to prefer nothing to the love of Christ" and to "cultivate, with great care, the attachment to the Lord."

After God revealed to Antony that his life was coming to a close, he prepared himself with great joy for his final encounter. He spoke to his disciples with tenderness, telling them: "I see the Lord calling me. I am now on my way to Him." He died as he lived, a humble pilgrim of Christ, a poor monk who was rich in his love for the Lord.

— JANUARY 18 —

Saint Antony: A Man Touched by Grace

It was said of Saint Antony that he was "Spirit-borne," that is, carried along by the Holy Spirit....Such men see what is happening in the world, as well as knowing what is going to happen.

ANTONY THE GREAT, APOPHEGMATA 30

For early monks and nuns, the essence of the spiritual life consisted in growing in grace from moment to moment. Grace is nothing else but the life of God in us. When we grow in grace, it is the divine life that grows and expands. Our Lady was called by the angel Gabriel "full of grace"; he meant that Mary's entire being was possessed by the life of God in her.

As a young man, when Antony received the call to the desert, God endowed Antony with the gift of his divine life. In doing so, God did not eliminate from Antony the poverty and limitation of his human nature, but by the power of his grace He transformed it and made it a vehicle to communicate his divine life. Antony became so filled with this divine life that he was called by other monks "*pneumantophore*": in other words, "Spirit-borne."

Through his desert experience, Antony learned that, in order to be filled with God's grace, one first had to acknowledge one's utter poverty before God, and stand empty and impoverished in his presence. He never boasted of himself, except of his sinfulness, knowing full well that all was grace, a free gift from God without which he could do nothing. Antony spent his years in the desert working out his salvation with humility and asceticism, acknowledging a total dependence on the God who was working in him. At the end of his life, having surrendered his entire existence to the Lord, he could see the transformation that the Holy Spirit had obtained within him, humbly saying: "I no longer fear God, for I love Him. And love casts out all fear." Grace had overcome fear, resulting in perfect love. Between God and Antony, barriers no longer existed, and all was love and light.

— JANUARY 19 —

Saint Antony: Work of Love

Our life and our death is with our neighbor. If we have gained our brother, we have gained God, but if we scandalize our brother, we have sinned against Christ.

ANTONY THE GREAT, APOPHEGMATA 9

S aint Antony retired to the solitude of the desert, not as an escape but as a means of learning to put into practice the teachings of the Gospels. He understood that the edifice of an authentic Christian life is built upon two pillars: love of God and love of neighbor.

Antony based his spiritual life on these two commandments. He knew that his relationship with God was tested by his encounters with other people and how he treated them. He recognized Christ in each. As Abba Apollo, another desert father, once said: "A person who sees his brother sees his God."

In our own lives, the only image of God we are permitted to see daily is that of our neighbor, a brother or a sister, made in God's image, and therefore deserving of all our love. Each encounter with another is a sacrament where we meet Christ. The smallest action we do to help or hurt a neighbor is done to Christ himself. This is the startling Gospel message uttered by the Lord: "Whatsoever you do to the least of my brethren, you do it to me."

For Antony, the love of God was an integral component of the love of neighbor. For him, as it should be for us, love was the purest criterion for all action. He lived and practiced daily the teaching of the Apostle John: "Beloved, since God loved us, we also ought to love one another....If we love one another, God lives in us, and his love is perfected in us" (1 Jn 4:11–12).

If, like Saint Antony, we make love the supreme rule of our own lives, we shall find great consolation when we reach the evening of life, for then love alone remains. It is on how much we have loved that we shall be judged in the end.

— JANUARY 20 —

A Wintry Day

The days are short, the weather cold,
By tavern fires tales are told.

NEW ENGLAND ALMANAC, 1704

This winter has been, thus far, a harsh one here in the northeastern United States. On the best of these cold winter days, I look at our garden through the kitchen window and see it full of snow. There, in the center, stands a statue of Saint Fiacre set inside a wooden shrine. His quiet presence protects the domain entrusted to him. In the winter sunlight, a glow springs forth from the statue, lifting high my spirit. Winter, in spite of its hardships, is not that bad after all. There are hidden treasures in the mystery of the season to be discovered by each of us.

Today, as the snow falls, I sit here in our monastery kitchen and continue with the daily morning task of writing. Because of the penetrating cold, I have lit the wood-burning stove. What joy and comfort to feel its warmth. Our wood stove contains a glass door in the front, which means I can watch the fire slowly burn. The stove is neatly located in the corner of the kitchen. Tending lovingly to the stove is one of the most inspiring activities of the day.

During these quiet hours of winter, I lift my heart to God, thanking him for the gift of immense stillness that winter affords and the joys of life's simple things. God seems more vividly present everywhere, and consequently it seems easier to enter into prayer on these days. Prayer becomes as natural as the twinges of frosty air we take into our lungs.

— JANUARY 21 —
Saint Agnes

What I longed for, I now see; what I hoped for, I now possess. In heaven, I am espoused to Him whom on earth I loved with all my heart.

ANTIPHON OF THE FEAST

During winter's bleakest period, we celebrate a feast full of light—Saint Agnes's day on which we remember a hero, martyr, virgin, and bride of Christ. The antiphons of the feast sing poetically of this virgin, of her soul aglow with love for her divine Bridegroom. Saint Ambrose recounted brilliantly the story of her martyrdom in his *Treatise on Virginity:*

> Today is the birthday of a virgin; let us imitate her purity. It is the birthday of a martyr; let us offer ourselves in sacrifice. It is the birthday of Saint Agnes, who is said to have suffered martyrdom at the age of twelve....A new kind of martyrdom! Too young to be punished, yet old enough for a martyr's crown; unfitted for the contest, yet effortless in victory, she shows herself a master in valor despite the handicap of youth. As a bride she would not be hastening to join her husband with the same joy she shows as a virgin on her way to punishment, crowned not with flowers but with holiness of life....
>
> In the midst of tears, she sheds no tears herself. The crowds marvel at her recklessness in throwing away her life untasted, as if she had already lived life to the full. All are amazed that one not yet of legal age can give her testimony to God. So she succeeds in convincing others of her testimony about God, though her testimony in human affairs could not yet be accepted....
>
> What menaces there were from the executioner, to frighten her; what promises made, to win her over; what influential people desired her in marriage! She answered: "To hope that any other will please me does wrong to my Spouse. I will be his who first chose me for himself. Executioner, why do you delay?" She stood still, she prayed, she offered her neck.
>
> You could see fear in the eyes of the executioner, as if he were the one condemned; his right hand trembled, his face grew pale as he saw the girl's peril, while she had no fear for herself.

One victim, but a twin martyrdom, to modesty and to religion;
Agnes preserved her virginity, and gained a martyr's crown.

— JANUARY 22 —

The Holy Martyrs

*The holy friends of Christ rejoice in heaven; they followed
in his footsteps to the end. They have shed their blood
for love of him and will reign with him forever.*

ANTIPHON OF THE OFFICE OF MARTYRS

The month of January is unusual in the choice of saints celebrated throughout its course. A bit of adjustment is needed
to jump from the beautiful Christmas season back into "ordinary time." But, then, most of life is not a feast, but a succession
of ordinary days. This being said, for the last several days, we
have been commemorating the martyr saints: Fabian, Sebastian,
Agnes, and Vincent. We are so far distant from the times when
these martyrs shed blood for the Lord that their lives seem to be
made up more of fantasy than of true accounts. Sadly, among
ordinary Christians, except perhaps for those in monasteries, little
attention is paid to the glorious stories of these martyrs.

There was a time when Catholics received at Baptism the
name of the saint on whose feast day they were born. This was a
good custom for keeping the memory of the saints alive, and it
helped the person hearing the name develop a warm friendship
and devotion towards his or her patron saint. Many of these
names were those of Martyrs: Agnes, Agatha, Lucy, Perpetua,
Felicity, and so on. Today's parents sometimes choose fashionable and secular names. Unfortunately, in my view, they forget
that what is fashionable today may not be so tomorrow.

Naming children after a certain saints who lived exemplary
holy lives is a praiseworthy custom now confined to fewer and
fewer Christian households. Of course, most monasteries hold
to this tradition: when a new monk or nun enters the monastic
life, they are given a saint's name. Very often, the name given to
the new monastic is that of a martyr, thus continuing the practice

of the early church, where monks were seen as successors and inheritors of the martyrs.

As we celebrate the memory of these martyrs, we do well to recall that through their martyrdom each became a confessor of the Lord and a true witness of the faith. We ought to pray daily for the grace to uphold our faith, the faith handed over by the Apostles and sealed by the blood of countless martyrs.

The heroic witness of the martyrs should also suggest that we too are called to witness Christ. We may not be called today to give up our lives as heroically as the martyrs did, but we can certainly give testimony to Christ in a pagan world such as ours, putting the Gospel into practice daily by living selflessly. This living example may become, as it was in the case of the martyrs, a seed of new Christians.

— JANUARY 23 —

Goodness of Trees

The trees of the LORD are watered abundantly,
the cedars of Lebanon that he planted.
In them the birds build their nests,
the stork has its home in the fir trees.

PSALM 104:16–17

Winters can be tough. Our well has frozen two or three times, something which did not occur at all last year. Then several times this winter we have had to do without water for twenty-four hours or so and electric power, which we occasionally loose during a heavy storm. And yet, life here in our small country monastery goes on. Over the years, we have learned to cope with all types of shortages and outages. Such situations can be unpleasant, but they never mark the end of things.

The days that we go without power makes me appreciate the things we make use of daily, but that are often taken for granted. For instance, our two gas stoves, which function the same with or without power, and the goodness of wood, which provides us with an alternate form of heating.

The silent trees that stand tall throughout our monastic property exude a natural goodness, one that we often overlook. In the summer, they provide shade from an otherwise intemperate sun. On hot summer days, our sheep readily seek relief from the oppressive heat by using the shady trees as shelter. In the fall, on a perfect autumn day, our maples parade a glorious red and golden tapestry. As I walk throughout the property, I find one tree's colors more startling than the next. I usually cut some branches and arrange a bouquet for the chapel. The colors of those leaves are in themselves a perfect song of praise to their Creator.

God, in his infinite wisdom, appointed a particular function to each component of his Creation. For the trees, there is a goodness in their generosity as they provide us with the wood to heat our homes, construct our houses, and build our furniture, while also purifying our air and performing countless other life-giving functions. During these wintry days, I see our bare tree boughs covered with snow or icicles; I look at them with renewed respect. Quietly, I utter a prayer: O *all trees of the Lord, bless the Lord.*

— JANUARY 24 —

Seize the Moment

Take my yoke upon you and learn from me; for I am gentle and humble in heart, and you will find rest for your souls. For my yoke is easy and my burden light.
MATTHEW 11:29–30

A carpet of snow covers our meadows and hills and glistens in the winter sun. A perfect day, I say to myself as I move swiftly around the barn, bringing food and water to the sheep and chickens; yet, something within me doesn't want to hurry. I wish to be totally present in the moment, in today's beauty, and watch it slowly go by. I have always regretted in the past hurrying along with daily duties. Time is such a precious gift from God. I do not wish to labor against it, but rather work with it. I always notice that when I take enough time to perform my daily work and do not rush, I enjoy my labor so much more, whatever it may be. On these occasions, I recall Saint Francis de Sales's counsel, whose memorial we keep today: "Let us try to make the present moment beautiful."

Ah, the wisdom of the saints! What wonderful lessons we can learn from them, and then apply them to our otherwise ordinary everyday life. Of course, all the saints, Saint Francis de Sales included, used the Gospels as their daily school and had the Lord himself as their teacher. The wisdom learned in the school of the Gospels was imparted by the Master who taught them well.

— JANUARY 25 —

Saint Paul's Journey

It was midday when Saul journeyed toward Damascus; suddenly a brilliant light from heaven flashed all around him.

ANTIPHON OF THE FEAST

About two months ago, we set out on our Advent journey towards Christmas, with the hope of meeting the Lord along the way. Today we celebrate the conversion of the great Apostle Paul, to whom the Lord revealed Himself on the road to Damascus. I marvel at the thought of how often the Lord mysteriously presents himself to us while we are "on the way": *in via*, as the medieval authors would describe it. It is as if he wishes to facilitate the journey and make it easier. As we reflect on the example of Paul on the road to Damascus, let us keep in mind another important New Testament journey, that of the two disciples on the way to Emmaus. The Lord shows himself to them as their companion on the road, and later reveals himself more fully in the breaking of the bread. The Lord seems to imply that if we embark on a spiritual journey, we will not be disappointed, for we can count on a gracious Lord who is eager to meet us halfway.

— JANUARY 26 —

Saints Paula and Eustochium

I exhort those of you who are virgins to preserve your chastity. Tell this story to later generations so that they may know that amid swords, amid wild beasts and desert regions, chastity is never taken captive, and that a person who is dedicated to Christ can die but cannot be defeated.

SAINT JEROME, *LIFE OF MALCHUS*

Today the Roman Martyrology honors the memory of the noble Roman widow, Saint Paula, an extraordinary woman and a jewel of early monasticism. Under the guidance of Saint Jerome, she and her daughter Eustochium set out from their home in Rome on a journey that would take them ultimately to Bethlehem in the Holy Land.

The Roman matron and her daughter first visited Jerusalem and then all of the other holy places mentioned in the Old and New Testaments. From Bethlehem and Jerusalem, to Nazareth and Mount Tabor, they carried out on foot one of the most arduous pilgrimages ever embarked on by women of the time. Motivated by an incredible faith, mother and daughter distributed alms along their way wherever they saw a need.

Deeply moved by the place where Jesus was born, they settled in Bethlehem and established their monastery near the Basilica of the Nativity built by Constantine. With her vast fortune, Paula was able to make plans for the foundation of two monasteries, one for men under the leadership of Saint Jerome and one for women directed by her. Attached to Saint Paula's monastery was a guest house, in memory of Mary and Joseph, who were without shelter when they came to Bethlehem. The guesthouse provided rooms for pilgrims, travelers, and the poor.

Life in Paula's monastery was arranged according to traditional monastic patterns. Her community of about fifty nuns was divided into three groups, each with a separate building. They worked and ate separately but gathered together as one community for daily worship. They sang daily the Canonical Hours at the prescribed time, but on Sundays and feast days they attended the Liturgy and Major Offices in the Basilica of the Nativity, much as did the Christians of Jerusalem in the Basilica of the Holy Sepulcher. A particular distinction in Paula's monastery was the attention she assigned among her nuns to the reading and study of the Bible.

Under the direction of Saint Jerome, she and Eustochium had developed an absolute passion for the Scriptures. In many ways, *lectio divina* was the primary occupation in their monastic day. Everything in their communal life was directed towards it. They not only wished to live close by the holy places where the Lord lived, but they wished also to relive the events of His life and put into practice His teachings. To obtain this knowledge, they had to study and pray over the Scriptures, the Gospels in particular. Paula, her daughter Eustochium, and their companions were truly pioneers of the cenobitic life among women.

— JANUARY 27 —

Indoor Gardening

Who loves a garden, loves a greenhouse too.
"THE GARDEN," WILLIAM COWPER, 1731–1800

This winter day shows itself to be stern, relentless, almost unforgiving. It is a day that calls for indoor seclusion. Since a ray of sunlight is shining into the greenhouse, I have decided to spend a few hours in what I call our "indoor garden." It is a pleasant winter activity that reinforces the feeling that I am not totally cut off from some sort of gardening during the long, cold winter months.

Our greenhouse plants suffer quite a bit with the harsh weather. Because of the cost of heating, I keep the temperature low at night, about forty degrees, and during the day the plants have to do with whatever heat they get from the sun, which can be plenty on clear days and sparse on those more overcast.

I start my "indoor gardening" by watering all of the plants, something I do about twice a week during winter. I try not to overwater, for large amounts of water in winter do more harm than good, inevitably rotting the roots of the plants. Once a month, I feed the plants with some sort of organic plant food as a tonic. Then, I start with the labor that I like least, that is, pruning and trimming the dead leaves from the stems. It is a tedious job, but a necessary one; otherwise the plants go to ruin. This cannot be done in one day, so I take different sections of the greenhouse one at a time.

Indoor gardening is a labor of love, and like all of gardening, requires much patience. God knows we need to learn to practice patience everyday, so I look to this task as training in the "school of patience." When I get a bit tired of the never-ending work, I remind myself of Saint Teresa's promise: "Patience gains all things."

— JANUARY 28 —

Bach's Cello Suites

Music has charms to soothe the savage breast,
To soften rocks, or bend a knotted oak.
WILLIAM CONGREVE, *THE MOURNING BRIDE*

One wintry day, when a severe snowstorm puts a stop to outdoor activities, I prepare to enjoy the rich and timeless music of Bach as I work at indoor tasks. Listening to Bach gives an incentive to try to accomplish a job in good fashion. Sometimes when I feel overwhelmed by the amount of work, Bach soothingly restores a bit of my common sense.

It has taken me a long time to learn how to listen to Bach's six cello suites all at once, without interspersing other music to break up what I once considered the monotony of the solo cello. But my years of practicing Bach on the piano and listening to his other music slowly ripened my ears for the delights of the cello suites. Today, as I listen, I begin to appreciate them as a synthesis of all the wealth of Bach's music. In these suites, we find a mirror of the varied experience of our own particular life story. All of life, from birth to death, is contained in this music. Bach purposely used these unaccompanied suites to convey vividly what he considered the fundamental aspects of life. He avoids the decorative effects which he so often used in his other music. When it came to the cello solo, Bach was uncompromising; he wished nothing to hamper its distinct, clear voice. Further, in his use and choice of the cello's continuo, that is, its uninterrupted playing, Bach portrayed without ambiguity the rhythm of human life as a continuum, a progressive whole.

Bach's cello suites, composed with a disciplined, ascetic directness, have a unique way of penetrating the soul of a person who is truly attuned. They comfort and nurture the human spirit and help us walk without fear, through all of the varied, mysterious, inner landscapes of the soul.

— JANUARY 29 —

Kyrie Eleison

He who has repented travels towards the Lord. The way to God is an inner journey in the mind and the heart.

THEOPHAN THE RECLUSE

The *Kyrie eleison* is a short prayer that comes to us right from the Gospel. The *Kyrie*, in its Greek form, is a relic from the early Church, when the liturgy in Rome was celebrated in Greek and not in Latin. In the monastery, we sing it in Gregorian chant at the beginning of the Mass, and then again in a simple litany form at the conclusion of the Offices, as prescribed by Saint Benedict in the Rule. Since we pray it over and over again in our daily offices, I have slowly learned to make this short prayer truly my own. It is so short, so simple. I see two movements in the prayer: our own part, as an expression of repentance and conversion, and the part of God, the bestowing of his mercy.

The *Kyrie* teaches us that we must repent daily and beg for God's mercy. Through the uttering of the *Kyrie eleison*, we focus our eyes on him who is all merciful. There is a twelfth-century ikon of Christ that speaks volumes to me. The name of the ikon is "Christ, the Merciful One." The Lord seems to be holding the

Gospel book in one hand, and with the other giving a blessing. To me, this gesture of blessing is an invitation to repentance and a never-ending assurance of His loving mercy.

As I gaze on the ikon of "Christ, the Merciful One," I find it easier to say the *Kyrie* and to pray for conversion. I know that conversion and repentance are the only ways to Christ. It is the type of conversion that demands a change of heart from arrogance to humility, from human efficiency to Gospel simplicity, from violence to nonviolence, from selfishness to selflessness, from judgment of others to nonjudgment. Before the conclusion of the offices, as we intone the *Kyrie*, I usually pause for a quiet moment and bring all of my petitions before the throne of God's divine mercy. Not only do I pray for the grace of conversion and true repentance, but I also pray for the people who suffer under national catastrophes, the sick, the poor, the victims of war, crime, and violence. After my litany of petition, I intone the *Kyrie*, and somehow feel at peace. Deep down, I am convinced that all shall be well because "His mercy endures forever."

— JANUARY 30 —

Signs of the Season

To him who in the love of Nature holds communion with her visible forms, she speaks a various language.

WILLIAM C. BRYANT

We have almost reached the end of January, and I notice that the long winter darkness is slowly but surely shrinking. The light is extending its duration by a few extra minutes each twenty-four hours, before the sun finally sets behind the hills and the mountains on the western side of the Hudson River. The longer daylight is one of those first few signs seen in Mother Nature that gives us a hint that spring cannot be far away.

I am particularly fond of the Gospel passages where our Lord uses the events in nature to announce the proximity of the next season. Take this passage from Matthew: "From the fig tree learn its lesson: as soon as its branch becomes tender and puts forth its leaves, you know that summer is near." (24:32). Those of us who spend our lives in the countryside experience a similar sensation, as we observe nature's announcement of changes in the seasons.

Here in the monastery we have a few signs of our own which announce the approaching spring. The earliest one is when our chickens begin to lay eggs again after a long winter rest. Toward the end of January, just before Candlemas Day, usually the first egg appears in some secluded, hidden corner of the barn where the chickens take winter with the sheep. For a while, even weeks at a time, I usually find just one egg per day in the nest. But as winter begins to shrink and the daylight is prolonged, two and three and even more eggs begin to appear daily.

Another sure sign of our approaching spring is when one of four ewes gives birth to the first lamb during late January or, preferably, in February. Sometimes a lamb may arrive on the coldest day of the season. On one hand, I tend to resent its arrival on a cold day, since it creates more work and hardship. Yet, on the other hand, the lamb's arrival fills us with hope and joy as it signals winter's exit and looks toward spring.

These are what I call our "mid-winter" days. Half of the season is over. The land around us is clean, pure, and white. The sheep make a path between the barn and the monastery, and I watch with joy to see the new lambs following their mother and treading over the clean snow for the first time.

— JANUARY 31 —

Blessed Are the Poor in Spirit

I have not a thing. I give you my heart.
WORDS OF AN OLD MONK

B lessed are the poor in spirit," the Lord counsels us in the Gospel. Poverty of spirit, frugality, moderation, and simplicity are all integral components of the monastic way of life. To a world that exalts riches, wealth, greed, and possessions, the way of the monk must be seen as totally absurd.

But the monk cannot be distracted by distorted notions of a

world wrapped up in its own selfish desires. This is not the aim of the monk's life. Instead, he must have his eyes fixed on Jesus, the only model. And what do we see when we look at Jesus? In the words of Saint Paul, we see him as someone who emptied himself of His glory at the moment of the Incarnation, and took the humble state of a servant.

Jesus subjected himself to the human plight. He embraced poverty, simplicity, and detachment from worldly comforts, and followed the way of the poor to the very end: *Mortem autem crucis*. He died on the cross as a poor man, repudiated by all except His Mother and a few disciples. All authentic monastic life cannot aim at being anything less than an imitation of the life of Christ, who was poor and crucified. For the monk, as for all Christians, it is not at all accidental that Jesus proclaimed, as the first of the Beatitudes: Blessed are the poor in spirit.

FEBRUARY

The Eve of Candlemas

Into the temple, like a vast ship, with glory, they entered
religiously.

RAYMOND OURSEL, *LES PÈLERINS DU MOYEN ÂGE*

Tomorrow is Candlemas, the feast of the Presentation of the
Lord in the Temple and one of the loveliest of February's
feasts. It occurs precisely forty days after the feast of the Nativity
of the Lord, a perfect crowning to the Christmas cycle. In the
monastery there is quite a bit of preparation for tomorrow's feast:
the many oil lamps in front of our ikons have to be cleaned and
refilled, old candles have to be trimmed and in some cases replaced with new ones, the chapel has to be dusted and cleaned,
and the last of the Christmas decorations put away for another
year. All must be completed by late afternoon, so that the chapel
is ready for the first Vespers of the feast. As I place the Festal
ikon on the main lectern, I rest my eyes upon the beloved famil-

75

iar faces: Mary, Joseph, the elder Simeon, Anna the prophetess, and at the center, the child Jesus. I am particularly fond of the elder Simeon, and I carry an image of him with the Child Jesus in his arms in my small French Bible. (I think I even named a recipe in one of my cookbooks after him.) The feast of the Lord's Presentation, in a way, is also the blessed elder's feast.

The oil lamps and the candles we burn during our worship are testimonials of our love and devotion. We burn them in front of the ikons of the Lord, of his Immaculate Mother, of the saints. I remember once being told by a visitor how well decorated the chapel was with those votive lights burning in front of the ikons. I quickly replied that they were not decorations. The ikons and the statues in our chapel, I explained to the visitor, are a form of presence, a presence contained in the mystery they represent. Through faith we enter in contact with that presence: we touch it, venerate it, and are comforted by it. The oil lamps and the candles are expressions of our devotion, prayer, and supplication to the presence represented in the ikon. And long after we have left the chapel, the lamps continue their watchful vigil in front of our beloved intercessors, pleading silently our petitions.

— FEBRUARY 2 —

Candlemas: A Feast of Lights

Adorn your bridal chamber, O Sion....Greet Mary, the gate of heaven, with loving salutation; for she carries the King of glory, the new Light. In the temple stands the Virgin, embracing in her arms the eternal Son begotten before the day-star. The elder Simeon receives him in his arms and proclaims to the nations.

ANTIPHON OF THE FEAST

On February 2, the churches of the East and West celebrate the beautiful Feast of the Presentation of the Lord in the Temple. This ancient feast originated in the Christian East, where it was known by its Greek name, the *Hypapante*, meaning "meeting" or "encountering." According to Mosaic law, forty days after the birth of a male child, the mother had to present him in the Temple while also making a sacrificial offering of a lamb or two turtledoves. This sacrifice served as purification for the mother after the birthing. Mary and Joseph were known for always being obedient to all the precepts of Jewish law. Thus, on the appointed day, they brought the infant Jesus to the Temple where, according to the Gospel story, he is received, blessed, and embraced by the elder Simeon and the righteous prophetess Anna (Lk 2:22–38). They both recognize in the young babe the savior promised by God to Israel. As they meet him for the first time in the flesh, their joy cannot be contained. The significance of the encounter of the elder and the recently born, helpless infant is expressed, I find, in terms of great tenderness in the Byzantine text for the Offices of the day:

> Simeon tell us: Whom do you bear in your arms that you rejoice so greatly in the Temple? To whom do you cry and shout: "Now I am set free, for I have seen my Savior?" This is he who was born of a Virgin; this is he, the Word, God of God, who for our sakes has taken flesh to save humankind.

This deeply touching feast of the Lord is celebrated in most monasteries with great solemnity. First, there is the procession with hymn, antiphons, and candles through the monastic cloister, as the monks proceed toward the church for Mass. The procession becomes a sort of cortege where the monks, united with Mary and Joseph, accompany the Lord as he enters the Temple to be offered to his Father. As the monks walk slowly in procession, we carry in our hands lighted candles that have just been blessed at the beginning of the rite.

Today's feast is sometimes known by its English name, Candlemas, for candles play an important role in the day's liturgy. The theme of light—based on the evocative words of Simeon, who calls the Christ Child "a light to enlighten the nations"—permeates the entire liturgy of the feast. Today the Church reaffirms the truth of Simeon's words that Jesus is the true light of the world by placing the blessed candle in our hands. Thus, we also

symbolically receive Christ in our hands and arms as the blessed
Simeon and Anna once did long ago.

Candles are very expressive of the devotional life of monasteries: there are the four candles of the Advent wreath, the Christmas candle lit on Christmas day, and the Easter candle lit during
the whole of Paschaltime. Then there are the everyday candles
used during the celebration of the Eucharist and the monastic
offices, the candle that accompanies the Eucharist taken to a sick
monk in his cell, and the candles and oil lamps lit in front of our
ikons. The dancing yet steady flames of the candles in our chapel
speak to me of those intangible realities the monk seeks during
long hours of prayer. The comforting, ethereal aura springing
from their light affirms the reality of a mysterious presence that
can be sensed only with the eyes of faith. Candles are, in a way,
messengers of him who is both mystery and the Invisible One.

— FEBRUARY 3 —

Simeon the Elder and Anna the Prophetess

O God-fearing Simeon, you lifted Christ in your arms,
whom the pure Virgin bore. Holy Anna, sober in spirit
and venerable in years, with reverence you confessed the
Master freely and openly in the Temple.
BYZANTINE MATINS OF THE FEAST

Today I give thanks to the Lord for another quiet, secluded
winter day—one which is a great help in promoting the work
of writing. I am presently working on two books simultaneously,
and at the same time correcting a third manuscript that shall see
the light of day early next year. Writing can sometimes be a struggle, especially when someone like me is caught in the midst of multiple duties that must be accomplished by day's end. I know I must
use time wisely, and I certainly need to take advantage of these
wintry days that allocate me a bit more time for the craft of writing.

I pause for a moment and add a couple of logs to the fire in
the wood-burning stove—always a pleasant task on a cold day
like today and one that provides a momentary change from steady

writing. I use the moment to reflect on yesterday's lovely feast, a feast that catches the imagination of the heart and continues to linger there long beyond its fixed date. In the Church of the East the feast is the equivalent of a Solemnity in the Church of the West. Luke's account of the event is one of the most touching stories in his Gospel, full of tender feeling and piety. The Troparion of the Feast expresses all of it in a beautiful manner:

> Hail, full of grace, Virgin Mother of God, for from you has shone forth the Sun of Justice, Christ, our God, giving light to those in darkness. And you, O righteous elder Simeon, rejoice, for you have received in your arms the Savior of our souls, who grants us the resurrection.

The elder Simeon and the prophetess Anna were given the privilege of beholding the Son of God and carrying him in their arms. They probably recognized Him the moment Mary and Joseph brought Him into the Temple. After all, they had been anxiously waiting for the promised Messiah for many long years, spending their days praying continually, fasting, and doing good to their neighbors. They were truly the "pure of heart," as the Byzantine Matins of the Feast expresses: *The Elder bent down and reverently touched the footprints of the Mother of God who knew no wedlock, and he said: "O Pure Lady, He who you carry is Fire. I am afraid to take God as a babe in my arms. He is the Lord of the light that knows no shadow and King of peace."*

— FEBRUARY 4 —

The Winter Wind

Do you hear the sounds of the winds that blow,
In the tempest wild across the snow?
They come in the shadow, they come in the storm
That darkens the sky with its awful form;
The bitter winds find no rest
On the sable cloud on the snow's white breast!

A SHAKER "WINTER SONG"

Because our monastery building is located on a hilltop, we can hear the wind blowing on all sides of the building. A gusty wind, such as the one we are having today, is one of those elements with which we must cope during our wintry season. I have a neighbor who is afraid to light up her wood stove on a windy day because of the danger of fire. She certainly has a point.

I notice that on one of these seemingly endless winter days, when the temperature is frigid and the wind extra heavy, our farm animals do not dare leave their barn shelter. Neither do they show their faces through the barn doors, as otherwise they like to do. They are as uncomfortable with a rough noisy wind as they are with a blizzard. Wind like today's, though not an enemy, is nevertheless seen by many country folks as intimidating. The streets in the nearby village tend to be empty on such days, as I witnessed this morning when I ran an errand there. I only saw a few sturdy souls; the village was practically asleep.

The bitter wind, often accompanied during the winter by blows of snowdrift, intrudes into the peace and serenity of the monastery. On such days, I realize how essential it is to cultivate a certain spirit of endurance, resilience, and sturdiness against intemperate weather. When the weather gets really nasty, I try to cope with it by simply repeating a friend's favorite slogan: "This too shall pass." Of course, deep inside, we know the Lord will see us through. And besides, tomorrow will be a new day, perhaps a calmer, gentler one.

— FEBRUARY 5 —

On Patience

Patience gains all things.

SAINT TERESA OF ÁVILA

The practice of patience is decisively a daily challenge for all of us, those living inside or outside a monastery. Our Lord, who endured much suffering, practiced patience every instant of his life. An early bishop, Saint Polycarp, frequently exhorted his disciples to look at Christ and how he exercised patience: "I exhort you all," he said, "let us be imitators of his patience."

But what is patience? Church father, John Chrysostom, gives us his own understanding of it in a homily he delivered to the Thessalonians: "Patience means that we should endure as Christ endured those things, and all of that without discouragement. Also, we should wait for him, that is, we should be prepared. Whenever Saint Paul speaks of patience, he, of course, implies affliction. For this is to love God, to endure and not to be troubled."

Today we honor the memory of Saint Agatha, an early virgin and martyr whose martyrdom is a living example of that "patient endurance" spoken of by Saint Paul. During the difficult time of persecution, she patiently endured suffering out of her love for God. And because of her great love, the Holy Spirit bestowed upon her the power to overcome fear. Thus, she triumphed over her persecutors.

— FEBRUARY 6 —

On Silence

Abba Joseph said to Abba Nistheros: "When you speak, do you find peace?" He replied: "No." The old man then said, "If you do not find peace, why do you speak? Be silent and when a conversation takes place, it is better to listen than to speak."

APOTHEGMATA PATRUM

Silence is something sacred. It ought to be greatly respected and avidly cultivated, for God abides in eternal silence. It is in that eternal silence that the Father uttered a Word. And the Word became flesh to communicate to us the meaning, the mystery of that divine silence. It is our duty, therefore, to keep a silent space within our hearts, so that we may be able to hear the Word.

In spiritual life, the practice of exterior silence and that of interior silence have always been intimately connected. One does not exist without the other. If Abba Joseph placed such emphasis on exterior silence, it was simply because he saw it as a prerequisite to interior silence of the heart. When the heart, by the grace of the Holy Spirit, reaches the point of being truly silent and pacified, the divine life hidden within is revealed. The heart then experiences a new reality: the life of God bursting within. Silence becomes a loving, intuitive, wordless dialogue between God and the heart. An ancient monk used to encourage in his disciples the practice and necessity of silence by telling them, "The love of silence ultimately leads to the silence of love."

— FEBRUARY 7 —

To Cultivate God's Presence

You must gather yourself together within your heart and stand there before the Lord. Pray, and may God grant you prayer.

THEOPHAN THE RECLUSE

A young student, who frequents our small monastery, asked me how one went about recalling the presence of God in daily life. He explained his difficulty in trying to think concretely about God. He wished to know if I could show him a method or some secret short-cut to achieving this. I told him that my understanding of the matter was that the continual awareness of God's presence sprung more from a deep faith on the part of the person and a grace from above—not on short-cuts or techniques. I added that God freely gives this grace to those who seek him with simplicity of heart.

The young man insisted that he needed a more concrete approach because he found it difficult to pray. After much insistence, I suggested that he could take fifteen minutes two or three times a day to recite a simple prayer that originated with the monks in Ireland. I said to him: "Seek a quiet place and try to calm down your whole being. As you slowly say the prayer, close your eyes. As you pray each phrase, each word, imagine it and linger over the words as much as possible. Cultivate the warm feeling you perceive, and surrender to it. Let the prayer take over, and let it become part of your being. Let go of all mental reservations and distractions. When you complete the prayer, continue to remain quiet a bit longer, both mentally and physically, with whatever feelings remain from the prayer." Since the student was quite serious about cultivating the awareness of God's presence in his life, I added this: "Do this three times a day: morning, noon, and evening. With the passing of time, the inner feelings springing from the prayer will take over and remain with you throughout the day and throughout the night. To discover God's presence, we must first take our eyes off of the outside world, enter our inner chamber as the Gospel counsels us, and attentively seek his presence deep within our very selves."

This is the simple Celtic prayer I offered to the young man:

God to enfold me, God in my watching,
God to surround me, God in my hoping.
God in my speaking, God in my life,
God in my thinking. God in my lips,
God in my sleeping, God in my soul,
God in my waking, God in my heart.

— FEBRUARY 8 —

The Evening Soup

Beautiful soup, so rich and green,
Waiting in a hot tureen!
Who for such dainties would not stoop?
Soup of the evening, beautiful soup!

LEWIS CARROLL, *ALICE IN WONDERLAND*

Nothing is so welcoming on a winter night as a bowl of hot soup. On cold days like today, I often partake of two bowls of hot soup and two slices of bread and that is very much my evening meal. I feel nourished, comforted, and warm, both in body and spirit.

The basic simplicity of soup gives it a timeless appeal. My own memories of growing up remind me how the "*souper*" always consisted of a good homemade soup and plenty of it. My family, descendants from the mountain people of the Pyrenees, were proud of their heritage, and one thing my grandmother often prepared was the local soup called Garbure. She would make enough of it to last for days, and we often feasted on it during our long and cold winter nights. It is in keeping with this tradition, both family and monastic, that I was inspired a few years ago to compile a book of soups entitled *Twelve Months of Monastery Soups*. It took me six years to complete this book, but because of my love of soups, I considered it a blessed and rewarding task.

Very often, when I make a simple, basic soup for myself I just look around and see what ingredients, mostly vegetables, are available. Tonight I found an onion, a carrot, celery, and a potato and decided to make a plain pea soup with all of it. First I sauteed the onion. Then I added a couple of cups of water, the diced carrot and potato, the thinly sliced celery (three branches), and the dried split peas. When the water began boiling I added one bay leaf (rescued from a bay plant in the greenhouse, a plant that we have grown here for over twenty-five years), a pinch of salt and pepper, a minced garlic clove, and some finely chopped fresh parsley. I allowed the soup to cook slowly over medium heat until the desired result was achieved. Soup-making is so simple, so basic, and the end result always so satisfying.

It is no wonder that soups were usually the chosen daily fare of monasteries throughout the centuries. It is also the daily fare of the poor and the homeless, in whose company a monk should feel at home. Often when hungry and cold, they seek relief in soup kitchens like those sponsored by the Catholic Worker movement. Dorothy Day, in whose company I was privileged to share many a bowl of soup, both in Tivoli and in New York City, had deep appreciation and reverence for soup. She used to tell me that soup was the one thing that was never missing from a Catholic Worker table. If we allow ourselves to discover the simple pleasure of soup-making, we shall find out that soup sharing and soup giving can become true occasions of endless joy.

— FEBRUARY 9 -

Grace

My grace is sufficient for you, for power is made perfect in weakness.

2 CORINTHIANS 12:9

G race is such an unfathomable mystery. It is God's life in us in ways beyond our human comprehension. Saint Thérèse used to love to repeat, "*Tout est grace*: All is grace." A guest, who last year made a retreat here, was deeply moved by the concept of grace. One day he asked me what grace was. I simply responded, "If you look with supernatural eyes, all is grace. Every occasion is grace." Recently, I received from him through the mail a piece of lovely writing entitled "The Personal Attraction of Grace." It is by Jean Mouroux and short enough to be quoted here:

> God then works within man, and the soul in its innermost depths experiences his action, which is both illumination and inspiration, a summons of light and love. It is grace which enlightens and attracts—and this is perfectly true; but it means that God himself...enlightens and attracts us by his grace. It is not the action of a blind force, an impassive sun shedding light without discrimination. It is a Person, who is light and love, who gives a little of himself to a person in need, one who craves that light and love.

— FEBRUARY 10 —

Saint Scholastica: Mother of Nuns

Let the Christian people rejoice in the glory of the gracious virgin, Scholastica; but, most of all, let the choir of virgins and nuns be glad celebrating the feast of her who, pouring forth her tears, entreated the Lord.

ANTIPHON OF THE FEAST

D uring mid-February, when winter begins to give us a hint of forthcoming spring, we celebrate the feast of the very quiet Saint Scholastica. I call her a quiet saint, for so little is known about her, and the little we know has come to us only indirectly through Gregory the Great's biography of Saint Benedict, her famous brother. The portrait that Pope Gregory gives is one of a very charming saint who makes the work of love and prayer the operative reasons for her life. Like her twin brother, Benedict, Scholastica received from God the call to monastic life. She entered a monastery of nuns near Monte Cassino where Saint Benedict was the abbot of a monastery of monks. Once a year she was permitted to have a visit with her brother, and they used this occasion to speak not only of family matters but, more importantly, to speak of God and their spiritual lives.

During one of those family visits, a most delightful episode took place. Toward evening, after a few hours of visiting with his sister, Saint Benedict was getting ready to return to his monastery; such was the rule. Scholastica, however, begged him to remain with her. Benedict refused his sister's request, reminding her of their obedience to the Rule and monastic custom. When Scholastica saw that her petition was of no avail, she laid her head in her hands on the table and prayed. A violent storm immediately broke, pouring out torrential rain and making Benedict's return to his monastery impossible. At this, Scholastica ceased her praying and, looking at her brother with a smile, said to him, "Go now, Brother. Return to your monastery and leave me alone, if you can." Benedict guessed what had occurred and, smilingly, reproached his sister, "What have you done?" To this Scholastica replied, "I begged you to stay, and you would not listen to me, so I made recourse to my Lord in prayer, and He heard me." Accepting the divine will, Benedict remained with his sister until the following morning. Gregory, commenting on the episode, said of her, "Greater was her power before the Lord, because greater was her love." Scholastica died three days after this visit. Upon learning of her death, Benedict ordered his monks to bury her in the monastery tomb prepared for him. So it was done, acknowledging that neither life nor death could separate these two.

Just as Saint Benedict is acknowledged to be the father of monks in the West, we can also rightly call Saint Scholastica the beloved mother of nuns. From the onset women contributed greatly to the monastic movement. We learn from the writer Palladius, for instance, that during the early years of the desert movement, twelve monasteries of women were established in the area around Thebes in Egypt. From the early monastic literature comes the names of such courageous women as the two Melanies, Macrina, Alexandra, Thais, Syncletica, Euphrasia, Mary of Egypt, Euphrosine, Paula, and Eustochium, along with many other early nuns who emulated their brother monks in fervor and sometimes surpassed them in virtue. The early monks acknowledged the extraordinary quality of these women monastics; some even came to recognize that it was the monks who were in need of imitating the sanctity and zeal of the early nuns instead of the other way around.

— February 11 —

Our Lady of Lourdes

Would you be kind enough to come here for fifteen days?

OUR LADY TO BERNADETTE

On February 11, 1858, an extraordinary event took place in a small village named Lourdes, in the foothills of the French Pyrenees. On that day, a young shepherdess named Bernadette, her sister Toinette, and her friend Balume decided to go in search of wood to heat their cold and damp home. With their sabots clomping on the cobblestone street, the young girls crossed the bridge over the River Gave and started to look for wood in the surrounding countryside. While the other girls were collecting bundles of sticks, Bernadette heard in the distance the church bells ringing the Angelus. She stopped and quickly recited the angel's salutation.

Suddenly, out of a perfect stillness came the sound of a gentle breeze. Bernadette saw nothing when she looked toward the place from which the sound had come. The rustling sound was repeated. This time Bernadette gazed toward what seemed like a grotto carved into a rocky hill. She rubbed her eyes in disbelief. A golden light appeared, pulsing forth from the obscure grotto. Then, in the center of the light there appeared a most beautiful young woman, brighter than the light that enveloped her body.

At first, Bernadette felt confused and inadequate in her proximity to such radiance. What could all this be? she thought. But the lovely young woman smiled tenderly and beckoned her to come closer. As Bernadette approached, she fell on her knees in front of the beautiful woman, whom she noticed was carrying a luminous rosary with a golden crucifix. Stunned, Bernadette saw the mysterious woman making the sign of the cross and so she did likewise, and together they recited the rosary. At the conclusion of the recitation, the beautiful woman seemed to disappear into the depths of the grotto. The apparitions continued for the space of several months, until the last occurrence on July 16 of the same year. When the beautiful woman revealed her name to Bernadette, she spoke in the patois language of the local people and said, "I am the Immaculate Conception."

From the moment the apparitions took place, thousands of people from nearby and from further away took interest in the events of the village. Among those people, most likely, were my great-grandparents who lived nearby and spoke the same patois dialect as Bernadette. My great-grandfather Francois (named after Bernadette's father) was born two years after Bernadette. In our family, Lourdes has always held a cherished spot. This family tradition continues, as some of my cousins still inhabit their ancestral home only four kilometers away from Lourdes.

I have often asked our relatives about the possibility of our forebears knowing Bernadette and the Lourdes of her time. They always assent, saying it is likely that the apparition was the most important event in the vicinity, and that the locals would not have missed being present. From my childhood, I remember all of our homes contained a small grotto built in a special garden corner, with small statues of Our Lady and Saint Bernadette in it. We prayed in front of the grotto and thus honored the distinguished Lady who once came to visit one of our own.

— FEBRUARY 12 —

Visiting Our Lady of Lourdes

Glory to you, Virgin Mary, humble servant of the Lord,
Mother of God, dwelling place of the Holy Spirit.

PRAYER TO OUR LADY OF LOURDES

It is a moving experience to witness the multitudes of pilgrims coming yearly to the holy place of Lourdes. They walk through the narrow *ruelles* or alleyways of Lourdes, approaching the grotto where Our Lady awaits them. They pray and sing in their own language, reverently touch the rock where Our Lady's feet once rested, and confide their pains and joys to her. Some pray for healing, others for strength to carry their daily crosses. Many of the pilgrims offer Mary a candle as a symbol of their devotion and petitions, while others silently drink from the fountain dug by Bernadette's fingers at Our Lady's insistence. When it is time to depart from Lourdes, they leave comforted by Our Lady's gentle presence.

They take with them prayers to Our Lady of Lourdes, perhaps like this one given to me by a student on my last visit there.

Mary, you showed yourself to Bernadette in the grotto of the rock. On a cold and grey winter day, you brought the warmth, light and beauty of your presence. In the often dark depths of our lives, in the depth of the world where evil is so powerful, you bring us hope.

Come to our aid, sinners that we are. Give us the humility to have a change of heart, the courage to do penance. Teach us to pray for all people. Guide us to the source of true life. Whet our appetite for the Eucharist, our bread for the journey, the bread of life.

The Holy Spirit has placed you near the Father in the glory of your eternal Son. Look with kindness on our miserable bodies and hearts. Shine forth for us like a gentle light at the hour of our death.

Together with Bernadette, we pray to you, O Mary, as your poor children. May we live our days in the spirit of the beatitudes. Then we will be able, here below, to sing together with you: Magnificat! Amen.

Humility

A brother asked Abba Tithoes, "Which way leads to humility?" The old man said, "The way to humility is self-control, prayer, and thinking yourself inferior to all creatures."

ABBA TITHOES

The Desert Fathers and Mothers struggled daily to achieve true humility. They knew from experience that the practice of humility is the way to inner freedom and union with God. Through humility we are given the grace to be able to look deep into ourselves with honest self-appraisal of where we actually stand in our spiritual journey. Humility gives us the courage to acknowledge that we are basically slaves: slaves of sinfulness, bad habits and vices; slaves of prejudices and intolerances; slaves conditioned by our present-day worldly culture; and slaves, especially, of the image we have created of ourselves, the idealized self which we falsely portray and anxiously wish others to believe is the real us. Nothing is more difficult, more painful, than to look at ourselves as we really are. It takes a great deal of courage and honesty, and, of course, humility.

Slowly we learn that the path of humility leads also to the path of wisdom; for humility not only helps us face our own sinfulness and occasional inner ugliness, but it also makes us capable of accepting our limitations. Humility, when taken seriously, can be a liberating experience. Yet the question remains: if humility is so infinitely desirable, so absolutely essential for a true Christian life, how can we work to acquire it?

Abba Tithoes recommends three time-tested ways that never cease to obtain results: self-control, prayer, and seeking always the last place below all others. Self-control helps us to acquire a measured perspective on all reality, especially on ourselves. Prayer, that is, unceasing communion with God, is the source of our strength in this struggle of self-confrontation. Finally, seeing ourselves beneath other creatures and accepting always the last place in all things keeps us attuned to the teachings of Jesus, who says that we must see ourselves always as useless servants, even after performing good deeds.

Like Abba Tithoes, Saint Clement of Rome, in his letter to the Corinthians, encourages all of us to cultivate the attitude of humbleness of mind and heart, putting aside all arrogance and foolish pride. He reminds us of the sacred words of the Scriptures, where the Lord says to each of us: "Whom shall I look upon with favor except the humble?"

— FEBRUARY 14 —
Saint Cyril and Saint Methodius

The awe-inspiring task of sowing the seeds of Christianity in so vast an area with two pairs of hands was a religious feat of strength unsurpassed by any who have labored for Christ. The architects of this awesome task were the brothers Cyril and Methodius, the Apostles to the Slavs.

GEORGE POULOS

This morning I gazed at our snow-covered vegetable garden, stark and symmetrical, with the outlines of the different raised beds delineated by the snow. One can imagine what the garden will look like in months ahead. In the meantime, it is peacefully resting, under the thick inches of snow, taking advantage of this well-deserved rest provided yearly by Mother Nature.

Today in the United States is Saint Valentine's Day, the day lovers celebrate their mutual bond. I don't know too much about Saint Valentine, except for the fact that he was a third-century martyr who was both a priest and a medical doctor. I don't know how legend ended up making him the patron saint of lovers. Be that as it may, lovers, of course, need their own patron saint, and an occasion to celebrate their love for one another.

For the rest of us and, more importantly, for the Church at large, we celebrate today the memory of two extraordinary saints, Saint Cyril and Saint Methodius, who were brothers by both faith and blood. Cyril and Methodius were of Greek origin. They used their education and intellectual talents to expand the work of evangelization to the Slavic people who, until then, had not received knowledge of the Christian faith. The two brothers translated the liturgical books and Scriptures, so that they could transmit the faith. They even created a new alphabet, which is still in use today, and is the basis for the written Russian language. For this very reason, Pope John Paul II proclaimed these two the co-patrons of Europe, along with our father Saint Benedict. Saint Cyril embraced monastic life but died a year after making his monastic profession. Saint Methodius survived him by quite a few years, and eventually became archbishop of a noted metropolis.

— FEBRUARY 15 —

Waiting Upon the Lord

One of the monks said: "Waiting upon the Lord consists of this: to have the heart turned towards the Lord while praying, 'Jesus, have pity on me; Jesus, come to my help; I bless you, Son of the living God, now and always,' and to raise one's eyes slowly while saying these words to the Lord."

LES SENTENCES DES PERES DU DESERT, HP. ETH. COLL. 13, 26

So much in the spiritual life consists in having the patience to wait for whatever designs God has for our individual lives. God wishes to be included in our personal lives, to be an integral part of them. But to grow into awareness of how close God really is to each of us demands time, patience, and perseverance. While God is never in a rush to act, we, on the contrary, are impatient and restless. We wish to see things accomplished immediately, including our own spiritual growth.

The Desert Fathers and Mothers teach us that to begin to grow in the spiritual life, we must first learn to slow down and wait, remembering that it is not so much our own activities that count, but the work that God is doing in us. True enough, waiting is not always an easy task. But waiting can become a time of spiritual grace, furthering the growth of God's life in us. While waiting patiently for the Lord, we allow his light to enter the

darkness of our hearts, those deep recesses of our innermost being, transforming us more and more into his image and likeness.

While cultivating this attitude of patient waiting, we must
follow the example of the Desert Fathers. We must have our hearts
turned toward the Lord in constant prayer, repeating humbly in
the petition of the Publican: "Jesus, have pity on me, a sinner."
The waiting may be long and tedious, it may require much
struggle, but in its midst, the continual repetition of the Publican's
prayer will be both a balm and a consolation.

— FEBRUARY 16 —

An Ordinary Wintry Day

Yet February suns' uncertain shine,
For rain and frost alternately combine.
EDMUND SPENCER

After Candlemas, our long winter nights slowly shorten, and
daylight stretches itself out just a bit, giving us a hint of
spring to come. Yet, the weather, at times, tells us that it is yet
too soon to let go of the cold reality of winter for a few weeks
longer. In our part of the country, we have been surprised by
snowstorms all the way to the end of April.

As I look at the horizon from the north-facing kitchen window, I see a sky darkened by storm clouds, announcing more
snow. The frosty air is bitter cold, and the cutting wind is felt to
the bone of anyone who ventures outside. Even our farm animals
show no desire to leave the shelter of their barn. As long as they
have enough food, for they get terribly hungry during the winter,
they remain comfortably content.

In late afternoon, as the light wanes and dusk approaches, I
peak once more at the view of our surrounding hills. The snow
still covers the monastic land with a lovely blanket of pure white.
All is peaceful. There is a rare, special calmness proper to this
time of year that seems to emanate from the quietude of winter.
All is silent. All is calm. Blessed is he or she who can enjoy the
graces of winter's quiet, silence, and peace.

— FEBRUARY 17 —

Quartets

Music is the art of the prophets, the only art that can calm the agitations of the soul.

MARTIN LUTHER

February has always been a month of uncertain weather and changing temperatures. The writer Leigh Hunt describes it this way: "If February were not the precursor of spring, it would be the least pleasant season of the year....The thaws then take place; and a clammy mixture of moisture and cold succeeds, which is the most disagreeable of wintry sensations."

Today is one of those dull winter days, with a cold and gusty wind sounding outdoors. I use this solitude to continue working on some writing and other household chores. While I work, I listen to some of Beethoven's quartets. One of my favorite winter occupations is to go through our collection of Haydn, Mozart, and Beethoven quartets in an orderly and systematic way. At times, I add the quartets of Schubert and Brahms. While listening to that music, I am transported to other realms of the spirit. I have always been attracted to what is called, in French, *musique de chambre*, and those quartets are quintessential examples. The time that I spend engulfed in this music is truly transcendental, an opportunity to touch the depths of human experience and nurture the human spirit.

Each season contains its own particular kind of blessings. To me, one of winter's blessings is the opportunity it provides me for listening to this type of music. I would go so far as to describe the quartets as "music for winter." They never sound better to me than during the long stretches of the winter months. All praise and thanks to the Lord for the joy of exquisite music, for the wordless surpassing beauty expressed in sound.

— FEBRUARY 18 —

Saint Bernadette

The Blessed Virgin chose me because I am the most ignorant of all. If she had found anyone more ignorant than myself, she would have chosen her. The Blessed Virgin used me like a broom. What do you do with a broom when you have finished sweeping? You put it back in its place, behind the door.

SAINT BERNADETTE

A week ago we were feasting Our Lady of Lourdes, and today we keep the memorial of her servant Bernadette, as do the faithful of the church of France. Bernadette Soubirous was born on a cold January day in 1844. Her parents were extremely poor. The father, a ruined miller, was often without a job to support his family. The family inhabited a damp, miserable room called *Le Cachot*, which today one can still visit in the center of Lourdes. Bernadette was a fragile child, so her parents sent her to the home of Marie Lagues, a few miles away, to be nursed. Later, when Bernadette was about eleven and contracted asthma, she was sent back to the farm of Marie Lagues, where proper nutrition and the care of her foster mother slowly helped her recuperate some of her health.

While at the farm of Marie Lagues, located in Bartres, Bernadette began catechism classes and learned the foundation of the Christian faith. On the farm, her daily occupation consisted in minding the sheep in the countryside, as many other children in the Pyrenees did. She loved helping with the sheep, and while pasturing her herd, she prayed the rosary.

She spent occasional summer months at the Bartres farmhouse, but always returned to her parents' home during the winter. She loved her parents and her siblings and, in spite of their dire poverty, she was always happy in their midst. Bernadette, a typical Pyrenees peasant, was outgoing and affectionate. She was encircled by friends and loved to play with them. She would try to help her parents, often taking any menial job available in Lourdes.

Food was always scarce at the Soubirous home, and she wanted to contribute to the family's welfare in whatever way she could.

Very early, she developed a strong trust in God and in Our Lady's protection. Every night, she would recite the evening prayers with the whole family, and on Sundays she attended Mass at the parish church. Everyone in the town of Lourdes knew that little Bernadette was a devout girl, who always carried her rosary in her pocket. She knew that she was, by the grace of her Baptism, a daughter of God, and knew herself to be loved by him.

An extraordinary series of events began for Bernadette on February 11, 1858, when a beautiful young lady dressed in white appeared to her in a grotto of Massabielle. The apparitions continued for several months, until the final one on July 16, 1858. Our Lady confided many secrets to the young shepherdess, but her main message was to invite all believers to prayer and conversion in the spirit of the Gospel.

After the apparitions, Bernadette continued living a life of prayer, gratitude, and intimacy with the Lord and His Holy Mother in Lourdes. She longed, however, to disappear from the limelight and aspired to a hidden, convent life. She was finally accepted as a novice among the Sisters of Charity of Nevers. In the convent at Nevers, far away from the grotto and her dear Pyrenees Mountains, she received the name of Sister Marie-Bernard and took her vows on October 30, 1867.

Bernadette suffered much incomprehension during her religious life, where one of her superiors considered her "good for nothing." She accepted all suffering that came to her without complaint, saying, "Following the example of Jesus, I will carry the cross hidden in my heart with courage and generosity." Fragile and often sick, Bernadette died on April 16, 1879, during Easter week, at the young age of thirty-five. Her last whispered words were: "Holy Mary, Mother of God, pray for me, a poor sinner."

Those who have the privilege of visiting the tomb of Bernadette at Nevers will see her laying peacefully asleep in a glass coffin. They leave consoled and strengthened by the simplicity and quiet beauty of the poor shepherdess, who once was favored to behold the Mother of God.

— FEBRUARY 19 —

Bernadette: The Little Shepherdess

She was entirely lost in God.

COMMENT OF A RELIGIOUS WHO RECEIVED HER HABIT ON THE SAME DAY AS BERNADETTE

A few miles away from Lourdes is the small village of Bartres. Bernadette spent part of her life there, and the charming little town preserves several souvenirs of the presence of Bernadette in its midst: the house where she lived with her wet nurse, the parish church she attended, and the sheep barn where she guarded her flock.

As one climbs the hill leading to Bartres and arrives at the village entrance, one discovers a long, sturdy path that leads across a wooded area before it empties into the pasture land. There, in the open prairie, stands a humble stone barn with a thatched-hay roof. The barn is called La Bergerie, and it is there that Bernadette kept her sheep. Today, as then, the stone barn is striking in its simplicity. One finds nothing superfluous about it. Inside the barn, there is a statue of Bernadette, surrounded by her sheep. It is a portrait of what her life was like in those days. In essence, the scene has not changed: same simplicity, same country peace, same profound silence.

Bernadette, as all true shepherds, was deeply attached to her ewes and their tiny lambs which she tended so lovingly. Working daily at the farm, spending hours on the prairie and in the rustic barn was a way of opening herself to God's special designs for her. While at Bartres, she used to confide to her cousin Jeanne Vedere: "I accepted whatever God wished for me. When one thinks about it, God permitted this, so I could never really complain."

The humble sheepfold and the rustic barn were the tools used by God to prepare Bernadette for the extraordinary events that were to take place in her life. Often, God uses the simplest elements and events to reveal himself to us. Through submission to God's will in the daily stuff of her life, Bernadette opened her heart to welcome the light from the divine apparition, thus entering into the joy that God prepared for her.

— FEBRUARY 20 —

The Daily Search for God

To draw close to God, to drive out demons—there is a task to be praised!

SAINT JOHN CLIMACUS, *THE LADDER OF DIVINE ASCENT*

Mistakenly, many people think that the search for God is reserved for certain special people, such as monks, theologians, or priests. Saint Benedict would affirm this, saying that the search for God is the primary reason for the embrace of the monastic life. He would quickly add, however, that this is also the fundamental quest for all Christians. "Seek first the Kingdom of God," Jesus proclaimed to all.

Today, the quest for God must continue through the ordinary events of our lives: through prayer and work, through our daily pains and joys, through our relationships and interactions with others, through our human incapacities and limitations, through our silence and solitude, through our study and reading. Every occasion and every event in our lives must become an incentive to intensify this divine pursuit, which ultimately is the sole purpose for all human life, the only reason for which any of us is placed upon the earth.

— FEBRUARY 21 —

A Winter Fireside

Praise be, my Lord, for Brother Fire,
By whom Thou lightest up the night:
He is beautiful, merry, robust, and strong.

SAINT FRANCIS OF ASSISI

One activity of a wintry day like today is to step outside and continue splitting the necessary wood to furbish our stoves which protect us from the freezing temperatures. This vigorous work consists principally of cutting, splitting, and piling wood. Later, the split logs are piled nearby for feeding the stoves. Occasionally, one of the young people from down the road will come to give a helping hand. I am always most grateful for their assistance.

Tending the stoves is a steady, full-time activity during the winter months. One has no chance of getting bored. I think we only experience boredom from not living deeply enough, by choosing not to enter into the diverse activities and mysteries that are the treasures of each season.

One of the joys of a winter day is to build a fire in our stove that will warm not only our tired bodies, but also our spirits. Tonight, after Vespers, I'll linger a bit longer in front of the fire, considering not only the events of the day, but also of those to come. I enjoy these quiet, nurturing moments. They have a particular quality all their own, inspiring reflection, prayer, and tranquility. If I am not too tired after Compline, I may return to the warmth of our stove and do a bit of extra reading. Reading, any reading, becomes significant in its own way when done by the heat of a woodstove. It reminds me of the words from Thomas De Quincey: "Surely everyone is aware of the divine pleasures which attend a winter fireside." In our case, sitting as it does in a corner of our kitchen, it becomes, in winter, the centerpiece of the room and inspiration for our labor.

— FEBRUARY 22 —

Chair of Saint Peter

*Blessed be the God and Father of our Lord Jesus Christ!
By his great mercy he has given us a new birth into a
living hope through the resurrection of Jesus Christ, and
into an inheritance...kept in heaven for you, who are
being protected by the power of God through faith for a
salvation ready to be revealed in the last time....*

1 PETER 1:3–9

One fine thing about our New York-New England winters is to have a day like today. There is a strong and bitter wind cutting across the property, the temperature is near zero, and all nature appears frozen. Yet, the sun rose this morning in all of its splendor, clothed in rare beauty. And though the frosty air is rather uncomfortable as I venture outdoors, I still admire the clarity of the sunshine as it falls upon the frosted fields and snow-covered hills. There is a brightness that dissipates any negative feelings I may harbor towards today's weather.

Today marks the feast of the Chair of Saint Peter. It is a feast of great antiquity, based on the veneration of a chair, the cathedra, from which Saint Peter taught and preached during the time he spent in Rome. The feast was ascribed to February 22 for its celebration, to replace an ancient pagan feast observed around the same date. Though this may be the origin of the feast, what the Liturgy commemorates today is Saint Peter's confession of faith. The Gospel according to Matthew tells us that when Jesus came into the region of Cesarea Philippi, he posed this question to his disciples: "Who do people say the Son of Man is?" The disciples replied in diverse manners. Then Jesus continued, "But you, who do you say I am?" Simon Peter responded, "You are the Christ, the Son of the living God," to which Jesus replied, "Blessed are you Simon, son of Jonah, for it was not the flesh and blood that revealed this to you, but my Father in heaven."

The faith of Peter is what we remember today, the faith that so pleased Christ himself that he made Peter the cornerstone of the structure that was to be his church. Today, as in the time of Peter, the foundation of the church is based on the confession of faith: that Jesus is indeed the Son of the living God, light from Light, true God from true God. This is the apostolic faith handed down to us on the day of our Baptism, the faith for which the martyrs died, the faith of the church, the faith that we cherish as our most precious treasure on earth.

By cultivating daily the faith that we professed at our Baptism, and later renewed at Confirmation, the Holy Spirit makes His presence felt in every segment of our lives. He quietly teaches us to learn from our daily experiences, and also inspires us to choose goals that instigate the work of our personal conversion.

— FEBRUARY 23 —
Saint Polycarp of Smyrna

When the Proconsul urged him and said, "Take the oath
and I will release you; revile Christ," Polycarp answered:
"Eighty-six years I have served Him, and He has never
done me wrong. How, then, should I be able to blaspheme
my King who has saved me?"

FROM "THE MARTYRDOM OF SAINT POLYCARP"

Saint Polycarp keeps company among those few called the "Apostolic Fathers." They are our fathers in the faith, having received it directly from the mouths of the Apostles. They are the indispensible link between the Apostles who saw and walked with the Lord and the great Fathers of the church who came into prominence later on. The Apostolic Fathers assured the continuity of the tradition in the church, making sure that the faith would be handed down intact to future generations. We who follow the Lord Jesus owe much to these giants of the early Church.

Young Polycarp was a disciple of the Apostle John. He was in his early twenties when he met his dear teacher. This providential meeting was the catalyst that instilled in him the ardent desire to follow the Apostle in his missionary work. He worked in close association with Saint John until the time that Saint John was exiled to the island of Patmos.

In his time, Polycarp was known for his literary talents. After being made bishop, he employed much of his time in prayer, preaching, writing, and attending to the poor. While he was known for his zeal and strength in preserving the purity of the faith, he was also revered for his goodness, gentleness, and charity towards all.

When the persecution of Christians peaked during Marcus Aurelius's reign, Polycarp was one of those brought to martyrdom. His arrest, imprisonment, and eventual martyrdom is eloquently related in a letter that he addressed to the other Christian churches. After his death, his disciples collected his bones, which they claimed were "more precious than costly stones and finer than gold," and placed them in a suitable area where they would often come together to celebrate the glorious martyrdom of their teacher.

As the soldiers were binding Saint Polycarp, preparing him for his death, the saintly bishop uttered this, his final prayer:

> Lord, God Almighty, Father of your beloved Son, Jesus Christ, through whom we have received knowledge of you, God of angels and powers of every created thing and all the assembly of the just who dwell before you, I bless you, because you have considered me worthy of this day and hour, to partake among the number of the martyrs in the cup of your Christ unto the resurrection of life everlasting both of soul and body....O undeceiving and true God, for this reason and for all these things: I praise you, I bless you, I glorify you.

— FEBRUARY 24 —

The Monastic Rhythm

I will sing to the LORD as long as I live;
I will sing praise to my God while I have being.
May my meditation be pleasing to him.

PSALM 104:33–34

Human life, on the whole, follows a methodical rhythm that directs its daily steps around a certain center. Most human beings rest during the dark hours of night, wake up in the early morning, and prepare for a day focused on work, education, tasks, and family life.

Similarly, the monk organizes his daily life around a center point, or what Saint Benedict calls the *Opus Dei*, that is, the chanting of the Canonical Hours. It is the daily office chanted at morning, noon, evening, and night that highlight the key moments of a monk's day. It is prayer, the time spent in church singing God's praises that marks the hours of the monastic day.

While work is vitally necessary for the sustenance of a monastery, it is not the center point of its daily routine. Prayer has the utmost priority. It transforms and sanctifies the life of the monastery, including manual tasks. When Saint Benedict organized the monastic day, he was mindful of the changes brought about by the succession of the seasons. Therefore, he changed the schedule of work, dinner, and supper, but not the hours assigned to the work of God. That was something sacred. The Divine Office was to be sung at the same appointed hours.

This quiet balance in the monastic day is due to the primacy given to prayer in the daily schedule. When prayer is put behind, the balance is lost; the monk suffers the consequence and the monastic perspective becomes eclipsed.

As the hours and days, months and years, pass, and the monk continues his daily life centered around the worship of God, he feels the healing yoke of this unique rhythm. The sometimes seemingly tedious monastic pattern of worship and work, allows the monk to witness the flux of time intercepted by the silence of the divine realm. The monk, then, remembers the words from the Psalm: O LORD *of hosts..../ Happy are those who live in your house / ever singing your praise* (Ps 84: 1, 4).

— FEBRUARY 25 —

Human Encounters

Human presence is a creative and turbulent sacrament, a visible sign of invisible grace.

JOHN O'DONOHUE, ANAM CARA

During January and February, our small guesthouse is closed to outsiders. I use this blessed winter solitude for more intimate, uninterrupted communion with God. Thus, January and February constitute a yearly journey into the wilderness. They are our "desert months," where, in the stillness of one's heart, God's voice may more easily be heard. It is his voice that gives birth to deeper silence and even deeper solitude. One is alone with Him who is alone, and the riches of that divine contact are slowly unveiled.

On the "temporal side," so to speak, I spend both months catching up with my writing, repairing furniture, and other things that need attention. I may mount icons, work in the library, or perform other chores which I have little time for during the months of good weather.

These months of great solitude, with little human contact, serve another purpose. They increase in me the awareness of the richness that every guest brings to the monastery. It is as if one needs to be deprived of human company for a while to fully appreciate it at a later date. Each guest who approaches the monastery brings his or her own gift. People of all classes, faiths, and national backgrounds have partaken in our monastic hospitality throughout the years. In most cases, during their transient stay, I have discovered a brother or a sister who, in their innermost being, reflect the image of the God who made them. When this occurs, one can almost hear God's voice speaking through God's life already present in each of them. Every human encounter can become a reinforcement of the divine life that nests deep within all of us.

— FEBRUARY 26 —

Mystery of the Snow

Stern winter congeals every brook
That murmured so lately with glee
And places a snowy peruke
On the head of each bald-pated tree.
WILLIAM HONE

W hen I awoke this morning, the entire monastery landscape was wholly clad in beautiful, spotless white. The land, seemingly asleep during these long winter months, is a silent reminder that all things in nature need a time of rest, a quiet chance to nurture the seed that shall come alive in the spring. This morning's beautiful snow, a heavy blanket of nurturance and protection, enriches the soil in preparation for the work of the next season. Nature is steadfastly at work, even when appearing dormant.

I enjoy watching snowstorms. Of the countless snowflakes that fall on the monastic ground, there are no two that are ever the same. A snowstorm is always an occasion to turn inward, to become reflective. As I watch the passing and fragile beauty of a snowflake, suddenly it dawns on me how much all of life tends to be the same. *"Todo se pasa,"* said Teresa of Ávila: All things pass. Indeed, they do, swiftly and at times inadvertently, but always permanently. Another message seems to be conveyed by today's snow: *"God alone remains."* The snow that landscapes the ground lasts for a while but, in the end, passes away, disappears.

— FEBRUARY 27 —

The Today of God

O that today you would listen to his voice!
PSALM 95:7

O ccasionally, throughout all of my years, I have been asked about my notion or conception of time. To such a dense question, I always respond that the mystery of time becomes concrete for me in one particular space: today. I only know today, the present. Of course, I am aware of yesterday and mindful of tomorrow. I know of its coming: in a strange way, it is already in the making. For the monk, as perhaps for everyone else, it is important to act in the present, to dwell in the *"hodie,"* the today of God. A fullness is hidden in each particular day, and we can only partake of it in so far as we remain attentive to the present *"now."*

When we pray the Our Father, we say "Give us this day our daily bread." Our Lord teaches us to pray for what we need today, not tomorrow. God dwells in an eternal present, and we are all invited to enter into communion with him. Through the simple or complicated events of today, its pains and joys, work and prayer, we enter into the realm of the Divine Presence. All that was yesterday, we must leave behind and place before God's mercy. All that shall be tomorrow, we can entrust to His providence. Today, however, we must allow the hours to unfold in the light of his love. *God is love, and those who abide in love abide in God, and God in them.*

— FEBRUARY 28 —

Arrogance

The LORD said to Moses, "I have seen this people, how stiff-necked they are. Now let me alone, so that my wrath may burn hot against them and I may consume them."

EXODUS 32:10

Both the Old and the New Testaments show us a God who detests the proud, the arrogant, the self-aggrandizer. God has had to deal with them, for better or worse, through both periods of salvation history. He has to continue dealing with them today. Times may have changed but, unfortunately, human nature has not. It is difficult to comprehend what it is about humans that makes us perversely enjoy contrasting ourselves against others for the sole reason of elevating ourselves above them. The temptation to pride and superiority is so subtle and shrewd that one doesn't always seem fully aware when one blindly gives into it. Monks as individuals, and monastic communities as a whole, are not exempt from this temptation. On the contrary, in our efforts to become spiritual beings, we are particularly vulnerable to the evil of self-pride, perhaps even more so than others.

I occasionally cringe when I hear the boasts of some monks or nuns that their community is better than others because they have vocations and others have none, or their liturgy is superior, or their observance is stricter and more authentic. These judgments about success are arrived at or based on worldly standards. And, yet, the only standard for true success lies in the Gospel's eternal paradox: "Unless a wheat grain falls into the earth and dies, it remains just a single grain; but if it dies, it bears much fruit. Those who love their life lose it, and those who hate their life in this world will keep it for eternal life (Jn 12:24–25). The devil is quietly but astutely at work even in good people, in God's servants. The demon of pride is so clever, so alluring, that if we are not vigilant he easily deceives and misleads us.

We often encounter passages in the Gospels where the Pharisees and scribes were horrified at Jesus' behavior. The Lord, with great spontaneity and without a trace of superiority, easily mingled with prostitutes, sinners, thieves, gluttons, drunkards, and tax collectors. No respectable religious person of his time would have ever consented to keeping such company. Jesus confounded all those around him by choosing as his disciples humans of all backgrounds, be they sinful or virtuous. When dispute arose among the disciples over who was the first among them, Jesus plainly told them that to become the first among others they must become the last in all things. He rejected squarely every form of arrogance, pride, and self-righteousness. Saint Isaac the Syrian, a true spiritual master, speaks to his disciples unmincingly about arrogance:

> By seeking the praises of his fellow men a man's mind is struck with madness, as he seeks to perform among them deeds which are above his measure, in order that the vainglory of his greatness may increase, and others may perceive that he is very near to God. Many who have excelled in virtue previously were rich in gifts from God....Later they gave in to pride and received thus a blow from God, those very men that before seemed so virtuous! The cause for this was that they were not able to bear the many gifts which they have received and were drawn towards haughtiness, and were thus rejected by God as dross and undesirables.

> Ultimately, one is judged by the amount of haughtiness which is found in one's soul. Thus, self-pride becomes the source of one's own spiritual ruin. For from none of the other sins does God withdraw from man, leaving him wholly alone. He does this only in those whom He finds the mind seized by haughtiness, pride, and blasphemy.

— FEBRUARY 29 —

A Blessing for the Close of the Month

Yet February suns uncertain shine,
For rain and frost alternately combine
To stop the plow, with sudden wintry storms—
And often fearful violence the month deforms.

EDMUND SPENCER

February in the northeast, in my opinion, is always a month of intemperate weather and uncertain temperatures. If February were not the obligatory prerequisite to spring, I would consider it a time of disagreeable dreariness. One fact that makes February melancholy and sometimes dangerous is the accumulation of ice throughout the property. The daily journey from the monastery to the barn to feed the animals can end up being quite precarious. I always feel relieved when the end of February arrives and I can readily venture out into March with its promise of a forthcoming spring.

A friend who knows of my love for gardening and my eager anticipation of spring sent me yesterday a copy of a beautiful blessing. It speaks volumes to me as we close the last page of the book of February. The blessing helped me reconcile all that February was and all the expectations that I have for March and the new season.

> May love be the gardener of your years bringing forth from you your grounding in God, a harvest of wholeness and peace, a bounty of courage and compassion. May your soul tower with the strength of the cedars, your heart pound with the power of the sea. May joy rise in you like the mountains and may it be the blessing you share with all those you love who this day make merry that in you the great love of God has found a home on earth. Amen.

MARCH

— MARCH 1 —

The Lenten Pilgrimage

Turn back to the Lord and do penance.
Be renewed in heart and spirit.

INVITATORY, MATINS, ASH WEDNESDAY

The season of penance has returned once more, inviting us to repentance, renewal, and conversion. As the words of one of our Lenten hymns illustrate: "Now is the acceptable time / Accorded us by God each year, / That moderation's strength may heal / An ailing world from sin and woe."

Our Lenten pilgrimage takes us across the desert for the forty days of preparation towards the celebration of the solemn Paschal Triduum. The pilgrimage begins with the ancient rite of receiving the ashes, which expresses emphatically what Lent is all about. When the priest, using the ashes, signs our foreheads with the cross of Christ, he says the words: "Repent, and believe in the Gospel." The ashes, accompanied by the strong evangelical

utterance, reminds us that the Lenten season is specifically de-
signed to call each of us to repentance.

Lent is indeed a school of repentance, where we are taught to
return to the Lord with humble sincerity and joyful compunction. We learn this through participation in the daily liturgy and
the offices, through assiduous practice of private prayer and holy
reading, through fasting and self-denial, and through performing acts of charity and almsgiving. Lent, with its invitation to
true conversion, provides us the opportunity to begin again a
new life in Christ. As we yield to the Lord through humble repentance, the Holy Spirit quietly accomplishes his work in us, re-
creating our minds and hearts unto the likeness of Jesus.

— MARCH 2 —

The Acceptable Time

*This is the time when you can win God's favor, the day
when you can be saved.*

LENTEN ANTIPHON

The Lenten pilgrimage is all about time, a time to renew our
relationship with God. During this journey, we must stand
back and look at time in a different light. We must manage it
wisely. We shall never profit spiritually from the Lenten season
unless we take time to live Lent thoughtfully. We need to make
time for the things that really matter and apply ourselves to them
during our Lenten pilgrimage. This effort may entail reprioritizing
of our values and a readjusting our schedules to make room for
those practices which nurture the life of the spirit—practices such
as prayer, holy reading (as Saint Benedict calls it), and perfor-
mance of the corporal works of mercy. This means doing some
serious planning to lighten our busy, tense schedules, so as to
leave room for our Lenten exercises. Let us keep in mind that
this is the acceptable period for repentance, and that God is patiently waiting for us. Lent is one season which allows no room
for the wasting of time. It demands that we fill our days wisely.

— MARCH 3 —

— MARCH 3 —

Early March Days

The stormy March has come at last, with wind and clouds
and changing skies; I hear the rushing of the blast that
through the snowy valley flies.

WILLIAM CULLEN BRYANT

We still have some cold days in March and, from time to time, the occasional snow. March is a month of contrasts, lovely sunny days changing suddenly into rain and wind. The rain, even though unpleasant, helps prepare the soil for the coming planting season. March also gives us intimations of the arrival of spring, as when the rays of a warm sun begin to melt the snow scattered throughout the property, and the first crocuses begin to appear from underneath it. On those early pre-spring days, with the sun warming our bodies as we toil outdoors, I breathe a sense of relief, aware that the cold months are now almost totally behind us. I drink deeply of the piercing fresh air with its promise of a forthcoming spring. I utter a prayer of silent gratitude while laboring under God's sun on a day of easy and pure joy.

— MARCH 4 —

Longer Days

You have made the moon to mark the seasons;
the sun knows its time for setting.
You make darkness, and it is night.

PSALM 104:19–20

Spring begins to arrive even before winter totally departs. Standing outdoors, I observe the metamorphosis taking place all around me: the greening of our pastures, the chanting of our lambs, the prolongation of the light which increases now in a noticeable way from day to day. I am thankful for these extra hours of natural light. God, in his wisdom, divided the seasons exactly. He gave us the reasonable amount of winter we need and no more. The same with the other seasons, and the same with the division and right proportion of light and darkness in the course of a day. Psalm 104, which is recited daily at the beginning of the Byzantine Vespers, extols beautifully God's wisdom in His creation: "O LORD, how manifold are your works / In wisdom you have made them all; / the earth is full of your creatures.

— MARCH 5 —

Lenten Practices

Wash yourselves; make yourselves clean;
remove the evil of your doings
from before my eyes;
cease to do evil;
learn to do good.

ISAIAH 1:16–17

L ent is a pilgrimage and partnership we embark on with God. He takes the initiative; we follow. The pilgrimage begins when we hear God's urgent invitation: "Return to me with all your heart now. Today, if you hear my voice, do not harden your heart." Our turning to him cannot wait until tomorrow. It must begin today. Throughout the centuries, the Church tradition, and in particular the monastic tradition, have encouraged certain practices to help us along the Lenten journey. These practices have been time-tested and retain their relevance today as much as they did in the past:

1. Attendance at Lenten services. Both the Eucharist and the daily Liturgy of the Hours are powerful aids to help us assimilate the spirit of Lent. Through participating in the Eucharist, we relive the mystery of the Lord's Passover, from his death to his glorious Resurrection. The Offices are truly a Lenten school where we learn day-by-day what is meant by "returning to the Lord in sincere repentance."

2. Making sufficient time for private prayer. This means the

sort of prayer that, in the words of Saint John Chrysostom, is "a conversation and partnership with God." This kind of prayer, he adds, "is a longing for God, a love too deep for words, a gift not given by man but by God's grace."

3. Daily reading of and meditation on the Sacred Scriptures. An ancient Father of the Church once said: "Whoever meditates on the law of the Lord will bring forth much fruit at harvest." One should spend extra time on the reading of the Scriptures, even a chapter or a page daily from a spiritual book.

4. Examination of conscience. It is extremely helpful for our spiritual progress to examine our consciences in the light of the Scriptures, especially the words of the Gospels as they are heard daily. The word of God is not just for hearing or reading; it must find a concrete application in our lives.

5. Works of mercy and almsgiving. From the earliest times, the Church has encouraged its members to give special attention during Lent to the corporal works of mercy and almsgiving. Saint Leo the Great says: "The works of mercy are innumerable. Their variety brings this advantage to those who are true Christians: that in the matter of almsgiving, not only the rich and the affluent, but also the poor are able to play their part. Those who are unequal in their capacity to give can be equal in the love within their hearts."

6. Self-control. Lent encourages us to practice control over our sensual appetites according to our individual possibilities. Fasting and abstinence from meat are traditional Lenten observances. In our modern era, we can also discover new ways of fasting, such as abstaining from popular entertainment and other worldly distractions. We can cultivate instead more time for God and for helping our neighbor.

7. Silence. To move into silence and refrain from unnecessary speech, especially gossip, is an absolute necessity for those wishing to undertake their Lenten journey seriously.

8. Saint Ephrem's prayer. Nothing expresses as poignantly the "inward attitude" we strive for during Lent as the Lenten prayer of Saint Ephrem. Why not recite it slowly, once or perhaps several times a day during the season?

9. Music. Listening to Lenten music, such as the Lenten cantatas and the Passions by J. S. Bach, the "*Stabat Mater*" by Vivaldi, or the seasonal Gregorian chant are an added stimulus to the Lenten spirit.

10. Inspiration. Choose an inspiring religious object: a cross, a crucifix, or an ikon that depicts the mystery of the Passion, and place it in the dining room or other prominent place in the home. Use it as the focus for your Lenten prayers and devotions, and for prayers before and after meals.

— MARCH 6 —

Lenten Prayer of Saint Ephrem

O Lord of my life, take away from me the spirit of laziness, faintheartedness, ambition and idle talk. But grant me rather the spirit of chastity, humility, patience and love. Yes, O Lord and King! Grant me to see my own sins and faults and not to judge my neighbor, for you are truly blessed forever. Amen.

SAINT EPHREM OF SYRIA

This prayer, composed by the great Father of the Church Ephrem of Syria, is recited from Monday to Friday throughout Lent after each liturgical office of the Byzantine rite of the Church. It is a prayer of great antiquity and is highly treasured in the Eastern Church. Saint Ephrem was a monk and a deacon, refusing like Saint Benedict to be ordained to the priesthood because of his profound humility.

Saint Ephrem's prayer is called "the Lenten prayer" because it encompasses the true spirit of Lent. It is like a check list of the virtues we ought to strive for during this holy season. The emphasis is on repentance and humility, the two essential elements of true conversion. In the practice of the Eastern Church, the prayer is accompanied by a deep bodily prostration after each petition. The prostration, besides being penitential, is symbolic of the repentance in which we hope to grow during Lent. After the last prostration, the prayer of "O God, cleanse me from my sins" is repeated twelve times. The faithful repetition of the prayer, three times daily throughout the forty days, sustains us in our daily efforts to work out our personal conversion. The prayer slowly grows in our hearts and helps create within us the necessary climate for true and humble repentance. I often think of Ephrem's prayer as a mirror, wherein we can look at ourselves honestly, with all of our daily failings and shortcomings, and yet take courage to continue the journey because we trust in God's loving mercy.

— MARCH 7 —

Saints Perpetua and Felicity, Martyrs

The holy friends of Christ rejoice in heaven; they followed in his footsteps to the end. They have shed their blood for love of him and will reign with him forever.

ANTIPHON OF THE FEAST

In the Christian society of our ancestors, many daily externals acted as reminders of the Lenten season. The community followed a rhythm of life closely connected to the liturgical seasons of the Church year. For example, the faithful, at the sound of the local monastery or church bells, would leave their homes or work in the fields to hurry to attend services—be they Mass, Vespers, or the Stations of the Cross. The whole family participated in other Lenten practices. For example, everyone, except the elderly, fasted and abstained from meat, so it was simpler and easier to go along and follow the course. But now we need to look elsewhere for those external reminders that encourage us to remain faithful to our Lenten pilgrimage. For that we can always turn to the Church's liturgy.

During Lent, the liturgy frequently invites us to meditate not only on the suffering and Passion of Christ but also on the role of suffering in our own lives. During our earthly pilgrimage, we all have to confront the mystery of suffering in one way or another. Paul, in his letter to the Colossians, affirms that we are called to complete what is lacking in Christ's sufferings for the sake of his body, which is the Church. Suffering, then, for the Christian, is not something useless or obsolete. When we look at it with the eyes of faith, as did the martyrs Perpetua and Felicity, we shall find that suffering, though harsh and dreadful, is charged with meaning.

In reading the documents that describe the martyrdom of these two women, one is deeply moved by their absolute heroism. They accepted the most vile form of suffering and death, as a supreme act of love for him who suffered and died on the cross for all of us. The example of these two friends of Christ should encourage us during this sacred time of Lent, as we, in a small and limited way, try to heed the words of our Lord and Master: If any want to become my followers, let them deny themselves and take up their cross and follow me (Mk 8:34).

— MARCH 8 —

The Joy of Spiritual Longing

During Lent, the monk ought to practice self-denial in food, drink, sleep, talk, and laughter, and look toward the holy feast of Easter with the joy of spiritual longing.

RULE OF SAINT BENEDICT

Often we look at Lent as a negative season, filled with prescriptions for abstaining from food, drink, and entertainment; we forget that the final goal of our Lenten pilgrimage is a joyful one. Saint Benedict in his Rule affirms that, yes, during Lent we all must learn to practice control over our bodily appetites, but he encourages the monk to do this in the joy of the Holy Spirit. In the view of Saint Benedict, Lent is never meant to be a negative experience. Instead, our Lenten observances, including self denial, are directed to creating an inner transformation that leads us to deeper communion with God, the source of all life and joy. As we walk through our Lenten pilgrimage, with its sometimes tedious and fatiguing elements, Saint Benedict invites us to never lose sight of our goal. He encourages the monk to undertake his pilgrimage toward the Paschal Feast, filled with the joy of spiritual desire. This spiritual desire is fulfilled in us on Easter Sunday, with the bursting of new life in joy, by the power of the Resurrection of Christ.

Saint Frances of Rome

I am the divine Lover who takes possession of those who love me, fills those souls with graces and with divine charity. I am the Love who, in taking possession of those souls, allows myself to be possessed by them...I am foolishly in love with souls.

OUR LORD TO SAINT FRANCES OF ROME

Hidden in the center of the city of Rome is a small medieval monastery with a charming old chapel filled with frescoes. The frescoes, painted by Antoniazzo Romano, tell the story of an extraordinary woman, the saintly Frances of Rome. Frances was born in Rome around 1384. From a very early age she was attracted to monastic life. However, her father was totally opposed to her vocation, saying that it was simply the imagination of a young girl. When she was only thirteen years old, her parents betrothed her to a young nobleman named Lorenzo Ponziano. The difficult early years of her marriage were totally the opposite of what she had prepared herself for. But she saw the will of God in her state of life and accepted it in a spirit of faith and sacrifice. She became an exemplary wife and mother during the forty years of marriage that followed. Besides taking care of her household, she devoted herself to works of charity, to the care of the poor, the sick, and the needy of the city of Rome.

A story in her life that portrays this vividly. One of her sons, Battista, married a girl named Mobilia, who had a violent temper. She complained about Frances constantly to her own husband and to Frances's husband. One day, in the middle of one of those habitual complaints, Mobilia was suddenly stricken ill. Frances stood by her during her illness and nursed her daughter-in-law with great tenderness until Mobilia recuperated. This act of loving devotion on the part of Frances changed Mobilia radically. She changed her hatred and contempt into acceptance and unconditional love. She sought to imitate Frances by giving generously of her time to the care of the poor and the needy.

After the death of her husband, Frances consecrated herself totally to God in the monastic life. She retired to the monastery of the Tor de' Specchi, which she had previously founded with a group of friends. While in the monastery, she intensified her life of prayer without neglecting her service to the poor, the sick, and the elderly, something her spiritual daughters continue to do today in the heart of modern Rome. Frances died on March 9, 1440, and was canonized in 1608. She, who was privileged to enjoy the continual company of her guardian angel throughout the years, uttered these last words: "Heaven is open, and the angels descend. He who is standing in front of me gives me a sign to follow him." During these Lenten days, Frances of Rome provides a worthy model for our consideration. She knew that the love given to our neighbor is also love given to God.

— MARCH 10 —

The Gift of a Sheep

You are worthy, our Lord and God, to receive glory and honor and power, for you created all things, and by your will they existed and were created.

REVELATION 4:11

On a cold, wintry day in February our first lamb of the season arrived. He was all black, and I called him Cyril, after the great Saint Cyril of Jerusalem. He is a beautiful, healthy lamb, in spite the fact that his mother had a hard delivery last year and our local vet, Dr. Mike Murphy, a good friend of the monastery, had to be called to assist her after the birth. This year, she showed no signs of difficulty, aside from the usual discomfort, and in almost no time I was able to admire the new addition to the flock.

Throughout yesterday, exactly a month after the first lambing, a certain ewe was showing all the signs that she was getting ready to deliver, so just before Compline, I separated her from the flock and placed her into her own pen in the barn. I retired to bed but around 11 P.M., in spite of the bitter cold and with little desire to get out of a warm bed, I put on my working habit and woolen hat, grabbed a flashlight and a jacket, and headed into the barn. I flashed the light into the pen, and two tiny white lambs were standing by their mother. One was nursing, while the other tucked his small head underneath his mother. They were born, I guessed, about half an hour before I got there. The mother had already began the usual ritual of cleaning up her little ones.

I never cease to marvel when one of our ewes gives birth to twins, even though it is not that uncommon. Since the two lambs were males, I gave them the names of Cossimo and Damiano, after Saints Cosmas and Damian, who were twin brothers. This morning, during the early Office, I thank the Lord for his gift of new life to our small monastery and to the mother ewe for her goodness to us. Right there and then, I promised her that one of her little ones would be the chosen Paschal lamb, to be blessed to the joy of all our guests after the Easter Vigil.

This evening I peeked into the barn for a last visit with the young twins before retiring, and there they were, bobbing their heads up and down. The only words that came to my mind were from the Benedicite Canticle that we sing at Lauds every Sunday: *All you works of the Lord, O bless the Lord.*

— MARCH 11 —

Prayer of the Lamb

Je suis votre agneau dans ma douceur de laine.

CARMEN BERNOS DE GASZTOLD

Not long ago, a French woman, a poet, lived and worked, as she described it, "under the shadow of an abbey." Her name was Carmen Bernos de Gasztold, and she chose to live in the Tower of the old *colombier*, as a dovehouse is charmingly called in French. The *colombier* was within the property of the Abbey of Limon of the Benedictine nuns, a bit southwest of Paris. There, Carmen breathed daily from the monastic atmosphere, from the prayer and chant of the nuns, which inspired both her own prayer and her poetry. She wrote two books of poetry, later published by the nuns, which she called *Prayers From the Ark* and *The*

Creatures' Choir. In the poems, prayers are offered by each animal to their Creator. These prayers, of utter charm and simplicity, have touched animal lovers all around the world, no matter what creed they profess or what cultural background they come from.

This morning, after living through the experience of the birth of the two lambs yesterday, an experience that forever seems to retain a freshness all its own. I felt drawn to re-read Carmen's exquisite poem about the lamb. It expresses the simple joy of the lamb and its tender natural attachment to the mother ewe. We have so much to learn from these humble creatures, if we only allow it. The prayer-poem of the lamb speaks for itself:

> A spindle on four legs
> leaving tufts of white in the thickets,
> I am your lamb,
> Lord, in my soft wool.
> My bleating sends its puny note
> into the ewe's heart;
> my fleece throws its curly shadow
> on the cropped grass.
> Look, Lord, how my joy must leap!
> Yet my need of my mother
> never sleeps in me.
> Let me run to her with my wavering steps
> and draw some of her tenderness.
> Oh, don't let it happen,
> Lord, that one sad day
> I will miss her.
> Amen.

— MARCH 12 —

The Rain

Bless the Lord, all you works of the Lord.
Praise and exalt him above all forever.
Every shower and dew, bless the Lord.

PRAYER OF AZARIAH

Today's steady March rain has a soft, drifting quality, full of melancholy. It is a day to remain indoors and work with the rapid approach of spring, I sometimes feel overwhelmed by the amount of labor that awaits me outdoors. But all of that will have to wait. Today's rain is a gift from the Lord, providing me with occasion to remain indoors and enjoy a quiet, golden day of greater solitude.

Since it is Lent, some extra time will be allocated to spiritual reading. No matter how much I read daily, it never seems to be enough. So much is available in our small monastic library and, yet, there never seems to be abundant time for it in our daily monastic schedule. This is one reason why I usually look forward to Sundays, to feast days, and to snowy or rainy days like today. They provide me with that extra bit of time for solid reading.

This afternoon, after the noonday meal, I shall build a roaring fire on the wood stove downstairs, pile some books to my right and to my left, and have plenty of time to spend on good, useful reading until the bell rings for Vespers. A warm fire and the steady, musical rhythm of the rain are both so soothing, so inviting to good concentration. All of this I count as extra blessings of a rainy day. A song of praise rises spontaneously from my heart: *Rain and dew, bless the Lord.*

— MARCH 13 —
First Step of Humility

The first step of humility is that a man keeps the fear of God always before his eyes and never forgets it. He must constantly remember everything God has commanded, keeping in mind that all who despise God will burn in hell for their sins, and all who fear God have everlasting life awaiting them.

RULE OF SAINT BENEDICT

Saint Benedict took Lent so seriously that he dedicated an entire chapter of his rule to the subject. Further, he declared that "the life of a monk ought to have always the character of a Lenten observance." For Saint Benedict, Lent is the season that mirrors most exactly what the life of the monk should be at all times.

Keeping in mind Saint Benedict's views on Lent, I decided during this holy season to concentrate on reading and meditating seriously on what Saint Benedict wrote in Chapter 7 of his rule. The chapter is dedicated entirely to humility, which obviously connects to the attitude or spirit we must seek to cultivate during Lent.

Humility's first step, as enunciated by Saint Benedict, seems clear and evident. It is a basic principle of all spiritual life. The fear of the Lord is the beginning of wisdom. It is also one of the seven gifts of the Holy Spirit. Saint Benedict makes us realize that God knows each of us through and through and that nothing escapes from his eyes. To him, we are like an open book where he can read every word, every line, every sentence. Humility's first step teaches us how to live in God's holy presence: in spirit of a humble repentance for our shortcomings and weaknesses, and in a spirit of gratitude for God's infinite patience with each of us.

Second Step of Humility

The second step of humility is that a man loves not his own will nor takes pleasure in the satisfaction of his desires; rather he shall imitate by his actions that saying of the Lord: I have come not to do my own will, but the will of him who sent me."

RULE OF SAINT BENEDICT

The essence of the Christian life consists in the imitation of the life of Christ. He is the model. He is also the master and we are the disciples to whom he utters the invitation: "If anyone wishes to follow me, let him renounce himself, take up his cross and then follow me." In order to follow Jesus, we must embrace the cross, the small crosses of everyday life, and follow the path of self-renunciation. This path is not easy, for we know it to be so contrary to human nature.

Jesus never promised us that the way to heaven would be easy. What he promised was to send us a Comforter who would remind us of Jesus' teachings and, at the same time, give us the strength and the necessary fortitude to follow the ways of the Gospel, no matter how perilous they may seem to be.

In the Our Father we pray daily, "Your will be done on earth as it is in heaven." This is precisely what Saint Benedict encourages us to seek through the practice of humility's second step: acceptance of the will of God in our daily life and in all of our actions. In accomplishing the will of the Father, we shall discover our true freedom, our only joy, our perfect peace. I think it was Dante who towards the end of his life stated, "In your will is my peace."

Third Step of Humility

The third step of humility is that a man submits to his superior in all obedience for the love of God, imitating the Lord of whom the Apostle says: "He became obedient to the point of death" (Phil 2:8).

RULE OF SAINT BENEDICT

The mystery of monastic obedience, and its only justification, is based on Jesus' submission to his heavenly Father. Throughout his thirty-three years on earth, he not only obeyed his heavenly Father but also his mother Mary and his stepfather Joseph. This submission to his Father was carried out to the end of his life, as he obediently accepted even death, death on a cross!

Following the example of Christ, the monk promises to remain obedient "even unto death" in the monastery. This monastic obedience implies fidelity and daily submission to the will of God, to the Church which is Christ's Body, to the Rule, to the monastic tradition, to the Father of the community, and to one another. Obedience allows the monk to become a servant as Christ became for our sake. Obedience, for the monk, is expressed ultimately in the humble respect he shows towards the abbot, the brethren, and all those he comes in contact with, seeing Christ in all of them.

Fourth Step of Humility

The fourth step of humility is that in this obedience, under difficult, unfavorable, or even unjust conditions, his heart quietly embraces suffering and endures it without weakening or seeking escape.

RULE OF SAINT BENEDICT

The practice of the fourth step of humility, according to Saint Benedict, is very demanding and painful. It is only in light of the mystery of the cross of Christ and of his supreme obedience to the Father that we can begin to apprehend the hardship entailed in this form of following the Lord. If we think that physical suffering is difficult to endure, we shall soon find out that mental and emotional suffering is many times more painful. Only those who have endured unjust persecution and the mental anguish that sort of suffering carries with it have experiential knowledge of how painful it is to assent to God's will under such circumstances.

We shall not be surprised, if in a moment of weakness and fear, we try to escape from the practice of this step. Jesus himself prayed: "Father, if it is possible, let this cup pass me by." It is precisely at this moment, though, "with a quiet heart" as counseled by Saint Benedict, that we try to submit to God's wishes as we utter the remainder of Jesus words: "Nevertheless, let it be as you, not I, would have it." In this submission, all natural resentment emanating from the source of this suffering begins to lessen, and a deep inner peace—a sure sign of the healing presence of God—settles in.

— MARCH 17 —

Fifth Step of Humility

The fifth step of humility is that a man does not conceal from his abbot any sinful thoughts entering his heart, or any wrongs committed in secret, but rather confesses them humbly.

RULE OF SAINT BENEDICT

Traditionally, a young monk who enters a monastery is put under the care of a spiritual father, either the abbot himself or another older spiritual teacher. The spiritual father forms, directs, and transmits to the new novice the principles of the monastic life. Further, the spiritual father has the delicate task of generating the inner life of the neophyte monk. This implies great trust on the part of both the spiritual father and the spiritual son. But it is impossible, in the eyes of Saint Benedict, to arrive to this level of profound mutual trust without first acquiring great humility of heart. The novice must look at the spiritual father as someone standing in the Lord's place, and open the innermost sentiments of his heart. A wise spiritual father is there not to judge, but to engender the life of the Spirit in his spiritual son. The spiritual son, on his part, with a humble attitude and without fear, can communicate to the father all that is within him, no matter how wicked or sinful it may seem. This step is absolutely necessary if the new young monk is going to make any progress in the spiritual life.

What is applicable to the new monastic aspirant is also applicable to anyone who wishes to grow in the spiritual life. We all need to open ourselves with sincere humility, either to a spiritual father or mother or to a confessor or a director, in order to be shown the light and the path that we must follow. As a result, those receiving this guidance shall experience a strengthening of their spiritual life and acquire a deep peace.

— MARCH 18 —

Sixth Step of Humility

The sixth step of humility consists that a monk is content with the lowest and most menial treatment, and regards himself as a poor and worthless workman in whatever task he is given.

RULE OF SAINT BENEDICT

Saint Benedict knew the dangers of self-aggrandizement, a common temptation among people who claim to be successful, either in the spiritual or secular life. These kind of people are all around us. Whenever people ascribe to themselves greatness of any sort, we know that what comes out of their mouth is not necessarily the wisdom of God, but pure praise for themselves and their self-proclaimed talents. Yet, in the words of Jesus, we must always seek the last place and make ourselves the servant of all.

The servant is not greater than the Master, says the Lord, and if he chose to empty himself by taking the form of a servant, it was to give us an example of how we must follow him. To choose therefore the lowest and the last place in all circumstances, to acknowledge oneself as the "useless servant" even when we think we have achieved some good, are the genuine signs of true discipleship. The Lord rewards the humility of the servant with the gift of inner freedom. For, in truth, one does not have to do battle for the last place, since very few aspire to such a position. In choosing to always be last, we are left alone with God, and no one can disturb this intimate communion.

— MARCH 19 —

Solemnity of Saint Joseph

Most Holy Joseph, you have delighted the hearts of the faithful and shown us the royal road to heaven. The heavenly powers were amazed as they beheld the heights of your unsurpassed glory. We, too, the faithful, sing a hymn to you: Glory to the One who honored you, O just man! Glory to the One who crowned you, O spouse of Mary! Glory to the One who chose you, Holy Joseph, as the intercessor of our souls!

MELCHITE BYZANTINE OFFICE

Much joy is felt throughout our small monastery for today is the feast of Saint Joseph. As one comes into the monastery, immediately after opening the front door, Joseph is there in the right-side corner, watching over the place. He has been embodied in a lovely statue made by a dear acquaintance of mine in the small village of Solesmes, Monsieur Grue, and was given to us by our close friend Frances W. Deleghanty, a descendant of George Washington and an oblate of Solesmes. The statue stands right on the top spot of our cornerstone, where a small statue of the saint was cemented in place the day Bishop Joseph Pernicone blessed the building's foundations. I still remember Bishop Pernicone's words on that occasion: "If you put your trust in Saint Joseph, he will bring to completion what has started today." Saint Joseph has been at work here ever since! It is not surprising that his quiet presence is detected everywhere. There are ikons of Saint Joseph in the chapel, refectory, library, and in practically every room of our small monastic house. And the herb garden is also dedicated to him!

Some people may ask why we make such a fuss about Saint Joseph? And I respond, "Why not?" From Sacred Scriptures, we gather the privileged role assigned by God to Joseph in the great mystery of the Incarnation. The Scriptures call him a just man, that is, someone sanctified by the Holy Spirit. And it is to this just, humble descendant of the house of David that the Eternal Father entrusted the care of the his only Son and that of his mother, the maiden of Nazareth. If God himself had such high regard for Joseph, such implicit trust in him, would he not inspire in us the same sentiments towards the saint?

I am also particularly fond of Joseph whom I affectionately call "our father," because he is a uniquely quiet, silent, laborious saint, the perfect model for a monk. Scriptures do not reveal to us any of the words uttered by Joseph. He was quiet and silent before the mystery unfolding in front of him. He communed with Jesus and Mary at the deepest of levels, but he did this in a very ordinary way. Like Mary, he kept his secret deep within his heart. He toiled daily to support his family and was known only as the carpenter, as his son Jesus was known as the carpenter's son.

Through the example of Joseph and Mary, the Lord shows us clearly that we need not accomplish great works in the eyes of the world to please him. An ordinary and hidden human existence, based on love, fidelity, and obedience to God's will, is more pleasing in God's eyes than all other works put together. This is the lesson the silent carpenter of Nazareth teaches us daily. *Saint Joseph, may we always rejoice under your protection.*

— MARCH 20 —

Arrival of Spring

My beloved speaks and says to me:
"Arise, my love, my fair one, and come away;
For now the winter is past,
the rain is over and gone.
The flowers appear on the earth,
the time of singing has come,
And the voice of the turtledove
is heard in our land."

SONG OF SOLOMON 2:10-12

The calendar seems to be correct this year. Today is a true spring day. Everywhere there are signs of it. A small amount of snow from the last storm still remains on the surrounding hills, creating a shining tapestry bathed in the soft light of the sun. Clusters of daffodils are open throughout the monastic property, and on both sides of the chapel's entrance we have crocuses showing their radiant yellow, white, and purple colors. It is a scene that I lovingly anticipate every year. All in all, it is a remarkable spring day, full not only of sunshine, but also of that intoxicating, fresh spring air. It is one of those days I believe to be stolen from heaven.

I always treasure our early springtime. It is somehow an anticipation of the eternal spring we all await. There, according to the Book of Revelation, we will never hunger or thirst again for the Spring Lamb who is at the center of the throne and who will be our shepherd and will lead us to springs of living water; and God will wipe away all the tears from our eyes (Rev 7:17).

— MARCH 21 —

Transitus of Saint Benedict

We think of Saint Benedict as the ideal monk, as one who lived as the Rule prescribes, and by this means discovered all the riches and excitement known to those who have penetrated to the heart of the Gospel message, that is, a true understanding of what it is to love God, and our neighbor as ourselves.

CARDINAL BASIL HUME, *IN PRAISE OF BENEDICT*

Today we celebrate the holy death of our father Saint Benedict, his departure to the heavenly Jerusalem. Benedict had received from the Lord the announcement of his death a year in advance—he knew the day and hour. He prepared for the long journey by receiving the sacrament of the Body and Blood of the Lord. Assisted by their monk, Benedict insisted on remaining standing while dying, with his open arms upheld in prayer until the final moment. Saint Gregory, his biographer, recounts lovingly Benedict's last days in his *Dialogues*. It is appropriate to quote him here:

> In the year that was to be his last, the man of God foretold the day of his most holy death to some of his disciples living with him and to others living at a further distance. In mentioning it to those who were with him in the monastery, he bound them to complete secrecy. And to those who were a distance away, he informed them of the special sign they would receive when his soul would leave his body.

Six days before his death he gave orders for his tomb to be dug. Soon after, he [Benedict] was seized by a strong fever and was made weak by a severe illness. Day by day his illness grew worse, so on the sixth day he asked his monks to carry him into the oratory, where he asked to receive the Body and Blood of the Lord to gain strength for the final departure. Then, while his weak body remained standing in the supporting arms of his monks, he raised his hands to heaven as he breathed his last.

That same day two monks, one of them in his cell in the monastery, and the other some distance away, received the very same revelation. They both saw a luminous road ascending in an easterly direction, a road made of rich carpeting and shining with myriads of lights. The road stretched forward from the monastery in a straight line until it reached the heavens. And there in the midst of the brightness stood the figure of a man of glorious appearance, who asked them, "Do you know who passed this way?" "No," they replied. "This," he told them, "is the road taken by blessed Benedict, beloved of the Lord, when he ascended to heaven...."

How beautiful, indeed, in the sight of the Lord, is the death of His saints! Like Christ, his Master, Saint Benedict dies while at prayer, with his hands outstretched in the form of a cross. Again, like his Master, Saint Benedict, six days before his death, ordered that preparations be made "in view of his burial," such as the anointing in the Gospels. At the end, like his Lord and Master, he announces in advance the hour of his death, and after his death he ascends to heaven in a glorious fashion that reminds us of the Ascension of the Lord.

— MARCH 22 —

Seventh Step of Humility

The seventh step of humility is that a man not only admits with his tongue but is also convinced in his heart that he is inferior to all and of less value, humbling himself and saying with the Prophet: "I am truly a worm, not a man, scorned by men and despised by the people."

RULE OF SAINT BENEDICT

S aint Benedict writes about humility in the rule right after the chapters on obedience and on restraint of speech. He knows that it is impossible to advance in any spiritual life without being rooted in the solid foundations of humility. Throughout the years, I have learned again and again to recognize someone as truly spiritual not by their outer gifts and talents, but by their profound humility: the type of humility where little is left of the self and only the light of God shines through the person. When one is given the grace to encounter such individuals, and they are indeed very rare, one is left with a profound sense of the presence of God.

In the seventh step of humility, Saint Benedict invites us to go one step deeper into the practice of humility, not just paying lip service to it, but admitting to ourselves our misery and nothingness, the fact that we are useless servants of no value at all. Saint Benedict invites us to rejoice in this fact and encourages us to wish that others will see us as such, and not as something we are not. It is when we become nothing in our own eyes and in the eyes of others that God turns himself towards us in mercy and finds his true pleasure in us.

In the Magnificat, which we sing daily at Vespers, Our Lady affirms this spiritual truth: Because He has looked with favor on the lowliness of his servant, the Almighty has done great things for me. A bit later she adds: He has scattered the proud in their conceit, he has cast down the mighty from their thrones, and he has lifted up the lowly. If we are indeed serious about pleasing God, about becoming his instruments, we must strive always for the last place in all things: what Charles de Foucauld would call the "dear last place."

— MARCH 23 —

Eighth Step of Humility

The eighth step of humility is that a monk does only what is endorsed by the common rule of the monastery and the example set by his superiors.

RULE OF SAINT BENEDICT

The eighth degree of humility has very subtle individual and communal implications. The temptation to think that we, either as individuals or as a community, are better than others is a very real one. How many communities succumb to the temptation that they are the only true faithful heirs to the ideals of their founders, and others are not? Others refuse to accept the liturgical reform approved by the Vatican Council, implying they know better than the Holy Spirit. I have sometimes heard monks in France state "We are true pillars of the Church." In repeating this to a very holy monk who has since died, remarkable for his wisdom as for his humility, he replied, "Son, when we monks start thinking like that, the best thing for us is to die and disappear. We are of no use to the Lord. The glory we should ascribe to Him alone, we ascribe to ourselves."

Pride and self-love are such strong powers in all of us that Saint Francis of Sales indicates they die in us only fifteen minutes after our own death. When Saint Benedict admonishes us to find our place within the common rule of the monastery or the society we live in, so as not to be distinguished from others, he is simply trying to remind us of the constant danger and temptation to pride, where we seek to be exalted above others. At a given time, when we are persecuted and real humiliations descend on us, we must see them as grace, as real signs of how much God cares for us. As Jesus mentions in the Gospels, some of his teachings are hard to accept, but at the end there is no choice. Either we choose the path of self-glorification that has no future, or we choose the path of God that leads to true life.

— MARCH 24 —

Ninth Step of Humility

The ninth step of humility is that a monk controls his tongue and remains silent, not speaking unless asked a question, for Scripture warns, "In a flood of words you will not avoid sinning," and "A talkative man goes about aimlessly on earth."

RULE OF SAINT BENEDICT

Silence and a certain amount of solitude are indispensable, according to Saint Benedict and the ancient monastic fathers, in order to pursue an authentic spiritual life. The voice of God can almost never be heard, except in deep silence and profound solitude. If Saint Benedict insists on the practice of silence as a means of achieving true humility, it is because he knows human nature. He knows the proud love to assert themselves, love to hear themselves speaking. How often we find ourselves in the middle of a conversation, anxious for the other person to end a sentence so that we can interject our own opinion. We sometimes don't even bother listening to what the other has to say. All we wish is to make ourselves heard. It is against such human temptations as pride, self-assertion, self-preference, and self-opinion that Saint Benedict counsels control over our tongues and the practice of silence. In paraphrasing the words of another great desert figure, Saint John the Baptist, the decreasing of the self in us is directly proportional to the increasing of the life of God within us. This is the wisdom and eternal paradox of the Gospels, authenticated throughout the ages by the example of the saints.

— MARCH 25 —

Solemnity of the Annunciation

Today the beginning of our salvation is made manifest, the revelation of the eternal mystery! The Son of God becomes the Son of the Virgin as Gabriel announces the coming of grace. Together with him let us cry to the Theotokos: Rejoice, O Full of Grace, the Lord is with you!

TROPARION OF THE FEAST

The mystery of the Incarnation begins at that moment when Mary utters her fiat in complete submission to the plan of God. Mary, of course, knew the words of the prophet Isaiah: Behold, a Virgin shall conceive and bear a Son, and his name shall be called Emmanuel. What she never knew, until then, is that Isaiah was speaking of her, that she was eternally destined to bear the Father's only Son. As one of the lovely antiphons of Advent tells us, "This is the good news the prophets foretold: the Savior will be born of the Virgin Mary."

On this day, the ikon of the Annunciation lays next to the lectionary in our chapel. Several times a day, as we enter or leave the Oratory, we offer it a profound homage. During the Liturgy and the Offices, candles are lit next to the ikon and incense is offered. As we gaze upon the ikon, we see Mary in deep prayer. Suddenly, she is visited by Gabriel, and in her profound humility she seems bewildered by his greeting. If Mary is startled by the vision of the angel, she is more so by the message he proclaims: "Do not be afraid, Mary, for you have found favor with God. And behold, you will conceive in your womb and bear a Son, and shall call His name Jesus."

"How can this be?" we can hear Mary asking the angel, "I do not know a man." She had promised to God to remain a virgin; was God asking her through the angel to do otherwise? Gabriel answered Mary quickly, reassuring her that the gift of her virginity to God would remain untarnished: "The Holy Spirit will come upon you, and the power of the Most High will over-shadow you; therefore, also, the child who is to be born will be called the Son of God."

Overwhelmed by the news given to her by Gabriel, Mary, a woman of deep faith, utters her fiat: "Behold, the handmaid of the Lord, be it done to me according to your word." At her fiat, the Son of God descends into the womb of Mary, uniting heaven and earth. At that precise moment, the Holy Spirit, through its mysterious power, accomplishes God's Incarnation: the Word is made flesh and dwells among us. Nothing will ever be the same. As the Akathist Hymn points out: "Gabriel stood amazed at the beauty of your holiness, and at the splendor of your purity, and he cried to you, Hail, O Mary, you are full of grace!"

— MARCH 26 —

Tenth Step of Humility

The tenth step of humility is that he is not given to ready laughter, for it is written: "Only a fool raises his voice in laughter."

RULE OF SAINT BENEDICT

This is not an easy part of the rule to interpret. As a matter of fact, one commentator on the rule says, "Since it is a short exposé, the commentary should likewise be short." This being said, I can't help but try to read some meaning into it, especially since I know that Saint Benedict is frugal and never wasteful in his use of words.

The first thing that comes to mind is that Saint Benedict, human as he was and always striving for moderation in all things, is not totally opposed to laughter, only to certain types of laughter that are not becoming to a spiritual person. Take, for example, a sarcastic type of laughter that implies a certain arrogance and putting down of a neighbor. Or the frivolous laughter that makes mockery of everything, and which again is not only a sign of intemperance but also of pride. And certainly, it seems perfectly natural that a loud laughter would be considered totally unbecoming to a quiet, recollected spirit. Moreover, it is usually the sign of a dissipated, scattered mind.

If the spiritual person is discouraged by Saint Benedict from exercising this sort of laughter, he says nothing whatsoever about forbidding a beautiful smile on the monk, which may reflect the peace and the joy of his union with God. A peaceful and radiant smile can do so much to reflect the presence of God in oneself. I think of Jesus' apparition to his disciples after the Resurrection. I am sure He smiled beautifully when he greeted them. And, in many apparitions of Our Lady, such as the ones at Lourdes, Bernadette often referred to her beautiful and tender smile.

— MARCH 27 —

Eleventh Step of Humility

The eleventh step of humility is that a monk speaks gently and without laughter, seriously and with becoming modesty, briefly and reasonably, but without raising his voice.

RULE OF SAINT BENEDICT

For Saint Benedict, an inner logic holds in the ascent toward attaining true humility. All the steps are connected in the one ladder. And so the eleventh step seems a natural extension of the tenth step. Saint Benedict, in this passage, not only advocates avoiding laughter; he goes further and counsels the monk to speak gently, briefly, with few words, and always with sincere modesty.

Saint Benedict is not only concerned with the inner workings of the monk, but also with his external behavior, which often becomes a reflection of his inner state. In the spiritual life, our interior and external conduct are intimately connected. Saint Paul, in his letter to the Galatians, gives us an insight into humility's eleventh step: "If you are guided by the Spirit, I say, and do not gratify the desires of the flesh. For what the flesh desires is opposed to the Spirit....Those who belong to Christ Jesus have crucified the flesh with its passions and desires. If we live by the Spirit, let us also be guided by the Spirit. Let us not become conceited, competing against one another, envying one another."

— MARCH 28 —

Twelfth Step of Humility

The twelfth step of humility is that a monk always manifests humility in his bearing no less than in his heart, so that it is evident at the work of God, in the oratory, the monastery, or the garden, on a journey or in the field, his head must be bowed and his eyes cast down. Judging himself always guilty on account of his sins, he should consider that he is already at the fearful judgment, and constantly say in his heart what the publican said with downcast eyes: "Lord, I am a sinner."

RULE OF SAINT BENEDICT

Saint Benedict makes reference in the twelfth step of humility to the story of the Pharisee and the Publican in Luke 18:9–14. This Gospel reading reminds us that the temptation to pride and self-exaltation remains with us until the end of our days. All we can do is to face the war within ourselves, as did the ancient Desert Fathers and Mothers. The weapon they used in the battle was the continual recitation, day and night, of the Publican's prayer: "God, be merciful to me a sinner."

Throughout the centuries the formula of that prayer developed into what has become now the Jesus prayer: "Lord Jesus Christ, Son of the living God, have mercy on me a sinner." The Jesus prayer allows us to confront ourselves daily, as in a mirror. We see the naked truth about our crude sinfulness, our failings, our shortcomings, our pride, our lack of charity, our passing judgment on others. Only the humility of recognizing our sinful state and our knowledge of God's abundant mercy lets us resolve this confrontation. There is a river of love and mercy for all who constantly say in their hearts what the Publican said in the Gospel. The time comes, after years of faithful praying, when by the grace of God the prayer takes hold of one's being. Then, no obstacles remain between the humble realization of our sinfulness and the gift of forgiveness received from a loving Father.

In this twelfth step, Saint Benedict also approaches the physical conduct and the bearing the monk, "whether he sits, walks, or stands" or "whether he is in the oratory or garden, on a journey or in the field, or anywhere else." Our physical bearing ought to be a reflection of our inner dispositions. This sort of behavior on the part of the monk is what the ancient fathers taught as monastic modesty. Modesty is the opposite to pride, the monk's great enemy. And by holding on in all things to the habitual practice of monastic modesty on a daily basis, little by little we let go of the false self. We die daily, to make room for God. We let go of ourselves, and in doing that we let God in.

— MARCH 29 —

Humility's Final Goal

Now, therefore, after ascending all these steps of humility, the monk will quickly arrive at that perfect love of God which casts out fear. Through this love, all that he once performed with dread, he will now begin to observe without effort, as though naturally, from habit, no longer out of fear of hell, but out of love for Christ, good habit and delight in virtue.

RULE OF SAINT BENEDICT

O ur Lenten journey through the different steps of humility at first seems repugnant and contrary to human nature. And, indeed, it is. But the value Benedict sees in the process is that these harsh and difficult steps are like strong medicine that we must take in order to get well. Saint Benedict knows that we are alienated from God by our pride, egocentrism, and lust for power. To remedy this fundamental depravity on our part, those hindrances to our relationship with God and with others, he suggests that we undertake the path of humility, the way proposed by the Lord Himself.

If the road to humility may seem at times nothing but struggle and futility, Saint Benedict readily comes to our rescue by reminding us of its ultimate goal. If we endure the struggle, and gradually let go of our pride, arrogance, self-importance, and judgment of others, it is so that we may "more quickly arrive at that perfect love of God."

The early monastic fathers and mothers claimed that the only purpose of their monastic life was to cling to that most excellent way which is love. Saint Benedict, a true inheritor of that tradition, passed on the same teaching to his disciples. He reminds each of us that to walk in the footsteps of Christ, whose love we must prefer above all things, we must learn to walk in the way of love and to learn to love as Jesus did. To do the work of love is our sole occupation. The work of love is real, imperative, and it must absorb our entire lives.

— MARCH 30 —

Saint John Climacus

Your abundant tears made the wilderness sprout and bloom, and your suffering made your labors fruitful a hundredfold; you became a shining torch over the world. O Holy Father John, pray to Christ our God to save our souls!

TROPARION OF THE FEAST

The Memorial of Saint John Climacus, kept today in this monastery, brings to a close the month of March in a very monastic fashion. Saint John Climacus, a true monastic teacher, is commonly known as the author of the book, *The Ladder of Divine Ascent*. No other book, except for the Bible and some liturgical books, has been as many times copied, translated, or printed throughout the history of Christian spirituality. It is a classic book of timeless appeal that can be found in every monastic library. I am always delighted when I discover an ancient version or an older translation of *The Ladder*, and can compare notes with a more updated present-day text.

There was a time, not so long ago, when reading *The Ladder* was de rigueur for every monk. I wonder if this is still so in many monasteries, especially with the influx of so many new books with a more contemporary approach to spirituality. Sometimes I feel a bit left out, for my reading has not moved much beyond the seventh century: I have been immersed so long in the Fathers and the monastic sources that I never seem to have enough time to go beyond them and embark upon new reading. There is so much wealth there, I can't quite yet take leave from those early centuries. One day, I hope to be able to have time to read the Cistercian Fathers. There is a unique, pure monastic intuition in their approach and return to monastic sources.

Little is known about John Climacus. It is thought that he was a teenager when he embraced monastic life at Mount Sinai, in a monastery established on the site where God revealed his face to Moses. There he shared with a small group of monks the life of *hesychia*, that is, a life of tranquil stillness. After making his monastic profession, Saint John retired to a small hermitage a few miles away from the fortress monastery. In this state of solitude he received from God the gift of tears and the grace of unceasing prayer. He remained in that solitude for forty years, except for a one-time visit to a large monastery in Alexandria. After forty years of solitude on the top of God's mountain, he was chosen by the monks of Sinai as the Abbot of their monastery.

It was during this time, as abbot of the large community, that he wrote *The Ladder of Divine Ascent*. He wrote it hesitantly, at the request of monks from another monastery. While he wrote his treatise with monks in view, he clearly transcended and extended his teachings to all of humankind. He was a true mystic, writing: "God is the life of all free beings. He is the salvation of believers or unbelievers, of the just or the unjust, of the pious or the impious, of those freed from passions or caught up in them, of monks or those living in the world, of educated or the illiterate, of the healthy or the sick, of the young or the very old. He is the outpouring of light, the glimpse of the sun, or the changes of the weather, which are the same for everyone without exception" (*The Ladder*). It is interesting to note that Saint John Climacus never sought to be ordained a priest. He was a monk, a seeker of God, and that was enough for him. Like many of the early monks, the mystery of his monastic vocation was enough to engage him entirely.

— MARCH 31 —

The Bridegroom

Look! Here is the bridegroom! Come out to meet him.
MATTHEW 25:6

During Lent, we place a special ikon of the Lord on the main lectern in the chapel, on the spot where we usually lay the festal or seasonal ikon for veneration. This particular ikon is sometimes designated by the title "The Holy Humility of Christ"; other times it is called "The Kenosis," that is, the self-emptying of Christ. Most commonly, however, the ikon is called simply "The Bridegroom."

I cherish this ikon deeply, for it truly represents the mystery of the Passion of the Lord in a profound way. It is the ikon that accompanies me on my Lenten pilgrimage, the ikon that brings me back to the center when I wander astray, as I often do.

At the beginning of holy week, the Bridegroom service is celebrated in churches of the Byzantine tradition. The ikon of the Bridegroom is solemnly enthroned in the center aisle of the church and the mournful singing begins, reminding us of the trial and

death of Christ and his patient endurance throughout. In the
words and ritual of the service we relive poignantly the hours of
the agony and sacred Passion. These are not the sufferings endured by an ordinary man; these are the sufferings endured by
the God-Man, in whose person the divine and human natures
co-exist. The Bridegroom service precedes the events of Holy Thursday, Good Friday, and Holy Saturday. The stanzas of the Bridegroom hymn are so expressive and beautiful, especially when sung.
Here are some of them for our own meditation and benefit:

> Behold, the Bridegroom comes in the middle of the night.
> Happy is that servant whom He shall find watching.
> On the contrary, unworthy is he who is careless and not ready.
> Let us, then, be vigilant and put aside the works of darkness,
> Lest we fall into deep slumber;
> For the Lord shall come as a thief in the night.

> O Bridegroom, more beautiful than all men,
> Having called us to the spiritual feast of Your kingdom,
> Now clothe us with the right wedding garment.
> That being adorned in the garment of your beauty,
> We may enter into your bridal chamber as your guests
> Shining with glory and joy.

> Let us cast aside the works of darkness
> And go to meet Christ, the immortal Bridegroom,
> Carrying sufficient oil in the vessels of our souls,
> Strengthened by prayer and fasting,
> Vigilantly let us await the Bridegroom, arriving near,
> For the bridal chamber is ready,
> and the wedding feast is at hand.

> Let us love the Bridegroom
> By readying our lamps, shining with virtues and deep faith,
> That like the wise virgins of the Lord well-prepared,
> We may enter with Christ into the wedding feast
> And receive from the Bridegroom the wedding garment,
> So that God may grant us an incorruptible crown.

APRIL

The Stuff of Daily Life

The ordinary is translucent with Jesus.

SISTER WENDY BECKETT

A young student once asked me to explain to him the mystery of monastic life. I paused and then said, "You see what I am doing?" The young man replied, "Yes, you are carrying manure from the barn into the garden." "Well," I continued, "doing what I am doing at each moment is what monastic life is all about."

Monastic life is indeed very ordinary. A romantic notion of the way monks live, as sometimes portrayed in novels and films, is a far cry from the reality of what a monastic day is all about. Monastic life is made of the same daily elements: prayer, work, reading, silence, cooking, eating, cleaning, gardening, tending to the farm animals, doing the dishes, and finally, sleeping. The same pattern gets repeated day after day, month after month, year after year. The monk cannot escape the daily sameness of his life, or the regularity of the daily schedule, or the routine of toil and prayer, just as much as he cannot escape the weather, the place where he lives, or those he lives with.

Yet it is within the confines of this daily monotony that the monk is called to seek and find God. The monastic life is not made of extraordinary things. There is no excitement, no agitation, novelty, or much variety in its daily unfolding. But as the monk slowly progresses in his monastic calling, he discovers the wealth hidden underneath his apparent everyday monotony. It is precisely this repeated sameness in everyday life that frees the monk from other concerns and allows him to concentrate wholly on the "one thing necessary" of the Gospel.

The true monk embraces his daily routine with simplicity of heart. This involvement with the minutia and mundane tasks presented to him daily allows him to escape daydreaming and other dangers to his spiritual life. In fact, it is a gift from God. The dailiness of his routine allows the monk to plunge directly, without distractions, into that vast ocean which is the mystery of God.

— APRIL 2 —

Saint Mary of Egypt

The life of Saint Mary of Egypt is not only an obvious ascetic triumph, a triumph of love, but also a triumph over preconceived notions of holiness.

MOTHER THEKLA, *IKONS: MEDITATIONS IN WORDS AND MUSIC*

If any saint truly embodies the spirit of Lent, it is our mother among the saints, Mary of Egypt. Lent is a privileged time given to us by God for the purpose of conversion, repentance, and Saint Mary of Egypt's life is a model of it. In the desert of Judea, where she was led by the Lord, she lived with an unusual attitude of deep repentance—a humble attitude of heart and mind that brings healing to all those who, moved by the Holy Spirit, embrace it wholeheartedly. Armed with the power of love and her tears, she made the desert fertile with the fruits of her holiness.

Mary of Egypt was a fifth-century prostitute from Alexandria who spent the early part of her life corrupting the young men of Egypt. She enjoyed entertaining all those who came her way, but she refused payment. Pleasure was the only motivation for her behavior. One day she joined a group of pilgrims who were going from Cairo to the city of Jerusalem to celebrate the feast of the Holy Cross. Curious about the true Cross, she followed the pilgrims to the church where it was displayed. However, a mysterious force somehow prevented her from entering the Church of the Holy Cross every time she tried to do so. While the crowd of pilgrims could move forward, she was paralyzed and couldn't move. Bewildered by her hopeless attempts to enter the church and glimpse the true Cross and feeling utterly rejected, she turned to an ikon of the Mother of God and prayed:

> O ever blessed Virgin and Lady, you gave birth to the Word of God in the flesh, I know that it is not proper for me, foul and corrupt, to gaze upon your holy ikon! But if, as I have heard, God became man, born of you, to call sinners to repentance, help me in my distress. Command the entrance into the church to be opened to me; do not let me be deprived of gazing upon the tree on which God in the flesh, born of you, was nailed and shed his own blood to redeem me. I call upon you to be my guarantor before your Son, that never again shall I defile his body with shameful fornication, but as soon as I venerate the tree of the Cross, immediately after, I shall renounce the world and all its vanities, and I shall go wherever you, the guarantor of my salvation, order me to go.

As Mary prayed so earnestly, she received the grace to move forward to the Cross of Christ, then forward to the River Jordan and into the desert, and, as Mother Thekla explains in her book *Ikons*, "forward into year after year of icy cold and burning heat, of temptation and carnal longing, of fear and despair, and, finally, of the peace above all understanding."

The example of the holiness of Saint Mary of Egypt, whose memory is kept today, has deep significance for all who follow the monastic way. Her life portrays the dramatic story of the

work of lust turned into the work of love by the mystery of grace
and repentance. For the Christian who embraces the monastic
state and receives the "habit of repentance," as the ancient monks
used to call the monastic garb, it is the abiding conviction that
humble repentance is the ordinary, real, and only way to God.
Repentance is an illumination and a grace, a humble attitude of
heart and mind that brings healing and inner freedom to whomever embraces it wholeheartedly as a genuine gift from God.

— APRIL 3 —

Sacrament of the Present Moment

A headache, work, dryness of spirit, fatigue. There was a
time when faced with such obstacles, I would say: "When
they are all over, I will begin to live again." Now I
understand otherwise: the moment to live is always the
present moment. It is the only way to be united with God.

MERE GENEVIEVE GALLOIS, *NOTES SPIRITUELLES*

Often we find ourselves immersed in the world of busyness,
unable to complete our task assigned within the appointed
time. We seem to be busy constantly. Someone once called it the
"sickness of our times." It is not surprising, therefore, that our
hearts are not at rest. We are not made to go on around and
around, nonstop, without getting hold of the one thing that matters. Sometimes it is difficult to escape from a busy occupation,
but we can at least approach it differently with another perspective.

We can try to rediscover the presence of God in the present
moment, at the very moment that our lives unfold. It is useless to
look for God in other places or at other times. We would not find
him. We must meet God in the present moment. The body may
be fully occupied with an engrossing event or occupation, but
the mind and the heart can find their own way to God. We must
honestly assess the task that occupies us, so that we can free the
mind and the heart for more important things.

At times, we try to escape this burden of busyness by making useless postponements or by arranging plans for the future. However, the future does not exist. We only have the present, and it is at that moment that God is waiting to give himself to us. It is today that we must listen to his voice. It is now that we must make ourselves available to him. It is easy to fix our gaze on the past, and it is easy to make plans for the future. But we don't live in our yesterdays or in our tomorrows; we only live in the present. The present is not ours to waste, for it belongs to God.

Abba Benjamin, one of the desert fathers, taught his disciples how to live in the present, in the now of God. As he was dying, he reminded them: "Be joyful at all times. Pray without ceasing and give thanks for all things."

— APRIL 4 —

Early April

In the month of March,	*Au mois de mars,*
Winter departs.	*L'hiver part.*
And in the month of April	*Au mois d'avril,*
The heat arrives.	*Le chaud arrive.*
April creates the flowers	*Avril fait la fleur,*
That May shows with honor.	*Mai en a l'honneur.*

AN OLD FRENCH PROVERB

April is beginning to show its face. The tender spring green is appearing in our meadows. This green is an April green, showing forth a brilliance that is hard to describe. With childlike glee, I delight in the gradual warming of the sun day by day, in the varieties of early flowers: crocus, anemones (windflowers), snowdrops, daffodils, and small Japanese iris. Of course, nothing is equal to the soft breezes of early spring. I feel rejuvenated as I breathe this air and clear the garden of some winter debris.

Some early April days give the impression that spring arrives reluctantly. On those days I make a point of recalling the fine weather we have had so far, knowing deep within that the promise of spring is here to stay. We may, from time to time, still have

days that remind us of winter, but there is no returning to it.
Early spring is a blessed time, a time of expectation, a time of
waiting, a time to practice patience. The snowdrops are blooming profusely around the statue of Our Lady in front of the chapel.
It is a visible sign of the season, a season that brings with itself
much joy and beauty to comfort the human heart.

— APRIL 5 —

Daily Efforts

*One of the Fathers asked Abba John the Dwarf, "What
is a monk?" He said, "He is toil. The monk toils at all he
does."*

ABBA JOHN THE DWARF, *SAYINGS OF THE DESERT FATHERS*

The early monastic fathers defined all spiritual life as a struggle.
I have been thinking about how we can understand this concept in more contemporary terms. I think the word that comes
closest to essentially expressing the same truth is the word "effort." We could say that the spiritual life implies a continual effort: sometimes small efforts, sometimes great efforts and, perhaps most of the time, efforts that are something in between.

The routine of daily life, be it monastic or otherwise, demands both physical and spiritual effort. From the first moment
of the day, when we are called to get up early to sing God's praises,
the question of making an effort arises. The spirit is ready but
the body is weak. It is the same with the rest of the day. On fast
days, to give an example, one often feels the sensation of hunger
and is therefore tempted to eat between meals, when on ordinary
days such thoughts do not even reach consciousness. We are then
called to make an effort not to give in to our bodily inclinations.
Think also of the growing season, when the weeds proliferate
abundantly in our gardens. There are days when one just about
has had it with them and one is tempted to give up. Instead, with
humble patience, one is called to make that extra bit of effort
and begin the arduous task.

I find that the effort required from us to accomplish these

not-always-so-pleasant tasks and the need for patience go hand in hand. And it is precisely through this struggle, through these constant daily efforts, and through much patience that we embrace the mystery of the Cross and share in the Passion of Christ. We may not all be called to be great martyrs or confessors of the faith, but we are all called to toil daily. As Abba John the Dwarf taught his disciples, we must toil to conquer ourselves through the multiple efforts demanded by life's daily situations. These constant efforts, these seemingly small struggles, this daily dying, are the backbone of a true spiritual life. It is the royal way of the Cross, the process by which the old self dies slowly so that the new life promised by Christ may be manifested in our very flesh.

— APRIL 6 —

On Cooking

Food should be treated with respect, since Our Lord left himself to us in the guise of food.
DOROTHY DAY

Cooking is different from other daily occupations, in that it has more of a human and universal character. All people, in one way or another, are interested in and in need of food. My own interest in cooking developed during my early years, watching my mother and my grandmother prepare delicious homemade meals for the whole family. In particular, I remember the Sunday noonday meal, the special meal of the whole week. As children, we used to eagerly await the arrival of Sunday, so we could join the entire family at our grandparents' home for the family meal. As was the custom in those days, everyone in the family was there, including all our aunts and uncles, and of course, all our cousins. The meal took several hours to be consumed, for besides the fact that the food was very special, there was a great deal of conversation and much fun around the table, as it is whenever large families get together.

Later, when I first entered monastic life, I was assigned to work in the kitchen as an apprentice to an older monk-chef. My main duties were to clean and peel the vegetables that came from the monastery garden, *eplucher les legumes,* as we used call it in French. From time to time, the older monk would allow me and the other young assistant to prepare the soup of the day—a very important task, for in a monastery monks eat soup twice a day. The soup prepared for the main noonday meal is again consumed during what monks call "collation," that is, the evening meal.

To prepare large amounts of soup in those days was quite an adventure. European monasteries then didn't have refrigerators. The other young monk and myself had to see what ingredients were available in the monastery. If it was winter and fresh vegetables were scarce, we went into the cellar to see what had survived from the autumn harvest. We could always find onions and potatoes, so they usually became the basis for our soup. We would add to it some carrots and turnips from the cellar. Finally, we put in some dried beans, peas, or lentils. We chose one of them as the main staple for the soup. When the water began boiling we would add bay leaves, a couple of minced garlic cloves, a pinch of salt and pepper, and, when available, some finely chopped parsley. We allowed the soup to cook slowly until the desired taste and consistency was achieved. When the soup was done, we waited with great expectation to see if our head chef approved of it. Needless to say, we sometimes failed in our attempts. The same can be said about other dishes, especially desserts. The kitchen chef, experienced as he was, usually was very understanding. He assured us that the art of cooking required much patience, experience, and creativity. It is only after one has mastered these three elements, he would say, that one can really call himself a cook.

As I look back at my experience of cooking for the many guests we receive here yearly, I can honestly say it has been both a challenge and an occasion of endless joy. From the Scriptures I have learned the importance that Jesus attached to food, so I look at it now as a pure and free gift from God. Food is meant to be good, delicious, enjoyable, nutritious, and appetizing, because God the Creator put all these qualities in the food that we partake of. Feasting on good food is a reaffirmation of the great mystery of the Incarnation, because as the Gospels tell us, the

Son of Man "came eating and drinking." If there is anything I have learned throughout these many years of working in the kitchen, it is the fact that cooking is an act of cooperating with the Creator. Saint Teresa of Ávila used to say to her Carmelite nuns: *Hijas, entre los pucheros se encuentra el Senor* (Daughters, among the *pucheros* [that is, a poor man's soup], the Lord can be found.) Looking from this spiritual perspective, daily cooking, either in a monastery or a family, can be a source of great satisfaction and a continual blessing.

— APRIL 7 —

Metanoia

For just as you were disposed to go astray from God,
return with tenfold zeal to seek him.

BARUCH 4:28

During these Lenten days we try, with the help of the Holy Spirit, to apprehend the meaning of what the early monastic fathers referred to as metanoia. Some spiritual writers describe metanoia as compunction, repentance, and sorrow for sin. It is all of that and more. I particularly like the sense given to the word by some of the later Fathers, who describe it in terms of "conversion of life." Conversion is at the origin of the spiritual life. It is a free act on the part of the Christian, who is moved by the grace of the Holy Spirit to renounce sin and all its of consequences, in order to return to full communion with God. Conversion implies change of mind, attitudes and habits, and heart. Saint Mary of Egypt is the perfect example of what true conversion is all about.

Conversion means change, and change does not come easily to us creatures of habit. Conversion makes us aware that we must work at changing ourselves daily, and that this effort must include every aspect of our lives, even the smallest and the most hidden. Conversion is an inexorable process from which there is no respite or escape. Guided by grace, we must learn to live according to the laws of the spirit.

The Desert Fathers, with their customary wisdom, used every situation to teach their disciples the meaning and importance of conversion. For instance, when Abba Ammonas was asked, "What is the narrow and hard way?" he, in all simplicity, replied, "The narrow and hard way (Mt 7:14) is this: to control your thoughts and to strip yourself of your own will for the sake of God."

In struggling to change the old self into the new, we must begin by first stripping ourselves of our own will in order to adhere to God alone. If the process sometimes is discouraging, let us bring to mind that metanoia is the surest and only way of ascending to God. In the words of Saint Isaac the Syrian, "Metanoia is fitting at all times for all persons—for sinners as well as the righteous who look for salvation. There are no bounds to perfection, for even the perfection of the most perfect is nothing but imperfection. Therefore, until the moment of death neither the time nor the work of conversion can ever be complete."

— APRIL 8 —

The Gift of Tears

A young monk asked Abba Poemen what he ought to do about his sins. The Abba responded, "He who wishes to be cleansed from his sins must do it with tears and he who wishes to acquire virtues must acquire them with tears, for weeping is the way of the Scriptures and our Forefathers."

ABBA POEMEN

It was said of the Desert Fathers and Mothers that they transformed the arid desert into fertile soil by the power of their tears. Yet, today, we find it rather unusual to approach the theme of tears in the spiritual life. It is an experience far removed from our contemporaries, including those who are considered themselves spiritual people.

Repentance and the gift of tears are closely related, though there is an important distinction between the two. Repentance is an act willfully chosen and assented to by us. While repentance demands our own personal consent and initiative, the gift of tears is a free gift from God who gives it to those whom he chooses. Many Fathers saw in the flowing water of tears an image of the waters of baptism. By the waters of baptism, we were cleansed from sin and initiated into the life of communion with God; and, by the waters of our tears, we are purified from the sins committed later on in life.

There is nothing pathological in those who, while at prayer, find themselves floating in a bath of tears. These are blessed tears which, paradoxically, are the fruits of true sorrow for our sins while, at the same time, they are a source of profound joy. Nothing is more liberating than this gift of tears, this transforming gift from the Holy Spirit. Tears purify our nature, free us from our anguishes and passions, cleanse us from our corrupted ways, and introduce us into the divine realm where we can meet our Savior, the Beloved of our hearts. Our Lord himself spoke of tears as a source of blessings when he said: "Blessed are you that weep now: for you shall laugh" (Lk 6:21).

Saint John Climacus, who himself received the gift of tears, wrote extensively about it in *The Ladder of Divine Ascent.* He counsels us: "Hold fast to the blessed and joyful sorrow of holy tears and do not cease laboring for it until it lifts you high above the things of the world to present you, a purified offering, to Christ."

— APRIL 9 —

Resurrection of Lazarus

In Lazarus, Christ is already destroying you, O death,
Where, therefore, O hell, is your victory?

BYZANTINE OFFICE FOR LAZARUS SATURDAY

This spring is one of the greenest I have ever witnessed in recent years. Rains pouring down in abundance turn everything green, making nature itself convey the image of resurrection and new life. We have arrived at the end of our Lenten pilgrimage, and now we proceed forward as we enter into the holiest of weeks. Palm Sunday marks the beginning days of Passiontide, the days that prepare us for the feast of feasts, the glorious Resurrection of the Lord.

The Church liturgy presents us the Gospel story of Lazarus's resurrection at the very end of our Lenten observance. The purpose of Lazarus's rising from the dead was, as the troparion of the day explains, "to confirm the universal resurrection." It is through the resurrection of Christ that we experience our own rebirth. If we listen attentively to the words of the Gospel, we hear the messenger's poignant words: "Lord, he whom you love [Lazarus] is ill." When Jesus arrives at Bethany, we hear Martha's gentle reproach: "Lord, if you had been here, my brother would not have died." Jesus' consolingly replies: "Your brother will rise again."

This Gospel causes us to ponder the mystery of our own earthly death and the promise of new life. For Jesus is announcing to Martha not only the resurrection of her brother Lazarus but also that of all his faithful followers. In a clear and solemn tone, he adds, "I am the resurrection and the life. Those who believe in me, even though they die, will live, and everyone who lives and believes in me will never die." At the end of the Gospel story, when Jesus summons in a loud voice, "Lazarus, come forth," he is not only summoning Lazarus but also each of us. It is each one of us he is asking to abandon the works of sin and darkness, to follow him through his suffering and crucifixion into the new life of the Resurrection. Like Lazarus, we are spiritually dead and in dire need of resurrection. The purpose of the forty days' journey is to awaken in us the desire for the new life offered by Christ. The predictable rhythm of our Lenten observance helps us to die daily with Christ, so that at Easter we may experience what it is to rise to new life with Our Lord. The story of Lazarus's resurrection, placed in liturgical context at the completion of the forty days, is the necessary link between a genuine Lenten preparation and a joyful Paschal fulfillment.

— APRIL 10 —

Palm Sunday

Glory and praise, and honor be yours,
Christ our King and Redeemer:
Children in the loveliness of youth,
Called out "Hosanna" to greet you!

GLORIA, LAUS, THEODULPH D'ORLEANS (D. 821)

As the Lord makes his solemn entrance into Jerusalem, we too enter into that special time: Passiontide. It is the final destination of our Lenten pilgrimage. By reliving each event of our Savior's last week before his death, we become participants in those very events. The Offices of Holy Week are a great aid to us in following the sequence of Jesus' last days, step by step, unto his cruel last hours. They portray how Christ honestly accomplished his redemptive work. By unfolding before our eyes the mysteries of Christ's suffering, death, and Resurrection, in all of its historical details, the liturgy allows us to witness to the supreme act of God's love. It is a love that has no equal.

Last evening, while the beautiful hymn *Vexilla Regis* was intoned at Vespers, I was almost instantly overtaken by the sacred drama awaiting us during the coming week. The Lenten chant, music, and text has served the double purpose of purifying us and of preparing us for what was to come. Now that we have arrived at the very doors of Holy Week, a week totally consecrated to the contemplation of Christ's death and Resurrection, the chant for Passiontide takes the place of the Lenten chant and opens for us the hidden meaning of the Paschal Mystery. The chant, mournfully, builds its crescendo to help us achieve an inner comprehension of the last events of Christ's life. The chant reaches its peak on Good Friday during the Liturgy of the Presanctified when we sing the whole of the *Christus factus est*. Quietly, decidedly, the chant works its way to the point where it leads us to encounter the Lord on the road to Calvary. It compels us to accompany him, with grief and tears of repentance, to his last hour—the hour which he awaited anxiously for our sake.

— APRIL 11 —
Early Days of Holy Week

More than thirty years he labored
In the finite course of time;
Having come on earth to suffer
He desired this bitter hour.
Lamb of God, in immolation,
Hung for us upon the Cross.

PANGE, LINGUA, GLORIOSI LAUREAM, VENANTIUS FORTUNATUS (D. 609)

The liturgical readings these days skillfully direct our steps from one event to the next in the last days before Jesus' death. We have journeyed from the resurrection of Lazarus to the entrance into Jerusalem, and today we are invited to contemplate the Lord's anointing at Bethany. Mary, Jesus' faithful disciple, anoints His feet with sweet spices in preparation for His burial. Afterwards, she dries those same feet with her hair. In contrast to Judas's presence at the same scene, and his imminent betrayal, Mary's devotion and tenderness must have been very consoling to Jesus in those final moments.

Our monastic life seems to be extra quiet during these days of Holy Week. A profound silence reigns throughout the monastery. I notice that even our farm animals seem to partake of this sorrowful silence. And why not? The sufferings of our Savior, His death and Resurrection, are cosmic events. The whole world should be weeping as we see Him, the innocent Lamb going to the slaughter. Throughout the years, I have grown particularly fond of a certain Crucifixion ikon that portrays both the sun and the moon crying at the sight of their Creator's suffering and death. That ikon, exposed on Good Friday in the chapel, always leads me back to that supreme moment at Golgotha, where everything was changed once and for all time, as the Office for Good Friday records: *All creation trembled with fear, when it beheld You suspended on the Cross, the sun was darkened and the foundations of the earth were shaken. The whole world suffered with Him who created it all. O Lord, of your own will you accepted death for us, Glory to You!*

— APRIL 12 —

The Passions of J. S. Bach: A Unique Contribution to Holy Week

O Sacred Head, surrounded by crown of piercing thorn.
O bleeding Head, so wounded, reviled and put to scorn.
Our sins have marred the glory of thy most holy Face,
yet angel hosts adore thee, and tremble as they gaze.

BACH'S CHORALE FROM SAINT MATTHEW'S PASSION

During Holy Week, no form of music, excluding our liturgical chant, is heard in this monastic enclosure. There is, however, one exception: the two Passions by J. S. Bach. This sacred music is listened to habitually during these days filled with sadness and woe. This music is not entertainment, but prayer.

The two compositions, the Passion According to Saint Matthew and the Passion according to Saint John, are sources of great inspiration and spiritual support . They also attest to Bach's personal and profound devotion to Christ, the Savior. These conjectures are well-grounded in the intimate details of the music, and, particularly, in Bach's faithful account of the Lord's sufferings. It is not surprising that some refer to Bach as the "Fifth Evangelist." For what Matthew and John conveyed with text, Bach did likewise with music. He never hesitated to use his prodigious creativity to communicate vividly to his contemporaries (as well as to the rest of us) his insights into the mystery of Christ's Passion.

The monumental work which became Matthew's Passion was first executed on Holy Thursday in 1729 in the church of Saint Thomas in Leipzig, where J.S. Bach was the choirmaster. Bach's genius conveyed the intense experience of reliving the suffering and crucifixion of Jesus. Bach's Passions possess the undoubted power to evoke in the listener the moving experience of those final hours. In a way, Bach's intent succeeded by making the listener intuitively present at the drama taking place at Calvary. Herman Scherchen, a contemporary of Bach, and also his collaborator, called Matthew's Passion a "crowning pinnacle of music." I am sure he would have spoken in the same terms about Saint John's Passion. Listening to both Passions awakens in our consciousness the deep sufferings of the Man-God. They summon us to bow before Him in awe and adoration. As Bach's Saint John's Passion ponders: *My heart, while the whole world suffers with the sufferings of Jesus, the sun dresses itself in mourning. The veil is rent, the rocks cleft, the earth shakes, the graves open, because they see the Creator grow cold. What will you do in your turn?*

— APRIL 13 —

Jesus: The Lamb of God

Without beauty, without majesty we saw him,
A thing despised and rejected by men,
A Man of Sorrows and familiar with suffering...
Harshly dealt with, he bore it humbly,
He never opened his mouth,
Like a lamb that is led to the slaughterhouse,
Like a sheep that is dumb before its shearers.

ISAIAH 53:2–3, 7

This past Saturday the last of our lambs was born, on the eve of Palm Sunday, just as were getting ready to enter into the most holy of weeks. This may be a simple coincidence, and I don't claim it to be more than that. But the presence of a new baby lamb cannot help but be an intimation of that other lamb, the Lamb of God, who, as Saint Paul appropriately puts it, "gave Himself for us as an offering to God, a gift of pleasing fragrance."

Jesus, our meek and humble Redeemer, is our Paschal lamb. For our sake, He offered Himself in sacrifice to the Father during the very time of the Jewish Passover, at the precise moment when the paschal lambs were being slaughtered in sacrificial offering in the temple. The Lord's self-offering, which took place once and for all time, was accomplished out of that ineffable, incomprehensible love of His, so that He might "take away the sins of many...and bring salvation to those who eagerly await Him."

The innocent Lamb of God is also the adult Man of Sorrows, the Bridegroom, whose particular ikon we have been venerating throughout Lent and, in a special manner, over the past three days. He, the Man of Sorrows, undergoes suffering to heal our passions by His Passion, to deliver our human nature from damnation by His life-giving sacrifice. *O long-suffering Lord, who accepted death for our sake, glory to you!*

— APRIL 14 —

Holy Thursday

Come, O you faithful,
With uplifted minds let us enjoy
The hospitality of the Lord,
Attending the Banquet of Immortality
Spread in the upper chamber.

BYZANTINE OFFICE, HOLY THURSDAY

This morning, at 9:00 A.M., we began singing the first of the three Offices of Tenebrae, much later in the day than the customary early morning hour assigned to them. In a way, these Offices mark an official entrance into the drama we are invited to relive in the next three days. The psalms for Matins speak poignantly of the sufferings endured by God's Servant. A peak moment in the Office arrives when Jeremiah's Lamentation is sung in its mournful Gregorian melody. In the Lamentation, we hear the cry of our sinful humanity lamenting the devastation caused by the sins of our forefathers, and our own. In the Lamentations, which we continue to sing until our last Tenebrae Office on Holy Saturday, we can hear the whole of creation groaning and weeping—downcast by its past sinfulness. Our only response is the profound admission that our sinfulness is at the root of our Redeemer's cruel suffering.

In the evening, the Last Supper of the Eucharist is the focal point of our liturgical celebration. As the Apostles once did at that moment, we gather around Christ, our Master, to celebrate with him his mystical supper, the Sacrament of his immense love for all of humankind. We approach this sacred banquet in the spirit of his disciples: a spirit of sincere love for our neighbor, a spirit of forgiveness and reconciliation towards all. Imbued with this love we chant at that precise moment the *Ubi Caritas*: "There where is love and fraternal charity, God is present. Let us rejoice and be glad in him. Let us fear the living God and love him, and with unblemished heart be bound to one another."

Love is the final testament of a dying Master. We, as disciples, cherish this testament, this new commandment, expressing and repeating it in song during the symbolic washing of the feet: *Mandatum novum do vobis: ut diligatis invicem, sicut dilexi vos, dicit Domini* (A new commandment I have given you: Love one another as I love you.)

— APRIL 15 —

Holy and Good Friday

The whole creation was overwhelmed by fear when it saw You, O Christ, hanging on the cross. The sun was darkened and the foundation of the earth was shaken, for all things suffered with the creator of all. Of your own will you have endured this torment for our sakes.

BYZANTINE SERVICE OF THE TWELVE GOSPELS

The monastery bells last rang during the Gloria of the yesterday's Mass, and they will not again be heard until the Gloria of the Easter Vigil. During these grieving days, we have recourse to a pair of wooden clappers to summon us to prayer and meals. Good Friday is a day of profound mourning, for we are accompanying the Savior on the way to Calvary and are about to witness his drinking of the cup of suffering to the full. This morning, during the Tenebrae Offices, the psalms related the intensity of Christ's pain, the loneliness of his agony. The Lamentations, in their grave and sorrowful tone, convey the God-Man's heart-rending cry of pain. The grievous torments of the Crucified Lord echo in our poor grateful souls, for it is the burden of our iniquities he bears. It is the price of our redemption for which he pays.

Reading the Passion account, we follow each step of the Savior's final hours: the agony and sweating of blood in the garden, the betrayal by Judas, His arrest by the soldiers, the trial before Annas and Caiaphas during the night hours, Peters's fears and denials, the court trial before Pilate, the scourging by the soldiers, the insults by the mob, the carrying of a heavy cross and the encounter with his Mother on the way to Calvary, and, lastly, a very cruel death and burial. Deeply moved, we fall down in adoration before the Crucified Lord: *Glory to Your Passion, O Christ. Glory to your long-suffering, O Lord!*

After a light repast of bread and water (today is a black fast day; no dairy is consumed), we keep vigil by the Cross from noon until three o'clock, when we attend the solemn Liturgy of the Presanctified. During the liturgy, we venerate and kiss the Cross, singing: *Before your Cross, we bow down in worship, O Master.* The veneration of the Cross expresses our repentance. Our kiss, in contrast to that of Judas, conveys our love and gratitude to the Savior for his selfless sacrifice: *Adore your Bridegroom covered with blood, and in your kiss give him your entire self!*

After reciting the intercessory prayers, we partake of the Body of the Lord. Through this sacramental communion, we share intimately in the Passion and Death of our Lord and Master as we eagerly await the glory of his Resurrection. Now that we are nourished for the remainder of the journey, we can continue the walk toward our final destination—with eyes fixed on the Cross.

Late in the evening, after a light collation of vegetable soup and a slice of bread, the only meal of the day, we return to the dark, bare chapel. A lonely candle flame flickers next to the stand holding the ikon of Christ's descent from the Cross. It is the only light in the austere setting. As we venerate the ikon, we recall the affliction of his Mother and the prophecy of Simeon the Elder. We watch her standing by the Cross, grieving as she receives in her arms the dead body of he whom she once bore and nursed as a tiny infant. Can anyone understand the depth of her emotions during those hours, the tragedy of her affliction? We seek to console the Mother of God, and join ourselves to her tragic sorrow by singing the mournful lamentations of the *Stabat Mater*. As we pray, sing, weep, and lament with the Theotokos, we witness Joseph of Arimathea taking down Jesus' body from the Cross. The dead body is deposed and presented to a sorrowful Mother, while we sing the old troparion: *The noble Joseph, when he had taken down your most pure body from the tree, wrapped it in fine linen and anointed it with spices, and placed it in a new tomb. But you rose on the third day, O Lord , granting the world great mercy.*

Preparation for the burial is now at hand. The Son's dead body is removed from the mother's arms. Two faithful disciples, Nicodemus and the "noble Joseph," carry their Master's body to a new sepulcher. The grieving mother follows the funeral procession, weeping bitterly, finding no consolation. An ancient tradition of the Christian East tells us that as the Son sees his mother's breakdown and is unable to bear her sorrow, he whispers in her ear the consoling words: *Do not lament for me, O Mother, seeing me buried in the tomb, the Son whom you once virginally conceived. I shall rise as God and be glorified, and shall raise in glory all those who partake of your sorrow in faith and love.*

As we accompany Mary to the tomb, Jesus foretells in that whisper not only his own glorious Resurrection, but also the final glorification of all those who share in His Mother's sorrow with faithful and undying love.

— APRIL 16 —

Holy Saturday

O happy tomb! You received within yourself the Creator and the Author of life. O strange wonder! He who dwells on high is sealed beneath the earth with his own consent.

BYZANTINE TEXT FOR HOLY SATURDAY

A profound stillness reigns throughout the whole monastic enclosure. It is Holy Saturday, a day of mournful silence. It is "the most blessed Sabbath on which Christ sleeps." The ikon displayed for our veneration portrays Christ lying in the grave, his Mother, the Apostle John, and the Holy Women standing by, weeping and mourning. With them, we also sit by the tomb and mourn as we pray and sing the last of the Tenebrae Offices. The lovely antiphons make reference to Jesus, who, after a most tormented death, now reposes in the tomb: *"In pace in idipsum, dormiam et requiescam. Caro mea requiescet in spe.* (I sleep and rest in peace. My body shall rest in hope." A responsory recalls the scene in Matthew 27: "They buried the Lord and sealed the tomb by rolling a large stone in front of it. They stationed soldiers there to guard it." Our hearts are numb as we consider that the Creator of all life is lying buried like a poor mortal creature. An ancient homily read during the Offices expresses some of this bewilderment: *Something strange is happening, there is a great silence on earth today, a great silence and stillness. The whole earth keeps silence because the King is asleep. The earth trembled and is still because God has fallen asleep in the flesh and he has raised up all who have slept ever since the world began. God has died in the flesh and hell trembles with fear.*

Keeping watch by Christ's tomb, we experience an incredible sense of peace. This is not an ordinary burial, another corpse or another sepulcher. This is a life-bearing tomb, containing within itself the Christ who brought victory over our mortality, and by his holy death and burial vanquished the corruption brought by sin. During one of the final responsories of the Byzantine Office, we join the faithful women who came to anoint the body of the Savior with myrrh and spices. With them, we mourn and weep: *This is the most blessed Sabbath on which Christ sleeps, but on the third day he shall rise again. Therefore, O Lord our God, we sing to you a hymn, a song to your burial: By your burial you have opened for us the gates of life, and by your death you have slain death and hell. O God, our deliverer, blessed are you!*

— APRIL 17 —

Easter: Glorious Pasch of the Lord

Today all things are filled with light: therefore, let the heavens rejoice and the earth be glad. Let the whole world, visible and invisible, celebrate the Feast. For Christ is indeed risen from the dead, our source of true and everlasting joy!

BYZANTINE PASCHAL CANON

Now that Holy Week has reached its conclusion, we can look with anticipation to the joy of Easter, a joy that cannot be attained except by passing through the sorrows of Christ's Passion. The Byzantine Liturgy makes this point categorically clear in the Canon sung at the Paschal night: *Yesterday I suffered and was buried with you, O Christ, and today I rise with you in your Resurrection.* The Passion of Christ is the necessary door one must go through in order to reach the triumphal victory of his Resurrection.

Shortly before midnight, deep in darkness, the Paschal Vigil begins outdoors with the blessing of the new fire. (The Resurrection of Christ is a cosmic event, therefore all natural elements participating tonight are blessed.) The large Paschal Candle, a symbol of Christ, is blessed and lit from the new fire. A procession forms, and all those present, holding lighted candles, solemnly follow the priest carrying the Paschal Candle into the dark church. The priest stops three times during the procession and intones the *Lumen Christi*, to which the faithful fervently reply *Deo Gratias.*

When the faithful finally congregate in the church, with only the candles and oil lamps in front of the ikons as light, the *Exultet*, the solemn proclamation of the Resurrection of Christ, is announced in song to the entire world. This chant, a haunting moment in the Paschal Liturgy, declares God's wonders in the Resurrection of his only-begotten Son. After the *Exultet*, the all-night vigil proceeds with the lessons, psalms, and antiphons. When we reach the moment of the Gloria, the bells of the monastery ring out in explosive joy, announcing to the surrounding countryside the glad tidings of the Resurrection. The solemn intonation of the triple Alleluia follows. Afterwards, we proceed with the incensing of the Resurrection ikon and the Gospel, followed by the ancient Resurrection response: *Having beheld the Resurrection of Christ, let us worship the Lord Jesus, the only Sinless one. We venerate your Cross, O Christ, and your Holy Resurrection. We praise and glorify. You are our God, and we know no other than you. We call on your Name. Come, all you faithful, let us venerate the Resurrection of Christ! For behold, through the Cross joy has come into all the world. Ever blessing the Lord, let us praise his Resurrection, for by enduring the Cross for us, he destroyed death by death.*

Next follows the Homily of Saint John Chrysostom, a patristic jewel from the early Church. Then follows the blessing of the new water and the renewal of our baptismal vows. Our long Paschal Vigil ends with the partaking of the Eucharistic banquet. In receiving Holy Communion, we the faithful are mystically united with the Risen Lord, for it is of his very Body and Blood, the food of immortality, that we partake. The Risen life of the Savior becomes our own and the pledge of everlasting life.

At the conclusion of our Eucharistic celebration, we gather around the dining room table, where all sorts of food, eggs, cheese, bread, and wine are blessed. Then, a tiny Paschal lamb, usually the youngest of our flock and a symbol of Christ, the immolated Lamb of God, is blessed with the new Easter water to the joy of all those present, young and old. The lamb is then taken back to the sheepfold, to rejoin the rest of the flock, as the rest of those present share the newly blessed food. Easter is the Feast of Feasts, when all creation partakes in the joy of the Resurrection of the Creator and Author of all life, so it seems natural that not only the monks but also the animals, the plants and flowers, in fact all those who inhabit the monastic land, partake in this extraordinary rejoicing.

APRIL 18

Bright Week

This is the day the LORD has made, let us rejoice and be glad in it.

PSALM 118:24

We cannot be content to limit our Paschal celebration to only one day. We need a whole season to celebrate the Resurrection. The privileged season of Eastertide opens up new horizons and brings a totally new experience to our Christian lives. The church, in her wisdom, gives us a special week, "Bright Week," to immerse ourselves in the new life of the Risen Lord. Here in the monastery, the joy of the Resurrection gives us a reprieve from our otherwise typical sobriety. This joy knows no bounds or limits, for Easter is the most thrilling and uplifting experience of the entire year. The monastery bells ring with Alleluias, the monastic church is dressed in splendor, filled with incense, flowers, and bright lights. The Easter music seems to inspire a planetary dance, for the chant does not cease proclaiming Christ's Resurrection. The monks greet one another with the traditional salutation: "Christ is risen." We reply: "Indeed, He is risen."

One of the most inspiring liturgical texts we sing throughout Bright Week is the "Hymn to the Resurrection" composed by Saint John Damascene. The author communicates to us the profound meaning of this sacred event:

> Today is the day of the Resurrection!
> O nations be illumined;
> It is the Passover of the Lord,
> In which Christ passed from death to life,
> From earth to heaven,
> As we sing the song of victory and triumph.
>
> Let us purify our senses
> That we may behold Christ shining as lightning
> In the splendor of his Resurrection,
> Hearing him say to us: Rejoice!
> As we sing the song of victory and triumph.

Come, let us drink a new water,
Not drawn forth from a barren rock,
But the new vintage from the fountain of incorruption
That springs forth from the tomb of Christ,
In whom we are established.

Let us rise early in the morning,
At the break of dawn and instead of fragrant ointment
Let us offer pure praise to the Master.
Let us behold Christ, the Sun of Justice,
Giving life and shining upon all.

— APRIL 19 —

Vespers of Bright Week

Christ is risen from the dead! By death he conquered death, bestowing life upon those in the tomb.

PASCHAL TROPARION

Easter gives us the occasion to celebrate life, for death has been conquered and we now know that life exists beyond the grave. During Paschaltide, at the beginning of all our Offices we sing three times the above quoted Easter Troparion. We also sing it before our meals and at every occasion where we are together. Every time we profess our faith in the Resurrection we affirm life, we say it is indestructible, we say it is everlasting. This is the good news of Easter.

Vespers of Easter Week, or Bright Week as it is called in the East, repeats that of Easter Sunday, as if the liturgy was quietly telling us, "You need all that time to absorb the great mystery just celebrated." Every evening, the monastery bells peal joyfully, calling us to sing the splendid and festive Vespers of the Resurrection. After the initial Easter Troparion, we sing "*Ad Caenan Agni Providi*," which I think is one of the loveliest hymns of the entire Gregorian repertory. Next, the exquisite antiphons with the assigned psalms are sung, recounting once again the Gospel scenes of Christ's Resurrection. One antiphon builds on the other, and so on, until the whole story is told in the chant. After the prayer of the light, the hymn "O Gladsome Light" is sung. Vespers reaches its climax with the reading of the Gospel account of Jesus appearing to his disciples after his Resurrection. A long silence follows. The flame from the Easter Candle seems to glow brightly in the darkness of the chapel. The presence of the Risen Lord in our midst is almost palpable. Afterward, we sing the beautiful responsory in its solemn tone: "*Surrexit Dominus de sepulchro, Alleluia, Alleluia.*" Vespers concludes, as it does always, with the singing of the Magnificat. With Mary the Mother of God, Our Lady of the Resurrection, we raise our voices in praise and thanksgiving to God for all the wonders he has done in the Resurrection of his Son. Fittingly at the end we sing, as we do after every Office during the Easter season, the *"Regina caeli."*

— APRIL 20 —

He Is Risen!

Today is the day of Resurrection. Let us shine with the light of the feast. Let us embrace one another, brothers and sisters. Because of Christ's Resurrection, let us forgive all things to those who hate us. Then, with joy let us sing: Christ is risen from the dead. By death he conquered death!

BYZANTINE MATINS

Fortunately, Easter in our hemisphere always coincides with the yearly arrival of spring—a season full of growth and promises. The magical glory of early spring speaks of warm, clear, sunny days, when our trees are dressed in their new foliage and when the splendor of a visible renewal is ongoing.

Nothing is so glorious to contemplate at this time of the year than the gradual greening of the pasture fields. Nurtured by March rains and warming sun, the fresh new tender green appears slowly in our meadows. What a sight that is on a clear day with the sun shining high above it! As I walk through the nearby countryside, and gaze at all sorts of newness appearing in the trees and in the fields, I delight in the springing up in our gardens, meadows, and woodland—a symbol of the springing up taken place in the depths of our hearts by the power of Christ's Resurrection. Jesus, our springtime Lamb, through his Paschal immolation, has planted the seed of divine life in our innermost being. This seed now begins to germinate, to show forth its luster. Spring and Easter harmonize to bring us from sorrow and death to the affirmation of life.

— APRIL 21 —
The Paschal Procession

This Jesus God raised up, and of that all of us are witnesses....Therefore let the whole house of Israel know with certainty that God has made him both Lord and Messiah, this Jesus whom you crucified.

ACTS 2:32, 36

Easter joy is expressed in multiple ways in a monastery, especially in one principally dedicated to the glorious mystery of the Resurrection, as ours is. In our small monastery, we have a morning procession around the church and the gardens on the first days following Easter Sunday. The monastery bells peal, summoning the guests present in our guest house to join us in our homage to the Risen Lord. Carrying the Resurrection ikon, made by a close friend and neighbor, we process around the property singing the Easter Troparion and the ancient monastic hymn, "*Salve Festa Dies.*" After completing the procession, we return to the church to sing the joyful hour of Lauds in praise of Christ's Resurrection. This procession is celebrated each year in remembrance of the solemn cortege once undertook by the Holy Myrrh-bearing Women, who went to Christ's sepulcher in search of the body of their Crucified Lord. We, too, as did these holy women, arise early in the morning and proceed to meet the Lord. Instead of myrrh, we offer to the Risen Christ our joyful song of praise.

> Hail, O noble festival Day!
> Blessed day that is holy forever.
> Day wherein God conquered death,
> And Christ arose from the tomb.

Lo, the beauty of the earth,
From the death of winter arises.
Every good gift of the year
Now with its Master returns.

Loving and Almighty God,
Let your word be assured to the doubting;
Light on the third day returns:
Rise, Son of God, from the tomb.

"SALVE FESTA DIES," VENANTIUS FORTUNATUS (D.609)

— APRIL 22 —

Set Your Hearts on Things Above

So if you have been raised with Christ, seek the things that are above, where Christ is, seated at the right hand of God.

COLOSSIANS 3:1–2

Christ's glorious Resurrection and triumph over the powers of darkness means that a new truth has entered our world, something which positively affects our ordinary everyday lives. If we, as Saint Paul counsels us in his letter to the Colossians, set our hearts on things above where Christ is seated at God's right hand, we shall discover a new life open to the spiritual powers that come from above—a new life that makes us see everything in a new way, as Christ sees it.

Our capacity for this new reality depends on us entirely. God himself sets no limits to the fullness of life and love with which he wishes to endow us. Jesus, by his Death and Resurrection, has opened for us this new pathway to truth and love. It is meant for all, and it is open to all of good will. It is also within the reach of all who drink from the fountain of incorruptibility that flows from the glorified wounds of the Risen Savior. In him, we are all invited to partake of this new Passover banquet where eternal life is being offered, and where we celebrate the feast "with the unleavened bread of sincerity and truth."

— APRIL 23 —

The Struggle

Clean out the old yeast so that you may be a new batch.
1 CORINTHIANS 5:7

Recently, I was speaking to a visitor who asked me, "Do you ever have bad days? Are things always so positive for you? Do you ever struggle?" I asked what prompted these questions. She replied emphatically, "You seem only to see the bright side of things; that to me is unreal." I told her if that were so, it would indeed be unreal!

"God manages very well to see that each of us undergoes a certain amount of suffering in this life," I told her. "He did not spare even his own Son. There are moments when one arrives at a point of despair and senselessness. But those moments are always God's hour. It is then that he is most at work in us. It is out of sheer despair that I gaze at Jesus, both Crucified and Risen. I see the marks of his Passion, the wounds he endured during his crucifixion, and, suddenly, I see this human body that endured so much suffering being transformed by the power of God into the glory of the Resurrection. He who in his body suffered as a mortal, as do the rest of us, is rewarded precisely because of his immense sufferings. He is now clothed with immortality, with the beauty of incorruption. It is this, I told the inquiring visitor, that gives me hope to look beyond my own struggles, my limitations, my own sense of despair. I could become very negative, I told our friendly visitor, if I allow those feelings to get hold of me. It is easier to give in to them than to continue the struggle, but, then, grace is given to us at that precise moment. I always call it God's hour, because I know how present he is to me then.

"As Christ's disciples, we are called to follow him through his death into his Resurrection. If I seem extra positive to you, it is not because I don't know suffering. Rather, it is through faith that I am able to see light at the end of the tunnel. I see a new dawn; I see the bright and radiant light of the Resurrection."

— APRIL 24 —

Doubting Thomas

But Thomas (who was called the Twin), one of the twelve,
was not with them when Jesus came. So the other disciples
told him, "We have seen the Lord." But he said to them,
"Unless I see the mark of the nails in his hands, and put
my finger in the mark of the nails and my hand in his
side, I will not believe." A week later his disciples were
again in the house, and Thomas was with them. Although
the doors were shut, Jesus came and stood among them
and said, "Peace be with you." Then he said to Thomas,
"Put your finger here and see my hands. Reach out your
hand and put it in my side. Do not doubt but believe."
Thomas answered him, "My Lord and my God!"

JOHN 20:24–28

On the first Sunday after Easter, its octave to be precise, we celebrate what is called "Thomas Sunday"—a title taken from the Gospel story of Thomas, who, not being present at Jesus' appearance to the other disciples, refused to believe in the Resurrection. Jesus returned once again, showing his wounds to Thomas and seriously rebuking him for his lack of faith. Thomas, no longer able to refute the truth, exclaims: "My Lord and my God!" Jesus then pronounces one of his great teachings: "Have you believed because you have seen me? Blessed are those who have not seen and yet have come to believe."

Several early church writers mention the fact that perhaps Thomas was jealous of the other Apostles who claimed to have seen the Lord. Others remark that perhaps Thomas resented the fact that Christ appeared to the group, knowing full well of Thomas's absence. Other commentators speculate that Thomas didn't feel obliged to believe the other Apostles, for they were not always trustworthy and had abandoned Jesus during his crucifixion.

Jesus, however, full of compassion, uses the occasion to teach Thomas and also the rest of us about the value of faith, the necessity of trusting in him. Faith will always remain a challenge for us as it will for future generations, but Jesus assures a blessing to those who without seeing him shall trust in him and believe in his words. The sixth-century Byzantine poet, Saint Romanus the Melodist, expresses this truth with great beauty:

> The doubt of Thomas was arranged as positive faith,
> O Savior, in accordance with your will,
> In order that no one would ever doubt the Resurrection.
> Only to him did you reveal yourself—
> Both the print of the nails, and the prick of the spear—
> So that he confessed you, saying:
> "Thou are Lord and God."

A long dialogue between the Risen Lord and Thomas follows, all of it in verse and too long to be included here. I just quote one of the last verses, where Christ responds to Thomas:

> Hear, then, and understand clearly:
> You have become the ally of the wise;
> I was recognized by men as the wisdom of the Father.
> Blessed are you in your faith. Still more do I bless
> Those who come to me merely on hearing of me.
> You yourself in touching me just now recognized my glory;
> But they worship me from the sound of words.
> Great is the insight of those who believe in me in this way.

— APRIL 25 —

Monastic Gardens

Thus says the LORD of hosts, the God of Israel: ...Plant gardens and eat what they produce.

JEREMIAH 29:5

A few years ago, a nice young man who makes periodic retreats at our monastery went off to France to spend the summer months. Before leaving, he asked me the addresses of some French monasteries so that he could visit them during his stay in France. A few months later, when he returned home, I asked what impressed him the most during his visit to the monasteries. The young man quickly replied, "The gardens. Those gardens cultivated and lovingly cared for by the monks and nuns who reside in those monasteries."

I was rather surprised by his response, for I was sure he was going to mention the splendor of the monastic Offices or the beauty of the Gregorian Chant. But what impressed him the most was the beauty and the enchanting sense of order in the monastic gardens. "There is real life in those gardens," he said, "and one can almost feel the pulse of the monks' life by the work that one sees accomplished in their gardens."

The young man's comments made me stop and reflect on the history, purpose, and the importance attached to gardens in the daily life of a monastery. In most monasteries, garden work is revered as sacred, as monks and nuns throughout the ages have held fast to the biblical story that God "took the man and put him in the garden of Eden to till it and keep it" (Gen 2:15). From the very beginnings of monastic life in the Egyptian desert, garden work was acknowledged as part of God's command to care for the earth. The lives and writings of these early monks and nuns are full of stories showing them as efficient and avid gardeners. Since their gardens had to be cultivated under difficult circumstances on desert soil, the monks patiently and with great wisdom went about elaborating the principles of monastic gardening, principles that would be followed by monks of later generations.

Some monasteries still keep the ancient custom of the famous "rogation days," three days of intercessions and procession through the monastic fields and gardens, beseeching God's blessing upon the newly planted seedlings. As the lines of monks chant through the fields, the main celebrant asperges the land with holy water, begging the Lord for a good harvest from the fruits of their labors. On a cool September day, a few months from now, as the monks reap the land's produce, they will recall this moment and say once more: *Deo gratias!*

Gardening in Early Monasticism

The first Christians to devote themselves entirely to the religious life were the third century cenobites, who retired to the desert to live solitary lives of prayer. They were also the first recorded Christian gardeners, so that Christian religious gardening is as old as the oldest form of Christian religious life. The Egyptian cenobites lived off bread brought to them by villagers, water, a supply of which was the only material requirement they made of their cave homes, and a few plants which they grew in the enclosures they made outside their caves. This is how Saint Jerome (342–420 A.D.), a desert cave dweller of long standing, began his instruction of a young man about to take up the same life: "Hoe your ground, set out cabbages, convey water to the conduits."

TERESA MCLEAN, *MEDIEVAL ENGLISH GARDENS*

In a fourth-century manuscript recounting the life of Saint Antony, we read a charming passage that relates the importance the early monks attached to their gardens: "These vines and these little trees did he plant; the pool did he contrive, with much labor for the watering of his garden; with his rake did he break up the earth for many long years." It is clear from this description that Saint Antony and the other monks engaged themselves wholly in the toil of caring for their gardens, a work they undertook in order to provide food for themselves as well as for the poor and the pilgrims who often traveled to the desert to seek advice from them. There was also another factor Saint Antony and his followers took seriously, and this was the biblical admonition that one must eat from the labor of one's hands (2 Thess 3:10).

A few centuries later, in Italy, Saint Benedict insisted on the same principle by writing in his rule that "they are truly monks when they live by the labor of their hands, as did our fathers and the Apostles." In practice, that meant the monks had to work hard cultivating their vegetable and herb gardens, caring for their orchards and mills, forever mindful that they had to produce sufficient food for the monastic table. And since the monastic diet according to the rule is a vegetarian one, for ascetic reasons, the cultivation of vegetable gardens was considered vitally important in the daily life of the monastic community.

— APRIL 27 -

Monastic Gardens: Images of Paradise

The diligent carry their fruits
And now run forward to meet Paradise
As it exults with every sort of fruit.
They enter the Garden with glorious deeds
And it sees the fruits of the just.
Surpass in their excellence
The fruits of its own trees.

SAINT EPHREM, HYMNS ON PARADISE

B esides their utilitarian aspect, gardens were held in high esteem by the early monks for a spiritual reason. According to the Scriptures, when God created the world he walked and conversed with Adam and Eve in the Garden of Paradise. When our first parents disobeyed God and were driven out of Paradise, the memories of their previous life in God's garden remained with them. Ever since, Adam and Eve's descendants, and that includes all of us, have tried to return to the experience of Paradise by creating gardens.

This idea of returning to Paradise through gardening was very appealing to the early monks, for it coincided with the very purpose of monastic life, which is to live in communion with God. The garden thus became for them a sacred place, where they encountered God, a holy place transfigured by the divine presence. The monks built a physical enclosure around their gardens, not only to protect them from hungry beasts, but primarily to symbolize the sacredness of the space.

Even today, the fence built around our own vegetable garden is a constant reminder that this is indeed a special place, a holy ground. Sometimes in the evening, after singing Vespers, I love to walk and quietly meditate in the garden. The work is over, and for a moment I can breathe and enjoy the unique presence that fills the entire space. Those are truly blessed moments in the course of the monastic day.

— APRIL 28 —

The Art of Monastery Gardening

Monks were natural importers and exporters, constantly improving their knowledge and resources by exchanging plants, personal and horticultural gossip with members of other monastic families. Monastic commerce was at once more international than any other in the Middle Ages.

TERESA McLEAN, *MEDIEVAL ENGLISH GARDENS*

Proper gardening in a monastery is both a task and an art. It relies principally on the solid tradition and experience handed on by the monastic gardeners who preceded us. For instance, we rely on certain methods and intricate little details that are the testament of our past master gardeners. These methods possess the advantage of being time-tested, frugal, and thus monastic. Again and again they prove successful.

One of the principles followed over the years here in our monastery is to synchronize our planting schedule with the rhythms of the liturgy. The seasons of Mother Nature and the seasons of Mother Church blend wonderfully in our daily experience. The stewardship of the monastic land and the care of our gardens receive their daily inspiration from the celebration of the liturgy. The liturgy, in turn, infuses each season with particular significance.

Living the mystery of the seasons in full measure helps the monk-gardener to become sensitively attuned to such things as the influence of the local weather, the proper nurturing of the soil, the knowledge of the right moment for planting and germination, the right time for expanding the cultivation, and when and how to collect the fruits of the harvest. Living in harmony with the seasons gives the monk-gardener the unique knowledge of the schedule and timing when certain vegetables will be available for use in the monastery kitchen. The monastic community and their guests are always grateful to the gardener for the wonderfully fresh vegetables presented at the table.

— APRIL 29 —

The Story of a Garden

As long as earth endures, seedtime and harvest, cold and heat, summer and winter, day and night, they will not cease.
GENESIS 8:22

Our first garden on this property was planted over twenty-four years ago, the year that our small monastery was established. We had some hard times at the beginning because of the poor quality of the soil: it was nothing but stones and rock. The location of the garden was also problematic, since it was easily accessible to the deer and to other animals. We were also overly ambitious, and the size of the garden was much too large. After a first year of poor harvesting, we decided to move the garden closer to the monastery building, right next to the barn occupied by our sheep. This had the advantage of discouraging the deer, who usually don't want to come too close to our quarters. It also facilitated the transport of sheep manure into the garden. Further, it gave the garden a certain protection from the heavy winds and other factors.

Here, our garden is 100 percent organic, and we are able to maintain it as such with the help of manure from our sheep and chickens and the compost we continue to build each year. After deciding on the structure, place, and size of the garden, little by little we started building the quality of the soil. This was a never-ending task, for the soil was poor and rocky. I remember our first carrots being small and flat since they could not grow deep enough. The same was the case with some of the other root vegetables. At that time we didn't even try to grow potatoes! With typical monastic tenacity and much patience, we persevered in tilling the land, much as other monks have done it in the past.

We have since managed many improvements in the soil. In the process of redesigning the garden, we decided to divide it into two equal sections. The first section consists of three long raised beds, where we cultivate mainly salads and root vegetables, sometimes combined with other things such as spinach, sorrel, peas, flowers, and some herbs. In the second section we grow on level ground those vegetables that are larger and thus demand more space: squash, pumpkin, cucumber, tomato, eggplant, pepper, pole beans, string beans, Swiss chard, cabbage, broccoli, Brussels sprouts, and cauliflower. On the right side of the raised beds, we plant a variety of potatoes, as well as butternut and zucchini squash. In the very center of the garden, between the two equal sections, stands a statue of Saint Fiacre, a monk and patron saint of gardeners. The statue is surrounded with pots of flowers and his protection over the garden is beseeched daily. There are two small patches built into equal squares, one in front of the statue and the other in the back. These special patches are dedicated exclusively to the cultivation of herbs for the kitchen: varieties of basil and parsley, thyme, oregano, cilantro, sage, dill, rosemary, and garlic. We have another herb garden in the monastery, but the one in the vegetable garden is exclusively for kitchen use.

Our monastery garden received a special distinction two years ago when it was chosen to be reproduced "as is" in France, at the Conservatory of the Chateau de Chaumont, which organizes a well-known garden display every year. It was one of thirty chosen from around the world. I was invited to go there in May to plant the garden, using French and American seeds, as we do here at Our Lady of the Resurrection. Since Chaumont is located in the Loire Valley, thousands of tourists visited our garden display. The Loire Valley, known for its chateaux, its wines, and other products, attracts many French and international visitors regularly. Because of that and because of my cookbooks, which are in great part inspired by the fruits from our garden, French, Canadian, and American television producers have visited here to film the original garden. A French TV station produced a beautiful documentary entitled *Paradis sur terre*, or "Paradise on Earth."

— APRIL 30 —

The Bounty of a Garden

*Get a garden! What kind you may get matters not, though
the soil be light, friable, sandy and hot, or alternatively
heavy and rich with stiff clay. Let it lie on a hill, or slope
gently away to the level, or sink in an overgrown dell!*

WALAFRID STRABO (D. 849), *HORTULUS*

Monks and nuns are usually frugal people, so we depend on
the produce of our gardens, orchards, and farms for our
food. This means canning and freezing some of our vegetables
and fruits, preserving them in cool cellars, and extending the growing season as long as possible.

Because the last few winters have been rather benign and
because we protected the vegetables on cold nights by covering
them, we have been able to extend the life of hardy vegetables
such as leeks, Brussels sprouts, cabbage, Swiss chard, beets, turnips, carrots, and salad greens until the end of the year. We always make a point of feasting on Thanksgiving, Christmas, and
New Year's Day with what is still available fresh from our garden. After that, the garden is put to rest until the next growing
season. The land needs a rest as does the monastic gardener.

During the winter months we rejoice and give thanks for what
the garden has provided for our daily sustenance. During these
months, when I open a jar of sauce from our own tomatoes, onions, and basil, I can distinctly recollect the original aromas from
the garden. The same can be said when we use our frozen spinach, chard, beans, or our canned beats, carrots, pickled cucumbers, or our winter squash and potatoes, which are all carefully
kept in our cool basement cellar. They retain the original taste if
not the texture. The bounty and goodness of a vegetable garden
does not end at the time of the harvest. It continues, in a different
fashion, to yield long beyond any appointed time. It remains for
the cook to use his talent, imagination, and good taste to create
dishes out of these winter vegetables that can be savored long
after the garden has been allotted its well-deserved rest.

MAY

Saint Joseph the Worker

Joseph, patron saint of workers, blending skill with charity, silent carpenter, we praise you! Joining work with honesty, you taught Christ with joy to labor, sharing his nobility.

BERNARD MISCHKE, O.C.S.

After a long winter and a very wet spring, the magic month of May has arrived. This morning, as I walk through the monastic landscape, I listen to the singing of the birds and the pulse of the forests and notice an apple tree in full bloom. What a gorgeous sight! I join Saint Francis in his moving prayer of praise: "Praised be Thou, my Lord, for our mother the earth, which doth sustain us and keep us, and bringeth forth divers fruits, and flowers of many colors, and grass." I lift my eyes to the nearby hills and silently agree with those who say it is well worthwhile to traverse the long winter in order to arrive at such glorious moments. The shining days of spring do not get repeated. Now is the time to enjoy them.

May is also the month of Mary, the Mother of God. We begin her month with an earnest Marian flavor as we celebrate the feast of Joseph the worker, her beloved spouse. Saint Joseph is one of those few saints, such as John the Baptist, the apostles Peter and Paul, and, of course, our Father Saint Benedict who are feasted twice in the Church's calendar. That suits me perfectly, for Saint Joseph is very dear to me. Today the lovely Office of March 19 is repeated and sung in its entirety in the oratory, where Saint Joseph's ikon holds a prominent place all year round.

A few years ago I was invited to do a book signing at another monastery and it happened to be May 1. In the morning, I arrived at the choir for the first Office expecting to be celebrating Saint Joseph. To my surprise, there was no mention of Saint Joseph in the office. Afterwards, I inquired of the monk in charge of the monastery's liturgy the reason for this, and he simply replied that the feast was optional and not mentioned in their ordo. I was disappointed, but, after all, individual monasteries arrange their liturgy as they see fit. However, and this may seem silly to some, I promised myself that in the future I would not spend another May 1 outside the boundaries of this monastery and risk being deprived of singing Saint Joseph's glorious praises.

I have always looked at Saint Joseph the Worker as a perfect model for monks. No one, outside of Jesus himself, lived more perfectly the monastic motto *Ora et Labora*. With a unique wisdom, Saint Joseph combined admirably his utter devotion to God with faithfulness to work and the ordinary duties of everyday life. The holiness of the "just man" Joseph is unequaled among the saints, for he blended the sublime task of caring for Jesus and his mother with the most humble of occupations: that of laborer and carpenter.

— MAY 2 —

Saint Athanasius

Jesus Christ...cries out, saying: See, I am with you always.
He is himself the shepherd, the high priest, the way and
the door, and has become all things at once for us. In the
same way, he has come among us as our feast and holy
day as well. The blessed Apostle Paul says of him: Christ
has been sacrificed as our Passover. It was Christ who
shed his light on the psalmist as he prayed: You are my
joy, deliver me from those surrounding me. True joy,
genuine festival, means the casting out of wickedness. To
achieve this, one must live a life of perfect goodness, in
the serenity of the fear of God, always practicing
contemplation in one's heart.

SAINT ATHANASIUS, AN EASTER LETTER

Throughout the surrounding countryside, the lilacs are showing their first blossoms, enticing all with their glorious colors and pure, intoxicating perfume. On a sunny day like today, a
day of unblemished beauty, it is a joy to work in the serenity of
the garden. This afternoon, I'll have the delightful pleasure of
adding some lilacs to the flowers already on display in the chapel.
The Paschal candle and the Resurrection ikon have been surrounded throughout the last few weeks by lilies, forsythias, daffodils, and tulips. Now, the lilacs will give their own touch.

Through many years of gardening one gets used to noticing
the gradual progression in the garden—which flower is the
season's first, which others follow, and so on. Unconsciously, a
true gardener seems to be always mindful of this. Our visitors
often remark about the seasonal flowers that make up arrangements in the chapel. The glory of the garden and the sublime
music of the Gregorian chant are both incentives to prayer, as
they enhance our daily praise in a distinctive fashion.

Today, the liturgy marks the feast of Athanasius the Great,
one of the great Fathers of the Church. Athanasius was only a
young deacon when he was asked to accompany his bishop to

the first council of Nicea. It was there that the Arian heresy was condemned and the dogma of the Incarnation proclaimed. For this reason, Athanasius is sometimes referred to as the "Doctor of the Incarnation."

Athanasius suffered enormously for the faith. Though already made bishop, he was sent into exile five times because, like the martyrs, he refused to compromise the faith. He guided his flock from his place of exile with the firmness of the faith and the love and compassion of the Gospel. Cardinal Newman referred to Athanasius as "that extraordinary man, a principal instrument after the Apostles by which the sacred truths of Christianity have been conveyed and secured to the world."

Among Scripture commentaries, letters, and historical works he wrote and left to us, nothing has as much value for monks and nuns as his *Life of Saint Antony*. This *vita*, Athanasius's particular legacy to the monastic world, contributed to the extraordinary expansion of monasticism in the East and in the West. Monks of all centuries owe much to Saint Athanasius, for in his picture of the life and figure of Antony, he portrayed the monastic ideal as it must be emulated by all. Saint Athanasius died in 373, after making his brother Peter his successor in the see of Alexandria.

— MAY 3 —

Saints Philip and James, Apostles

Philip said to him, "Lord, show us the Father, and we will be satisfied." Jesus said to him, "Have I been with you all this time, Philip, and you still do not know me? Whoever has seen me has seen the Father....Believe me that I am in the Father and the Father is in me; but if you do not, then believe me because of the works themselves."

JOHN 14:8–9, 11

This morning, at Lauds, we sang the praises of two apostles of the Lord: Philip and James. Not too much is known about James, and sometimes one confuses him with the other apostle James, who is commemorated on July 25. The Gospel tells us not much more than that he was one of the twelve chosen by the Lord, and was a son of Alphaeus. Was he also the author of a letter in the New Testament attributed to James? Or was it the other James? We shall probably never know with absolute certitude. About Philip, however, we know a bit more. He is frequently mentioned in the Gospels. We know that he was from the town of Bethsaida, like Peter and Andrew. We also know that previously he was a disciple of John the Baptist, probably first hearing about Jesus through him. After becoming Jesus' disciple, it is Philip who is requested by Jesus to provide food for the multitude. Obviously, Jesus trusted Philip in a particular way. The dialogue between them implies a certain closeness.

I am forever grateful to Philip for some of his questions to Jesus, because it is in response to Philip's request, "Lord, show us the Father," that Jesus elaborates on his relationship to his Father, one of the most beautiful texts in the Gospel of John. I am grateful to Philip for that particular text because it has sustained my prayer for so many years. Often, when at prayer, I seem to get nowhere. I then glance at the large ikon of Christ, the Pantocrator, in our chapel and reflect on Jesus' response to Philip: "Whoever has seen me has seen the Father."

I know I cannot comprehend God, that his mystery is beyond me, but I know that in the ikon I see Jesus. Trusting his words, I know in an inexplicable way that in seeing Jesus I also see the Father. That suffices, for it nurtures my prayer and restores my hope. God is no longer a stranger but simply Jesus' Father, and Jesus is nothing other but the "Father's image and substance." I recall then the words from the Athanasian creed, which we used to say once a year at Prime on Trinity Sunday: *Immensus Pater, Immensus Filius, Immensus Spiritus Sanctus. Aeternus Pater, Aeternus Filius, Aeternus Spiritus Sanctus.*

— MAY 4 —

Light in the Garden

You give them drink from the river of your delights.
For with you is the fountain of life;
in your light we see light.

PSALM 36:8–9

A monk, living in harmony with the seasons, is most sensitive to light at every moment of the day, the month, or the year. In early morning, we joyfully greet the light of day. At evening, we thank God for the light given us on that day. At night prayer, we ask God to protect us from dark shadows as we long for light's arrival on the following day. The monks' attentiveness to light and its effects is prompted by the Christ whom we serve and who said, "I am the Light of the world," and who admonishes us through the Scriptures to be "children of the light."

In early May, as I complete some garden tasks, I become aware of the splendid light the sun provides during these mid-spring days. Gazing on the monastic landscape, I seem to see farther than I do during our stark winter days, when no visible obstacles stand between me and the beyond. Now I realize how much I missed this type of light during the winter months. I find winter's light attractive in its own right, but May's light has its own sort of brilliance, its particular type of warmth. It inspires my work in the garden and allows me to take strength from it.

Continuing with the sometimes tedious garden chores, I reflect on how fortunate we are to enjoy the blessings of country living with its wide open spaces and natural light. Citizens of crowded cities sometimes are deprived of the simple pleasure of contemplating the light at different moments of the day or year. How many city people get to contemplate the slow rising of the sun or one of those unforgettable sunsets we often witness here in the country?

Today, as I bask under this glorious May sun, I feel reinvigorated by its warm rays shining into the whole of the garden. For several reasons I linger outdoors. The work is ample at this time of the year, when one is just beginning to plant the seeds or transplant the seedlings into the garden. I secretly rejoice in the fact of that extra hour of exposure to the light of day. The truth is, one really doesn't wish to let go of it. Of course, there is always tomorrow's light to look forward to. In the meantime, as I prepare for Vespers, I find comfort that shortly we shall be singing praises to the Author and Giver of Light. As Saint Gregory of Narek prays: *Creator of Light and fashioner of the night, / thou, life in death, and light in darkness, / hope unto those who wait, / and forbearance unto those that doubt; / thou, who with skillful wisdom, / turns the shadow of death into morning; / thou unending dawn, / thou sun without setting.*

— MAY 5 —

The Paschal Light

In the heavens he has set a tent for the sun....
Its rising is from the end of the heavens,
and its circuit to the end of them.

PSALM 19:4–6

Today no strong wind inhabits the land. The tree shadows are quiet, and the sun is warm. The verdant hills show their tender green which I like so much. They reflect somehow the subtle colors of today's light. It is no coincidence that the light at this time of the year is particularly exquisite. The pallid light of late March has now been transformed into the beautiful, brilliant full light of spring. It is the light of Easter here in our northern hemisphere; or, as I prefer to call it, the Paschal Light. The grayness of winter is now but a distant memory.

If I spend a considerable amount of time describing the light at this time of year, it is because I am deeply affected by it. Another reason, however, is the fact that this superb light is a constant reminder of the Risen Christ. On the Easter vigil we lit the Paschal candle from a roaring fire, proclaiming the victory of life over death, of light over darkness. The light emanating from the Paschal candle, the light of the Risen Lord, is the force that dispels all darkness and enlightens our journey. Now we can face life again with renewed dynamism, for the light of Christ is pointing the way toward the Father, toward the day that shall have no end. And while on the journey not only are we enlightened as we proceed on our path, but we are also nurtured and sustained basking under the Sun of God's pure holiness. We ask for a blessing from Him who said "let there be light" before time began. We pray that the Paschal flame, the light of Christ, will shed its rays upon us, shining on those who dwell in darkness and the shadow of death, and guiding our feet into the way of peace.

— MAY 6 —

The Month of Mary

It is easier to depict the sun with its light and its heat
Than to tell the story of Mary in its splendor.
JACOB OF SERUGH, *ON THE MOTHER OF GOD*

I am so absorbed almost every moment of these gorgeous early May days with multiple tasks in the garden that I have not allotted time for other duties: writing, correspondence, laundry, house maintenance, the care of guests and the guesthouse, and jobs on the farm. But the Lord knows full well how limited we are in terms of time, and how time in a monastery comes as a scarcity. Many demands are placed upon us, and we cannot always meet our daily goals. All of these concerns, all of these unfinished jobs and projects, I entrust daily to the care of the Mother of God. She, the Theotokos, is our assigned guardian, in charge of watching over our interests.

I am filled with renewed gladness these days because May is Our Lady's month. Each day, after the Noon Office and just before lunch, we sing her litany. I love Mary's litany just as much as I love the Akathist hymn, which is sung here during Lent and on special Marian festivals. There is something about this daily repetition which fills our souls with serenity, trust, and confidence. After completing the litany, I leave the chapel and head for the kitchen and lunch. Quietly, I feel reassured. Those beautiful salutations to Our Lady remain steady in my mind, like the notes of a lovely melody which one does not wish to hear fade away. Invariably, they pop up during the rest of the monastic day, sweetly echoing something like the chant of the angels in heaven: *Mater Christi....Mater purissima....Mater castissima....Regina Angelorum....Regina Martyrum....Regina Pacis....*

The litany of Mary marks the month of May in a special fashion, at least for me. By singing Mary's praises, in the words of Jacob of Serugh: *We sing of the maiden who became like the heavenly chariot, and solemnly carried that Mighty One, bearing Creation. The Bride who conceived although the bridegroom had never been seen by her; and gave birth to a baby without her coming to the place of his Father. The image of her beauty is more glorious and exalted than any words can express.*

— MAY 7 —

A Special Garden

There was a garden in the place where he [Jesus] was crucified, and in this garden there was a new tomb in which no one had ever been laid. And so, because it was the Jewish day of Preparation, and the tomb was nearby, they laid Jesus there.

JOHN 19:41–42

Gardening actually is a very contemplative activity. I never tire of watching the plants grow. One seems to detect something new at every stage of each plant's development. In early spring, our plants seem so tiny and fragile, especially the seedlings grown indoors. I often wonder, after transplanting them outdoors, if they will be able to survive a late storm. Sometimes I cover them at night. I protect them as if they were my own children. During the steamy days of summer, gardening is often a real struggle, yet that contemplative dimension remains. The inner dialogue between myself and the plants, and even with the tools used in gardening, goes on and on. During those precious moments I recall another dialogue that took place in a very special garden, long ago:

But Mary stood weeping outside the tomb. As she wept she bent over to look into the tomb, and she saw two angels in white, sitting where the body of Jesus had been lying, one at the head and the other at the feet. They said to her, "Woman, why are you weeping?" She said to them, "They have taken away my Lord, and I do not know where they have laid him." When she had said this, she turned around and saw Jesus standing there, but she did not know that it was Jesus. Jesus said to her, "Woman, why are you weeping? Whom are you looking for?" Supposing him to be the gardener, she said to him, "Sir, if you have carried him away, tell me where you have laid him, and I will take him away." Jesus said to her, "Mary!" She turned and said to him in Hebrew, "Rabbouni!" (which means Teacher). Jesus said to her, "Do not hold onto me, because I have not yet ascended to the Father. But go to my brothers and say to them, 'I am ascending to your Father, to my God, and your God.' So Mary Magdalene went and announced to the disciples, 'I have seen the Lord'; and she told them that he had said these things to her (Jn 20:11–18).

— MAY 8 —

The Prayer of a Gardener

Here is a translation which I have made of a prayer by a thirteenth-century Cistercian monk Guerric D'Igny:

> Lord Jesus:
> You are the true gardener;
> You are its creator and cultivator,
> And the guardian of your garden.
>
> You plant the seeds by your words,
> You water them by your Spirit,
> And you make them grow by your power.
>
> Lord, who is allowed into your garden,
> Becomes himself a well-watered garden
> That keeps growing and blossoms,
> And its fruits are multiplied.

— MAY 9 —

Symphony in the Garden

Two lovers stray in a forest green,
And there they talk unheard and walk unseen,
Save by the birds, who chat a louder lay,
To welcome such true lovers with the month of May.

ANONYMOUS

Certain days in the garden are memorable. One of those days is the first time I hear our recently returned birds, singing loud and clear from the top of our flowering trees. They love the apple trees and the lilacs, and they also have a preference for our dogwoods. As I work in and around the flowerbeds, I see them by the hundreds, flashing in and out of the garden, flying from treetop to treetop. They play and amuse themselves and, of course, I am amused and distracted by their company.

They deliberately seem to go for trees and shrubs with a sweet-scented odor. Like stars in vast open spaces, our visitors seem to move from orbit to orbit. They glow brilliantly against a cloudless blue sky, reiterating again and again their joyful singing. I say to myself, with beautiful sounds such as this, who needs other music while garden laboring? All of a sudden, the garden has become an enchanted place. There is something more. As I take my spade and fork and move to another corner of the garden, I receive a strange sense of fulfillment, a sort of contentment from my experience of complete absorption in the birds' song. Somehow, it reminds me of the monastic chant and our instinctual need to praise God in song. The birds, in their own inimitable way, make a continuous joyful noise unto their Creator, acting as reminders of our indispensable exigency to praise God. As the psalmist points out: *It is good to give thanks to the LORD, to sing praise to your name, O Most High* (Ps 92).

Spring Gardening

The garden is the life-breath of this diseased world that
has been so long in sickness: That breath proclaims that
a saving remedy has been sent to heal our mortality.

SAINT EPHREM, *HYMNS ON PARADISE*

N o trick of the weather shall be enough to deprive me of my
daily rendezvous with the garden. Spring gardening occupies a special place in my heart. What makes it particularly unique is the fact that spring, in our hemisphere, usually coincides with the Paschal season, a special time in a monastery consecrated to the Resurrection of the Lord. Furthermore, the reality of spring and the celebration of the Resurrection seem to me inseparable. They naturally go hand in hand. The miracle of the Resurrection, at least symbolically, gets repeated every spring! Today, as I approach some of my gardening chores, I sense the mystery of renewal all around me. It is the garden's own way of telling me that creation is again made new by the power of the Resurrection of Christ.

The ninth-century poet Sedulius Scotus, in his *Carmen Paschale*, expressed beautifully this intimate connection between the festival of the Resurrection and spring's arrival:

> Christ, our true Sun,
> Last night from darkness rose,
> And in the Lord's garden,
> The mystic harvest now is springing up.
> The wandering clans of bees,
> Happy in their chores,
> Murmur far through scarlet flowers,
> Gathering their honey about.
> How many birds now soften the air with melody,
> And as dusk falls the nightingale
> Modulates her song,
> While in the church choir
> Monks chant the praises of Sion!

— MAY 11 —

The Holy Abbots of Cluny:
Mayeul, Odilon, Odon, Hugh, and
Peter the Venerable

Our fathers in monastic rule,
We gladly celebrate this day,
For they left the world to follow Christ,
And tread the narrow Way of life.

TWELFTH-CENTURY VESPERS HYMN

The feast we celebrate today takes me back to a place I have often visited and for which I hold fond memories: Cluny, an ancient abbey located in the hearty of Burgundy, a place noted for its Romanesque art and its medieval churches.

In the past few years, my return visits to France have been short in duration and extensive in demands, leaving me no time to visit many places, such as Cluny, which I deeply cherish. Fortunately, the fast train that runs between Paris and the southeastern part of France, the TGV, on which I am often obliged to travel, passes by Cluny. Each time the train goes past that lovely place, I manage to give a quick glance, *un coup d'oeuil,* as one says in French, to the relics of the old abbey. There, in the distance, stands the majestic and justly famous octagonal church tower and the remnant buildings. From the distance, I can watch for a few precious minutes those beloved monuments. There is so much to the history of Cluny, including the fact that there was a time when the Cluny abbatial church was considered the largest of all Christiandom, and competed with Saint Peter's in Rome.

During the early Middle Ages, monastic institutions were profoundly influenced by the cultural changes sweeping across Europe. Reforms and new monastic institutions were emerging: the Carthusians, the Camaldolese, and the Cistercians, primarily. One of the most notable and successful monastic reforms was begun by the monastery of Cluny and guided by their wise and holy Abbots. Later, this reform extended to all the monasteries affiliated with Cluny. This reform called for returning to the Gospel, to the Rule of Saint Benedict, and to the early monastic sources.

The holy Abbots, in spite of the extraordinary burden it required, undertook the work of the reform in the spirit of absolute fidelity to Christ. They knew full well that for any monastic reform to succeed, it had to be firmly rooted in the Gospels, in the example and words of Christ.

As monks study the history and experience of Cluny, they can learn much from it. Reforms, throughout the history of monasticism, come and go. They are usually tied to a certain period or a charismatic personality, as they succeeded each other across the centuries. There are some today who, in an effort to purify what they consider the present ills of the monastic institution, would wish to return to what they conceive of as the monasticism of the Middle Ages—as if the medieval monasteries, or those of any other era, were ever perfect. In my view, that sort of idealism is nothing but a naive approach to the problem. In truth, monastic life would not profit from a so-called literal return to the past, but rather from actualizing today the values learned from the past. For monastic life to survive, it must show the same versatility as the Gospel: it must be able to adapt itself to each epoch, to each place where it is implanted or lived.

Monastic life is essentially charismatic, and thus totally dependent on the gifts and grace from the Spirit of God. And as we all know, the Spirit breathes where he wills, not being bound by preconceived notions of what is projected as a perfect past. Yes, we draw life from the past, from the living monastic tradition, then we actualize that tradition in the present and move forward. Filled with the grace and light that shines forth from the Gospel, we move forward seeking God daily with purity of heart, with true simplicity and authentic poverty of spirit, in the silence and solitude of the desert, where God always dwells. Monastic renewal, in essence, is all about this and all else is superfluous.

— MAY 12 —

Saint Epiphanius

The blessed Epiphanius was one day told by the abbot of a monastery situated in Palestine, "By the help of your prayers we do not neglect our appointed sequence of psalmody, and are careful to recite Terce, Sext and None as prescribed." Then Epiphanius corrected him with the following statement: "It is clear that you do not trouble about the other hours of the day, if you cease from prayer. A true monk should always have prayer and psalmody continually in his heart."

ABBOT EPIPHANIUS OF CYPRUS

Today we commemorate a notable Desert Father, Epiphanius of Cyprus. Epiphanius was a Palestinian by birth and eventually migrated into the Egyptian desert to be trained in the ways of monastic life. He became a disciple of Saint Hilarion, also a Palestinian monk, and a beloved friend of our father Saint Antony. Eventually, Epiphanius returned to his native Palestine and settled in a monastery in a place called Besanduk, somewhere between the strip of Gaza and Jerusalem. Because of his great holiness and pastoral care for others, he was chosen as bishop of Cyprus, where he continued to impart the Gospel lessons learned in the desert.

For Epiphanius, as for all the Desert Fathers, the Christian Scriptures were the primary inspiration for their monastic life. In the solitude of the desert, the early monks used the technique of continual rumination of the Scriptures, so as to memorize them and dig deeper into their meaning. The daily praying, reading, and studying of the Word was done with a fine inner attention, it took place at the deepest level of their being. It was there that the sacred seed of the Word was planted, and there it was meant to fructify. Saint Epiphanius strongly emphasized this particular teaching. He held that reading of the Scriptures is a great safeguard against sin, and ignorance of the Scriptures is a precipice and a deep abyss.

To the monks and nuns who were scrupulous about acquiring books, seeing it as a violation of their evangelical poverty, he gently reassured them: "The acquisition of Christian books is necessary for those who can use them. For the mere sight of these books renders us less inclined to sin, and incites us to believe more firmly in righteousness." Saint Epiphanius, in his profound wisdom, knew how to combine desert austerity with human flexibility and went always to the heart of the matter. If Christian books, the Scriptures in particular, were a helpful tool to inner growth, he counseled monks and nuns not to hesitate in their procurement. What mattered for Epiphanius was that the monk or nun be occupied at all times with the essentials of the monastic life: unceasing prayer, psalmody, charity, manual work, humility, and an assiduous reading of and meditation on the Scriptures. To be concerned with anything else, according to the Epiphanius, was trifling and inconsequential.

— MAY 13 —

Monastic Instinct

The way to do is to be.

LAO TZU, CHINESE, 600 B.C.

I have often been asked what I call "the large questions" by those whom I meet: What is monastic? What is a monastic attitude? What is the monastic way of being, acting, behaving? From time to time, when I am invited to give a talk or do a book-signing at a bookstore or a monastery, one of these questions always seems to pop up. I usually reply to the inquirer that what is often meant by "monastic" is such a deep question that I cannot give a response in a few simple words. Then, I always seem to proceed with "Well, there is such a thing as a monastic instinct...."

A monastic instinct is first of all something that develops innerly throughout the years of the monk's life, as he is more and more totally seized by God, by Christ, his Lord and Master. Through the course of time as the monk responds to God's call, he develops a certain life perspective that in turn determines his behavior, feelings, judgment; in a word, all of his life's actions. One could perhaps say that the monastic instinct is a form of sensitivity, an intuition, which when nurtured by the Spirit of God grows and develops quietly in the monk throughout the length of his monastic life. This monastic instinct, this particular approach to acting and viewing reality is heavily influenced by the lifestyle proclaimed in the Gospels, in particular, by Christ's example of frugality and simplicity. Its growth and development in the heart of the monk is the work of grace, of God's acting and illuminating each step of the monk's life. The daily asceticism, the assiduousness to prayer, the lectio divina, the exercise of humility, and all of the other monastic practices contribute in the formation and expansion of the monastic instinct. Eventually, a day arrives in the life of the monk, when he can instinctively recognize in each particular situation what is monastic and what is not, when he may clearly identify diverse life experiences and assimilate them to the degree that they positively impact his monastic calling. The great wisdom of a monastic instinct consists in the gift of discernment that it instills in the monk. It allows him to see all reality from God's perspective and in God's own light, as Saint Benedict once did in a vision.

— MAY 14 —

Daily Trust

Do not look forward to what might happen tomorrow;
the same everlasting Father who cares for you today will
take care of you tomorrow and everyday.

SAINT FRANCIS DE SALES

We are still in Paschaltide, basking in the light and warmth that flows out from the presence of the Risen Lord in our midst. Sometimes I wish these days of Paschaltide could be prolonged for a while longer. Sunday's Gospel passage from John always makes me feel a bit nostalgic: "In a short time you will no longer see me, and then a short time later you will see me again."

Though I love the Feast of the Lord's Ascension, I am never anxious for it to arrive. As far as I'm concerned, its arrival can wait a bit longer. I try to imagine what must have been the feelings of the disciples at the immediate departure of their Master. It is not easy to be orphaned. Where does one go to find comfort?

This morning, as I was reading the Scriptures, the comfort I was seeking came from Jesus himself, from the last discourse in John's Gospel: "Do not let your hearts be troubled. Trust in God and trust in me. If I go and prepare a place for you, I will come again and will take you to myself, so that where I am, there you may be also" (14:1–3).

The daily work of one's monastic life is the living out of this trust in God and trust in Jesus' words and promises. The monk, in his poverty, knows himself entirely dependent upon God's unfailing love and mercy. And this dependance equally demands from the monk a complete, absolute trust in our Heavenly Father, in his designs for our lives. We may not have an idea where our lives are headed, where the road is leading us, or what is awaiting us at the road's end, but we do know that we are not traveling alone, that God is beside us. With Saint Paul, the monk repeats daily: *I know the one in whom I have placed my trust.*

— MAY 15 —

Saint Pachomius

The fame of our father Pachomius and of his charity reached everyone. His name was heard even abroad and among the Romans, and they came to become monks with him. And the man of God Pachomius treated them well in word and deed, like a nurse comforting her children. When the men of the world saw Pachomius, a man of God in their midst, they were very eager to become Christians and faithful. For he was full of mercy and a lover of souls.

BOHAIRIC LIFE OF PACHOMIUS AND THE GREEK LIFE OF PACHOMIUS

In the monastic calendar, we honor today the memory of Saint Pachomius, an early Desert Father and a pioneer of the *primitif* monastic movement. In our chapel, his ikon stands next to that of Saint Antony, symbolizing how much we owe to these two fathers of monastic life. Pachomius, like Antony, was Egyptian by birth, being born of pagan parents around 292 A.D.

Perhaps one of the most touching episodes in Pachomius's life is the origin of his conversion to Christianity. While serving in the Roman army, Pachomius encountered a group of people whom he came to admire greatly because of their inspiring charity toward everyone and their willingness to help whoever was in need. Pachomius inquired about these selfless and heroic people. He learned that they were Christians, disciples of a master called Christ, who left as trademark to his followers that they must love one another as he has loved them. Immediately, Pachomius decided that he, too, would become a disciple of Christ and a servant to others.

After leaving the army, Pachomius sought refuge with a humble Christian community. There, he received baptism and requested guidance in his spiritual pursuit from a hermit named Palemon. Pachomius had a vision of God's grace passing through his hands, and flowing out unto the entire world. This vision impelled him to spend the first three years after his conversion working and serving those most in need in the local villages. It is only after these three years of training in the "school of charity" that he felt moved to embrace the monastic life.

Pachomius founded a monastic community that was based upon service and the practice of charity towards all. His fellow monks, following the example of the Apostles, were to be united in love and to serve one another after the model of the first Christians. They were to be particularly known for their generosity and concern towards strangers and the poor. Pachomius's great gift and contribution to the monastic movement was being able to combine this insistence upon Gospel charity with the most traditional monastic values practiced in the desert: silence, fasting, vigils, continual prayer, humility, obedience to the elders, study, and the reading of the Scriptures.

Pachomius was such an excellent monastic organizer that his monastery continued to grow to the point that he was obliged to found six other monasteries nearby, all of them under his spiritual direction. One of these new foundations was a monastery exclusively for women. Pachomius's own sister was the first to enter and later became the mother of the monastery. For all of them, the saintly monk wrote a simple rule to guide his monks and nuns in their continual search for God. The Koinonias, or monastery, founded by Saint Pachomius attached great importance to the role of the Scriptures and the Eucharist in its monastic life. The monks and nuns were fed by the Word of God which they heard and chanted in their daily Offices, and by the Body and Blood of Christ, which they received at least once a week. Thus, the Pachomian monks and nuns strove to remain united perfectly in their communion in the Word of God and the Body and Blood of Christ.

Saint Pachomius, humble monk and God's servant, died around 345 A.D., the victim of an epidemic illness that ravaged the Egyptian countryside. Before dying, he exhorted his monks to remain faithful to the monastic life they embraced, and to seek in all things the perfection of charity. He died in peace, in the joy of knowing that he was going home to the Lord he faithfully followed and served for many, long years.

— MAY 16 —

The Daily Significance of the Incarnation

The fact that Christ shared our human condition gives significance to every human life wherever it is....In becoming man, Christ became all men.

ABBOT BASIL HUME, *SEARCHING FOR GOD*

Up until now we have had a steady line of clear days. There are those who would count that as a blessing. But here, in a farming monastery, where water is needed and prayed for daily, I find myself longing for darker days, with a hint of rain in them. The response so far has been negative. I don't wish to get discouraged, so I place all my hope in the Lord. We have lived on this hillside spot now for many years. The monastery has seen the changing of the seasons again and again, and I know that sooner or later the Lord, sometimes in unexpected ways, always comes through. Today I continued planting in the garden, as I would do usually, some leeks, beans, brussels sprouts, and cauliflower. Despite our present drought, the planting and the watering continues.

Throughout this time of water anxiety, I reflect on of the mystery of the Incarnation, how God, in becoming man, embraced all human and earthly conditions. Nothing is foreign or strange to him, not even sin. The Incarnation implies to me that God, in Jesus, is present in everything, even if hidden. As I go about my daily toils, I look for him for whom our hearts yearn. As I seek to encounter Him in the small events of the day, I reflect that both the rain and the garden are God's gift, and that eventually the Almighty will provide in His own manner whatever is necessary for our survival. Often, when God closes one door, he opens another.

To be alive today, to toil, to pray, to long for rain, and to ultimately trust and depend upon God for whatever the outcome, is to affirm that God, in becoming man, knew full well the limitations of our condition and our utter dependency upon him. *Christus, veritas et vita, semper nobis benedicat.*

— MAY 17 —

The Resurrection Ikon

Even if Thou didst descend into the tomb, O Immortal One, still Thou hast overthrown the power of Hades and Thou hast arisen as victor, O Christ, our God. To the women bearing incense Thou hast said, "Hail," and on Thy apostles Thou has bestowed peace, thou who dost offer resurrection to the fallen. Death was swallowed up in victory, and always celebrating it we rejoice, as with jubilation we cry out: Truly, Christ is arisen.

SAINT ROMANUS THE MELODIST, "ON THE RESURRECTION"

In this small monastery, during the days of Paschaltide, we pay particular attention to the ikon of the Anastasis, the Greek name for the ikon of the Resurrection. This ikon is positioned right next to the tall Paschal candle and is always surrounded by fresh flowers. Each time we enter or leave the chapel, we devoutly kiss and venerate this image of the Risen Lord.

The Gospels tell us nothing about the Resurrection moment itself. It is something that happened in the silence and darkness of night, in God's own mysterious space and immense solitude. Perhaps only the angels were witnesses to the awesome event. The Anastasis ikon respects that description from the Gospels, and thus we only have two distinct representations of the Resurrection in the ikonographic tradition of the church: *The Descent into Hell* and *The Myrrh-bearer Women by the Empty Tomb*. The specific Resurrection ikon we honor in the oratory, a gift from a dear friend and neighbor, is the one that depicts the Lord's descent into hell in search of Adam and Eve. Our first parents and all the souls of the just have been waiting throughout the course of time for this blessed moment when the Risen Lord would come to fetch them from their captivity.

In the ikon, the Lord is dressed in luminous white clothing, radiant and enveloped by light, symbolic of his glorified body after the Resurrection. In a tender gesture, he lends his hands to Adam and Eve, as to bring them forth from their captivity. These are the same hands that Christ, in his boundless love, gives to each of us in his effort to free us from our own sinful captivity.

— MAY 18 —

A Paschal Homily I

I adore your Cross, O Christ, our God, and I shall glorify your tomb, O Immortal One. And in celebrating the festival of you Resurrection, I cry to You: "The Lord is risen."

SAINT ROMANUS THE MELODIST, "ON THE RESURRECTION"

In less than a week we shall be celebrating the Lord's glorious Ascension. As our Paschal days rapidly come to a close, I re-read the gracious and illuminating homily by Saint John Chrysostom, truly a jewel among all Paschal homilies, and a great sustenance to our sometimes tired spirits. I read and refer to the homily often during these forty days of Paschaltide, for it is a perennial reminder of the meaning and joy of the Feast of Feasts. It also reminds us that in the new dispensation Jesus has abolished social distinction among people: rich and poor, saint and sinner, learned and ignorant, weak and powerful; all are equally invited into the Feast of Feasts. Unlike us, God is not intolerant and makes no distinction among his children. To prove this to the world, he extends his hospitality to all on the day of the Resurrection.

Several translations of the Saint John Chrysostom's homily are available. However, this is my own particular version, taken from different sources, including a French translation. Because of the length of the homily, it has been divided into two parts. Today we read Part I:

> If anyone is devout and loves his God, let him rejoice on this radiant festival. If anyone is a faithful servant, let him enter rejoicing into the joy of his Lord. If anyone be weary from the hardships of fasting, let him receive his humble reward. If anyone has toiled from the first hour, let him receive his just dues. If anyone has come after the third hour, let him join the feast with gratitude. If anyone has come after the sixth hour, let him not be agitated, for he shall not be punished. If anyone has delayed until the ninth hour, let him come without fear. If anyone has arrived at the eleventh hour, let him not be upset by his delay.
>
> The Lord is liberal and of great generosity, and welcomes the last the same way he welcomes the first. He provides rest for the one arriving at the eleventh hour in the same manner as he provides for the one laboring from the start of day. He shows pity on the last to arrive just as he does with the first; the latter he welcomes in justice and the former he welcomes with charity. He honors the good works and the good intentions from both. Let all, then, enter into the joy of our Lord. Let the first and the last receive their recompense. Let rich and poor rejoice in harmony

together. Let both the sober and the slothful celebrate the feast today. Whether you have kept the fast or not, rejoice today. The table is full, eat plenty, all of you. Be nourished at the feast today, the fatted calf is served, and let no one go away hungry. In faith, let all partake of the cup and abundance of God's goodness.

— MAY 19 —

A Paschal Homily II

Spare, O Christ, our God, those who believe in your Cross, tomb, and Resurrection. Grant us forgiveness of sins, and whenever the awakening trumpet sounds for all, consider us worthy to see your face, and to hear with confidence your voice saying: "Welcome, alongside my saints, enter into the joy of my kingdom."

SAINT ROMANUS THE MELODIST, "ON THE RESURRECTION"

Here is the second part of Saint John Chrysostom's Paschal homily.

Let no one lament his poverty, the kingdom banquet is offered to all. Let no one bewail his transgressions, for forgiveness has come from the tomb. Let no one surrender to the fear of death, for the Savior's death has obtained our freedom. He endured death, and in that manner he has overcome it. He descended into hell and destroyed its powers. Hell was embittered when it encountered his flesh; Isaiah had prognosticated this, when he foretold: Hell below was in uproar at your coming (Isa 14:9).

When it encountered you below, hell was made bitter. It was embittered for it was overturned, embittered for it was mocked.

It took flesh and instead it received God. It seized the earth and instead it ran into heaven. It received that which was visible and instead fell into that which is invisible. O death, where is your sting? O Hell, where is your victory? (1 Cor 15).

Christ is risen and death is overcome. Christ is risen and the devil is crushed. Christ is risen and the angels rejoice. Christ is risen and there are no dead left in the tombs. Christ rising from the dead has become the first fruits of those that sleep.

To him be glory and power throughout all ages. Amen.

— MAY 20 —

May Flowers

No flower around the garden fairer grows than the sweet
lily of the lowly vale, the Queen of flowers.

AUTHOR UNKNOWN

In the past few days I have been anxious about the lack of rain. It has been almost a month since it rained last. Is our work, Lord, meant to be futile? I tease the Lord half-seriously. I know God has a plan for everything. I just wish that sometimes he would give me a hint about what may be happening, especially concerning the weather.

The other day, when it looked as if it was going to pour at any moment, I transplanted myriads of leek seedlings into their permanent beds. I also transplanted cauliflower and other seedlings, and then didn't bother to water them. It was late and I thought the rain would do the job. After dinner and Compline, I retired to bed. The next morning, I looked out for signs of the rain. I was afraid I might not have heard it during my sleep. To my regret, I saw no indications of rain. The storm had eluded us again! Mother Nature, like its Creator, is often unpredictable. Nevertheless, deep down I know God is acting out his plan and all he demands from us is humble submission, complete trust.

This morning, after spending a long chunk of time watering our gardens, I went flower picking for an arrangement to put in the chapel. There were not many flower varieties to choose from. I picked a few irises, peonies, and some wild phlox for the main bouquet. Since it is May, Our Lady's month, I managed to gather a small bouquet of lilies of the valley to place in front of the twelfth-century statue of Our Lady of the Resurrection.

This lovely flower has been known for centuries as a Mary flower, for according to ancient tradition, it suggests the virtues of humility and purity. In some countries, it is called "Our Lady's tears" and in others it is referred to it as "the Virgin's flower." In France, where people are particularly fond of this flower, they often use it to cheer loved ones or someone who is ill. The humble lily is also a favorite for bridal bouquets. It is fitting, therefore, that this May flower growing in abundance in our garden be chosen to pay homage to the Mother of God, the *Regina Caeli* of our Easter season. The bouquet is not only symbolic of our homage to her, but also a plea for her continual intercession on our behalf. *Holy Theotokos, save us!*

— MAY 21 —

On Contemplation

If we try to contemplate God without having turned the face of our inner self entirely in his direction, we will end up inevitably by contemplating ourselves, and we will perhaps plunge into the abyss of warm darkness which is our own sensible nature.

THOMAS MERTON, *THOUGHTS IN SOLITUDE*

In most of my spiritual reading, I try to stick with monastic authors, especially the early Fathers. Whenever they write about prayer and communion with God, they always do so with that singular realism which is typically monastic and which obviously comes straight from the Gospels.

Lately, I have been rereading Saint Silouan, the Athonite. A few years ago, I read him in French and instantly became very attached to him. In many ways, Saint Silouan reminds me a great deal of our father Saint Antony. As I reread him, this time in English, I found a passage on contemplation which particularly struck me. This excerpt containing the words of Saint Silouan was edited by his disciple Archimandrite Sophrony:

> Divine contemplation is accorded to man, not in those precise moments when he seeks it, and it alone, but when his soul descends into the hell of repentance and does really feel that he is the meanest of creatures. Contemplation forcibly attained, as it were, through reasoning is not true but only seeming contemplation. To accept such contemplation as truth creates a condition in the soul which may prevent the action of grace and make genuine contemplation impossible.

Knowledge revealed in the contemplation which proceeds from grace surpasses even the most sublime creations of the imagination, as Saint Paul affirmed when he said, "The things that no eye has seen and no ear has heard, things beyond the mind of man, all that God has prepared for those who love him."

— MAY 22 —

A Prayer by Saint Silouan the Athonite

All day, all night, my soul is taken up with you, O Lord, and I seek you. Your Holy Spirit draws me to seek you, and the remembrance of you makes my mind glad. My soul came to love you, and rejoices that you are my God and my Lord, and I yearn after you till my heart is filled with tears. And though all the world be beautiful, no earthly thing can occupy my thoughts—my soul desires only you, O Lord.

— MAY 23 —

Vigil of the Ascension

Do not let your hearts be troubled, and do not let them be afraid. You heard me say to you, 'I am going away, and I am coming to you.' If you loved me, you would rejoice that I am going to the Father, because the Father is greater than I. And now I have told you this before it occurs, so that when it does occur, you may believe.

JOHN 14:27–29

This morning I found in a corner of the garden a radiant yellow iris blooming, filling the air with sweet fragrance. It glows like a flame in the midst of the surrounding greenery. I am usually reluctant to remove such a beauty from the garden, but tomorrow is Ascension day, and all that is best in our gardens shall be offered to the Lord. I was hoping that there would also be some early roses in bloom to join the irises and the other flowers, but I am afraid we may have to wait until Pentecost for that. After all, it is still the month of May, and roses almost never begin to bloom here until June makes its entrance.

The quotation from John is perhaps the best biblical text to prepare us for tomorrow's feast. Our Lord minces no words: I am going away and I will come back for you. If you love me, you will rejoice that I am going to the Father. Those words, uttered in the ears of our hearts today, are as true now as they were when they first were pronounced, and they shall remain true in the future. Jesus explicitly adds: I have told you this before it happens, so that when it happens you may believe.

— MAY 24 —
The Ascension of the Lord

Christ's Resurrection is our hope, and his Ascension is our glory. It was with his human nature that Christ entered heaven and sat on God's throne. This, therefore, is the raising and glorification of our human nature.

SAINT AUGUSTINE

After the blissful and much needed rain of the last two days, this morning I welcomed the dawn with joy. The early light was serene, unspoiled, perfectly apt for Ascension day.

I went to sing Lauds this morning, enchanted by the tranquility of the early hour. There is nothing akin to praising the Lord in that deep stillness, when the rest of the world is still asleep. Today's feast is truly majestic, for it concerns the final glorification of our Lord, King, and Master. Jesus is returning to the Father, exalted in glory, because of what he endured for our sake. He has fulfilled the Father's plan and now he is being received back into his bosom. All we can do is to lift up our hearts and desires to him, *sursum corda*.

I think it is Saint Bernard who says that through desire we already possess the object of our longing. The feast of the Ascension also intensifies the realization of our earthly pilgrimage. We are still here on earth, *in via*, but we still have miles to go to reach our destination. We can be comforted and strengthened, though, by the knowledge that Christ, our Savior, has reached the end of his earthly pilgrimage, and now is waiting with open arms for us to join him. As he once spoke: I am going to prepare a place for you, so that where I am you may be also.

— MAY 25 —

The Splendor and Glory of the Ascension

I think no better way exists than to praise the Lord on this splendid feast with the words from the Byzantine Vespers of the Ascension:

> The Lord ascended into heaven to send the Comforter into the world. The heavens prepared his throne, and the angels marveled at his sight. Today the Father receives in his bosom him who was always with him. The Holy Spirit commands the angels: "Lift up your gates, O you Princes." O you nations of the earth, clap your hands, for Christ has ascended to the place where he was before time begun. O Lord, the Cherubim were amazed at your Ascension. They were dazzled as they beheld You, O God, Rising upon the clouds higher than they could rise. We sing a hymn of praise to you: On this day of your glorious Ascension, we glorify your tender mercy.
>
> O Christ, splendor and glory of the Father, as we behold your Ascension on the holy mountain, we sing a hymn to the beauty of your countenance: We bow down to your Sacred Passion, we venerate your Resurrection and glorify your noble Ascension. O Lord, ascended into glory: have mercy on us!
>
> O Lord, life-giving Christ, when the apostles saw you ascending upon the clouds, a great sadness filled them. They shed burning tears and exclaimed: O dear Master, do not leave us orphans! We are your servants whom you loved so tenderly, as you promised to send your Holy Spirit to enlighten our souls!
>
> Lord Jesus Christ, while you lived on earth you were God inseparable from the Father, yet a real man. Through your Ascension, you filled your Mother and the apostles with a joy that surpasses every other joy. Through their intercession make us worthy of your elect, for you are all-holy and infinitely merciful.

Purity of Heart

Let us aim at our principal goal, at that purity of heart which is love.

SAINT JOHN CASSIAN

According to the teachings of Saint John Cassian, the primary aim of the monastic journey is to work to achieve the purity of heart to which the Gospel promise is attached: "Blessed are the pure of heart, for they will see God" (Mt 5:8). This task demands humility, renunciation, constant vigilance, unceasing prayer, and, most of all, grace from the Holy Spirit. Purity of heart is not achieved in a single day, month, or year. It is rather the result of a long, slow process, a process sometimes tedious and cumbersome, by which the monk learns to die daily so that he may live in God alone.

Purity of heart allows the monk to return to the center of his being, where God dwells and where he is most himself. In that center, all things converge and come together. The Gospel never ceases to remind us that "the kingdom of God is within us," and not anywhere else. To loose sight of that unique center is to diminish our capacity for the genuine purity of heart required for the vision of God. During these days that precede Pentecost, our constant petition to the Holy Spirit must be to enable us to travel ever deeper into that center where he is our most delightful Guest. It is there, according to Jesus' promises, that the Spirit will teach us all things. Through the power of the Holy Spirit, the true dynamic force in the life of the Christian, we shall be able to slowly make progress into the ways of love, and eventually arrive to the final vision of he who is Love itself.

— MAY 27 —

Spring Music

*All one's life is music, if one touches the notes rightly and
on time.*

JOHN RUSKIN

I am very much a seasonal listener, that is to say, I usually spend
time listening to a particular type of music depending on the
season. In the winter, for example, I enjoy listening to chamber
music, specifically to quartets. I detect that musical sounds, over-
all, reverberate in consonance with the reality of the moment.
More than any other medium, they can express the unspoiled
beauty hidden in the depths of a particular season. Invariably, I
find music to be the most effectual tool to express the inexpress-
ible.

When spring arrives, I turn my ears to the joyful and sublime
music of Mozart. I have heard musicologists describe Mozart's
music as "divine," "heavenly," or "out of this world." It is probably all of that and more. The appreciative listener is susceptible
to the wide range of feelings and emotion the music of Mozart
inspires: joy, serenity, lightness, graciousness, civility, refinement,
melancholy, a sense of longing for the inner world. In the music
of Mozart, one seldom confronts the sense of tragedy or struggle
of other composers. Mozart, deeply human as he was, used his
music in a positive manner. He wished to affirm all that was
good in creation, such as it came from the hands of God.

Every spring, as we relive the mystery of Christ's Resurrection and feel the resurgence of new life taking place all around
us, I am quietly drawn to Mozart. His music, a metaphor for
God's life in us, inspires us to incorporate in our daily lives a
sense of sobriety, beauty, goodness, godliness, joy, and all other
positive attributes connected with the divine. Thus, through listening to Mozart and through the mysteries celebrated during
the season, we may experience the truth hidden beneath the words
of the Cure d'Ars: *It is always spring in the soul united with
God.*

— MAY 28 —

The Mozart Sonatas

A painter paints his pictures on canvas. But musicians paint their pictures on silence. We provide the music and you provide the silence.

LEOPOLD STOKOWSKI

The constant rain of the last few days has forced me to work indoors for most of the time. With a quiet mind, I have been able to enjoy listening to Mozart piano sonatas as well as to his sonatas for violin and piano. Mozart, ingeniously, always transports me into a world of wonders and delight, especially during this time of year. I feel miles and miles removed, at least for the time being, from any sort of agitation or disturbance. This experience makes me agree with what Martin Luther once said: "Next to theology I accord to music the highest place and honor. Music is the art of the prophets, the only art that can calm the agitations of the soul; it is one of the most magnificent and delightful presents God has given us."

Mozart's sonatas seem to be an intensely personal effort on the part of the composer. There is no doubt in my mind that somehow Mozart utilized these sonatas to reveal something of himself to the listener. The meticulous genius of the composer is apparent in every phrase of the sonatas, in every note. In sonata after sonata, it becomes evident to me that Mozart was supremely capable of expressing every form of feeling, without resorting to the tragic. He also enjoyed the fact of not taking himself too seriously. There is a certain humor in the sonatas that is altogether absent in most composers of the German school. There is also unrestrained joy—a trademark of Mozart's music.

During these midspring days which breathe new life into the cosmos, into each of us, Mozart's music seems to divulge in a lyrical fashion the sublime sense of renewal and amazement taking place in our midst. I can't help but to make an obvious identification between Mozart and the current season. So much of what I perceive as the mystery of spring is contained in his music. Mozart, in his own incomparable way, affirms our faith in the reality of the Resurrection. Life is worthwhile and there is meaning to it after all, for Jesus is indeed risen!

— MAY 29 —
A Prayer to the Holy Spirit

When the Advocate comes, whom I will send to you from the Father, the Spirit of truth who issues from the Father, he will testify on my behalf. You also are to testify because you have been with me from the beginning.

JOHN 15:26–27

The days of Pentecost are quickly approaching. Eastertide has been a joyful and consoling season, a sort of preparation for the climax of Pentecost. Before leaving us on Ascension Day, Jesus foretold the arrival of the Holy Spirit who shall be sent by the Father and the Son to enlighten our souls, to reveal to us the meaning of all that Jesus taught while still on earth. The Holy Spirit comes into the soul that is prepared to receive him and, through his grace and light, he infuses new life into the soul. The Holy Spirit is both immaterial and invisible and yet, like a gentle wind, he touches our being and penetrates the innermost of our hearts. At his presence, fear, doubt, all the forces of evil are dispelled, and the soul experiences the consolation of this most delightful Guest. As we prepare to welcome him on Pentecost day, may he grant peace and perfect stillness to our souls, so that we may perceive his subtle presence in the depths of our hearts. We pray: *O Holy Spirit, Eternal King and Giver of life everlasting: Look down in your infinite mercy upon the weakness of our human nature. Illumine and sanctify our souls. Let the light of your knowledge shine forth in our darkened hearts. In our earthly nature show forth your invincible strength and power.*

The Source of All Holiness

A wonderful explanation of the Holy Spirit was written by Saint Basil the Great. Here is an excerpt from one of his treatises:

All creatures turn to the Holy Spirit in their need for holiness. All living things seek him according to their capacity. His breath empowers each to achieve its own natural end. The Holy Spirit is the source of all holiness, a spiritual light, and he extends his own light to every mind to help it in its search for the truth. By nature, the Holy Spirit is beyond the reach of our mind, but we can know him by the experience of his goodness. The power of the Holy Spirit fills the entire universe, but he gives himself only to those who are worthy, acting in each according to the measure of their faith.

Simple in himself, the Holy Spirit is manifold in his mighty works. The whole of his being is present to each individual; the whole of his being is present everywhere. Though he is shared by many, he remains unchanged; his self-giving is no loss to himself. Like the sunshine that filters through the whole atmosphere, spreading over the land and sea, and yet is enjoyed by each person as though it were for him alone, so the Holy Spirit pours forth his grace in full measure, sufficient for all, and yet is present as though exclusively to everyone who is willing to welcome him. To all creatures that share in him he gives a delight limited only by their own nature.

The Holy Spirit raises our hearts to heaven, guides the steps of the weak, and brings to perfection those who are making progress. He enlightens those who have been cleansed from every stain of sin and makes them spiritual by communion with himself....

From the Holy Spirit we receive foreknowledge of the future, comprehension of the mysteries of faith, insight into the hidden meaning of the Scriptures, and other special gifts. Through the Holy Spirit we become citizens of heaven, we are admitted to share in the company of the angels, we enter into eternal happiness, and abide in God. Through the Holy Spirit we acquire a likeness to God; indeed, we attain what is beyond our most sublime aspirations—we become God.

— MAY 31 —

The Visitation

In those days Mary set out and went with haste to a Judean town in the hill country, where she entered the house of Zechariah and greeted Elizabeth. When Elizabeth heard Mary's greeting, the child leaped in her womb. And Elizabeth was filled with the Holy Spirit and exclaimed with a loud cry, "Blessed are you among women, and blessed is the fruit of your womb. And why has this happened to me, that the mother of my Lord comes to me? For as soon as I heard the sound of your greeting, the child in my womb leaped for joy. And blessed is she who believed that there would be a fulfillment of what was spoken to her by the Lord."

LUKE 1:39–45

The glorious month of May, dedicated to honor the Mother of God, concludes, as it started, with a strong Marian flavor. Today we celebrate the feast of the Visitation. It is a feast that evokes the charity of the maiden of Nazareth as she journeyed through the hill towns of Palestine to offer help to her pregnant cousin, Elizabeth. It is a feast full of joyful serenity and gentleness, for we get to see how much Mary and Elizabeth loved and cared for each other. It is also a feast that portrays the human context and climate in which the mystery of the Incarnation took place. Suddenly, we can get a glimpse into why God chose Mary to be the mother of his only-begotten Son. She was a woman full of virtue, being selfless, humble, and of exquisite charity. As always, these are the factors that attract God towards one of his creatures. It is in people such as these that God is free to do great things, as he did for Mary. Jacob of Serugh, a Syrian church father, plainly states:

Because God saw her, and how good and pure was her soul, He wished to dwell in her who had been purified from every wickedness, for no other woman had ever appeared like her....Had any other woman pleased him more than Mary, he would have chosen her instead.

JUNE

Early June

And what is so rare as a day in June? Then, if ever, come
perfect days....Whether we look or whether we listen,
we hear life murmur, or see it glisten....

JAMES RUSSELL LOWELL

After a four-week draught, the Almighty had pity on us farmers and gardeners, and he sent rain in abundance. It poured
almost nonstop for over a week. But who am I to complain? I
think the Lord, with a humor all his own, answered our petitions
abundantly. I can almost hear him whispering: "O ye, of little
faith, you know I am always watching over your interests, and
yet you didn't trust that I would come through for you."

This incident reminds me of what an old monk once said:
"When you pray, watch out what you ask of the Lord, for he may
answer your prayer in an unexpected fashion." One thing I have
learned, throughout long years of praying, is never to complain

about the responses I get from above. The Lord always hears us, but he is also unpredictable and playful. He enjoys surprising us. All we need to do is to align ourselves to his holy will, even when it may be beyond our understanding. Whatever he wishes for our lives, he always provides us the means to accept and bear it.

As we get ready for Pentecost, I delight in the fact that June, one of the most alluring months of the year, is here. The flowers in our gardens begin to appear in their true splendor, and the hay-making scent that permeates the local air is utterly delightful. With the arrival of June, in the words of Leigh Hunt, we leave spring behind and enter into the "complete summer": "The hopes of spring are realized; yet the enjoyment is but commenced; we have all summer before us."

— JUNE 2 —

Eve of Pentecost

O Holy Spirit, O Light inscrutable, Light beyond all name: Come and abide in us. Deliver us from the darkness of ignorance; and impart upon us the stream of your divine knowledge.

BYZANTINE PRAYER

Early June continues to be a time of great activity in the garden. Because of the long rains, I was unable to complete planting the vegetable garden until now. It is over a month since the first plantings started, and yet only now does that part of the work come to a gradual conclusion. The last two days I concentrated on planting several varieties of tomatoes, as well as peppers, eggplants, cucumbers, basil, pole beans, and sunflowers. I also added some annuals wherever they were needed, both in the cut-flower garden and among the vegetables. June's weather is kind to plants, and thus these do well when transplanted during the early part of the month.

This morning I spent a considerable amount of time cutting and arranging the peonies for the chapel in preparation for tomorrow's feast. In some countries, peonies are called Pentecost roses, for they invariably bloom for Pentecost. That is certainly true here. For over a week now, since Ascension day, we have begun our spiritual preparations for tomorrow's great solemnity. The liturgical readings and the chant at the Office have been making steady allusions to the Holy Spirit, whom Jesus promised to send after his earthly departure. In the history of God's dealings with his people, Jesus' return to the Father was a necessary prelude to Pentecost.

As Jesus promised, the Holy Spirit remains today in our midst, to help and direct our Christian journey toward God. He works in and through us, as long as we are totally attuned to his subtle movements in the depths of our souls. It is in the most obscure recesses of our own souls, that we are called to experience the intimate presence of the Holy Spirit. He is the light of our souls, the true *lumen cordium* that imparts new life into our entire being. He is also the most tender and ineffable of guests, the *dulcis hospes animae* that gently draws us into communion with the eternal Father, and his only-begotten Son.

— JUNE 3 —

Pentecost

O heavenly King, the Comforter and Spirit of Truth, you are everywhere present and fill all things. Treasury of blessings and Giver of life, come dwell within us, cleanse us from every stain, and save our souls, O Gracious Lord.

BYZANTINE PRAYER

The Solemnity of Pentecost usually arrives in June, a month of almost perpetually perfect weather. Today is no different, the countryside seems transformed by the light of June. It is no longer the pale light of winter or the resurgent, magical light of spring. Under a blue, cloudless sky, the rays of the sun shine with the exuberance and warmth that provide June with a brilliant radiance. The early days of the month, from dawn to dusk, seem bathed in this infused, burning light. It is the light of Pentecost, the sweetness of the Holy Spirit. It reminds me of the lines from Gerard Manley Hopkins, so appropriate for our celebration today:

> Oh, morning, at the brown brink eastward, springs—
> Because the Holy Ghost over the bent
> World broods with warm breast and with ah! bright wings.

Early this morning, during the solemn Office of Lauds we sang the beautiful Hymn *Beata Nobis Gaudia*, ascribed to Saint Hilary of Poitiers. The music and the text are lovely in describing the mystery we commemorate today. My only regret is that it is sung only once in the entire liturgical year.

> The cycle of the Christian year
> Completes our happiness today,
> As we recall with joy the morn
> The Spirit Paraclete came upon the Church.
>
> The parted tongues of flaming fire
> Enkindled each disciple's zeal,
> And now would prompt his eager lips
> In spreading far and wide the faith.
>
> Most tender Father, hear our hymn,
> As low before your throne we bow:
> Send down your Holy Spirit's gifts
> To fill our souls with light and strength.

Pentecost is a time of plenitude and fullness. Today we complete the days of the Easter cycle—exactly fifty days after the Resurrection of Jesus. Today, we experience the descent of the Holy Spirit into our lives. Today, he comes to reveal to each of us the hidden meaning of all that Jesus taught during his earthly years: "I have said these things to you while I am still with you. But the Advocate, the Holy Spirit, whom the Father will send in my name, will teach you everything and remind you of all I have said to you" (Jn 14:25–26).

Today, the Holy Spirit is given to us as he was once given to the Apostles: to understand with greater clarity and depth the teachings of Jesus. This gift of understanding is essential if we are to continue, in our own small way, the work of Jesus. The Holy Spirit descends upon the entire universe. We realize that he descends upon people of different places, races, cultures, tongues, and times. He fills all things with the gift of himself.

In spite of the extraordinary diversity that exists in the world, we all share the one life in God. The Holy Spirit is the common tie that binds not only the Church, the Body of Christ, but also the vastness of the universe. Today, both creation and the Church are renewed by the Holy Spirit who sustains all life. For the Christian, there is no "life in Christ," or any other experience of God, except by the grace and energies of the Holy Spirit. It is no surprise that the humble nineteenth-century Russian mystic, Saint Seraphim of Sarov, never ceased reminding his disciples that, "The only purpose of the Christian life consists in the acquisition of the Holy Spirit."

— JUNE 4 —

Pentecost Sequence

The liturgical texts do so much to enhance our conception of the celebrated mystery of Pentecost. We feel overwhelmed by their richness. The hymn for Vespers, the *Veni Creator*, is so full of majesty and grace, imparting inspiration and holiness to all who in one way or another partake of it.

Among the rich chants for the solemnity of Pentecost none is more beautiful, more inspiring, than the Pentecost Sequence— truly a jewel of the Pentecost liturgy. It helps us understand the mysterious presence of the Holy Spirit in our own souls, and how his graceful company brings the supreme gift of God into our personal lives. In years past, we kept the Octatve of Pentecost, and thus were able to sing the Sequence for a whole week. With changes in the liturgy, however, the season now ends on Pentecost Sunday. From then forth, it is Ordinary Time.

Ordinary Time, in my modest view, is the prolongation of Pentecost. It is the time assigned by God for the particular work of the Holy Spirit. In a way, we do not digress altogether from the rhythms

of the liturgy by concentrating today on the text of the Pentecost
Sequence. The sequence is such a support to one's prayer that one
can fruitfully feed on its words every day of the year. The translation that follows is my own adaptation from the original Latin:

> Come, Holy Spirit,
> And from the high heavens
> Shed a ray of light divine!
>
> Come, Father of the poor,
> Come, Giver of gifts,
> Come, Light of our hearts!
>
> You are the best of comforters,
> You are the soul's sweetest guest
> And pure refreshment here below!
>
> In our labor, welcome rest;
> Tempering heat with coolness sweet;
> Solace in the face of trials.
>
> O most blessed Light,
> Shine in the hearts of your faithful
> And fill their innermost with yourself!
>
> Without your presence, we are naught;
> Nothing good in deed or thought;
> Never free from ill or affliction.
>
> Wash our sinfulness away;
> Pour your dew in our arid souls;
> Heal the depths of our wounds.
>
> Bend the stubbornness of our rigid hearts;
> Melt the frozen, warm the chill;
> Make straight all that is devious.
>
> To your faithful,
> Who in you put their trust,
> Grant your gifts in abundance.
>
> Grant them virtue's sweet reward;
> Grant them salvation, O Lord,
> Grant them eternal joy. Amen. Alleluia.

— JUNE 5 —

The Pentecost Sticheras

The Pentecost liturgical tradition, both in the East and the West, is so profound that it is impossible to absorb all of it in a single day. In the Byzantine East, the Sticheras sung at Vespers are intertwined with the verses from Psalm 140, the preeminent Vespers psalm. We are privileged in our small monastery to combine in our Offices elements from both traditions.

The two traditions complement each other perfectly and make us partake, on a deeper level, of the mystery and reality of the one, undivided Church. It seems to me that only through prayer can we one day regain the unity willed by Christ. Prayer alone can heal and overcome the pride, prejudice, and misunderstanding created throughout the centuries, for prayer is the supreme work of the Holy Spirit. The Sticheras, as do the Pentecost Sequence yesterday, reveal not only something of the mystery of Pentecost; they help us to pray that mystery.

Behold, we celebrate today the feast of Pentecost, the descent of the Holy Spirit, the fulfillment of a promise and the realization of our hope. How noble and awesome is this great mystery! Therefore, O Lord and Creator, we cry out: Glory to You!

You renewed your disciples, O Christ, by giving them a variety of tongues with which to proclaim that You are the Immortal God, the Word, who bestows great mercy upon our souls.

The Holy Spirit provides every gift: He inspires prophecy, perfects the ministry, gives wisdom to illiterates. He makes simple fishermen become wise theologians, and establishes perfect order in the structure of the Church. O Comforter, equal to the Father and the Son, glory to you!

We have seen the true light and received the heavenly Spirit, we have found the true faith in the worship of the Trinity. O Christ, through the prophets You have shown us the path to salvation, and by the grace of the Spirit You have enlightened your Apostles. You are eternal God unto ages of ages!

— JUNE 6 —
Saint Hildebert's Hymn

An early hymn to the Holy Spirit by Hildebert, Bishop of Tours, is another jewel of the Pentecost liturgy.

Holy Spirit, merciful Paraclete.
Love of the Father and the Son,
You are he who begets and is begotten,
You are their eternal bond.

You are the Prince of Goodness and Love
For you unite one and the other.
You are the purity of their essence,
You are all tenderness, sweetness, and delicacy.

Holy Spirit, you are the link
That reunites God and humankind.
You are the power
That brings forth this union.

Eternal glory to you, worthy of adoration,
And also to the Father and the Son.
Endless honor be offered to you
Who proceeds eternally from God. Amen.

— JUNE 7 —
On Prayer

Hear me, O God, in your mighty goodness. Answer my
prayer with fire, as you did once for Your holy Prophets.
BISHOP THEOPHAN THE RECLUSE

Yesterday, a woman who is spending a few days here on retreat asked me what I considered to be the principal occupation of the monastic life. *Deo Gratias!* I said to myself. At least that is not too difficult a question to answer. At times, some of our guests ask questions well beyond my competence. In reply to her I said, "It can all be summarized in one word: prayer."

Prayer is the beginning and the end of the monk's life. By

cultivating humility of mind and heart the monk strives daily for unceasing prayer. He musk seek it with a pure and humble heart, not for the sake of consolation or delight, but solely for the sake of finding God and finding himself in God. In the midst of despair, persecution, or desolation, prayer is an anchor of joy for the monk. Prayer is his only home.

Prayer is the kindling fire that brings forth a new birth in the soul of the monk. Through prayer, he receives from above the pure and free gift of a continual awareness of God's presence. This is a great mystery, but one that suffices for the monk. He wishes only to surrender completely to a God that pours his life into every inch of the monk's being. God loves to be sought and pursued by his creatures. Prayer incites us to seek him daily. It is through prayer that the Holy Spirit feeds into us that extraordinary longing, that almost unspeakable craving, to see God's face. Prayer is the beginning, the in-between, and the end of a monk's life. It is the one reality that answers all his needs.

— JUNE 8 —

Conversation on Prayer

I fall at the feet of my Master, begging, beseeching, praying, worshiping and calling out to him with love and fear.

THEOPHAN THE RECLUSE

Yesterday's conversation about prayer continues today. The guest who seems to be very serious about prayer asked this morning if we could go a bit further into the subject. Back in her home state, she belongs to a group that practices what is called "Centering Prayer." Throughout the years, she told me, she has had many fruitful contacts with a variety of monasteries. It seems therefore natural that she would be interested in the topic of prayer, and in particular, monastic prayer.

After listening to a few of her questions and reflections, I responded that inner prayer is a very personal experience, not always easy to talk about. Monks by nature recoil from such

personal revelations. "Prayer," I said, "is the most precious activity in the monk's life, in the monk's day. It is that most intimate of relationships which is kept secret within the heart's enclosure, where the monk is most alone with his God. How can
one, then, dare speak about it?"

She, in spite of my short response, wished to continue and
inquired about the role of solitude and silence in the prayer. "Are
they absolutes?" she asked. "Are they really essential and necessary for an authentic prayer life?"

"God alone can answer those questions," I said to her. "It is
certainly true that He can reveal himself to a soul in manifold
ways, anywhere. Often, he enjoys meeting us in the most unexpected places." She appeared perplexed, so I continued: "The
monastic tradition has always emphasized the necessity of both
solitude and silence as requirements for those who apply themselves exclusively to prayer. Silence and solitude are indispensable tools for a solid life of prayer. Silence, interior and exterior,
pave the road for communication with God. Without silence, the
road is not accessible."

I could sense she craved to hear more about the virtues of
aloneness. "Solitude frees us from our particular attachments to
others, to ourselves, from our strong dependence on security and
worldly values. It compels us to look at God alone for our sustenance, for friendship, for comfort. In solitude, the monk never
ceases praying, never ceases knocking and calling upon him who
is the only one left to him. Solitude, seen from this perspective, is
not a negative experience or a deprivation. On the contrary,
monastic solitude can be incalculably rich, immensely positive.
When cultivated properly, humbly, it creates the right climate
that makes unceasing prayer possible. Just as silence paves the
way for closer communication with God, solitude leads the soul
to the harmony and joy of intimacy and communion with him."

— JUNE 9 —

Saint Ephrem the Syrian

Thanks to the Fountainhead sent for our salvation.
Thanks to the Compassionate One who bore our pain.
Glory to your coming that restored humankind to life.
Glory to the one who came to us by his First-born. Glory
to that silent one who spoke by means of his voice, glory
to that sublime one who was seen by means of his dawn.
Glory to the spiritual one who was well-pleased that his
Child should become a body so that through him His
power might be felt.

SAINT EPHREM, HYMNS ON THE NATIVITY

June is the month of perennials and wildflowers. As one drives along the local back roads, varieties of wildflowers seem to emerge from almost nowhere. The wildflowers that catch our eyes are exceptionally lovely in their natural habitats. They seem eager to show their rare beauty on the very spot where the Divine Gardener has planted them! I am especially fond of the ox-eye daisies. At present, they are blooming profusely, not only beside the back roads and in the fields but also in our vegetable and herb gardens, where they were never planted. I frequently combine them with other flowers for the chapel floral arrangements.

Today, we celebrate the feast of Saint Ephrem, a great monk and poet of the Syrian church. Ephrem was born in Nisibis, early in the fourth century. There he received classical training needed for the prodigious amount of writing and teaching he was to accomplish throughout his life. For Saint Ephrem, his sole purpose was to be a worthy instrument of the Holy Spirit and thus continue to build the Church, the Body of Christ.

Saint Ephrem is often described as "the harp of the Holy Spirit." He is principally appreciated for his various hymns on the Nativity of Christ, paradise, the Church, and in praise of virginity. He wrote with exquisite tenderness about the Theotokos, the Mother of God. In fact, according to Saint Ephrem, Our Lady was chosen to give birth to the Son of God because she was the human creature most pleasing in his sight. From all eternity, says Saint Ephrem, Mary was assigned to give birth, nourish, and care for he who himself gave life, nourishment, and care to her:

> By power from Him Mary's womb became able
> To bear the one who bears all.
> From the great treasury of all creation
> Mary gave to him everything that she gave.
> She gave him milk from what he made exist.
> She gave him food from what he had created.
> As God, he gave milk to Mary.
> In turn, as man, he was given suck by her.

In his hymns, Ephrem portrayed vividly God's radical identification with his own creation as a result of the Incarnation. Through the mystery of the Incarnation, says Ephrem, God transcended his own creation and imprinted himself onto it like a seal. God acted thus not because of a particular need, but simply out of his unfathomable, passionate love for every being he created. God never loves in the abstract, only in the concrete. For Ephrem, love is the sole explanation for the Incarnation of the Word into the concrete body of a humble maiden from Nazareth.

— JUNE 10 —

O Beata Trinitas

O God, we offer you our praise and worship, unbegotten Father, only-begotten Son, Holy Spirit, constant friend and guide; most holy and undivided Trinity, to you be glory for all ages.

VESPERS ANTIPHON TRINITY

L ast evening, the monastery bells summoned us to Vespers, greeting joyfully the arrival of today's glorious Feast of the Most Holy Trinity. A week after Pentecost's abundant pouring of the Holy Spirit upon us, we are led by this same Spirit into the contemplation of the mystery of mysteries that is so far above our minds, so how can we dare speak of it? I gladly leave to Saint Athanasius, one of our giant Fathers in faith, the task of deciphering something of this august mystery:

> We acknowledge the Trinity, holy and perfect, to consist of the Father, the Son, and the Holy Spirit. In this Trinity there is no intrusion of any alien element or of anything from outside, nor is the Trinity a blend of creative and created being. It is a wholly creative and energizing reality, self-consistent and undivided in its active power, for the Father makes all things through the Word and in the Holy Spirit, and in this way the unity of the Holy Trinity is preserved. Accordingly, in the faith of the church, one God is preached, one God who is above all things and through all things and in all things. God is above all things as Father, for he is principle and source; he is through all things through the Word; and he is in all things in the Holy Spirit.

Each time we make the Sign of the Cross we bless ourselves in the name of the Father, and of the Son, and of the Holy Spirit, and thus confess, again and again, our adherence to the Trinitarian mystery. At every Sunday liturgy, we are invited at the moment of the *Credo* to profess our faith in the eternal reality of the three divine Persons: Father, Son, and Holy Spirit. Through finite words, we try to express that which is beyond any human comprehension: the mystery of three distinct Persons, yet only one God. That is as far as our minds can go. Beyond that, lies God's own mystery, the intimate life of love between these three divine Persons.

The *Credo* must never be recited lightly. On the contrary, we must be diligent when we profess our faith in the mystery, for this attentiveness leads simultaneously to an attitude of deep inner prayer. And it is through prayer alone that we can experience something of the ineffable presence of the three divine Persons abiding within us. It is in our innermost solitude that they communicate with us, for Jesus promised: *If anyone loves me, he will keep my Word, and my Father will love him, and we shall come to him, and make our home with him.*

June Roses

O, my love is like a red, red rose that's newly sprung in June.

ROBERT BURNS

Today, as I step out into the cut-flower garden, I am blissfully dazed by the glorious rose blossoms. During this time between the solemnity of the Holy Trinity and that of Corpus Christi, I look at the roses as God's generous gift to us, to the garden, to the whole world. The roses make our garden look as if it were recently rearranged by the angels; it bespeaks of God's presence in our midst. The newly bloomed roses have such a sweet and fragrant scent, and they possess a certain magic in themselves, linking in unusual harmony what we see and smell with what we feel. Truly, roses are unique among flowers!

An ancient flower, the rose is found in all sorts of climates and continents. It was already known in biblical times, for it is mentioned in the Scriptures. The prophet Isaiah, in particular, makes allusion that the desert shall "blossom as the rose," and the bride of the Song of Songs describes herself as "the rose of Sharon." During the Middle Ages, many monasteries specialized in the cultivation of roses, for the rose was often considered a symbol of the Mother of God. One often notices in medieval imagery that Mary is holding the child Jesus in one hand and a rose in the other. Medieval monks also believed that after Our Lady's Dormition roses blossomed over her tomb as a symbol of her glorious Assumption into heaven. Mary was often referred to as the *Rosa Mystica*, and in many of her hymns the allegory endures. One of the stanzas in the lovely Akathist hymn starts with these words: *Hail, from whom alone there springs / The unfading Rose; / Hail, for you have borne / The sweetly-smelling Apple. / Hail, unwedded Mother, nosegay of the only King / And preservation of the world.*

In the Christian tradition, the rose is also a symbol of the martyrs, who spilled their blood for confessing Christ. In medieval and early Renaissance paintings, martyrs are often depicted with a crown of roses on their brows, a symbol of their victory. Today, the liturgy recalls the memory of one of them, Saint Barnabas, a disciple and martyr of the Lord.

Originally named Joseph, he was given the name Barnabas, which means "son of encouragement." He was thus called, for in his great generosity he sold a piece of his land and put the money at the disposal of the early Christian community. As portrayed by Luke in Acts, it was also Barnabas who introduced the newly converted Paul to that same Christian community. The Book of Acts also relates how Barnabas was chosen by the Holy Spirit to complete the number of the Apostles. After closely collaborating with Saint Paul in strengthening and comforting the local churches, he shed his blood for Christ. According to tradition, his martyrdom occurred in Cyprus, which was also his country of origin. The Lauds hymn, sung at dawn this morning, joyfully acclaims his praises: "With the Apostles, Barnabas, the Levite, shines in glory won by many labors. Through love of Jesus, he despised as nothing all that he suffered. Land and possessions he abandoned also, charity's ardor marked his earnest teaching."

— JUNE 12 —

Capital Punishment

Thou shall not murder.

EXODUS 20:13

This week, as the federal government approves the death penalty for suspected terrorists, may well be considered a time of infamy in the United States. This fact may not be as surprising as it seems, for, ultimately, to people of faith, no government has the power to execute another human being. God alone gives life, and he alone has the right to take it away.

As a Christian monk and pacifist, I have always been in total opposition to capital punishment, war, or any other form of violence. I find it difficult to comprehend why the United States, where we enjoy God's abundant blessings, continues to be the only Western nation to uphold such a cruel and inhumane system of justice. In Europe, abolition of the death penalty is a firm reality and requirement for membership in the European Union.

When I am confronted with such sinister evil, the only recourse remains prayer. As I prayed the psalms and the Jesus Prayer, I wove humbly into my prayer the person facing the possibility of this punishment and those who wished to punish him. Ultimately, all of us are in dire need of God's loving mercy.

I'll never forget the man who once told me he stood for the three G's: God, guns, and guts. When I asked him what he meant by guts, he responded, "It takes courage to support the death penalty." I simply replied, "And it takes faith to be against it. I don't see how you can join the holy name of God with guns and killing, when Jesus preached exactly the opposite."

Recently, I encountered a man whose parents were cruelly killed about twenty years ago. Since then, all he could do was hate—not only the perpetrator but almost everyone he came in contact with. One day, almost by an act of Providence, he found himself in the very jail where the killer of his parents was imprisoned. Once he realized this, he asked to see him. They met, spoke a few words, and suddenly, without any previous design or preparation, he heard himself saying to the killer, "I forgive you." When he left the prison, he told me, he felt an extraordinary sense of liberation. The horrible burden of hate he had been carrying all those years was suddenly lifted. He said, "At that very instant, for the first time in years I felt light, alive, free. It was as if I were a new person. Abruptly, I recovered my old appreciation for nature: I noticed the beauty of the light and the blue sky, I heard with joy the song of the birds, I realized the wonder of the trees around me. For almost twenty years I had lost all of that. For the first time, in a very long time, I was at peace."

I then interjected, "You were at peace because you were able to forgive." And he simply nodded. No other words were uttered, for how can one explain the mystery of forgiveness, the grace and immense peace that is imparted with it?

Indeed, forgiveness is never easy. God asks much of us when he asks us to forgive, but he also rewards abundantly those who forgive in his name. Every day, I continue to pray that the Lord may gradually change our hearts and inner attitudes, so that slowly we all recognize the evil of capital punishment. Then one day we will break down this barbaric and senseless law. We must never cease praying, for only prayer and fasting can overcome certain evils.

— JUNE 13 —

A Heavy Burden

A good portion of the evils that afflict mankind is due to the erroneous belief that life can be made secure by violence.

LEO TOLSTOY

This week I feel both physically and emotionally tired, as if I were carrying a heavy weight (in French, a *fardeau*, or burden). Encountering violence in any form is exhausting and a cause for dislocation. It is difficult for me to understand how capital punishment is taken so lightly and accepted by so many. The death penalty, in my eyes, be that of a criminal or an innocent person, is always a violent act. It is the killing, for whatever reason, of another human being who is made in the image and likeness of God.

Perhaps what is so difficult to bear is the justification given by some for their approval of capital punishment. Without judging anyone in particular, these people seem to be blinded by an inner violence that makes no room for compassion, forgiveness, or reconciliation. I recently mentioned to a visitor that both compassion and forgiveness, as taught in the Gospels, are immensely powerful experiences. They become a source of inner release to those who yield to their influence. "In contrast," I added, "when we support capital punishment or retribution, we insist on a rationality of justice that is based on anger, hurt, vengeance, and hate. This perspective denies victims the healing power that springs from forgiveness and compassion and make it impossible for victims to experience the inner healing they so need. Only forgiveness and compassion can ultimately lead to healing, to solace, to acceptance, to peace."

Compassion and forgiveness do not deny our own personal suffering, nor that of the victim. Indeed there is no disputing that when someone hurts or kills someone we love, we all suffer: the victim suffers, the perpetrator suffers, everyone suffers. What Christian forgiveness and compassion do is to allow us to move beyond our dark feelings and negative judgments into a different realm: one of stillness and light. They inspire us to transcend our brokenness, our hurt, our tragedy, and strive instead for wholeness and redemption. This is the testament Jesus left us from the cross: "Father, forgive them, for they do not know what they do."

Saint Francis, a faithful disciple of the Lord, knew well the secret of true joy found in compassion and forgiveness. He taught it thusly:

> Lord, make me an instrument of your peace,
> Where there is hatred, let me sow love.
> Where there is offense, pardon.
> Where there is discord, reconciliation...
> For it is in forgiving that we ourselves obtain pardon,
> It is in dying that we rise to eternal life.

— JUNE 14 —

Sheep Shearing

As shepherds seek out their flock when they are among their scattered sheep, so I will seek out my sheep. I will rescue them from all the places to which they have been scattered on a day of clouds and thick darkness. I will bring them out from the peoples and gather them from the countries, and will bring them into their own land....I will feed them with good pasture, and the mountain heights of Israel shall be their pasture; there they shall lie down in good grazing land, and they shall feed on rich pasture on the mountains of Israel. I myself will be the shepherd of my sheep, and I will make them lie down, says the Lord GOD. I will seek the lost, and I will bring back the strayed, and I will bind up the injured, and I will strengthen the weak, but the fat and the strong I will destroy. I will feed them with justice.

EZEKIEL 34:12–16

Here in the monastery, June is the usual month in which we shear our sheep. It is a ritual, part of a yearly routine. By now, most of the lambs have been weaned from the mother ewes, and before the heat of summer arrives, it is time to remove the sheep's heavy fleece which has been growing longer and heavier since winter. In our monastic calendar, the yearly shearing usually takes place around June 15, the feast of Saint Germaine, a humble shepherdess from the south of France.

In times past, the sheep were washed in a stream before their fleece could be shorn. This custom still continues in certain areas of the world, such as the region of the Pyrenees in France. Here, however, the fleece from our sheep show little signs of filth, so we can dispense with this extra chore.

I used to shear the sheep myself, and then sold the wool in a nearby town. With the years, however, I discovered that it was more practical to have the sheep shorn by somebody else, who then takes the wool as compensation. For years, I have relied on the talents of a local man who faithfully comes to do the job within days of receiving the request. His name is Mr. Fink, and he always demands that I lay aside whatever else I may be doing and concentrate instead on being his assistant. I usually start the task by rallying the sheep into an enclosed pen. Then, we connect several long electric cables for the shears to an outlet in the monastery. (The electric power in our barn has been disconnected for years to save on the use of electricity.)

While I am connecting the cables, Mr. Fink spreads on the ground a large plastic sheet in order to keep the wool clean. Then, one at a time, I carry each of the sheep to Mr. Fink. He places the sheep in such a way as not to move them too suddenly, supporting their weight with his thighs. I stand close by as he neatly labors with his shears through every one in our flock, except, of course, the lambs. At first, the sheep show their displeasure, but once firmly positioned, they allow Mr. Fink's expert hands to accomplish the task. As each sheep gets shorn, I separate the dark black fleece from the lighter one and then place each in different plastic bags. The fleece is usually very oily and pleasant: a good sign. As he finishes shearing each of the sheep, he also cuts their long nails. After hours of heavy laboring, the job is completed and the sheep are ready to face the heat of summer. As I help carry the bags of wool into Mr. Fink's van and share with him some produce from our garden, (he always insists on inspecting the garden!), I can't help but hope that once the wool is sold and spun, it shall provide clothing and comfort for other human beings, perhaps for a poor family.

Today, as one more daily duty reaches it conclusion, I express my gratitude to God for the excellent weather he granted for the shearing. It helped enormously with the task. I thank Mr. Fink for always coming to our rescue. Lastly, I thank our humble sheep for the gift of their wool. I know somehow, that in God's own mysterious Providence, it shall serve to make someone happy.

— JUNE 15 —

A Garden of Simple Pleasures

Earth's crammed with heaven and every common bush afire with God.

ELIZABETH BARRETT BROWNING

More and more I become conscious of the simple details that make a garden an enchanted place. Today, as I strolled through the garden during the early morning hours, I saw dew drops on the leek tops and on the Swiss chard leaves that shone like precious pearls. As I proceeded through the paths to inspect other plants, I was mindful of the first sunrays beginning to shine in the garden's enclosure. Filtering through some of the trees' shadows, the sunrays rested gently on the lovely French marigolds, making them shine like diamonds. In an unobtrusive corner, there is a patch of wild daisies blooming, unbearably bright. They are so becoming to that spot, yet I do not recall having planted them there.

In the garden, beauty is always found intertwined between the sublime and that which is most humble, most ordinary. This should not be surprising, for gardening is a collaborative effort between the Creator and us, his humble creatures. I have ceased, a long time ago, to labor in the garden solely for aesthetic reasons. Instead, I find joy in the small and seemingly insignificant wonders the garden renders daily. Even the tedious task of weeding can provide a joyful experience. Today, after weeding for a couple of hours, I looked at the spot just cleared and suddenly viewed the garden differently. I saw a garden transformed by loving care and persistent devotion. In my mind, I hold no doubt that a garden is in a very special way a tabernacle of the Most High, a place where he delights in his own creation.

— JUNE 16 —

The Herb Garden

Every flower of the field, every fiber of a plant, every particle of an insect, carries with it the impress of its Maker, and can—if duly considered—read us lectures of ethics or divinity.

THOMAS POPE BLOUNT

From the very beginnings of monastic life, the first monks collected herbs from all sources—the desert, the woods, the fields, the waterfront—and transplanted them into their own little gardens. These basic herbs were primarily used by monasteries for healing purposes, to relieve the pain of an older monk, and to provide cures for people of the surrounding villages. In those early centuries, monasteries indirectly served as local health clinics where people often went for help. Mindful of this tradition, Saint Benedict insisted in his Rule that "Special care must be taken of the sick so that they may be looked after, as Christ said 'I was sick and you visited me.'" In another paragraph, Saint

Benedict wrote: "The abbot must ensure the sick are never neglected."

To my mind, however, those early monks, thrifty as they were, also extended their use of herbs for cooking and flavoring their food. They concocted herb teas, both for medicinal and culinary purposes. They manufactured soap and other toiletries, combining herbs and natural oils. They recognized the invaluable and multiple herb uses, and hence they were deeply thankful to the Lord for providing such a pure gift to them.

Our small monastery cultivates an old-fashioned herb garden where the crops are later preserved and sold in small bottles. The bottles contain a combination of dried culinary herbs, something similar to *herbes de Provence*, but containing an expanded variety. The products of our small herb industry are sold via a small business that sells monastic products nationwide. Besides this traditional herb garden, herbs are also cultivated in our vegetable garden and in some corners of the flower gardens. The herbs in the vegetable garden are strictly for culinary usage. Some botanists believe that combining vegetables, herbs, and flowers renders a healthier harvest. Because of past proven experiences, mine and those of others, I wholeheartedly adhere to this theory.

Until recently, the vegetable garden has demanded almost all of my undivided attention. I perceive myself a bit neglectful of the herb garden, where most of the herbs are perennials and thus survive from year to year. Lately, I have noticed the tremendous intrusion of weeds into the otherwise lovely herb enclosure. Today, leaving other cares behind, I dedicated all possible time and energy to the cleaning, weeding, and restoration of our Saint Joseph herb garden. I prayed to the saint to assist me in the task and then single-mindedly applied myself to the chore. I love renewing my acquaintance with these aromatic plants. Working with herbs, one gets to know their essence and understand their subtle qualities. Herbs are earthy and unpretentious in their rare humbleness. They teach the gardener to remain firmly rooted in the soil, in this holy ground where the Lord left his footsteps as an imprint of his creation.

— JUNE 17 —

Corpus Christi

Lord! You showed your goodness to your children by giving them bread from heaven. You filled the hungry with good things, and the rich you sent away empty.

VESPERS ANTIPHON OF THE FEAST

The Rule of Saint Benedict makes no specific mention of the celebration of the Eucharist. From other sources, however, it is commonly understood that the Eucharist was only celebrated in the monastery on Sundays and on special feast days. This was the common observance of most Eastern and Western monasteries, having both evolved from the same desert monastic tradition. Saint Benedict, much as the Desert Fathers and Mothers, was almost reluctant to expand upon the Eucharistic mystery. He would have been terribly uncomfortable with many of today's so-called Eucharistic devotions, with almost no relation to the specific and only purpose that the Lord gave to this sacrament. Saint Benedict was a man of the Bible, and all of his understanding about the Eucharist proceeded from that unique source. He also found support for his approach in the common patristic tradition of the Church. He knew that Christ has given Himself as food to us and that He said, "Take and eat. Take and drink," and that the Lord added no more.

The great, inexhaustible mystery of the Eucharist, for Saint Benedict, lied in the sacred act of communion. Christ, the Son of God, had this burning desire to share his intimate life with each of us, and thus he gave himself as food and drink. Nothing, in the experience of our Christian lives, is comparable to the supreme mystery of eucharistic communion. It is God's incomprehensible gift, the gift that allows us to say with Saint Paul: "It is no longer I that live, but that Christ lives in me."

For Saint Benedict, as for all early monks, Eucharistic communion was a participation in the totality of Christ. It transformed the communicant, in the words of Saint Athanasius, "into the Word," the second Person of the Blessed Trinity. "Through sacramental communion," says Athanasius, "the Christian is Christified." Holy Communion, in the language of the Fathers, is the "food of immortality," the food that contains the promise of eternal life for all. "The one who eats my flesh and drinks my life has eternal life," says the Lord. Saint Theodore of Cyrus goes as far as to claim that "through consuming the flesh and the blood of the Spouse, we enter into a union of marriage with the Lord." Christ comes to us in holy Communion to make our lives complete, radiant, and God-filled. Indeed, it is no longer us, but Christ who lives in us.

To me, nothing portrays better the "monastic approach" to the Eucharist, if one can describe it so, than the attitude conveyed by Saint Mary of Egypt. Just prior to dying, after spending more that forty years in the desert, she expressed her one wish to the monk Zossima:

> At sunset, on the day of the Holy Supper of the Lord, bring me the life-giving Body and Blood of Christ in a holy vessel worthy of such mysteries, and wait for me on the bank of the Jordan, on the inhabited side, so that I can receive and make my communion with the life-giving gifts. From the time on when I made my communion in the church of the Holy Precursor, before crossing the Jordan and entering into the desert, up to this day I have not received the Holy Sacrament. And now I hunger for it with a love which cannot be restrained. This is why I beg and implore of you to fulfill my request.

At the moment of holy Communion, the Mystical Supper of the Lord, all is recapitulated in that one act: Christ is truly present in us, and we are in him. And only with him, only through him, can we enter into the eternal Trinitarian communion of the Father, the Son, and the Holy Spirit.

The Wonder of New Life

You show me the path of life.
In your presence there is fullness of joy.

PSALM 16:11

This morning, in the quiet stillness of the early hours, I approached the barn to check the sheep. Once inside, I noticed a mother hen on her nest; beneath her, three bright young chicks had just hatched. For weeks she has been hiding under a makeshift crib used to feed the sheep during the winter months. About two weeks ago, totally by accident, I discovered where she has been sitting on her eggs. This particular hen is what the neighbors call a "Polish chicken," and a bit wild one at that. Often these sort of chickens hide their nests and their eggs, particularly when they are hatching them. This way they feel safe, secured, protected.

This morning, as I faced the wonder of new life, I was once more reminded of the orderliness and harmony God bestows upon his creation. The miracle of new life, renewed today in clandestine fashion in a humble barn, was an intimation of the interrelationship that exists among all of God's works: man, animals, plants, soil, weather, and seasons. We do not exist in isolation. Life comes hidden, wrapped in the mystery of each living organism. These mysteries, no matter how small, reveal our deep interconnectedness. Through faith, we accept living as God intended from the very beginning: respecting that living stream springing from multiple sources and bringing all things into one.

So much of one's daily monastic life consists in the living out, in a humble fashion, of this intimate connection with all the works of the Creator. Whether cultivating the soil, caring for animals, attending to guests, preparing meals, or entering into a sacred silence of prayer, the monk rediscovers the inner force within that connects all elements of life. Through the wonders of God's graciousness, life's web continues to pattern rhythmically our daily existence, recapturing something of the serenity, harmony, and joy of the first moments of creation.

— JUNE 19 —

Saint Romuald

While the eremitical life doubtless claimed adherents in the Western Church, yet for a time no one actually organized it. Its first founder was a man of wondrous holiness and admirable life, Saint Romuald. He was the first to transmit to his contemporaries and to bequeath to future generations the constitutions and rules of eremitic life, not in written form, but by the example of his life and teaching.

PAUL GUSTINIANI

Today, the monastic calendar celebrates the memory of Saint Romuald, founder of the Camaldolese hermits. The Roman Martyrology sings his praises in these terms: "Athirst for the living God and desiring the desert life, he left his monastery of Saint Appolinar—in Classe near Ravenna, his home town, three years after making monastic profession. His personal experience and the Holy Spirit's inspiration led him to Camaldoli in Tuscany, where he organized a new form of eremitical life."

Saint Romuald reminds us that the monk must at all cost cherish silence as a most intimate friend. Solitude and silence have but one only aim: the pursuit of unceasing prayer, the facilitation for continual conversation and dialogue with Christ, who inhabits the depths of our hearts. Solitude is this immense space that sets us free to be our true selves in the presence of the living God. One of the early Desert Fathers used to repeat to his disciples: "Stay put in your cell and your cell will teach you everything."

One of Saint Romuald's disciples, Blessed Paul Gustiniani, wrote in praise of solitude something that could have come from Romuald's own mouth:

O blessed solitude which teaches humans to come to their senses and to desire to see, as much as men can, the Divine Majesty. O solitude, the foretaste of heaven's delight, the sample of celestial joy, granted to men living in the flesh! When holy souls weep in exile, impatient for the eternal joy that they hope to attain in the homeland, you alone, beloved solitude, relieve their long wait by glimpses of the bliss to come. O solitude, not well appreciated by those who have not lived in your company! O solitude, never sufficiently praised: you change human misery into angelic bliss. You enable the soul to adhere always to God the Creator, all good and almighty, who caresses the soul like a cherished bride. You delight it with divine words, as sweet as the kisses of a bridegroom....Truly, until I was alone, I never really lived. Until I was alone, I was not with myself. Until I was alone, I never drew close to my Creator.

Saint Romuald insists on the value of physical solitude as a practical aid to entering into the inner chamber, where one can be alone with God. Solitary places have a great role to play in one's spiritual life, for such formal solitude leads to true solitude of the soul. The first Egyptian and Palestinian monks chose the desert as a way of safeguarding this "blessed solitude." In later centuries, monks chose remote solitary places, sometimes in the mountains or in a deep forest, for building their monasteries and hermitages. The aim was always the same: the preservation of physical solitude for its dwellers, a solitude conducive to continual recollection and silence, a solitude like that of Mount Sinai where, in the stillness of the mountain, the Creator reveals his name to His creature.

— JUNE 20 —

Heavenly Breath of Summer

Oh, bring again my heart's content, thou Spirit of the summertime!

WILLIAM ALLINGHAM

Tomorrow marks the official entry into the summer season. *La belle saison,* as summer is called in France, is a time of profound changes in the garden, a time when vegetables begin to ripen, a time when the flowers love to show the best of their texture and colors. As the season advances, under the influence of a hot sun, the flowers become brighter and our vegetables more succulent and immensely desirable at the table. At present, the strawberries are rapidly being consumed, and the blackberries shall soon follow.

The sound of mowers can be heard throughout the countryside, as farmers continue their hay-cutting in the surrounding fields and meadows. The sweet scent of summer is all around us: in the air, in the gardens, and in the woods and meadows. I am particularly struck by the intoxicating smell arising from the alfalfa field as it is slowly trimmed. Whenever I look at those fields being worked, and inhale the sublime scent they emit, I recognize the glory of God being solidly manifested on our earth, across our green meadows and into our nearby hills. The farmer and the gardener may be busy at work, but so is God. From a close distance, I quietly observe the wonders of God's acting out in our universe, concretely in our gardens and meadows, in our farms and fields. Quickly, I feel enveloped in a sentiment of gratitude and thanksgiving. *Sursum corda.* With gratitude I lift my heart unto the Lord, offering him endless praise. *Gratias agamus Domino Deo nostro.*

— JUNE 21 —
Summertime

Season of mists and mellow fruitfulness
Close bosom-friend of the maturing sun;
Conspiring with him how to load and bless
With fruit the vines that round the thatch-eaves run.

JOHN KEATS

The summer days grow steadily hot and dry. The best times for work in the garden are the early morning hours or late afternoon into the evening. If a grave necessity arises, I may return after Vespers to do some extra work among the vegetables. This is not my preference, but the reality of the weather and the demands of the garden are such that often I have no choice.

One of summer's subtle changes is clearly manifested in the light which is intense, heavy, and at times almost unbearably bright. The clear, cool spring skies are now but a distant memory. Living in the country makes one deeply sensitive to light changes. Sometimes even the slightest and most subtle of changes are noticeable. Once we become habituated to a certain light quality, we expect it to remain thus for a long time.

For farmers and gardeners, summer is a time when we begin to gather the first fruits of our labor. For a few weeks now I have been harvesting diverse salad greens, radishes, sorrel, and fresh herbs from the garden. They have grown at a record speed! Now I am beginning to pick the sweet peas, for which I have earnest feelings, also some tender *haricots verts*, and even some early small white turnips whose seeds I brought back from France. It is important to pick frequently, for the more you pick, the more the plants yield. If it doesn't rain, it is imperative that one waters the garden often. Some vegetables, more than others, need frequent watering. This is particularly true of cucumbers, zucchinis, peppers, yellow squash, and others. Maintaining a garden is indeed a full-time job! But the task becomes a fraction easier by the exuberance and beauty of the season, by the realization of our close collaboration with the Creator, and, most certainly, by relishing the taste of the garden's produce at the table!

— JUNE 22 —

The Sacred Heart

Love, by a certain instinctive movement, longs to put itself forth and transfer the good it possesses to someone it loves with all its love.

BALDWIN OF FORDE, EARLY CISTERCIAN FATHER

The feast of the Sacred Heart of Jesus is an invitation to celebrate God's indescribable love—the love that motivated the Son of God to become incarnate and the love that makes God continue to pursue each of us. When Our Lord appeared to Saint Margaret Mary, he uttered these words: "Behold, the Heart that has loved mankind so much." These words make us realize that love, in reality, is a Person. It is the person of Jesus Christ, who is himself love incarnate, and the most pure manifestation of God's love for each of us. God so loved the world that he sent into it his only-begotten Son.

The mystery of Christianity, of the good news of the gospel, is summed up in that one word: love. It is the one response from God to everything. Without always knowing or being conscious of it, love is that which we are constantly seeking.

The feast of the Sacred Heart is an invitation for us to focus solely on that ultimate and timeless reality. It is an invitation to welcome Jesus, the lover of humankind, into our lives and to become one with him. As we receive his loving embrace, we are led to the source of all that love, the mystery of the Trinity, where we are given a taste of the oneness of Divine Love: "When Love is in me, I am one with Love...."

The feast of the Sacred Heart of Jesus is an inspiration to us to become totally free and at home with the boundless truth of God's love. Today, we pray to the Holy Spirit to continue to captivate our hearts by the love that springs forth from the heart of Jesus. Following in his footsteps and example, we shall learn daily from Jesus, our Master, to love as God alone loves and to love all that God loves. There are no degrees or limitations to this love. There is only the supreme ecstasy of knowing ourselves at one with him whose very nature is love.

— JUNE 23 —

A Summer Poem

Go forth, my heart, and seek delight
In all the gifts of God's great might,
These pleasant summer hours;
Look how the plains for thee and me
Have decked themselves most fair to see,
All bright and sweet with flowers.

The trees stand thick and dark with leaves,
And earth o'er all her dust now weaves
  A robe of living green;
Nor silks of Solomon compare
With glories that the tulips wear,
  Or lilies' spotless sheen.

Thy mighty working, mighty God,
Wakes all my powers; I look abroad
  And can no longer rest;
I too must sing when all things sing,
And from my heart the praises ring
  The Highest lovest best.

CATHERINE WINKWORTH

Today is the feast of the Immaculate Heart of Mary, one of the very few feasts of Our Lady in June. The only other one I know of is the feast of Our Lady of Perpetual Help at the end of the month. The poem by Catherine Winkworth, translated loosely from the German, seems to me so appropriate to today's feast. Didn't Mary, after all, exalt the mighty works of God in her Magnificat?

— JUNE 24 —

Saint John the Baptist

Offspring of a barren mother and friend of him who was born of a Virgin, you have worshiped him by leaping in your mother's womb and have baptized him in the waters of the Jordan. We entreat you, intercede with him, O Holy Prophet, that we may escape from the mighty tempests to come.

FROM THE SYNAXIS OF SAINT JOHN THE BAPTIST

One of June's glorious events, a celebration that makes June and early summer special, is the feast of Saint John the Baptist—a feast that brings great joy to this small monastic corner. Monastics through the centuries have professed an affinity for John the Baptist for many reasons. He is a desert saint and thus a model for monks. He was particularly close to Jesus, a friend of the Bridegroom, as a monk or nun aspires to be. He was dear to the heart of Jesus who went so far as to state: "No man born of a woman is greater that John the Baptizer."

Fittingly, since John the Baptist is Jesus' precursor, the story of his birth is told just before that of the birth of the Savior in Luke's Gospel. This is the pedagogy of the Scriptures, which arranges the sequence to explain God's great mystery of the Incarnation of the Son of God. From the very first moment of his conception, John reveled in his unique relationship with the Son of God. Filled with the Holy Spirit, even from his mother's womb, he leaped for joy at the proximity of the Word Incarnate, present in Mary's womb. John was one of the first to greet the Savior's arrival in our midst!

From the moment when the angel announced John's conception to his father, Zachariah, John was entrusted with a special mission. He was going to be God's messenger—the one assigned to prepare the way for the Lord. This unique role as herald of the Messiah is one that John continues to play today. In the apse of our chapel we have a life-size ikon of what is commonly called the Deesis. In this ikon, Christ Pantocrator stands at the center, to his left and right sides are the Theotokos and John the Baptist. In the ikon, I see the Mother of God and the faithful Precursor pointing Christ to me, announcing him, speaking quietly into the ears of my heart about him, revealing his name to me. Not only do they point and speak to me about Christ, but they also speak to him about me; they plead and make intercession for me. Praying with the help of this ikon makes each of the three—the Lord, his Holy Mother, and John the Baptist—all very present and very close in real life.

It is a given that one should pray to the Lord unceasingly, and that one should always count on the protection of the Mother of God. Few, however, think of imploring John the Baptist's intercession. Throughout the years I have become used to doing it in a very short and simple way. Just as I make recourse to the Jesus prayer often, I also like to call upon the Mother of God with a short prayer, "Holy Theotokos, save us," and to Saint John the Baptist with "Holy Precursor of Christ, intercede for my salvation." I repeat these very short invocations throughout the day, even when far from the ikon (though I do, however, keep a small ikon of the Deesis in the car which helps me to pray when I drive). Through recourse to these short simple prayers, the Lord, his Mother, and John the Baptist seem always present in the fabric of daily life. In the ikon, both Mary and John gaze at Christ, and simultaneously they seem to look at me. For my part, I try not to wander too far or too long from their benevolent sight.

In the Eastern Church, every Tuesday of the week is dedicated to Saint John the Baptist. He is honored with the following troparion: *With praise the holy man is remembered, yet for him who has prepared the way, the praise of the Lord himself suffices. For you, O John, are higher in honor than the prophets, since you were chosen to baptize in Jordan's stream him whom you foretold.*

— JUNE 25 —

Garden Weeds

Working outdoors pulling weeds in the spring is a very different proceeding from puttering around doing the same job in the balmy days of summer or early fall.

THALASSA CRUSO

Frequent weeding is part of the daily practice of gardening. It can be a monotonous activity and certainly always a challenge. There is a lot of physical activity involved: one must bend and pull, bend and pull, until the task is accomplished. Because it is rigorous physical labor, I usually spend about one to two hours weeding nonstop, and then change to another needed task in the garden. From time to time, one needs a shift of scene and position, after which one can safely return to more weeding.

Throughout many years of weeding, I have found that the early morning and evening hours are the best suited for me. Those particular moments of the day I recommend because there is usually a cool breeze in the garden, often accompanied by the sweet singing of some of the local birds. I also often weed right after a rain, since the loose ground makes pulling much easier. As I pull the weeds, I assemble them into a large gathering basket. And since the barn is right next to the garden, the sheep are the beneficiaries of the proceedings! Sometimes, when certain weeds are small and tender, I share some of them with our chickens and ducks. Thus, all our farm animals partake of the banquet!

Weekly weeding will continue a bit longer, for the next three or four months or so. I must accept the fact and not procrastinate every time I am confronted with the task. Part of the monastic ascesis is to accept the inevitability of certain chores. What would gardening mean without weeding, I say to myself, as I continue cleaning up around the vegetables. Pulling those weeds seems but a small job in comparison to the delight our vegetables and flowers bring into our daily life.

One sign of contentment in the garden is the seeming disappearance of the sense of time while weeding. It is as if the weeder is completely absorbed in the task and the repetitiveness of the hand movements, suddenly and without noticing, transport me into another realm, one where the hours and moments of the day seem to dissolve into the eternal now, into God's sense of timelessness. This is one of the many paradoxes of a simple, ordinary, menial job, such as weeding. It is one of the many blessings of the monastic day.

— June 26 —

On Writing

Setting down in writing is a lasting memory.
Henry Fielding

The daily habit of committing one's thoughts to writing doesn't come easily. Writing is a craft that demands daily cultivation and application. One's mind begins to expand the more one submits oneself to this notion of rigorous, constant craftsmanship.

It is often difficult to leave behind multiple obligations and apply all of one's soul, mind, and time exclusively to writing for several hours. There is also the matter of the monastic schedule that can at times put a limit on these hours. Fortunately, I am glad to have the precedent of the long monastic tradition which portrays writing as one of the principal occupations of a monk. Dom Jean Leclercq's classic *The Love of Learning and the Desire for God*, which I read many years ago, was a great help in reaching this understanding. Father Leclercq, who visited here up until the time of his death, calls monastic writing "the literature of silence." Monastic writing, according to him, is "perfected in the school of silence, *silentium loquendi magister*, and they [the monks] are destined to give it preference." A heavy responsibility therefore lies with the monk to communicate to others the mysteries of silence.

Whenever possible, I sit down at the desk for close to two hours in the morning or afternoon and allow myself to be engrossed by writing. The craft has become somewhat easier since I began working on the computer, though I still write longhand occasionally. There is something unique about handwriting that cannot be duplicated by the computer. There are days, of course, when nothing seems to burst from one's imagination. It is better then to turn to other occupations and not waste considerable time. On occasion, I feel a bit frustrated not having accomplished as much as expected within the short hours assigned, or by the fact that the schedule sometimes forces me to leave whole sentences incomplete. In spite of these trivial frustrations, I often feel a sense of exhilaration. No one has robbed me from the feeling of fulfillment which comes from being absorbed in the task of writing. It is the same sort of feeling one experiences while working in the garden, making music, preparing a meal, showing empathy towards someone in need, or praying in silence. It is intense, sacred, all-encompassing. One savors the experience of being totally and completely "at one" with the task. One is captured in the beauty of the moment, in the blessing of illumination that springs forth from profound quietude and peace.

— JUNE 27 —

Our Lady of Perpetual Help

Today, we the faithful rejoice, sheltered as we are, O
Mother of God, by your presence. While gazing on your
beloved ikon, we humbly say: Defend us by your
protection, and deliver us from all evil, praying your Son,
Christ our God, to save our souls.

TROPARION TO THE MOTHER OF GOD, OUR DEFENSE

Gardeners, in general, love to talk about their gardens and to compare notes and information with other gardeners. It is no different here in the monastery. I often receive requests from writers who wish to inspect and write about our humble gardens. Since these visitors also wish to photograph the gardens, it means I must continually keep busy weeding and tending to small minutia, as one prepares them to greet the prospective visitors. Thank God a garden is always a happy and cheerful place, and the hours spent there are not only productive but also blissful ones, for a garden is a vivid image of the world as God first created it, a prototype of all that is good upon the land.

Today, the spiritual family of Saint Alphonsus Liguori, the Redemptorists and Redemptoristines, celebrates the feast of Our Lady of Perpetual Help. I try to celebrate whenever I can this feast with our good neighbors, the nearby Redemptoristine Nuns.

The ikon of Our Lady of Perpetual Help was one of my first introductions to ikons, for her image held a prominent place in our home. An ikon of Our Lady is distinguishable from other representations of the Mother of God by its specific forms of expression and by the feeling of holiness it imparts. Those who have become accustomed to praying in front of ikons, be it of the Savior, the Mother of God, or the saints, encounter there the reality of a divine presence, to the extent that our human limitations allow us to understand it.

Through the ikon, the grace from the Holy Spirit goes further and communicates to us the light of God's truth. That truth becomes visible to our fallible human eyes through the symbolism of the ikon. Those who frequently share in our worship here know of the powerful inspiration that ikons provide to our daily prayer. When I am sometimes asked why there are so many ikons in our chapel, I always respond that the ikons, in their humble physical presence, express God's loving presence in our midst. I do not go any further. Words are always poor tools, never sufficient to express a mystery.

— JUNE 28 —

Saint Irenaeus

The glory of God gives life; those who see God receive life. For this reason God, who cannot be grasped, comprehended or seen, allows himself to be seen, comprehended and grasped by men, that he may give life to those who see and receive him.

SAINT IRENAEUS, *A TREATISE AGAINST HERESIES*

Today we keep the memory of Saint Irenaeus, a great and most influential Church Father. He was born in Smyrna early in the second century. Irenaeus was a disciple of the great Saint Polycarp, Bishop of Smyrna, who in turn was a disciple of the Apostle Saint John. This is very important for understanding Saint Irenaeus's teaching, for his greater claim was always the continuity of the apostolic tradition, which he inherited directly from his predecessors: Irenaeus knew Polycarp, Polycarp knew John, and John knew Jesus, the Eternal Word of God.

Saint Irenaeus spent most of his life in France and thus became one of the true fathers of the Church of God in that country. His influence has certainly been a powerful inspiration in my own life. Saint Irenaeus was sent to preach in Lyon and it seems certain that he was ordained a priest there. Shortly thereafter, he succeeded Saint Pothinus as bishop of that city. As bishop, he showed special care for the poor and those in a great need, be they pagan or members of his flock. Saint Ireneus continued the preaching of the Gospel as he had received it from his early teachers. Burning with a zeal to preserve the purity and integrity of the apostolic faith, he became its great defender against the errors of the Gnostics. At the end, when his work on earth was completed, Saint Irenaeus received the crown of martyrdom.

In many ways, our present times are not unlike those of Ireneus. The temptation to diverge from the apostolic faith remains as strong today as during the time of the saint. Threats to the faith are sometimes confusing and hard to fight. There are those who, for example, idealize the Middle Ages, thus prefer returning to the liturgy of those days. They promote the Tridentine Mass as the only true Mass (as some of the French *integristes* call it, *la Messe de toujours*, or "the eternal Mass"). I ask myself, what happened to previous liturgies such as those of the early Church or of other rites? What about the first Eucharist as it was celebrated by Jesus himself, in Aramaic and not in Latin? Where do they fit into their schemes?

Sometimes such groups refuse to worship with the rest of the Christian community which follows the general Church norms, and demand instead that special dispensations be granted to them. Saint Irenaeus reminds us today, in a timely fashion, that the true apostolic faith is not encapsulated in a particular time or culture. Faith, by its very nature, comes from God, is a gift from God, and even if revealed at a particular moment of history, transcends all times and given cultures. Thus our Christian faith is neither Greek nor Roman, neither Jewish nor Arab, neither European nor American, neither Eastern nor Western, but only the result of the gratuity and largess of God for all times and all peoples: Go and announce the Good News to all nations, and baptize them in the name of the Father, and of the Son, and of the Holy Spirit.

— JUNE 29 —

The Apostles Peter and Paul

*How glorious are the apostles of Christ. In life they loved
one another. In death they rejoice together forever.*
VESPERS ANTIPHON OF THE FEAST

Saint Augustine, in his sermon for today's feast comments: "This day has been made holy by the martyrdom of the blessed apostles Peter and Paul. We are, therefore, not talking about some

obscure martyrs. For their voice has gone forth to all the world....
These martyrs realized what they taught: they pursued justice,
they confessed the truth, they died for it."

Jesus chose his own disciples and, during the three years of
his public life, he gradually introduced them to a particular intimacy with him. He prepared them for the crisis they were to
undergo when they would see him humiliated and crucified. They
didn't do very well at this moment, especially Peter. However,
through the experience of the death and the Resurrection of Jesus,
the apostles achieved the maturity needed for the mission that
Jesus was going to entrust to them.

The difficult hour of Jesus' Ascension arrived. It was the
moment of separation, the hour of their Master's departure to
his Father. What was to become of them? Their sole consolation
was Mary's continuing presence and the impending arrival of the
Holy Spirit, who their Master had promised to them.

Each of the apostles was missioned to announce the good
news of God's kingdom and be witnesses, to the point of death
and martyrdom, to the truth of Jesus' Resurrection. What they
saw while living with him during those last three years of his life,
they were now to announce, teach, and proclaim to the whole
world. This was no easy task, especially for simple, unlettered
fishermen. But Jesus promised to be with them until the end. He
also promised them the Holy Spirit, who would inspire in them
every word and deed.

As we look back now on the development of the early Church
we see that all of the Apostles (not only Peter and Paul), in spite
of their weaknesses and fears, fulfilled the mission entrusted to
them. Above all, they confessed and proclaimed with their lives
Christ the Lord, the Son of the living God. At the end, adhering
faithfully to the teachings of their Master, they were able to give
their lives for the sake of his name. Today, as we keep the memory
of the glorious Apostles Peter and Paul, we can also look to the
example and witness of their lives. We can take courage from
them, learning of their human weaknesses, very much like ours,
and yet always ready to confess and die for their Lord. As Saint
Augustine exhorts us at the end of his sermon: "Let us embrace

what they believed, their life, their labors, their sufferings, their preaching and their confession of faith."

Today is also a good day to pray for all the shepherds of God's Church. I am afraid the example of the apostles is not very visible in many of our bishops and prelates today. Too often we pay lip service to the apostolicity of the Church, without feeling obliged to live and to act as did the apostles of Jesus. A Gospel lifestyle remains a must for everyone that takes his or her Christian life seriously, including those in positions of authority. One can only claim to be a disciple of the Lord or to represent Jesus to the extent that one tries to follow the example of the Master. As the Lord himself taught us, "The disciple is no greater than the Master."

— JUNE 30 —

Out in the Fields With God

Much of our summer is spent outdoors. The days are longer and more inviting. Therefore, we tend to linger with our outside summer activities. There is so much pleasure working in the garden, with our farm animals, with watching things grow. God seems present everywhere in nature. Every element speaks his name, reveals his face, incites us to pray. Today, I took time to reread and enjoy a poem (whose author is unknown) that expresses all of this with simplicity and clarity:

> The little cares that fretted me,
> I lost them yesterday,
> Among the fields, above the sea,
> Among the winds at play.
> The foolish fears of what may happen,
> I cast them all away
> Among the clover-scented grass,
> Among the rustling of the corn,
> Where drowsy poppies nod,
> Where ill thoughts die and good are born—
> Out in the fields with God.

JULY

— JULY 1 —

A Sultry Month

*July is a large portion of the year, which is made glorious
summer by the sun.*

ANONYMOUS

As July, the seventh month of the year, advances, the heat
increases dramatically. In ancient Rome, the period between
July 1 and August 15 was known as the *Canicula*, the "doggy
days of summer," or the famous *jours de la Canicule*, as the French
call it. Occasionally, though seldom, we may get a cloudy or rainy
day, and as long as the humidity is bearable, I can put in my
normal hours of work in the garden. The work is intense at this
time of the year, for everything, especially weeds, tends to grow
rapidly. From time to time, it is wise to take a moment of rest in
a patch of shade. It renews one's energies, which tend to diminish under the weight of a scorching heat.

Early July is the "middle age" of the year. Its days are warm, robust, and lively, thriving with health and promise. Mother earth is ripe with good products. The local growers show the best of their produce at the farmers' market. I remember the days when we ourselves used to sell our produce at the Saturday market. Undeniably, in those early July days, the farmers and local growers would always show their best smiles, displaying an utter contentment with the ripened fruits of their labors. Those were moments of pure joy for them. None of the commercial crops sold in the local supermarkets can compare in quality or freshness to those grown by our farmers and gardeners. Surely, a good and prosperous harvest at this time of the year is a clear sign of God's blessing, a sign of his loving concern for all of us.

— JULY 2 —
Wildflowers

Anyone who knows where rare wildflowers grow would be wise these days to keep this information to himself. This sounds selfish, but...a natural stand of a rarity is such a fragile matter that the less general knowledge there is of it the better.

THALASSA CRUSO, *THE GARDENING YEARS*

It seems only yesterday that I was gazing at some of the jewels of the surrounding countryside: its wildflowers. In actuality, it has been a full year since I glimpsed this sight, but to a gardener's memory (which is akin to that of a desert monk), "a day is like a thousand years." I revel in the fact that so much of the local acreage that has not yet been destroyed by greedy developers still unravels for us the secret of its yearly mystery: the radiant, plain, unspoiled beauty of its wildflowers. Nothing is so full of majesty as the flowers that proliferate in our fields, our woods, our wetlands, and the borders of our country roads. They are such a feast to our eyes!

Wildflowers are called wild, I suppose, for the simple reason that they were not deliberately cultivated by the hands of humans. I am not sure that human beings are always the best stewards of the gifts God has entrusted to them. We continue to witness constant biological and ecological abuses, and yet there are so few who even blink an eye at the destruction of our environment. When we finally take notice of what has been done to the stability of our ecosystems, it will be too late. We will not have the ability to restore our planet to its original harmony and purpose, as God once created it and entrusted it to our stewardship.

One of July's extra joys is the exuberance of the wildflowers that seem to overtake the countryside. They fill the contours of the local *paysage* with astonishing colors and a delicate fragrance. In the woods, where the foliage is at times dense and a bit unfriendly, the wildflowers render it bright and lively. They humanize the woods and make them approachable. In these spots, I often gather daisies, buttercups, black-eyed Susans, phlox, and other wild species to fill the pottery vases for the chapel. The fields, woods, and gardens, through the constant flow and succession of the seasons, gratefully provide means to render praise to their Creator.

— July 3 —

Saint Thomas

Saint Thomas, whom the Savior chose
When here on earth, as special friend,
Accept our joyous hymn of praise
And to our earnest prayers attend.

Your love for Christ made you desire
To die with him and share his plight;
His love for you gave you a throne
Of glory in his realm of light.

Lauds Hymn for the Feast of Saint Thomas

If the feasts of the saints have a particular meaning in the monastery, it is because they bring all of us together. Those in heaven and those still on earth are conjoined in the immense family of God. Through the celebration of those dear to God, and dear to us as our intercessors, we enter into that marvelous communion of saints. The *turba magna* of the Book of Revelation comprises not only the angels, prophets, and apostles but also the martyrs and saints, the monks and nuns of all ages. It includes all of us here, as we await the moment of the eternal encounter.

I derive so much strength, inspiration, and encouragement from the presence of the saints in heaven. They are truly our brothers and sisters, because we have the same Father in common. They are also our friends, because they are friends of God. When their particular feast comes around yearly on the calendar, we then celebrate their memory and rejoice at their victory in having achieved their goal.

Today we keep memory of Thomas, one of the Lord's famous Apostles, well known in the Gospels for his lack of faith in the Resurrection of his Master. Refusing to believe what the other Apostles told him about the risen Savior, he demanded to place his fingers in Jesus' wounds to verify that it was really the same Jesus who had died on the cross. Thomas would not change his mind until Jesus himself appeared to him and said: "Put your finger here; look, here are my hands. Give me your hand; put it into my side. Doubt no longer but believe." Thomas then replied, "My Lord and my God!" It took Jesus' appearance, his own personal intervention, for Thomas to come around and believe.

How often are we also slow in affirming our faith, in coming around to Jesus' invitation to follow him? The Lord, however, shows the same patience toward us as he did with Thomas. This patience should be a great encouragement to all of us. God is never surpassed in patience, in kindness, in understanding, in forbearance, in mercy. We can learn much from this Gospel episode about ourselves. In the end, though we may be a bit late in coming around, let us pray that we, like Thomas, will never cease praying and never cease proclaiming: "My Lord and my God!" It is this confession of faith that ultimately rescued Thomas, and one day, it shall do the same for all of us.

— July 4 —

Some of July's Favorite Flowers: Daylilies, Hostas, Phlox

You visit the earth and water it,
you greatly enrich it;
the river of God is full of water.

PSALM 65:9

Some of America's most popular perennials bloom during the heat of July. There is no denying that these growing things excite the heart of the gardener everywhere. Sometimes I get letters from distant gardeners inquiring about every small detail in our gardens: What type of soil do you cultivate in? How much spading do you do or how much mulch you use? When do you add your compost? What are your favorite species? Do you use chemical fertilizers? The questions go on and on. I wish I could reply to all of them, but a gardener never has enough time for letter writing, certainly not during July.

The perennials most popular in the Northeastern landscape seem to be the stupendous daylilies, the hostas, and my all-time favorite—phlox. For any ornamental border, they complement the list of other lesser-known perennials. One must pay special attention to the requirements of each particular species, such as how much water to give them during a drought. I try to meet their needs as closely as possible. The hostas, for example, love shady areas and it would ruin them to be exposed to a full sun all day long. And the daylilies, which spring up all over the landscape, make for a great deal of work: since they don't last long, I face the task of having to remove their dead flowers each day. It is all a part of the gardener's experience.

As I face garden work in July, I try to think about its beautiful seasonal aspects and less about the prospects of a hot sun or rising temperature. A flourishing garden of phlox, daylilies, hostas, and others is a delight to the eyes. It exhilarates my heart. My belief is that they are faithful flowers. They return yearly, and each year they seem more glorious, more radiant, and more appealing! It is a joy to commune with God in their midst, to see his face in every flower. These moments of communion are worth all of the work the garden demands.

— JULY 5 —

Saint Athanasius the Athonite

I never read of a hermit, but in my imagination I kiss his feet; never of a monastery, but I could fall on my knees and kiss the pavement.

DR. JOHNSON

Mount Athos holds a fascination for all those interested in monasticism. No one is sure when the first monks arrived at Mount Athos, but by the eighth or ninth century, small colonies of hermits began populating the famous peninsula. An English tourist, John Julius Norwich, describes a first encounter with Athos:

> Within a day or two of his arrival he [the tourist] begins to feel its influence. It touches him at all levels. Just as his physical perception seems contained by the mountain and the encircling sea, so his spirit is swathed in the beauty and serenity he finds around him, and his grateful mind adjusts to the deceleration of time. Miles and kilometers are forgotten; distances from one monastery to the next—and no other distances exist—are reckoned in hours or days.

Saint Athanasius, the monk we honor today, is one of the most influential figures in the monastic development of Mount Athos. Athanasius was born at Trebrizond of pious Antiochian parents who baptized him with the name Abraham. As a youngster, he was sent to Constantinople to pursue his studies where he discovered monastic life and joined the monastery of Saint Michael at Bithynia—a fervent monastic laura, where the monks lived in solitary seclusion around a communal church, under the direction of an abbot. In Bithynia, the young Abraham took the monastic name of Athanasius. Soon his reputation for wisdom and holiness became known and the monks wished to make him their abbot. To escape having to accept such a position, Athanasius left his native monastery and retired to Mount Athos. There, after several trips accompanying an old friend named Nicephorus Phocas, he began around 961 A.D. to build the first monastery at Mount Athos.

Athanasius was greatly helped financially by Phocas, who by this time had become Emperor Phocas and had the means to support the monastic undertaking of his dear old friend. In spite of great opposition by the local hermits, who twice tried murdering Athanasius, he continued building his monastery and gathering the community that was to inhabit it. In due time, he became the abbot of over fifty-eight lauras of monks on the Holy Mountain of Athos. Athanasius died tragically, when an arch of a church collapsed on him and some of his monks.

Today, the monastery of Saint Athanasius, called the Great Laura, still remains standing—a self-sufficient and self-contained monastic community, faithful to the ideals and traditions implemented by its holy founder. It is considered the oldest and the largest foundation on the peninsula.

— JULY 6 —

The Opus Dei

Prayers, as everyone knows, ought to be said at the third, sixth and ninth hours, at dawn and in the evening.
LETTER OF SAINT JEROME TO THE NUN EUSTOCHIUM

All life entails an inner rhythm around which daily living is centered. The physical universe has the rhythm of the seasons. Mother Nature, guided by the solar system, creates her own rhythm through a sequential succession of months, weeks, days, and hours. In daily life, people organize their living arrangement around a schedule of work, recreation, eating, and rest.

Similarly, daily monastic life is organized around a life-giving rhythm: the daily celebration of the work of God, as Saint Benedict calls the Canonical Hours. It is this punctuation of liturgical prayer at precise moments of the day that constitutes the daily rhythm of a monastery. This schedule of prayers creates the throbbing beat of the days, which transforms the daily monotony of the monk into something of rare beauty.

Often, people who visit monasteries tend to think that it is work which shapes the daily monastic schedule. They are misguided. As important as work is for the monk's daily sustenance, it does not constitute the center of his monastic existence. Prayer, adoration, the praise of God: these are the main occupations that mark a monk's day. Anything else is an outgrowth of this most central precept.

When Saint Benedict writes in the Rule about the organizing of the daily monastic schedule, he does it in direct reference to the hours of the *Opus Dei*. The hours of work, reading, study, and dining may change according to the nature of a particular season, but the hours of the Work of God do not. They remain firmly established. They are not replaced. In the life of a monastery, all the rest is there to accommodate and respect this unique schedule, this unchanging rhythm.

— JULY 7 —

Psalmody

The true monk should have prayer and psalmody continually in his heart.

ABBA EPIPHANIUS

The psalms occupy a pivotal place in the *Opus Dei* of the monastery. The Book of Psalms, commonly called the Psalter or in Hebrew the Book of Praises, comprises the traditional poetry and prayers addressed to God by his chosen people of Israel. These prayers were used daily in the worship of Israel: in the synagogue, in the Temple, and in the context of ordinary home worship.

Of all the elements that comprise the monastic Offices, nothing is more adequate for the monk's own inner prayer than the psalms. In reading the sayings of the Desert Fathers and Mothers, we learn of the importance attached by them to psalmody. In an arid and empty desert, the psalms were their daily bread. They would have not survived the desolation of the desert without this daily nourishment. The psalms, far more than any other form of prayer, express the extraordinary interaction that has been going on between God and his people from the very beginning of creation. That interaction, which peaked with the Incarnation, continues today. As Thomas Merton points out, "The psalms bring us in direct contact with Him whom we seek."

For me personally, throughout all these years, the psalms have been a "true school of prayer." They are God's inspired words, heartening us to pray according to the Holy Spirit's own summoning. If it is the moment to glorify God, the psalms teach us to praise him. If it is the moment to ask God for pardon, the psalms convey to us the meaning of true repentance. If we are traversing a moment of pain and suffering, the psalms teach us how to ask for help. If we face a moment of temptation, the psalms inspire us to cry out for assistance. If it is the moment to render God thanks for past kindness, the psalms moves us to sing and dance for joy in his presence.

There are many ways of praying and singing the psalms during the monastic Offices. The most ancient form is what is called direct psalmody. Here, a soloist sings and prays aloud while the others listen and absorb the words. This is a contemplative way of praying the psalms and it was the preferred method of the Desert Fathers and Mothers. During these privileged moments the monk rests in God and remains open to the action of his Spirit in his soul.

A most common form of praying the psalms in the community consists in what is called alternating psalmody. The verses from the psalms are alternated between two choirs. Prayer becomes an ongoing dialogue of two groups. Today, this is often the practice in many Western monasteries. It has the advantage of giving time to the monk to breathe and reflect between the verses.

The third form of praying the psalms during the Offices is the one called responsorial psalmody. During this form of executing the psalms, the soloist sings a certain part of the psalm and, at the end, everyone responds with a common refrain. For instance, when Psalm 136 is sung, the soloist sings, "O give thanks to the LORD for he is good," and everyone joins in a refrain of "For his steadfast love endures forever." This is also an ancient approach to the praying of the psalms. By the end of the fourth century it became a universal part of the monastic cursus of both the East and West.

The very nature of the psalms, as simple, blunt, and direct as they are, calls for them to be sung in the everyday language of the people. Nothing is more remote from them than an obscure language that makes them distant and unapproachable. Sung mechanically, they are no longer the psalms of the Bible as Jesus knew them. They were composed as poetry in song, and they attain their true meaning when they are sung in a contemplative fashion as pure praise of God. It is not necessary that they be sung in a beautiful and perfect manner, though this can enhance them as we try to pray. What really matters is that the psalms be sung humbly, prayerfully, slowly, and fervently. Only then can we begin to savor their richness, absorb their wisdom, and capture something of the pure joy of praising God.

— JULY 8 —

Vigils

I rise before dawn and cry for help;
I put my hope in your words.
My eyes are awake before each watch of the night,
that I may meditate on your promise.

PSALM 119:147-148

From the early beginnings of monasticism, the first monks rose before dawn and awaited the arrival of the new day in prayer. This was nothing new, for the first Christians, following Jesus' counsel, observed what was then called "the watches of the night." Alertness, watchfulness, and vigilance were teachings that came straight from the Gospels, admonitions which the early monks took seriously.

Today, the Office of Vigils is observed in different fashions depending on the custom of the particular monastery. Some anticipate their Vigils the night before, others observe them in the middle of the night, and others pray them just before the arrival of the dawn. No matter how and when the Vigils are prayed, they always retain their nightly character. Saint John Chrysostom recalled the night vigils of the early monks and described them thus: "Just as they rise, they intone the psalms of David, and sing them with such sweet harmony! There is no harp, or flute, or any other instrument that can render a similar sound to theirs! In the silence and solitude of night, their prayer rises like that of the saints. They sing with the angels, yes, with the angels, the *Laudate Dominum de coelis*, while the rest of us are still in our deep sleep, or semi-asleep, dreaming of worldly cares."

The Office of Vigils always starts with the *Domine labia mea aperies* ("O Lord, open my lips"). The monk faces the altar, a symbol of Christ, and repeats it three times as prescribed in the Rule. The others respond: "And my mouth shall proclaim your praise." The Invitatory, Psalm 95, follows. Since Vigils is the first Office of the day, a great deal of its opening consists of an invitation to worship and adoration. A hymn follows and the psalmody starts. The psalmody at Vigils keeps a restrained character, vigilant and appropriate for that hour of day. In many cases the psalms are recited by a monk alone, by the light of a flickering candle, while the others listen and pray. There are long, silent pauses in between psalms and readings. After the psalmody, lessons from the Scriptures and the Fathers are read, followed by the responses. On Sundays, a Resurrection Gospel is proclaimed, followed by the *Te Deum* or *Te Decet Laus*, which brings the Vigil Office to conclusion. As the Office of Vigils comes to an end, the first light of day begins to appear on the horizon. A new day begins, a day full of promise, a day to be lived for God, for our brothers and sisters in Christ scattered around all corners of the globe. The monk awaits the light of day in prayer and in joy, for he knows himself to be one of "the children of light." As we sing in our Vigil Office at Our Lady of the Resurrection Monastery:

Awake all you who are asleep,
And rise from among the dead.
For Christ is risen from the dead
And he shall give us light.

The night is dark for unbelievers, O Christ,
But for the faithful there is light in the truth of your words.
Therefore, we keep vigil for you.
Awaiting your coming, O Lord.

— JULY 9 —

Lauds

The beauty of the rising sun
Begins to tint the world with light,
Awakened nature glows with life
As form and color reappear.
Lord Jesus Christ, you far surpass
The sun that shines since time began;
We turn to you with joyous song
That You may bless us with your smile.

PERGRATA MUNDI, LAUDS HYMN FOR TUESDAY

Saint Benedict points out in his Rule that Lauds, the office of morning praise, must be sung at the moment one receives the first rays from the sun, *illucescente aurora*. It is a blessed moment of the day, for the sun, a symbol of the eternal Sun of Justice, is just appearing on the horizon. It recalls another early morning, when Christ, our true light, rose from the dead. The office of Lauds, especially on Sundays, is enfolded in the mystery of the Resurrection. With the holy myrrh-bearer women, we approach the tomb that held life. We sit by its side, and with joyful voices we proclaim to the world that Christ is indeed risen.

The Office begins with the *Deus in adjutorium meum intende* ("O Lord, come to my assistance"). The choir replies: "Lord, make haste to help me." The doxology and hymn of the day follow. The hymn can be from the ordinary of the day, depending on the day and week; it can be seasonal, as for Advent, Lent, or Paschaltime; or it can be from the proper of a feast or a saint. The hymn serves as an introduction to the Office; it conveys its theme and opens our hearts to praise. Some monasteries postpone the singing of the hymn until the psalmody is completed. (Saint Benedict places the hymn after the short reading-response following the psalmody.) After the liturgical adaptations from Vatican Council II, the Church reassigned the hymns to the entry of all the Offices, where they properly belong. I think Saint Benedict, were he here today, would have been the first to conform to this arrangement. When the time comes to decide the format or time of a certain office, he gives a great deal of latitude to the abbot or the person with responsibility for the *Opus Dei*. As he states in his Rule: "If this arrangement is unsatisfactory to anyone, he may do otherwise if he has thought of a better one."

After the hymn of the hour or day, we proceed to psalmodize until the moment of the lesson from the Scriptures. While the psalms are sung in English here, the antiphons are sung in Latin. They are simple and basic to understand, and besides, they provide us with the proper Gregorian mode for singing their corresponding psalm. After the lesson from the Scriptures a few minutes of silence follow for meditation on the Word of God. After the meditation on the Scripture lesson, a simple or solemn response follows depending on the feast or occasion. The Gregorian response is always sung in Latin.

Lauds concludes with the Benedictus Canticle, which lovingly proclaims: "In the tender compassion of our God the dawn from on high shall break upon us, to shine on those who dwell in darkness and the shadow of death, and to guide our feet into the way of peace." The intercessions and the Our Father follow. Our morning praise closes with the prayer of the day. The sun is erstwhile on high, shining on the world. *Jam lucis orto sidere.* People everywhere are awakening to face the pains and joys of a new day. The monk carries in his heart, in his prayer, the needs and sufferings of the entire world. This is his particular call. This is what God asks of him. Gazing at the light from on high, the monk is confident that all is well. For He, the Giver of light, Who makes the sun shine on the virtuous and the malevolent, is mindful of the individual needs of all His children. As morning begins, and the day proceeds through its course, we pray often: *Exsurge Christe, adjuva nos.* Rise, O Christ, quickly, and come to our aid.

— JULY 10 —

Sext

O true noon-day
When warmth and light are at their peak
And the sun at its zenith
And no shadows fall.
When stagnant waters dry up
And their fetid odors disperse.
O never ending solstice
When daylight lasts forever.
O noon-day light,
Marked with the mildness of spring,
Stamped with summer's bold beauty,
Enriched with autumn's fruit,
And (lest I seem to forget)
Calm with winter's rest from toil.

SAINT BERNARD

Noon has arrived. A profound silence fills the monastery. The bells peal the *Angelus,* beckoning us once more to the Office. After several hours of intense work, it is a welcome pause. I thank God for the gift of the past hours, for what was accomplished, and for all that is waiting to be done: "Almighty Ruler, God of Truth, / From whom the ordered seasons flow, / The splendor of the morning sun, / The noonday heat which you bestow" (Hymn for the Hour of Sext).

Noonday reminds one of many things, in particular, that life is often a struggle. And noontime accentuates the weariness, the burdens of the day. The monk has humbly cast his lot among the poor and the lowly, among those who occupy the last place in society. We have nothing to count on except God's mercy. We only find rest, shelter, refuge, and comfort under the shadow of his wings. I delight in having this noonday pause for prayer. Though short, it lifts up my spirit and soothes it. I find peace and tranquillity in prayer. This is perhaps why I wish prayer on everyone. Prayer grants me the good fortune to bathe my tired spirit in God's presence, in the luminous rays of his light.

— JULY 11 —

Saint Benedict

Saint Benedict wished to please God alone.

SAINT GREGORY'S *DIALOGUES*

Today we celebrate the solemnity of our father Saint Benedict. The French monks call it *la Saint-Benoit en ete* to differentiate it from the winter feast of his Transitus on the twenty-first of March. It is a feast of great joy for the entire monastic family, as it gets celebrated by both black (Benedictine) and white (Cistercian) monks alike. We are all children of Saint Benedict and owe to him the inspiration for our monastic lives.

Saint Benedict's presence is strongly felt in this small monastic enclave. It seems to me as if I have been living with the saint for umpteen years. It is not only his Rule, or the monastic tradition, he imparted that is so deeply felt here. There is another uniquely subtle influence, something more enriching to me than anything else. It is Saint Benedict's own example of a faithful Gospel life.

Saint Benedict was thoroughly evangelical in the best sense of that term. He was Christlike, for him the imitation of Christ was the supreme ideal of his life. He taught his monks to "prefer nothing to the love of Christ." The Rule he wrote for his monks is nothing but a distillation of every single page in the Gospels. He would have never thought to add something besides what the Divine Master had already taught or lived. If the Rule contains today a certain resilience, a certain feeling of timelessness, it is simply because it is a lucid condensation of Gospel wisdom. The Rule remains as timely as the Gospels it wishes to incarnate. This is Saint Benedict's gift to us today, to all his children, to the Church at large, and to the world he embraced in his mystical vision.

After being forced out of his beloved solitude on Monte Subiaco, Saint Benedict, a poor and humble pilgrim, undertook the road to Monte Cassino. There he wrote his famous Rule for monks; and there, too, he spent the remaining of his days. He wrote the Rule, first of all, to hand on a living tradition to his monks. Human and wise as he was, Saint Benedict made a point of avoiding in the Rule all formalism and legalism that would otherwise taint a monastic experience meant to be pure and free and rooted in the simplicity of the Gospels. The power of the Rule, when properly lived as Saint Benedict conceived it, can lead to a life of fullness where the monk, in the words of Saint Paul, is "hidden with Christ in God." This is the heart of the monastic life, its only purpose, as proposed daily.

— JULY 12 —

Vespers

Let my prayer be counted as incense before you, and the lifting up of my hands as an evening sacrifice.

PSALM 141:2

The sun begins to go down, the end of the day is near at hand. In the early days, Christians in Jerusalem used to rush at this precise time to the church of the Holy Sepulcher and spend the remaining evening hours in prayer. It was the *hora incensi*, the hour to offer the evening incense as Saint Ambrose describes it. It was also the time of the *lucernarium*, when the first evening lamps were lighted. The Office of Vespers is an ancient rite of prayer, rooted in the prayer of the synagogue itself, where it has its origins. After the Resurrection of Jesus, the Apostles and the first disciples continued to pray in the evening, following the Jewish custom. Soon that prayer became a commemoration of the sacrifice of Christ on the cross.

The hour of Vespers is observed in the monastery at the most solemn hour of the day. At sunset, when the rays from the sun begin to withdraw from our sight, the bells of the monastery summon us to our evening praise. The candles and the oil lamps in front of our ikons are lit. The sweet scent of incense pervades the air. Chanting begins slowly with the Byzantine invocation: "Blessed is our God, now and always, and unto ages of ages." We all respond with a solemn "Amen." The opening hymn and the psalmody follows, just as we did at morning Lauds, with the antiphons in Latin and the psalms in English. Psalm 141, which speaks of the "evening sacrifice," is sung everyday in the Byzantine tradition. After Psalm 141, a special prayer of the light is offered, followed by the *Phos Hilaron*, one of the oldest hymns to Christ and one of the most beautiful of all the Christian hymnology. The hymn praises Christ as our "evening light" who comes to enlighten our darkness.

An appropriate lesson from the Scriptures is read, then the electric lights are put out for a few minutes of silent meditation. In the evening darkness, we are alone with God, surrounded by the Theotokos and the saints as our only company. There is only a response on solemn festival days. On ordinary days, we offer the depth of our silence as our sole response. The lights are lit again, and the *Magnificat* is intoned. We sing the *Magnificat* accompanied by the Byzantine antiphon: "More honorable than the cherubim, and more glorious beyond compare than the seraphim. Remaining a virgin you gave birth to God the Word, true Theotokos, we magnify you." This antiphon is sung here daily, following the Byzantine usage. On feast days and solemnities, the Latin Gregorian antiphon or the proper Troparion replaces this otherwise daily antiphon.

Our eventide Office is completed with final intercessions, the Our Father, and a concluding prayer. A final blessing and a hymn to Our Lady closes the evening Office, followed by the veneration of our ikons, something which is part of the daily ritual of this monastery. The last rays from the sun have vanished, and dusk starts to descend. The early shadows delineate the silhouettes of our trees, our buildings, and the cross high on the bell tower. There is no room for fear. Christ, our Light, is among us, to protect us from the gloom of our own darkness, from the advances of the evil one. The Lord is palpably there, close by, to guide our feet into the ways of peace.

— JULY 13 —

A Byzantine Prayer at Eventide

*Receive the prayers, thrice Holy Savior, of those who stand
on earth and sing your praise. Look down with sleepless
eye, O Lover of the human race, and overlook our
weakness, and grant us peaceful rest. Receive our prayer,
raise up our souls, lest our sins frustrate our prayer.
Deliver us, your servants, from the grief of Judgment,
and make us worthy, who sing to you now, to stand in
the chorus of saints. Glory to the Father, and to the Son,
and to the Holy Spirit, unto ages of ages. Amen.*

ANONYMOUS, FIFTH CENTURY

— JULY 14 —

Compline

*God, who made the earth and heaven, darkness and light:
You the day for work have given, for rest the night. May
your angel guards defend us, slumber sweet your mercy
send us, holy dreams and hopes attends us, all through
the night.*

REGINALD HEBER

It is an exquisite July night. A poet certainly would feel inspired by the magic of the moment and the fragrance emanating from our gardens. As I look at the wide open sky, every star
seems to have taken its rightful place in the heavens. A bright
moon bathes the darkness with its own startling clarity. There is
something calming about the night that inspires silence, recollection, and peaceful reflection.

The evening meal has finished and the dishes are piled up in
the sink. The day's journey approaches its conclusion. The monastery bells ring for the last Office of the day, summoning us to
Compline. Afterwards, the bells and everyone within the monastic enclosure remain silent until the following day. In the chapel,

the only lights are those in front of the main ikons of the Savior and the Theotokos. Compline is a short Office. There is no pomp in its ritual, only a sense of spareness and simplicity. To enhance the simplicity of this Office, Saint Benedict deliberately makes it repetitive in its format and content. There is no variation in the psalms. The three assigned psalms (5, 91, and 134) are repeated every night. The only small variation occurs occasionally in the choice of the hymn.

In the quiet of the church, Compline begins with a brief examination of conscience. We look back at the events of the day: its joys and sorrows, our conduct and failings. We acknowledge our sinfulness through the *Confiteor* and humbly beg for pardon from the Father of all mercies. The hymn follows.

After the hymn, the three abovementioned psalms are sung and repeated night after night. Since eventually one learns them all by heart, Compline is sung in the dark shadows of the night. After the psalmody, a short reading from the Scriptures follows. There is a pause for silence after which the short response is sung: *In manus tuas Domine, commendo spiritum meaum* ("Into your hands, O Lord, I commend my spirit"). How often have I made recourse to this short prayer. How consoling it has always been!

Compline reaches its peak with Simeon's canticle, the *Nunc Dimitis* and its accompanying antiphon: "Save us, O Lord, as we stay awake, and guard us as we sleep. That awake we may keep watch with Christ and asleep rest in his peace." After the canticle, a short prayer follows and the final blessing brings Compline to its conclusion. At the end of Compline, we tend to the ikon of the Theotokos and sing one of her seasonal antiphons, usually the *Salve, Regina*. With much love and devotion, the monk commends his life, his concerns, and all the intentions entrusted to him to the care of the Mother of God. We can take leave for the night and still feel secure, for we place our trust in her unfailing protection.

After Our Lady's antiphon, as we bow to the altar and leave the chapel, we are asperged with holy water. Silently, we depart for the repose of the night. The day's journey has ended by our singing God's praises and commending ourselves to the intercession of the Holy Mother of God. As we enter into the secrecy of the night silence, we seek quiet repose for our tired bodies and spiritual refreshment for our souls.

— JULY 15 —

Chant: Vehicle of Prayer

When sung in Gregorian chant, the Divine Office is supported by the best music there is for nourishing the soul, music which is also an artistic masterpiece. The music expresses the thoughts and feelings that are at the origin of prayer. Its richness and beauty give rise to prayer.

DOM JACQUES HOURLIER,
REFLECTIONS ON THE SPIRITUALITY OF THE GREGORIAN CHANT

M onks have always made recourse to special music for their worship of God. This music is the chant—specifically consecrated to exalt the sacred and, in its simplicity, awaken the monastic heart to prayer. There is an intimate connection between the chant and the texts of Scripture used in our Offices. Here at Our Lady of the Resurrection, we combine both English and Latin in our daily worship, and the Gregorian chant is a superb vehicle for the expression of our humble praise in both languages.

The genius of the Gregorian chant, according to Père J. Y. Hameline, is that in singing it we realize "it is not a question of adding music to the words, nor even of setting words to music....Instead, it is a question of making the words bring forth the music they already contain. We do not have the text on the one hand and the melody on the other...but rather a unique monody in which the melody sings the words correctly, precisely, because these words gave the music its initial motion. The words, in turn, support the melody and cause it to sing because of the melody's role, which is to transfigure the text's meaning, rhythm, and elemental sonority."

The objective purity of the chant is an excellent means to make our Offices conducive to contemplation. Singing chant repeatedly throughout the years, the monk eventually finds it dwelling ever more deeply within himself. It is in the air he breathes, the bread he chews, the water he drinks, the words he hears. The chant remains in the ears of his heart long after the Offices have concluded. At times, it returns to haunt him with the sound of heaven, with the vision of the eternal. It is prayer that has become music and music that has become prayer. Singing it daily, the beauty of the chant never wearies the human mind or heart. On the contrary, it lifts our tired spirits to intimate communion with our Creator. The chant liberates us from earthly cares to instead explore and penetrate the divine realms of God's supreme majesty.

— JULY 16 —

Our Lady of Mount Carmel

Guiding Star of Ocean,
Heaven's welcome haven:
Holy Mary, now we greet you,
God's own Virgin Mother.

VESPERS HYMN FROM THE COMMON OF THE BLESSED VIRGIN MARY

Our mid-July days seem extra long, perhaps because of the weight of the heat and the heavy brilliance of the sun. Occasionally, an echo arrives from a motorist or the tumult outside. Otherwise, a quiet silence pervades the hazy beauty of our summer days.

In the beauty and quiet of this summer scene we celebrate today Our Lady of Mount Carmel. Though only a memorial on the calendar, it is Our Lady's only feast in July. In addition, it is a solemn feast for the Carmelite family, who honors Mary today as their special patroness. The origins of the order goes back to the twelfth century, to Mount Carmel in Palestine, where Our Lady and the prophet Elias inspired the lifestyle of their first hermits. These hermits, following Mary's example, applied themselves to the cultivation of inner prayer and contemplation. She was their model, their protector, and their mother. Later on, when she appeared to Saint Simon Stock, she promised her special blessing to all those who would wear the habit of the order. It is not surprising, therefore, that an order singularly blessed by Our Lady has rendered great fruits of holiness throughout the centuries. One has only to think of the great Teresa of Ávila, John of the Cross, Thérèse of Lisieux, or Edith Stein.

Today, we rejoice greatly, *Gaudens gaudebo*, in honoring the memory of the Mother of God. Her white mantle covers all of her children, in every generation, and this includes both saints and sinners. As we move forward with life's destination, we entrust ourselves to her intercession. No matter how many times we may have sinned or fallen along the way, she, who is Refuge of sinners, is there to assist and sustain us. We pray: "Holy Mother of God, Queen and Beauty of Carmel, we rejoice today in your presence. Shelter us always under your mantle and save us from the power of evil. Amen."

— JULY 17 —

The Shrines in Our Gardens

The sculpture you place in your garden is your signature on the face of nature.

AUTHOR UNKNOWN

The ancient Romans had the custom of adorning their gardens with shrines to their pagan gods and goddesses. Because of this association of gardens with pagan gods, it took a long time for monastic gardens to incorporate Christian statuary and symbols. With the passing of time, monks slowly began incorporating other Christian symbols and outdoor shrines into their otherwise traditional gardens. Today, it is inconceivable to find a monastery garden that does not contain a shrine to the Mother of God or one of the saints.

Here in our monastery, we name our gardens after their specific shrines. For example, a large composite of two attached flower gardens accommodates two statues of the Mother of God and is consequently called "Our Lady's Garden." The herb garden contains a shrine to Saint Joseph and is named after him. The vegetable garden holds in the center a statue of Saint Fiacre and hence that specific garden is confided to him. Saint Antony, the father of monks, presides over the humble rock garden and naturally that garden is entrusted to him. A long perennial border has as its patron Saint Francis, the humble friar from Assisi. Christian sculptures endow our gardens with a vibrant presence. Because of the solidity of the statues and the strategic place where they are set, they add to the gardens a certain feeling of timelessness, of the eternal.

The shrines in our gardens tend to be rather rustic. They create a definite focus that allows the gardener to scale and delineate the right proportions in his garden. And, of course, they accentuate its monastic appearance and style. There is another substantial aspect to the importance attached to these shrines in our gardens. They become pivotal places of prayer and recollection for the gardener, the monk, the guest, and the visitor. The presence in the shrine invites a certain dialogue, inspires a motion to prayer and a summons to praise. It anchors our restless feelings in something concrete that emanates tranquillity and peace. In a way, they serve as reminders that prayer is what gardening is all about.

During these peaceful, balmy July days, I often take an evening walk around the gardens. I stop in front of the shrines and pray the *Angelus* or utter a simple prayer. It is a moment that intersects with heaven, that allows the monk to regain and relive the ancient idea of a garden as "paradise on earth," where the Spirit of God fills the entire space.

— JULY 18 —

On Judging Others

The Abba said, "If a man practices humility and poverty, and if he does not judge others, the fear of God will dwell in him."

ABBA EUPREPIUS

Many years ago, when I was first exposed to the wisdom of the Desert Fathers, one thing that struck me most was their stress on the refusal to pass judgment. I was aware of the

Gospel teaching, "Judge not, that you too may not be judged" (Mt 7:1), but it was a point not emphasized on my early monastic training. Later on, I finally concluded that I could no longer keep sidestepping this particular Gospel teaching. On average, it doesn't bother us Christians in the least to pass judgment on others, especially on those with whom we disagree. Yet Jesus, in no uncertain terms, tells us we must not judge.

Of all the Christian virtues we are called to practice, perhaps one of the most difficult is cultivating this nonjudgmental attitude. It is painfully difficult, almost as much as the command to love our enemies. It is doubly difficult, for most of the time we do it automatically, without truly realizing what we are doing. In a word, we have become so accustomed to judging others that it has become our second nature. Yet the Scriptures remind us that the only judgment is the Lord's. He alone has the prerogative to render it. The Desert monks and nuns observed that it is impossible to enter into communion with God while possessing a judgmental bearing towards our neighbor. Besides, when we honestly consider it, the act of passing judgment upon others is a supreme act of pride. It connotes that we consider ourselves superior and better to others.

Saint Paul, in his letter to the Romans, says that every time we judge others we condemn ourselves. And the Desert Fathers, with that unique, penetrating perception of theirs, recall to our attention what we have in common with others: weaknesses and sinfulness. They reproach us for even daring to judge others made in the image and likeness of God, when we are equally as weak and sinful. Furthermore, there is always an added problem of judging a neighbor's action about which we know nothing. Who really understands, except God, what is behind certain conduct?

Monastic life, in many ways, is a daily struggle to live in a manner worthy of the Gospel. The temptation to pass judgment upon our neighbor is always present. We are encouraged, however, by the very example of Christ. When others demanded that he judge the woman caught in adultery, he offered her instead love and forgiveness. Love is the way of the Christian, the way of the monk. And love is never static. On the contrary, it is active and dynamic. It overflows when focused on God's personal plan and demand for each of us. Love, and love alone, can be the sole response to an otherwise critical and judgmental demeanor.

— JULY 19 —
Saint Macrina the Younger

Macrina and her companions lived apart from all worldly trivialities and their life was brought into harmony with the life of the angels.

SAINT GREGORY NAZIANZUS

Today, the monastic calendar marks the feast of Saint Macrina, one of the cherished women of the early monastic movement. Macrina was born into an extraordinary family of saints around 327 A.D. in Cesarea of Capadoccia. She was the granddaughter of Saint Macrina the Elder and the sister of the great saints Basil, Gregory of Nyssa, and Peter of Sebaste. From an early age, inspired by the example of holiness in the members of her own family, she applied herself to a life of piety and devotion. She intended to get married, but the sudden death of her fiancé changed her plans drastically. She saw it as a sign that God wanted her totally for himself, and right then she made the resolve to embrace the monastic life.

Upon the death of her father, she and her mother Emmelia retired to a large family property in Pontus. There she organized a communal form of monastic life, centered on liturgical and private prayer, the study of the Scriptures, and manual and intellectual work. She was quite intransigent about the monastic community supporting itself and not living off the wealth of others. Macrina herself worked daily in the bakery, baking bread for the community and the poor of the surrounding area, as well as the bread for the Eucharist. Upon the death of her mother, she became the head of the monastery, continuing to counsel and direct her nuns as well as the many who sought her advice. She had a tremendous impact on the early development of feminine monasticism. What her brother Saint Basil did for monks, Saint

Macrina did for the nuns. In the end, when death came near, she asked that her bed be turned toward the East from whence Christ shall return. On those last days she stopped speaking with others, saving every word for God alone. Gifted with the grace of mystical prayer, she stretched out her hands in a sweet welcoming of her Lord and Spouse, gently murmuring her last prayer:

> Eternal God, for whom I was snatched from my mother's womb, whom my soul loved with all its strength, to whom I consecrated my flesh from my youth until now, entrust to me an angel of light, who will lead me by the hand to the place of refreshment, where the "water of repose" is, in the bosom of the holy patriarch.
>
> May you, who cut through the fire of the flaming sword and assigned to paradise him who was crucified with you and entrusted to your pity, remember me too in your kingdom, because I too have been crucified with you; from fear of you I have nailed down my flesh and have been in fear of your judgment.
>
> May you who have the power on earth to forgive sins, forgive me, that I may draw breath and that I be found in your presence, "having shed my body and without spot or wrinkle" in the form of my soul, and that my soul may show itself humble and spotless, and may be received into your hands like incense in your presence.

— JULY 20 —

Saint Elijah

O prophet of great renown, O holy Elijah, gifted with the wisdom of God's wonders, as you held back the rain by the power of your prayers, so now intercede for us with our Savior, the Lover of mankind.

KONTAKION OF THE FEAST

The Fathers of the Eastern and Western Churches wrote prodigiously about the prophet Elijah, whose memory the monastic martyrology keeps today. In the figure of Elijah, the Fathers saw an image of "a man similar to us" who was invited to walk with God.

Some of the Fathers emphasized the life of Elijah as a model of true asceticism. The basic elements in Elijah's life became an archetype for the future Christian monastic movement: zeal for the glory of God, obedience to his Word, yearning for his presence, poverty, celibacy, fasting, vigilance, solitude, silence, and the exercise of the gift of spiritual paternity.

I hold no doubt in my mind that the great Elijah is a true exemplar for all those who embrace the monastic way. Since the ikon of the saintly prophet rests right behind my place in the chapel, I have the occasion to gaze upon and think often about him. He is very dear to me and important in my life. Every year, when his feast arrives, I find no better way to honor him than to reread 1 Kings 19:9–14, which poignantly describes Elijah's journey to the mountain of Horeb and his encounter with God:

> At that place he came to a cave, and spent the night there. Then the word of the LORD came to him, saying "What are you doing here, Elijah?" He answered, "I have been very zealous for the LORD, the God of hosts; for the Israelites have forsaken your covenant, thrown down your altars, and killed your prophets with the sword. I alone am left, and they are seeking my life, to take it away."
>
> He said, "Go out and stand on the mountain before the LORD, for the LORD is about to pass by" Now there was a great wind, so strong that it was splitting mountains and breaking rocks in pieces before the LORD, but the LORD was not in the wind; and after the wind an earthquake, but the LORD was not in the earthquake; and after the earthquake a fire, but the LORD was not in the fire; and after the fire the sound of sheer silence. When Elijah heard it, he wrapped his face in his mantle and went out and stood at the entrance of the cave. Then there came a voice to him that said, "What are you doing here, Elijah?" He answered, "I have been very zealous for the LORD God of hosts; for the Israelites have forsaken your covenant, thrown down your altars, and killed your prophets with the sword. I alone am left, and they are seeking my life, to take it away."

— JULY 21 —
Psalm of Repentance

Out of the depths I cry to you, O LORD,
Lord, hear my voice.
Let your ears be attentive
to the voice of my supplications!

If you, O LORD, should mark iniquities,
Lord, who could stand?
But there is forgiveness with you,
so that you may be revered.

PSALM 130: 1-4

Psalm 130, commonly called *De Profundis*, is usually associated with the Office for the Dead or the funeral liturgy. It is also prayed daily in the Byzantine Vespers. Yet, it is above all a prayer that opens new horizons, for it is a prayer that expresses conversion. Conversion is a long and arduous road, a road that demands all the inner energies of our being as we seek to traverse it. *Out of the depths I cry to you, O Lord.* The more our cry leaps out from the depths of our misery, the more honest the cry and the more genuine our heart's attitude. It is then when we find who and what we truly are.

Often, prayer tends to be from the lips, from the mind, or from a sheer act of our will, and not always from the depths of our hearts. It is painful to descend into our own hearts, to risk finding things there that would make us uncomfortable. Frequently we avoid the prayer of the heart to protect ourselves from true self-knowledge, vulnerabilities, and misery.

Psalm 130 is a learning vehicle that teaches us to pray from the depths of our hearts, from the deepest center of our being. As we descend into that abyss, we discover it to be a place in which the vital functions of feeling, sense, and intelligence converge. Furthermore, we discover the heart to be a wide open space that explores all eternal possibilities, such as the mystery of a final encounter with God. Paradoxically, as we begin to uncover God's presence in our hearts and embark upon praying from there, we find ourselves containing all the realities that are woven into our daily existence: joy, suffering, fear, longing, love, hate, hope, surrender, fulfillment, death, and life. All these complex human realities are deeply rooted in the soil of our hearts, and as we try to pray and relate to God in intimate friendship, we incorporate all of them into our prayer. They express to God who we are. We carry them, burdensome as they may sometimes be, to the throne of all mercy, crying all along in supplication: *Let your ears be attentive to the voice of my pleading.*

— JULY 22 —

Saint Mary of Magdala

Today, let us sing a special hymn in honor of that friend of the Lord who was the first to anoint him after his death. Let us praise Mary Magdalen for being the messenger of joy for his disciples. Let us fall before the Lord himself, filled with wonder, that he should lavish on the world such a fountain of grace.

KONTAKION OF THE FEAST

Today we celebrate the feast of a Gospel saint, Mary of Magdala. Her personal story runs through the four Gospels. Matthew, Mark, Luke, and John portray her as a prominent figure among Jesus' disciples. The Gospels convey to us the idea that Mary was indeed very dear and very close to the Lord. She was there, next to him, at all the important events in his life. After encountering Jesus and her subsequent conversion, Mary abandons all worldly vanities in pursuit of her one vocation: to be a true disciple of the Lord.

The Gospels recount how Jesus cast out several demons from Mary. Strangely enough, the Gospel does not spell out what these demons were. But no matter of what evil, sin, or illness they might have been, this direct contact with Jesus alleviated Mary from her heavy burdens and restored her to complete health, both of soul and body. She was not the only one to be healed by the

Lord. The Gospels relate how often the Lord exercised his healing gift toward both men and women.

Mary of Magdala's role becomes even more prominent at the moment of Jesus' crucifixion and later on at the hour of his glorious Resurrection. During the time of Jesus' Passion, most of the Apostles deserted him, abandoning Jesus during those crucial hours of his agony and death. Only his mother Mary, the disciple John, Mary of Magdala, and a few other women remained with him till the end. Mary, a grateful disciple, stood by the cross of her Lord and Master until his death came.

Three days later, after waiting by Christ's tomb, Mary was the first one to receive the glad tiding of the Lord's Resurrection. She experienced the unsurpassed joy of seeing her Lord and Master, in his very flesh, triumphantly risen from the dead. She also received the command to go and announce to the Apostles the good news of the Resurrection. Performing this role she became indeed an apostle to the Apostles. From then on, the Easter story would be forever connected to the person of Mary of Magdala—and by the Lord's own choice.

The story of Mary of Magdala is a love story. The moment she met Jesus, she left all things to follow him. When she heard him pronounce her name in the garden, there was the instant recognition only love alone can bring. Mary lived the mystery of love her teacher taught her. Love alone gave her the strength to stand by him in the cross at that fateful moment. Love alone bid her to be the first to return to the tomb and weepingly seek his sacred body.

Like Mary, the Mother of God, Mary of Magdala was chosen to be an instrument of God's infinite mercy to the entire universe. Without her, the Resurrection story would have never been told. She witnessed with her very eyes the first appearance of the Risen Lord. For this, she shall be remembered forever as the herald of good tidings to the Apostles and to the whole world. Today, with Mary of Magdala we pay tribute to our faith in the Resurrection and continue to proclaim to the entire world: Christ is Risen from the dead. Indeed he is Risen!

— JULY 23 —

Saint John Cassian

Since you were open to God in all things, you received the light of precious insights, O Holy father John. Like the sun in high heavens, you enlighten your devoted followers with the wisdom of your instructions.

KONTAKION OF THE FEAST

When I think of the evils of our times—war, intolerance, poverty, hate, discrimination, hunger, greed, cruelty, and materialism—I am reminded of the first Christian centuries, particularly of the times of Saint John Cassian, whose memory is kept today in our monastic calendar. Fervent Christians of that period, intent on preserving the integrity of the gospel, retreated to the desert in open rejection of the false values of their world.

Although John Cassian left us a legacy of an incredible amount of writing, details of his personal life are sketchy. It is said that he was born in Dacia, around 360 A.D. As a youngster, he was educated in the classics, studies which would serve him well later on. Fascinated by the monastic experiment in the Egyptian desert, he spent ten years there learning the basics of monasticism and receiving training from some of the renowned ascetics of his time. During the time Cassian spent in Egypt, he became a close follower of Evagrius—a famous spiritual teacher of the Egyptian desert. Subsequently, he and a faithful companion named Germanus migrated to Constantinople, attracted by the reputation of its charismatic bishop, Saint John Chrysostom. There he was ordained deacon. From Constantinople John Cassian eventually made a trip to Rome to confer with Pope Innocent and while in Rome he was ordained to the priesthood.

After leaving Rome, John Cassian made his way to Lerins, in southern France, and there he founded two monasteries, one for monks and another for nuns. Here he dreamed of perpetuating the desert monastic tradition that he inherited while in Egypt. Through the direct ties to Saint John Cassian, the monasticism of France can rightfully make the claim to an uninterrupted tradition going back to the Desert Fathers and Mothers. Through his writings, the "Institutes" and the "Conferences," Saint John Cassian was able to introduce the monastic ideal to the West, especially the tradition of inner prayer as it had been practiced in the deserts of Egypt and Palestine.

Today, we see in our midst a renewed interest in the works of Cassian. This can perhaps signify better things to come for the future of monasticism. Perhaps, too, new expressions of monastic life will arise for a world and culture that seems to change before our very eyes. The classic forms of monasticism, based on the model from the Middle Ages and a nineteenth-century renewal, served well through the twentieth century. But the times may call for simpler and more Gospel-oriented expressions of monastic life.

— JULY 24 —

A Summer Evening

Now the fair traveller's come to the west.
His rays are all gold, and his beauties are best;
He paints the sky gray as he sinks to his rest,
And foretells a bright rising again.

ISAAC WATTS

On late summer evenings the sun seems to delay its departure. Slowly, the shadows begin to show their faces, mysterious, inanimate beings that suddenly extend over and intercept the earth. Adding to the intoxication of the time of day, certain flowers give off their delicate scent only during the evening interval. I deliberately take time to smell those flowers, such as the phlox, certain lilies, the monarda, the nicotiana, the four o'clock, and others. Even the roses seem to emit their sweetest fragrance at dusk.

Something refreshing is in the air—the peace of the evening hours, the calm after sundown. All is quiet, only the last "baahs" are heard from the sheepfold before our friendly creatures retire for the night. Vespers has just been completed, and the first stars appear over the horizon, announcing the night to come. The poet

Isaac Watts paints this picture of a sinking sun: "His rays are all gold, and his beauties are best; / He paints the sky gray as he sinks to his rest."

— JULY 25 —

Saint James

Now let the earth with joy resound
And heaven the chant re-echo round;
Nor heaven nor earth too high can raise
The great Apostles' glorious praise.

Sickness and health your voice obey,
At your command they go or stay;
From sin's disease our souls restore,
In good confirm us more and more.

HYMN OF THE FEAST

Today we celebrate the feast of a great Apostle of the Lord, Saint James the Great. His name distinguishes him from the other Apostle, James the Minor, who was a cousin of the Lord and seemingly the author of the Letter of James. The James we feast today was the brother of the Apostle John and, like his brother, enjoyed a close relationship with the Lord.

James was chosen to be one of the few to witness the glorious Transfiguration of the Lord on the mountain; and when Jesus saw his imminent end arriving he again selected those closest to him, John, Peter, and James, to accompany him into the garden of Gethsemani.

After the Resurrection and Ascension of Jesus, most of the other Apostles migrated to other regions of the world to preach the Gospel, as they were commanded. This was not the case with James. A constant Church tradition relates that James remained in Jerusalem and that he became its first bishop. The history of Saint James is also linked with Spain where, according to an old tradition, his body was transported and buried at the site of Compostela. Throughout the centuries, Compostela has become one of the most famous sites of Christian pilgrimage, a true center of devotion to the Apostle James. From there, he continues to inspire today countless numbers of people in the ways of the Gospel, instilling in them the Master's message that the power of God's love rests in the powerlessness of the cross.

— JULY 26 —

The Ancestors of God: Saints Joachim and Ann

Ancestors royal, patriarchs and prophets, Abraham, David, none would have such glory; You and no other would deserve the title, parents of Mary.

VESPERS HYMN OF THE FEAST

Today we celebrate the intimate family feast of Saints Joachim and Ann, parents of Mary and grandparents of Jesus. They represent the just of the Old Testament. They worshiped day and night, eagerly awaiting the hour of deliverance for all of Israel. In the church of the East where today's feast originated, Joachim and Ann are remembered several times daily at the conclusion of all the Offices. The Eastern Fathers have beautifully eulogized the Ancestors of God, as the following excerpt from a sermon by Saint John Damascene demonstrates:

Ann was to be the mother of the Virgin Mother of God, and hence nature did not dare to anticipate the flowering of grace. Thus nature remained sterile, until grace produced its fruit. For she who was to be born had to be a firstborn daughter, since she would be the mother of the firstborn of all creation, in whom all things are held.

Joachim and Ann, how blessed a couple! All creation is indebted to you. For at your hands the Creator was offered a gift excelling all other gifts: a chaste mother, who alone was worthy of him. And so rejoice, Ann, that you were sterile and have not borne children; break forth into shouts, you who have not given birth. Rejoice, Joachim, because from your daughter a child is born for us, a son is given us, whose name is a Messenger of great counsel and universal salvation, mighty God. For this child is God.

Joachim and Ann, how blessed and spotless a couple! You will be known by the fruit you have borne, as the Lord says: By their fruits you will know them. The conduct of your life pleased God and was worthy of your daughter. For by the chaste and holy life you led together, you have fashioned a jewel of virginity: she who remained a virgin before, during and after giving birth. She alone for all time would maintain her virginity in mind and soul as well as in body.

— JULY 27 —

Wisdom From the Desert

A few of the monks came to visit Abba Lucius and they mentioned to him, "We do not do manual work; we obey the apostle Paul's command and pray all the time." The old monk replied, "How do you manage that? Don't you eat or sleep?" They said, "Of course, we do." Then he continued to inquire, "But who prays while you sleep? Forgive me, dear brothers, but it seems to me that you do not practice what you claim. I shall show you how I pray without ceasing, while still continue to work with my hands."

"With God's assistance, I gather a few palm-leaves and sit down to weave them, praying, 'Have mercy on me. O God, in your goodness, in your compassion, blot out my offense.'" He said to them, "Do you think this is honest prayer or not?" They replied, "Yes, it is."

Then, he went on, "After I have worked and prayed thus in my heart all day long, I make about sixteen pence. Two of these I place outside the door of my cell and with what remains I buy the food I need. He who finds the two coins outside the door, I ask him to pray for me while I eat and sleep. And so, by God's help I go on praying without ceasing."

THE APOTHEGMATA PATRUM

— JULY 28 —

A Prayer From the Desert

Strengthen me, O God, by the grace of your Holy Spirit;
grant me to be strengthened with might in the inner man,
and to put away from my heart all useless anxiety and
distress, and let me never be drawn aside by inner desire
to possess anything whatever, whether it be worthless or
precious; but may I regard all things as passing away,
and myself as passing away with them.

Grant me prudently to avoid the one who flatters
me, and patiently to bear with the one who contradicts
me; for it is a mark of great wisdom not to be moved by
every wind of words, nor to give ear to wicked flattery of
the siren; for thus we shall continue securely in the course
we have begun. May your Holy Spirit penetrate my inmost
being, and take possession of my soul and body.

Without you I cannot be saved; therefore, I yearn
deeply for your salvation. With your wisdom, guide my
heart, O merciful Lord, that I may always remember your
loving presence day and night.

ADAPTED FROM A PRAYER ATTRIBUTED TO THOMAS À KEMPIS, 1380–1471

— JULY 29 —

The Friends of the Lord: Saints Martha, Mary, and Lazarus

After Jesus had raised Lazarus from the dead, they gave a dinner
for him at Bethany, and Martha served at the table. Mary took
a pound of costly perfume and anointed the feet of Jesus.

RESPONSORY OF THE FEAST

Today's feast is a true homage to the place assigned to friendship and hospitality in the Gospels. The name Bethany resounds with warmth, tenderness, and a feeling of comfort. It was there that Jesus, wearied from much traveling and preaching, often sought refuge in the tranquil household of Martha, Mary, and Lazarus. Jesus found solace in the their company and especially cherished those three friends. As the Apostle John describes it in his Gospel: "Jesus loved Martha, her sister Mary, and Lazarus."

The story of Bethany and its inhabitants also portrays the total humanity of Jesus. For he, like any other human being, enjoyed the personal attention, the caring, and the warm hospitality provided to him by these beloved friends. Martha was the mistress of the household and often spent hours preparing to welcome the Lord in a worthy manner. Jesus, half-teasing, often reproached her for fussing too much! And yet, it was this very spotless and convivial hospitality provided by Martha that he sought whenever he stopped in Bethany.

Mary, Martha's sister, loved the Lord in her own particular way. She was totally entranced by the personality of her Master, her Lord and God. While Martha would spend so much time attending to Jesus' physical needs, Mary would simply rest at the Master's feet and absorb every word he uttered. She was totally oblivious to the world around her, so much so that her sister would complain about her lack of cooperation in entertaining the Lord. But Jesus, human as he was, loved both manners of attention. It is not surprising, therefore, that he chose that place to perform one of his most admirable miracles: the resurrection of his friend Lazarus.

The story of Lazarus's resurrection is one of the most beautiful and touching stories in the Gospel of John. Upon Jesus' arrival at Bethany, he hears Martha's complaint: "If you had been here, my brother would have not died." She adds a word of complete trust in Jesus, saying "But I know, even now, that whatever you ask of God, he will grant you." A few minutes later, it is Mary's turn to repeat the same complaint. Jesus, deeply touched by both the death of his friend and the sorrow of the two sisters he loved, began weeping. The Jews present at the scene couldn't help as to remark, "See how much he loved him." To show the might of God's power, and so that others may believe he was indeed the Lord of the living and the dead, Jesus performed the resurrection of Lazarus.

When the hour of his death was drawing near, Jesus came back once more to Bethany to find comfort and courage in the company of his friends. In the intimacy of that blessed household, he would find strength, support, and understanding in facing what he often called "his hour." While Martha was serving him at the table, Mary brought a costly ointment and anointed the feet of Jesus, wiping them later with her own hair. The ointment was to be a symbol of the one to be used at his forthcoming burial.

Once more, Jesus found much consolation in the faithful company of these friends. He cherished them to the very end. With gratitude for their friendship, he consecrated them some of those last remaining days before undergoing his Passion. The story of Bethany reminds us of the unique role that oasis of peace, repose, and warm hospitality had in Jesus' life.

— JULY 30 —

Contentment

The LORD is my chosen portion and my cup;
*   you hold my lot.*
The boundary lines have fallen for me in pleasant places;
*   I have a goodly heritage.*

PSALM 16:5-6

One of the tests of a true monastic vocation is reaching the state of simple contentment. I have been asked on more than one occasion if I am truly happy. In reply, I say that I don't sort out what happiness is or what others mean by it. It is not part and parcel of my own life in the way others understand it. I find the worldly conception of happiness to be ephemeral, fleeting, and transitory. I would rather talk about serenity or steady contentment. They offer some real possibilities, and something that all of us can apprehend.

Contentment and serenity go hand in hand to make us feel as if time has disappeared. This is a paradox, for in one way we are rooted and grounded in time, yet as we begin to experience something of the eternal, we sense that time and all earthly realities have been transcended. Contentment is basically a state of being as harmonious as a Bach fugue. There may be much turmoil all around us, but nothing can intrude into our inner sanctuary and destroy its integrity. *Nada te turbe, nada te espante, todo se pasa, Dios no se muda,* Saint Teresa would say. Contentment grants us the freedom to be totally absorbed in whatever we are involved at that moment, be it prayer, work, reading, eating, cleaning, making music, writing, gardening, cooking, or any other creative activity. This absorption renders us unaware of the hours, days, or months. It transcends time and finds its rest in eternity.

— JULY 31 —

Our Lady of Nazareth

When they [Mary and Joseph] had finished everything required by the law of the Lord, they returned to Galilee, to their own town of Nazareth. The child grew and became strong, filled with wisdom; and the favor of God was upon him.

LUKE 2:39-40

The daily life at Nazareth, more than any other episode in the Gospels, is the profound inspiration for a monastic lifestyle. Mary, Joseph, and Jesus, simple peasants in an otherwise almost forsaken town, led quiet, hidden lives, observing rituals of prayer and work within their home. In Nazareth, they were not known for being achievers, or famous, or anything impressive. Joseph was known by his trade as a carpenter, and Jesus as the carpenter's son. Mary, Our Lady of Nazareth, applied herself to the daily care and maintenance of her family: cleaning, cooking, sewing, gardening, and tending to Jesus' education. From her lips, he learned to pray the Psalms of David and to read the prophecies. Mary loved the Word of God: she lived by it, and above all, she kept it in her heart. She instilled in Jesus this same attachment to the Scriptures.

In Nazareth, their daily lives were so ordinary that one day Jesus, while preaching in the local synagogue, utterly surprised his neighbors by the wisdom of his discourse. "Is he not the carpenter's son?" they would ask, astonished at what was coming out from his lips. I am sure Mary and Joseph were probably standing nearby, smiling quietly but acting unsurprised at what was taking place in their midst. Slowly, the Father's plan was beginning to unfold.

Whenever I read in the Gospels about those quiet years in Nazareth, I feel reassured that our daily monastic life must humbly try to mirror the mystery of Nazareth and receive all its inspiration from the simplicity of the life once lived there. Just as in Nazareth, our days consist of much routine, monotony, repetition, and silence. Like the Nazareth family, the fabric of our lives consists of worship and prayer, manual labor, reading and study of the Word of God, eating, gardening, farming, and a much-needed rest at the end of day. This gets repeated day after day, be it summer or winter, spring or fall. There is no glamour or any other special allure to make it sound spectacular. It is a life that requires faith and fidelity to the will of God.

Through faith, inspired by the Word of God, we open the eyes of our hearts to the mystery of the everyday. It is there that we uncover God's designs for each of us. We encounter him not in the rare splendor of Tabor, but rather in the humble reality of Nazareth. The Lord somehow weaves his interactions with us through plain events. Each day, each moment, each event or action, if we are inwardly attentive as Our Lady of Nazareth, can become an opportunity to make direct contact with the Lord. If we only knew the gift of God in simple things, we would steadily grasp and hold them, retreating inwardly with Mary to ponder God's wonders in the innermost of our hearts.

The lingering memory of Our Lady of Nazareth is a unique grace in the life of the monk. He looks at her not only for inspiration and direction, but even more for her motherly intercession in all life's circumstances and events. In Nazareth, she stood close by Jesus and Joseph, supporting, encouraging, and protecting them. Today we beg her to do the same for us. *Our Lady of Nazareth, Mother and Model of monks, pray for us now and at the hour of our death.*

AUGUST

— AUGUST 1 —

Early August

The eighth (month) was August, being richly arrayed,
In garments all of gold, down to the ground...
EDMUND SPENCER

With the arrival of August, we find ourselves midterm in our summer journey. In ancient times, the Anglo-Saxons named August "Weod-monath," that is, the "weed month," for weeds are usually plentiful at this time of the year. They seem to grow at a more rapid pace and, quite frankly, they are found sprouting everywhere in our gardens.

August is not always kind to a gardener. It can often be a very testy time when one can easily get discouraged, not only by the abundance of weeds but also by the lack of rain, which makes garden work most difficult. Nothing is so depressing to a gardener as a relentless drought halfway into the growing season. I have had this unlucky experience several times throughout the years. At times, under duress from the drought, I felt tempted to give up gardening for the remainder of the season. This temptation, I learned later, is not uncommon among gardeners! With God's help, however, we go on, we continue. This sometimes means watering the gardens twice a day: once in the early morning and once in the late evening. Watering may not require considerable physical effort, but it does consume a lot of time that one may have to steal away from other activities.

Another aspect this time of the year is the scorching heat which usually affects some people more than others. I happen to be among the ones affected. I don't bear well the burden of the heat. In fact, sometimes I don't seem to function at all under its spell. To make things worse, the Hudson Valley is renowned for its hot, humid weather.

Just when August flounders in heat and drought, I am reminded that it is also the month of the Transfiguration of the Lord and the Dormition of Our Lady—two very cherished monastic feasts! Midsummer is also the time when the annuals in our gardens bloom in steady profusion: zinnias, sunflowers, marigolds, dahlias, and snapdragons. Their bright colors add a touch of beauty to the late summer garden. August's lush abundance also becomes visible in the vegetable garden. The first tomatoes begin to ripen and, of course, there is nothing to compare with their taste. The delicious new potatoes are also harvested at this time, to say nothing of the basil and some other herbs, whose aromatic scent permeates the whole of the garden and the kitchen! All of this, when I think about it, compensates for the nuisance and setback of the intense heat.

— AUGUST 2 —

A Summer Ramble

The quiet August noon has come;
A slumbrous silence fills the sky,
The fields are still, the woods are dumb,
In glassy sleep the water lies.

Away! I will not be, today,
The only slave of toil and care;
Away from the desk and dust! away!
I'll be as idle as the air.

Beneath the open sky abroad,
Among the plants and breathing things,
The sinless, peaceful works of God,
I'll share the calm the season brings.

Come, thou, in whose soft eyes I see
The gentle meaning of thy heart,
One day amid the woods with me,
From men and all their cares apart.

WILLIAM CULLEN BRYANT

— AUGUST 3 —

Monastic Hospitality

All guests who present themselves are to be welcomed as
Christ, for he himself will say: "I was a stranger and you
welcomed me."

RULE OF SAINT BENEDICT

The origins of monastic hospitality are in the Gospel and the
earliest of the monastic tradition. The Desert Fathers and
Mothers welcomed all those who came to the desert in search of
advice, counsel, or simply a word of encouragement. Who can
discern but God alone the mysterious reasons that prompt a pilgrim or guest to approach a monastery? These multiple reasons

were a challenge to the early monks and nuns, as they are to us today.

Saint Benedict clearly counsels that guests must be received as if they were Christ himself. The monk is called to recognize the face of Christ in every stranger who knocks at the monastery doors. Behind that face, the hidden Christ is present. Often, monastic hospitality entails a readiness to listen to someone in distress or to provide a space of silence to someone in turmoil or transition, or simply to supply a bed for the night to a poor homeless person.

The monk-guestmaster must exercise vigilance and wisdom in assisting those who, for whatever reasons, arrive at the monastery gates and request to be received. Many visitors come here to share our life of prayer. Such guests are never a burden beyond the physical work it entails to lodge and feed them. Then, there are those who arrive here, not necessarily seeking God, but primarily because of mere necessity or some sort of difficulty. These guests demand a special sort of attention. I'll mention one case, just to give an example.

A few years ago, I was awakened in the middle of the night by two women, mother and daughter, crying by the window. I got dressed and descended the stairs to open the doors. When we had a chance to sit down, the mother explained that they desperately needed a place for the night. She explained that her present husband usually got drunk after work on Fridays and then would return home to abuse her daughter. This was a Friday night and he had called, already drunk, saying he was on his way home. Fearful of what might again happen, she got her daughter into the car and drove with her to the monastery. She had never been here before, so I asked her why she choose to come here instead of going elsewhere. She answered, "I read about you in the newspaper, and I knew that if I came here I would not be turned away."

After making sure they were all right, I led them into our small guesthouse and quickly prepared their beds. They were safe for the night. Unfortunately, there was no more I could do except to pray for them. The following morning, after breakfast, I suggested that we call social services and seek the advice of a social worker. After making an appointment to see the social worker, they left and I never heard from them again.

People like these are no different from some of the guests and pilgrims who, for reasons of their own, request to partake of our monastic hospitality. The important thing, however, is not their diverse motives but that during the short time they spend here they come to experience something of the peace of God—the peace that everyone seeks, even when not aware of it.

— AUGUST 4 —

Rest

Our foster-nurse of nature is repose.
SHAKESPEARE

During August the demand is steady for our monastic hospitality. People come here to the country for repose. Rest is as much a law of life as work, though in a frantic world such as ours, we often forget it.

I often tell new arrivals, "You are in the house of God, a place of peace. Be simple and free with yourself. Take time to pray, to enjoy nature, but also take plenty of rest. If you feel like it, get your hands daily into the soil. Gardening may not be your only work. You can also work on the farm with our animals, or at another task. Just don't be compulsive about work. Do it in a meditative and restful way. Contemplate the trees, the flowers, the blue sky. Listen to the birds, to the sounds of our animals. Rejoice in it. Make ample time for reading, and if you wish, for writing. Breath deeply, and enter into the monastic rhythm of prayer, silence, work, and rest, without fear or hesitation. Let the rhythm work in you and carry you daily. It may be all that you need to find serenity."

Often, this works. Those who come here, from all the tramp and bustle of the world, have the good fortune to discover the treasure of monastic silence and quietude. They delight in the fact their spirits can bathe in a sea of tranquillity and find rest in an ambiance of peace. The monastic atmosphere helps them a great deal to come to grips with what is superfluous and unwarranted in their lives. Thereafter, they proceed to let go of certain encumbrances. When they return home, they usually sent a note of gratitude attesting to the fact. John Henry Cardinal Newman begged from God the timeless need for rest, both physical and spiritual, as he prayed:.

> May he support us all the day long, till the shades lengthen and the evening comes, and the busy world is hushed, and the fever of life is over, and our work is done. Then in his mercy…may he give us a safe lodging, and a holy rest, and peace at the last. Amen.

— AUGUST 5 —

Vigil of the Transfiguration

Let us journey into the heavenly and holy mountain,
And let us gaze with our minds and hearts
At the spiritual Godhead of the Father and the Holy Spirit,
Shining forth in the only-begotten Son.

BYZANTINE HYMN FOR THE FEAST

When August arrives, I feel as if the year has made another full circle. Once again the sublime season of the Transfiguration returns. Today's readings from the Letter of Paul to the Colossians seems especially pertinent:

> So you have been raised with Christ, seek the things that are above, where Christ is seated at the right hand of God. Set your minds on things that are above, not on things that are on earth, for you have died, and your life is hidden with Christ in God. When Christ who is your life is revealed, then you also will be revealed with him in glory (3:1–4).

As I prepare for the feast of the Transfiguration, which in fact starts today with first Solemn Vespers, I am reminded of a lovely custom kept on this feast by many monasteries of the East.

To appropriately celebrate Christ's Transfiguration, the monks from monasteries near a mountain, along with hundreds of other pilgrims, undertake a climb of several hours in order to reach the mountain's summit. They usually keep an all-night vigil, watching in prayer throughout the entire night, awaiting the dawn when the Divine Liturgy is celebrated. The journey up the mountain is part of the pilgrimage and thus done on foot, no matter how rough or precarious the terrain may be. Then the vigil follows, which lasts for hours unending. This is prayer, true prayer, continual prayer, as undertaken by Peter, John, and James when they followed their Master up the mountain to pray. It was while praying that they saw that his face "shone like the sun, and his clothes became dazzling white" (Mt 17:2).

We seem to find every excuse these days to abandon the ways of prayer. Yet, prayer is God's chosen path for us to find him. "Pray always and don't get discouraged," our Lord often counseled his disciples. It is true that prayer is work, that it demands everything from us: faith, humility, renunciation, conversion, and a steadfast fidelity to its practice. But prayer is also the greatest consolation of all. If anything, the mystery of the Transfiguration is a validation for mystical prayer, the prayer of continual union with the Lord. Alone with the Lord, in the solitude and silence of the mountain, the monk perceives daily the glory and transfigured presence of Christ; not in a cloud, but in the innermost of his heart.

— AUGUST 6 —

Transfiguration of the Lord

The sun which makes the earth bright sets once more; but Christ has shone as lightning upon the mountain and has filled the world with joy.

VESPERS ANTIPHON OF THE FEAST

Today's feast is a preeminently monastic one. Monks and nuns throughout the ages identify with the feast of the Transfiguration of Christ. In fact, many monasteries, both in the East and the West bear the Transfiguration title and observe their titular feast today. Further, it is also the day that many monks and nuns make their monastic profession. In the monastic setting, the Transfiguration is celebrated as a radiant feast, since it honors Jesus' appearance at Mount Tabor clothed in the divine light of his own divinity!

Many years ago, I undertook a pilgrimage to the Holy Land, prompted by the monastic profession of a dear friend who was being professed at the Carmel in Jerusalem. Besides this event, an invitation also came from an Eastern rite monastery to come and share their life for a while. I was in Rome at that time, so it was simpler, shorter, and cheaper to fly directly from Italy to the Holy Land. While in the Holy Land I had the occasion of visiting the various places associated with the life of Christ, and also some very ancient monasteries and monastic ruins. Every place I visited, as expected, I found to be deeply moving.

Nothing, however, prepared me for the experience I was to have as I climbed Mount Tabor, the mountain of the Transfiguration. As we reached the top of the mountain, where the church of the Transfiguration stands majestically, I felt enveloped by its profound silence. The extended view of the surrounding mountains and countryside was ravishing. Mount Tabor, under a cloudless sky, was wrapped in a bright, clear light. In the few hours spent there I could somehow get an intuition of why God had chosen this spot. God has an affinity for mountains, and this mountain, among all others, was very dear to him. Tabor was the place where I felt most at home in the Holy Land. It attracted me more than any other location.

The memories of my visit there remain clear and vivid to this day. Often, when Psalm 87 is prayed in the morning Office, my thoughts automatically return to Mount Tabor: "On the holy mount stands the city he founded; / the LORD loves the gates of Zion / more than all the dwellings of Jacob. / Glorious things are spoken of you, / O city of God."

When departure time arrived, I told the priest friend who drove me there that I was not quite ready to leave. I said to him, "How can one leave a place like this? It feels so good to be here!"

Suddenly, the words from Saint Peter came to my mind: "Lord, it is good for us to be here"—words uttered on that very spot many centuries ago. Indeed, I felt good being there, just as Peter, James, and John once felt, gazing upon the Man-God, seeing him not only as man but also as God. This was exactly the privilege that was accorded to the disciples: to behold the flesh of Christ transfigured by his divinity, and to hear the mysterious voice in the cloud say, "Listen to him." What a glorious vision was unveiled to the humble disciples. As they, spellbound, descended from the mountain, they were given the mission to share one day, with the world at large, the transfiguring glory of the Father's only-begotten Son.

In the Gospel accounts of the Transfiguration, we see the explicit desire on the part of the eternal Father to glorify his Son before he undergoes the sufferings of his Passion. For a moment, the veil covering his divinity is lifted and, suddenly, Jesus appears clothed in unsurpassed beauty. He is luminous, translucent with the Father's glory. The disciples present at the event instantly recognize the glory of God shining from that human face. From the mysterious, enveloping cloud, they hear the solemn declaration: "This is my Son, the Beloved; with him I am, well pleased; listen to him" (Mt 17:5). This is the Father speaking, with nearly the exact words he spoke from on high at the baptism of Jesus. He bears witness to the fact that Jesus is the only Son of God, true God from true God, as we believe and assent in the Credo.

For the monk as for the ordinary Christian, the feast of the Transfiguration is rich in meaning. By the grace bestowed on us in baptism, we are called to share in the mystery of the Transfiguration, to become inwardly transformed by the same divine light. In the churches of the Christian East, where today's feast is kept in great solemnity, the faithful bring to church the fruits from their orchards and the vegetables from their gardens to be blessed after the Divine Liturgy. Here in the monastery we keep this lovely custom, and every year after the liturgy we have the traditional blessing of the produce from our garden. This is symbolic of the earth itself being renewed by the presence of Christ and offering in homage its first fruits to its Lord and Master.

The Transfiguration Sticheras

Extol the LORD our God,
and worship at his holy mountain;
for the LORD our God is holy.

PSALM 99:9

The mystery of the Transfiguration is so rich in theological meaning that many saints spent their entire lives in its contemplation, trying to live by its message. Certainly, the monks of the East, such as Saint Gregory of Palamas and others, saw in the mystery of the Transfiguration an added dimension, that of the cosmic transformation of the world at the end of time. As one of the Byzantine hymns asserts:

> To show the transformation of human nature at your second and fearful coming, O Savior, you did transfigure yourself! And you have sanctified the whole world by your light.

The world at large—which is now under the lure of sin, shall be freed and transformed when the Savior returns in glory at the end of time. The blinding light of Tabor, the light which shone from Jesus' face, sanctifies those that come close to him as did the disciples. Today, that same light nurtures our best hopes about the future of the cosmos that God created at the beginning of time. The light of the Transfiguration points to the path of a new future in which God shall be all in all. Thus, we praise the Father together with the Son and the Holy Spirit:

> Let all the earth be moved to praise Christ, our God, Lord, both of the living and the dead. For when he was divinely transfigured on Tabor, the Savior of our souls was pleased to have at his side the leaders and preachers of both the Law and Grace.
>
> The shining cloud of the Transfiguration has taken the place of the darkness of the Law. Moses and Elijah were found worthy of this glory brighter than light and, taken up with it, they said unto Christ: "You are our God, the King of ages."

— AUGUST 8 —

Thirst for God

O God, you are my God, I seek you,
my soul thirsts for you;
my flesh faints for you,
as in a dry and weary land where there is no water.
So I have looked upon you in the sanctuary,
beholding your power and glory.

PSALM 63:1-2

Once when I was asked to explain the mystery of the monastic vocation, I answered rather simply: "To be a monk means to be always thirsty, it means to live in a state of permanent thirst for God."

It is the thirst for God that somehow colors every instant, and every movement in the monk's life. It is the reason for his prayer, it is what sustains and supports his daily work. The psalms, perhaps more than anything else, gently nurture this condition in the monk. They express our thirst, our desire for God, in a way that no other prayer does. The psalms, in that sense, constitute the daily drink of the monk. Paradoxically, they increase the thirst as they simultaneously help to quench it.

If the monk no longer feels the need to trot around the world looking for God, and instead settles in his humble solitude, it is because he realizes that he whom he thirsts and pines after already abides in him. In his monastic solitude, the monk then concentrates wholeheartedly on the Divine Guest. Leaving behind all that is worldly, futile, useless, selfish, and vain, the monk cherishes this aloneness with his God.

The monk's thirst for God finds its sole comfort in intense prayer. In the deep and penetrating silence, the monk applies himself to the discovery of the Presence that he longs and thirsts for daily. Prayer facilitates this marvelous discovery, this utterly splendid encounter. The monk confides to his God, in the words of Psalm 63:

I think of you on my bed,
    and meditate on you in the watches of the night;
for you have been my help,
    and in the shadow of your wings I sing for joy.

— AUGUST 9 —

Humility

The way of humility is this: self-control, prayer, and thinking yourself inferior to all creatures.

ABBA TITHOES, SAYINGS OF THE DESERT FATHERS

It seems almost taboo to speak of humility in today's narcissistic world where pride and self-glorification are the rule of the day. Today, glory is no longer ascribed to God but to oneself. Sometimes I see certain persons walk extra miles in efforts to show themselves off to others (*se gonfler* in French). How terribly tiring it must be to exert oneself in such a way. In contrast, the monastic virtue of humility is incredibly liberating.

To be humble means to accept one's vulnerability and one's limitations. It also means to recognize one's sinfulness and, therefore, be willing to occupy the last place in all things. More important yet, it is to seek contentment in that last place. One no longer has to fight or compete with anyone, for no one wishes to assume the role of the useless servant. Embracing humility means we deliberately take the last place in all situations. As an old monk used to tell me: "There is a great deal of freedom in being considered 'null and good for nothing,' for when you truly accept this, no one wishes to bother with you or is jealous of the state you assume."

Our lives make sense only so far as we follow the example of our Master. Toward the end of his life, in the final moments of the Last Supper, Jesus gave his disciples a supreme example of humility, with the express command that they must do as he did. After washing their feet he went back to the table and said: "Do you know what I have done to you? You call me Teacher and Lord—and you are right, for that is what I am. So if I, your Lord and Teacher, have washed your feet, you also ought to wash one another's feet. For I have set you an example, that you also should do as I have done to you" (Jn 13:12–15).

— AUGUST 10 —

Saint Lawrence

Lawrence cried out: I rejoice greatly because I have been considered worthy to be a sacrificial victim for Christ.

LAUDS ANTIPHON OF THE FEAST

On these quiet summer days, daylight stays on until late. In fact, the light is still apparent as one enters into the chapel for Compline. It is midsummer, the middle age of the year. As we traverse mid-August we seem to have reached a time of fullness, fulfillment and completion. The harvest is abundant, and one hears distant echoes of a rare bird song, which becomes true delight to one's ears! Today, I reflect upon the beauty of a hazy summer day: the meadows are lush as are the trees; the nearby hills seem dressed in an enchanting pale blue, almost violet shade; the flowers in the garden, though barely surviving the consequences of the heat, still manage to show the brilliance of their colors; and there is that lovely misty fog in the early morning that seems to come right out of a Monet painting. Yes, though the temperature is unnerving and disagreeable, when I consider all things in a proper perspective, I can still count my August blessings.

Monastic solitude, when one is called to it, is certainly a blessing. However, it also contains certain dangers, and it takes a certain amount of humility and good common sense to recognize them. In solitude, one could easily give in to depression, anxiety, fear, laziness, or some other destructive feeling. This is especially true when things don't go our way or we lose control over our emotions.

God, however, provides help via his grace, which helps us to overcome what could otherwise become negative and extremely dangerous for our spiritual lives. This grace demands that we cooperate with God by adhering to time-tested monastic values:

vigilance, humility, moderation, and prayer. This monastic asceticism imparts a wonderful resilience, magnanimity, and courage on our sometimes tired spirits. We may now continue the inner journey in peace, for with God's help we have made life-giving choices that steer us toward the course of what is fully positive, toward He who is perfect joy himself.

Today, the martyrology celebrates the memory of Saint Lawrence, a great martyr of the Church of Rome. Born around 210 A.D., he was arrested during Valerian's persecution, together with Pope Sixtus II and other Christians, for professing their allegiance to Christ. They were all put to death in 258 A.D. Young Lawrence, a deacon, was given the charge to help the poor and the widows, the indigent, homeless, and orphans—a ministry entrusted to deacons and deaconess in the early church. In a sermon for the feast of Saint Lawrence the great Saint Augustine wrote:

> Just as Christ laid down his life for us, so we too ought to lay down our lives for the brethren. My brethren, Lawrence understood this and, understanding, he acted on it. Just as he had partaken of a gift of self at the table of the Lord, so he prepared to offer such a gift. In his life he loved Christ; in his death he followed in his footsteps. Brethren, we too must imitate Christ if we truly love him. We shall not be able to render better return on that love than by modeling our lives on his.

— AUGUST 11 —

Saint Clare

O Clare, endowed with so many titles of clarity! Clear (clara) *even before your conversion, clearer* (clarior) *in your manner of living, exceedingly clear* (praeclarior) *in your enclosed life, and brilliant* (clarissima) *in splendor after the course of your mortal life.*

FROM THE "BULL OF CANONIZATION"

More years ago than I can remember, I had the privilege of spending three months on retreat in Assisi, the Umbrian town of Saint Francis and Saint Clare. The kind sisters where I was staying gave me a room with a balcony overlooking the monastery of the Poor Clares, where the saintly foundress sleeps in peace awaiting the eternal resurrection. Every day, from that little balcony, I would gaze at the lovely valley below Assisi and at the monastery's tall, majestic bell tower. It was an occasion that moved one's heart to praise God, as one watched the last rays of an unforgettable sunset.

While in Assisi, I was able to meet up with a friend of a friend, a remarkable woman named Nesta de Robeck. Nesta, a devout English woman, had settled in Assisi after her conversion to the Catholic faith. She told me her conversion was due to the influence of Saints Francis and Clare, and so she had decided to settle in Assisi. Nesta gradually introduced me to Saint Clare, whose life she was putting into writing. Once I told her of the soothing influence the tower and bells of Saint Clare's monastery had on me during those three months, she remarked: "I had lived here many more years than I can recall, and still, every day, I am charmed by the beauty of that tower, by the sounds of those bells." Her living accommodations were not far from Saint Clare's church. I think she attended daily Mass there, where she was well known and loved by the friars and nuns. At the end, when she could no longer attend Mass because of her age and physical condition, a saintly friar brought holy Communion to Nesta on a daily basis.

Once, as I was preparing to take my leave, she told me to anticipate the forthcoming appearance of her Saint Clare book. When this occurred a few years later, I purchased the book, and in reading about Saint Clare relived the memories of that extraordinary summer in Assisi. A paragraph, in particular, touched me profoundly:

> The tower which guards the shrine of Saint Clare is tall, and strong and beautiful, even as she was; and the pearly gray and rose of its stone reflect all the light in the sky. It catches the first rays of the sunrise, and its bells ring for the new day. Throughout the hours it waits upon God's pleasures in sunshine and storm, and its midday recalls us to his Presence in his world. Its face is turned to the sunset, and while many birds fly round it singing, it joins with all the other bells of the valley in echoing the Angelus; the time for rest has come.

Today, as we keep the memory of Saint Clare, the "little plant of our father Francis," as she loved to describe herself, we ponder the wondrous work of the Holy Spirit in her life. She fought courageously to maintain the rule of holy poverty among her sisters, the very testament she had received from her father and mentor Saint Francis. Through her efforts, the Franciscan ideal survived the many attacks it received after Francis's death, both from within as well as from outside her religious order. The example of Saint Clare's own life became the most eloquent witness to the testament entrusted to her by Saint Francis. It is because of the humble Clare of Assisi that the spirit of the *Poverello* continues to shine today throughout the entire Christian world.

— AUGUST 12 —

The Work of Unceasing Prayer

Grant us, Lord, to cling to you, not in our outward beings but in our hidden selves, and may we follow you until we behold your face. For in this world, a person continues to follow after you as he becomes perfected, but in the New World you will manifest your very face to him.

PRAYER OF A SYRIAC MONK

A disciple once inquired from Abba Agathon what the most important occupation was of the monk in the desert. Abba Agathon, with his usual simplicity, replied: "I think there is no labor greater than that of prayer to God. For every time a man wants to pray, his enemies, the demons, want to prevent him, for they know that it is only by turning him from prayer that they can hinder his journey."

From morning until dusk, and again from night until morning, prayer was the one continual occupation of the desert monk. Prayer, an unceasing colloquy with God, was the work above all other works, and this demanded undivided attention. The desert monk or nun, were he or she to be here today, would not feel terribly comfortable with the way prayer is relegated to an almost a trivial level. We are engrossed in novelty, in materialism, in the news of the world. We continue to swim in the icy waters of a pagan culture. We seek enlightenment from those whose life is not necessarily prayer; so how can we catch the divine fire of prayer that Christ prayed for and wished for us? Jesus' admonition to Martha of Bethany resonates today with a great deal of actuality: "Martha, Martha, you are busy about too many things. Only one thing is necessary."

True, prayer does not come always easy. It takes practice, patience, perseverance and, above all, a great deal of humility. But if we do this, day in and day out, without discouragement and with complete trust in God's promise, we can be sure that one day we shall discover that our contact with God in prayer is the best recompense a human being can ever imagine. In prayer, the Holy Spirit reveals to us the Face of the living God, the Face of He who is the sole object of our desires.

Prayer's intensity may serve to prolong it. What seems to the soul like a few short moments may indeed encompass several hours. In the end, instead of feeling tired or exhausted, one feels light, rejuvenated, and reenergized. Prayer is not a matter of verbal communication, but the living experience of Someone we love, Someone we revere, Someone we adore.

The monk's life, then, proceeds into a continuous, harmonious unfolding of this intimate friendship with God. This relationship grows daily through unceasing prayer and the practice of the Gospel counsels. Worldly demands, from time to time, may knock at the doors of the monastery or the hermitage, or even at the very heart of the monk, and try to distract him from his one purpose. But he, guided in all simplicity by the Holy Spirit, not looking back at worldly cares, will continue to gravitate towards the one thing necessary: a conscious, uninterrupted communion with his God. This is his only goal, and by necessity, his sole occupation.

— AUGUST 13 —

Syriac Mysticism

O Christ, the ocean of our forgiveness, allow me to wash off in you the dirt I am clothed in, so that I may become resplendent in the raiment of your holy light. May I be covered with the cloud of your hidden glory. May the things which divert me from gazing upon your beauty not be visible to me. May wonder at your glory captivate me continually, may my mind become unable to set in motion worldly impulses. May nothing ever separate me from your love, but rather may that desire, which is to behold your countenance harrow me continually.

JOHN THE ELDER, SYRIAC MONK

Early Syriac mysticism, distinct from the Greek or Latin tradition, was the product of intense and fruitful attachment to the Scriptures. The Syriac monks used as their source a Syriac translation of the Bible, which contained nuances not found in either the Greek or Latin Bible. After the fifth century, the Syriac monastic-mystic tradition more or less mingled with that which originated in the Egyptian desert. The richness of the mysticism found in the Greek, Latin, and Syriac traditions have their common roots in the one Gospel message. Though they are distinct, they have intermingled and interacted with one another for centuries. I am deeply attached to the tradition of the Syriac Fathers, in particular to Saint Isaac of Nineveh, commonly called Saint Isaac the Syrian. For years their writings have inspired and nurtured my own approach to prayer. As one reads their texts, so rich and illuminating, one is almost immediately moved to an attitude of prayer.

— AUGUST 14 —

Vigil of the Dormition

Let us celebrate the most holy Dormition of the Mother of God: For she has delivered her spotless soul into the hands of her Son. Therefore the world, restored to life by her glorious Assumption, in radiant joy celebrates this feast with psalms, hymns, and spiritual songs.

VESPERS OF THE FEAST OF THE DORMITION

We are on the eve of mid-August. Starting with first Vespers this evening, we shall be celebrating all day tomorrow the great solemnity of the earthly Dormition and heavenly Assumption of the Theotokos. This feast is considered, especially in the East, the most prominent of all of the feasts celebrated in honor of the Mother of God. It is also one of the most ancient. In the Christian East, the feast is kept with great solemnity and is preceded by a two-week fast as preparation.

Some Christians, not of the Orthodox or Catholic tradition, have a difficult time trying to comprehend the mystery we are about to celebrate. After all, there is no testimony in the Scriptures concerning the death and Assumption of the Mother of God into heaven. Our belief is founded on sacred tradition, the belief of the ancient, undivided Church. Although reliable information is lacking concerning Our Lady's last earthly years, there is some mention in the patristic literature of the East which recounts her Dormition and Assumption. Saint Juvenal, bishop of Jerusalem around the time of the Council of Chalcedon, relates the tradition as it was believed by the Christians of Jerusalem: *Mary died in the presence of all the Apostles (except Thomas), but when her tomb was opened at the request of Saint Thomas, it was found empty; where from the Apostles concluded that her body had been taken up to heaven.*

Later on, some Church Fathers, such as Andrew of Crete and John Damascene, expanded on this short and very simple belief of the early Christians. One of the most touching texts of the Byzantine Vespers of the Dormition expresses the mystery thus:

At your departure, O Virgin Theotokos, to him who was ineffably born of you, James, the first bishop and brother of the Lord was there, and so was Peter, the honored leader and head of the disciples, and the whole sacred company of the Apostles. In discourses that showed forth heavenly things, they sung the praises of the divine and amazing mystery of the benevolence of Christ our God; and they rejoiced, O most holy Virgin, as they buried your body, the origin of the Life and bearer of God. On high the angelic powers wonder before this marvel, and said to one another: "Open wide your gates and receive her who bore the Creator of heaven and earth. With songs of praise let us glorify her precious and holy body, dwelling-place of the Lord on whom we may not gaze." Therefore we, too, as we keep your festival, cry out to you: "Most blessed Lady, Protector of Christians, intercede for the salvation of our souls!"

As we keep vigil today, commemorating both Mary's earthly death and her glorious Assumption into heaven, let us keep in mind that this is a feast full of hope for all of humanity. In the glorification of the Theotokos, all of human nature is transformed. Redeemed as we are by the precious blood of her Son, we too await the day that our human nature shall be carried up and received into the heavenly realms.

— AUGUST 15 —

Assumption of the Mother of God

While giving birth, you remained a virgin, and in your Dormition, you did not forsake this world, O Theotokos. For you, who are the Mother of Life itself, have yourself passed into life. And by the help of your prayers, you delivered our souls from death.

TROPARION OF THE FEAST

Just as the Dormition is the crowning of the earthly life of the humble maiden of Nazareth, her Assumption into heaven is God's glorification of she who was chosen to be the mother of his only-begotten Son. A few years after the Resurrection and

Ascension of her Son into heaven, Mary was called to join him body and soul, there where he sits above the stars: *In quo Rex regum stellato sedet solio.* When I think of this mystery, I am always in awe of the thought of that blessed encounter, that first reunion between Son and mother. As the Peter Damian's hymn for the vigil of the feast beautifully describes it:

> She gazes on her Son divine,
> In whom both God and Man combine;
> He whom she cradled with delight
> Now reigns as King in Godhead's Light.

Only in heaven shall we be able to understand something of it. Through faith, we sometimes get a glimpse of it. The liturgical texts, both from the East and the West, especially the Sticheras of the feast, have much to enrich our faith and piety:

O marvelous wonder! The Source of Life is laid in the tomb, the grave becomes a means of ascent to heaven! Rejoice, Gethsemani, holy chamber of the Mother of God. Come, O faithful, and with Gabriel let us cry out aloud: "Hail, O woman full of grace, the Lord is with you. Because of you the Lord bestows on the world great mercy."

Glorious are your mysteries, O pure Lady. You were made the Throne of the Most High and today you ascend to heaven. Your glory shines with grace and majesty, surpassing every splendor. Therefore, all you virgins, ascend with the Theotokos, and cry out: "Hail, O woman full of grace, the Lord is with you. Because of you the Lord bestows on the world great mercy." The dominions, the thrones, the rulers, principalities and powers, the cherubim and the fearful seraphim glorify your Dormition. Those who dwell on earth rejoice beholding your glory; kings together with the angels and archangels, sing out to you: "Hail, O woman full of grace, the Lord is with you, because of you the Lord bestows on the world great mercy." She who is higher than the heavens and more glorious than the cherubim, is also held in greater honor than all creation. Today commends her most pure soul into the hands of her Son who once took flesh from her most pure body. With her, all things are filled with joy, and she bestows great mercy upon us.

— AUGUST 16 —

Seek God Above All

Imagine that there is nothing else in front of your eyes—
as though you were not among mankind—because you
are seeing nothing else but God, for God is the entire
reason for your way of life.

JOHN THE SOLITARY

Saint Benedict's Rule indicates that the sole purpose for the
monastic vocation is to seek God above all. In the monastery
or hermitage, the monk must not waste time or energy seeking
human approval. Only God's approval matters. Saint Benedict
measures the advances a monk makes in his spiritual quest by
the level of detachment from earthly approvals, popularity, con-
tests, and especially by the degree of the monk's self-surrender
into the Father's loving hands. For Saint Benedict, to seek God
alone means to abandon one's former life completely and to entrust oneself to the Father's will as Jesus did. While Jesus was
making his entrance into our world, he uttered: "Behold, I come
to do your will." During his earthly days he prayed daily, humbly: "Your will be done on earth as in heaven."

There is a certain pedagogy in Benedict's Rule. He wishes to
show the monk that, just as Jesus lived for God alone, the monk
must act likewise in his daily monastic search. After all, the disciple is no greater than the master. This implies that the example
of the master defines the path the disciple must follow. All authentic monastic life is thoroughly theocentric. Just as Jesus committed his life radically to God alone, even to the point of death
on the cross, so must the monk commit himself to a life of full
communion with God in all times and in all places. Prayer is the
monk's daily tool in his search for fullness of life with God. The
Holy Spirit, through continual prayer, guides the heart of the
monk towards the living waters of God's love. Only when we
begin to love God as he really is, above all things, do we discover
the true joy that can replenish all the desires of the human heart.
No other but God can fully satisfy the human heart.

— AUGUST 17 —

Salad Days

Salads taste good. What's more, they're in the "good for you" category.

MARYE DAHNKES

During these brutally hot, sultry summer days, nothing is more appetizing and calming to our nerves than a healthy salad that springs fresh from our garden. Some days I really don't feel up to lighting the stove or the oven. On those days, a good, hearty, refreshing salad is the perfect solution. Nutritionists have always recommended raw vegetables and fruits in one's daily diet, and what better way to heed their advise than by eating the delicious, fresh treats from the bounty of our gardens?

A well-made salad is indeed a treat. A good salad can be assembled at the last minute, just before dinner. On the days I decide to have a salad as a complete meal (*un repas complet*), I pick up a basket after Vespers and approach the garden to see what it has to offer. Since I work daily in the garden and am mindful of what is ripening at that time, I have an idea of what to look for. I usually begin by picking one or more varieties of tender lettuces, to which I add other greens: arugula, mâche, mesclun, whatever is available. This shall constitute the base of the salad. I go on to pick some gorgeous looking tomatoes, cucumbers, peppers, string beans (which can cook in three minutes!), onions, and a wide range of herbs: basil, chervil, and parsley to garnish the salad.

Salad-making is essentially a simple task, but it still requires attention and careful planning. I usually begin by washing and drying the salad greens. I then place them at the bottom of the salad plate. On the top, I add the tomato and cucumber slices, finely chopped onion, thinly sliced pepper strips, and some olives. To be sure it is a complete meal and that one gets sufficient protein, I add some cubed cheese, feta or mozzarella. On other occasions, instead of the cheese, I add slices of hard-boiled eggs. This adds variety in the daily preparation. One always needs to be imaginative about the salad ingredients, for the whole secret of a good salad consists in the right combination of its ingredients and dressing.

When this part of the preparation is completed, I drizzle the right amount of olive oil and vinegar (or lemon juice), a dash of salt and pepper, and garnish the top with the freshly chopped herbs. Accompanied by good bread, a fresh salad becomes an entire meal.

Moreover, after consuming such a salad one feels light, restored, and well satisfied. It gratifies not only the stomach but also the intellect and the heart. A fresh salad from our own garden reinforces our attachment to the earth, to nature, and to the Creator of all good things. As Saint Paul assures us, all perfect gifts come from above. *Benedicamus Domino!*

— AUGUST 18 —

Monastic Frugality

Once some robbers came into a monastery...and said to one of the elders: "We have come to take away everything that is in your cell." And the elder replied: "My son, take all you want." So they took everything they could find in the cell and started off. But they left behind a little bag that was hidden in the cell. The elder picked it up and followed after them, crying out: "My sons, take this, you forgot it in the cell!" Amazed at the actions of the elder, the robbers brought everything back into the monk's cell and did penance, saying: "This one really is a man of God!"

FROM *SAYINGS OF THE DESERT FATHERS*

Monastic frugality springs directly from the example of Jesus and is as much countercultural as was Jesus himself. There is an enormous contrast between a culture of consumerism which worships spending, expanding, wasting, and the abuse of God's creation versus the humble life in the monastic desert which offers another alternative to the people of our times. This alternative is to scale back on possessions, to avoid cluttering, to spend and consume less so that others may not be deprived of what is necessary, to share and give away to those in need, to build small dwellings, and to conserve all natural resources. This contrast is immensely refreshing to those of good will who genuinely seek alternatives to a society made of consumers.

The slavery of greed and possessions blinds us to the precious gift of frugality and simplicity, which can truly liberate our souls for God, for others, and for the things that really matter in life. Often I notice that when one succumbs to the temptation to own and possess more instead of less, one begins to feel enslaved by the chains of our own accumulations. We experience the terrible weight of the burden we have created for ourselves. Caught in this state of restlessness, one finds it difficult to transcend the situation.

Frugality, on the contrary, provides the monk with a spiritual perspective. It inspires him to place his priorities on what is really important, on the "one thing necessary" of the Gospel. It makes him appreciative of the blessings of the present moment. One does not have to wait until tomorrow to find joy or achieve peace and contentment of spirit. Every moment is unique and therefore precious in God's presence. The present moment is a treasure that can never be recaptured. To connect with it is the grace given to those who seek to efface themselves, those who deliberately choose the path of true frugality and simplicity for the sake of the Kingdom.

— AUGUST 19 —

An Exquisite Gift From the Garden: Tomatoes

No vegetable can sell people on home gardening faster than the juicy, ripe tomato. Simply everyone loves vine-ripened tomatoes. They are easy to grow, productive, and delicious.

L. BURROWS AND L. MYERS

A yearly miracle takes place in the garden at this time: the tomatoes seem to ripen overnight and the garden presents us with a real deluge of them. Tomatoes, the most popular of products from the garden, are usually the pride and joy of all gardeners. If nothing else goes well in the garden that particular year except for the tomatoes, the gardener still seems pleased.

This year I have planted twenty-four tomato plants, of all varieties and sizes, including some new species to our garden whose seeds were brought from Italy. A superb year for tomatoes, the plants look wonderful, and at present they are yielding magnificently. For weeks now I have been eating them fresh every single day. I also serve them to those here on retreat, and we still have enough to share with friends. Soon, I will have to start canning them, for nothing compares in flavor or texture to preserved tomatoes from one's own garden. Canning them involves a bit of extra effort, and sometimes I tend to delay the task, for I know well once we start the process it will go on for weeks until the season ends. Sometimes, like now, I don't feel quite up to it yet, so I linger and just enjoy the fresh tomatoes at the table. All one needs to add is a drizzle of olive oil, a dash of salt and pepper, a few sprigs of fresh basil, and one has a feast for the palate.

When the tomatoes are in season, such as now, the best time to pick them is just before eating, when they are still warm from the sun. Tomatoes are loaded with vitamins, especially vitamins A and C. They also contain lots of potassium. Some recent research even seems to indicate that the yellow substance that surrounds the tomato seed is quite effective in preventing blood clots, and consequently proves good for one's heart. If a cook ever advises the removal of seeds in a particular recipe, I no longer pay attention to it. Even when canning, I preserve the entire fruit, except the for peel, which may be discarded.

Part of the magic of August are those fresh, ripe, succulent, juicy, fabulous tomatoes that provide endless delight to a summer table. They are an exceptional gift from the garden, a heavenly blessing bestowed upon us. As our summer days begin to wane and autumn hovers over the horizon, now it is the time to enjoy our daily blessings and to make the most of those gorgeous tomatoes.

— AUGUST 20 —

Saint Bernard of Clairvaux

Saint Bernard, the Holy Spirit blessed your lips,
That words of truth from them should flow,
As sweet as honey to the taste,
Yet burning with a seraph's glow.

HYMN FOR VESPERS OF THE FEAST

Today, we honor Saint Bernard, perhaps one of the most remarkable monks of the Middle Ages. He was barely twenty
years old when he entered the abbey of Citeaux, in the heart of
Burgundy. When he knocked at the doors of the monastery, the
monks were surprised to see that he did not come alone. Saint
Bernard was being escorted by thirty other men, relatives and
friends, who were eager to join the new monastic reform at
Citeaux. Citeaux was founded a few years earlier by a group of
monks determined to return to an authentic monastic observance
based on a faithful interpretation of the Rule of Saint Benedict.
This reform held a great appeal for Bernard and his companions.
Years later, he was chosen as founder and abbot of a new monastery at Clairvaux, also in Burgundy. From there, other monastic
foundations inspired by the example of Saint Bernard followed.
Filled with zeal for the things of God, he exerted an enormous
influence among the Christians of his time, leading and guiding
many of its most powerful people, among them popes and kings.

More and more people, not only the Cistercians, are drawing benefit from the depth of Bernard's wisdom. Of course, how
could I forget how much we owe in all of this to our cherished
friend, the late Dom Jean Leclercq, who from 1948 on spent a
great part of his life researching the entire work of Bernard? Dom
Jean Leclercq lived and breathed Saint Bernard. He was a frequent visitor and *bienfaiteur* to our monastery. As his sometimes
private chauffeur for years, I was able to benefit from many of his
personal insights into the complex person that was Saint Bernard.

Saint Bernard was also a great guide on the ways of prayer. I
happen to use a small book called *Saint Bernard et la priere*. The

book contains selections of Bernard's writings about prayer. As one reads them, they help expand our hearts into the mystery of prayer. They open us to the immense possibilities and ways on how, through prayer, God can reach each of us and enhance our lives. These little vignettes are true incentives to prayer. To quote one of those selections: *Let us breathe a bit, my brothers! For if we are nothing of value in our own sights, perhaps we count for something in the depths of God's heart!*

— AUGUST 21 —

A Kiss of the Lord

This beautiful excerpt from Bernard's *The Song of Songs* (Sermon 4) is typical of his mystical thinking:

> When God endows us with the more ample grace of a sweet friendship with him, in order to enable us to live with a virtue that is worthy of such a relationship, we tend to raise our heads from the dust with a greater confidence for the purpose of kissing, as is the custom, the hand of our benefactor. It is essential, however, that we should not make this favor the occasion of self-glorification, we must give the glory to him from whom it comes. For if you glory in yourself rather than in the Lord, it is your own hand that you kiss, not his, which according to the words of Job, is the greatest evil and a denial of God. If, therefore, as Scripture suggests, the seeking of one's own glory is like kissing one's own hand, then he who gives glory to God is quite properly said to be kissing God's hand....
>
> The heartfelt desire to admit one's guilt brings a man down in lowliness before God, as it were to his feet; the heartfelt devotion of a worshiper finds in God renewal and refreshment, the touch, as it were, of his hand; and the delights of contemplation lead on to ecstatic repose that is the fruit of the kiss of his mouth. Because his providence rules over all, he is all things to all, yet, to speak with accuracy, he is in no way what these things are. If we consider him in himself, his home is in inaccessible light, his peace is so much greater than we can understand, his wisdom has no bounds. No one can measure his greatness, for no man can see him and live.

— AUGUST 22 —

Queenship of the Theotokos

The Most Holy Virgin opens her merciful arms to all, all humankind receives from her fullness: the sinner receives pardon, the just receives grace, and the angels receive joy.

SAINT BERNARD, 12 PRI, 2

Today, we celebrate the Queenship of Mary, which is the prolongation and completion of the feast of the Dormition and Assumption of the Mother of God. Our Lady is the new ark of God. She is the one who once contained He who is the source of life, and later gave birth to Him who is life itself. This is why the Christian never ceases honoring the Theotokos, never ceases singing her praises. In this small monastery consecrated to her under the title of Our Lady of the Resurrection, the memory of Mary is kept alive in multiple ways: not only in our prayers and song but also in the garden where several of them are dedicated to her. In mid-August, as I pay a visit to her in the garden, I usually sing her litanies and some other Gregorian hymns such as *Tota pulchra est Maria, Ave, Maris Stella,* or possibly, the *Salve, Regina* in its solemn tone. The *Salve*, as is the *Memorare*, is attributed to Saint Bernard, who was renowned for his filial piety toward the Mother of God. Today, I find no better way to keep remembrance of the Theotokos than by translating from the French some of Saint Bernard's tender praise to the Mother of God:

> Let us follow in the footsteps of Mary, let us throw ourselves at her feet, let us plead with her insistently! Let us keep her close by us, and may she not depart before granting us her blessing, for she is all-powerful.
>
> O Holy Mother of God, Mistress of the world, Queen of heaven, all generations proclaim you blessed. For them you have given birth to Him who is their Life and Glory! In you, the angels rejoice without ceasing, the just find grace, and the sinner obtains pardon. All creatures have their eyes fixed on you: through you, in you, and from you, the hand of the Almighty has re-created that which he once created for the first time.

— AUGUST 23 —

Saint Bernard on Prayer

H ere are some of my translated quotes on prayer from Saint Bernard.

Go to the mountain of prayer, and there pray with perseverance, following Jesus' example who often spent the entire night in prayer. Then, your good heavenly Father, shall give you his good Holy Spirit (S. Asc. 4:11).

He who prays should do it as if he already were in heaven, in the presence of him who sits among the angels...Yes, he should act and pray as such in the presence of the Lord of all majesty (S. Div. 25:8).

Happy, indeed, and blessed is the heart that hears the voice of God murmur in silence! Happy is he who often says with Samuel: Speak, Lord, your servant listens (S. Div. 23:7).

When you pray and sing the Psalms, be mindful of the presence of the Angels. Be reverent and rejoice in the thought that your Angels gaze without ceasing into the face of the Father (S. Cant. 7:4).

None among you should belittle the value of your prayer, for him to whom the prayer is addressed doesn't look at it as something insignificant (S. Car. 5:5).

It is of utmost importance to him who truly wishes to pray to arrange ahead of time the place and the time he allocates exclusively to prayer (S. Cant. 86:3).

— AUGUST 24 —

Saint Bartholomew

Philip found Nathanael [later called Bartholomew] and said to him, "We have found him about whom Moses in the Law and also the prophets wrote, Jesus son of Joseph, from Nazareth." Nathanael said to him, "Can anything good come out of Nazareth?" Philip said to him, "Come and see." When Jesus saw Nathanael coming toward him, he said of him, "Here is truly an Israelite in whom there is no deceit." Nathanael asked him, "Where did you get to know me?" Jesus answered, "I saw you under the fig tree before Philip called you." Nathanael replied, "Rabbi, you are the Son of God! You are the King of Israel!" Jesus answered, "Do you believe because I told you that I saw you under the fig tree? You will see greater things than these." And he said to him, "Very truly, I tell you, you will see heaven opened and the angels of God ascending and descending upon the Son of Man."

JOHN 1:45-51

Bartholomew is one of Jesus' twelve Apostles. He is mentioned as such in the four Gospels. The Gospel of John describes the first encounter between Jesus and Bartholomew (then called Nathanael), wherein Jesus called him a "true Israelite in whom there is no deceit."

From John's Gospel, we become aware that Bartholomew was someone who knew and lived by the teaching of the Scriptures. He awaited the Messiah, and he was ready for him. The moment the occasion came to encounter Jesus, he was immediately illumined, touched, and consoled by Jesus' recognition of him. Instantly he decided to leave all behind and follow Jesus.

There is no doubt that Bartholomew, as much as the other disciples, displayed traits that showed the conflict between faith and human weakness. This example should be reassuring to all of us. Discipleship is not an easy task. It does not happen or come readily. We see in the Gospels how often the Apostles were

uncooperative and unreceptive towards their Master's teaching.
They even quarreled among themselves about who was to occupy the first place in the Kingdom. As are many of us today,
they were desirous of prestige and anxious for power. How distant they were from the truth, from what Jesus was all about!
And yet, these ignorant, weak human beings were the ones chosen to announce the good tidings to the whole world. God always uses weak instruments to confront the strong and the mighty.
This Gospel lesson should provide a great deal of consolation to
us all, who, in spite of our weaknesses and sinfulness, try to tread
on the footsteps of the Master.

Today, in listening to the story of Bartholomew, we are invited
to receive the grace of conversion, the grace to change ourselves
gradually and become more like Jesus. Then, like Bartholomew,
we shall be able to share the good news with others, to tell the
Jesus story with the example of our own lives.

— AUGUST 25 —

Lectio Divina

*The nature of water is soft, that of stone is hard; but if a
bottle is hung above the stone, allowing the water to fall
drop by drop, it wears away the stone. So it is with the
Word of God, it is soft and our heart is hard, but the one
who hears the Word of God often, opens his heart to the
fear of God.*

ABBA POEMEN, *SAYINGS OF THE DESERT FATHERS*

As a monk undertakes the practice of what some consider to
be the most important activity of the daily monastic routine, the period of *lectio*, he may benefit from the example of the
ancient desert monks. They held in high esteem the reading of
and meditation on the Sacred Scriptures. Their daily lives were
fashioned by the study of God's Word, which informed and per-
meated their prayer while inspiring and giving incentive to their
search for God. In the words of Douglas Burton-Christie:

The Scriptures were experienced as authoritative words which pierced the hearts of the monks, illuminated them concerning the central issues of their lives, protected and comforted them during the dark times of struggle and anxiety, and provided practical help in their ongoing quest for holiness.

At all times and in all circumstances, the desert monk made recourse to the Scriptures as the basis for his prayer, as light in moments of darkness, as nourishment for his soul.

Lectio divina is as weighty a component of the monastic day as the *Opus Dei* and the *opus manuum* (manual work). Saint Benedict's Rule specifies that the monk's daily routine must make room for *lectio* at assigned times. In fact, Saint Benedict goes a step further, recommending that the leisure of the Lord's Day be spent in additional hours given to the work of *lectio divina*.

Some guests occasionally ask me to explain the practice of *lectio divina* to them. In reply I say that *lectio* is much more than just a simple reading of the Scriptures, or a method of grasping its meaning. "*Lectio*," I tell them, "is an ancient technique of reading the Bible that ultimately leads to inner prayer. Through the understanding of the word we are given during the sacred time of *lectio*, we enter into the mystery of God's presence. In a word, *lectio* is a holy reading that ultimately leads to communion with God in deep prayer. One must approach *lectio* with the same attitude one approaches prayer. The sole goal for *lectio* is prayer and nothing else but prayer. It alone explains it all."

John the Solitary, one of the Syriac Fathers, clarifies an exact approach to the exercise of *lectio*:

> Pay attention to the reading of the words of Scripture, in order to learn from them how to be with God. Do not choose for yourself just standing in prayer and neglect reading, for it is not required of you that just your body should be at labor, while your mind is idle. Intersperse your way of life with various kinds of occupations: a time for reading, a time for prayer. In this way you will be illumined in prayer as a result of your reading. For the Lord of all does not require of us an outward stance, but a mind that is wise in its hope for him, and which knows how to draw close to perfection.

— AUGUST 26 —

Saint Caesarius of Arles

Brothers and sisters, which to you seems the greater, the word of God or the body of Christ? If you want to give the right answer you will reply that God's word is not less than Christ's body. Therefore, just as we take care when we receive the body of Christ so that no part of it falls to the ground so, likewise, we should ensure that the word of God which is given to us is not lost to our souls because we are speaking or thinking about something different. One who listens negligently to God's word is just as guilty as one who, through carelessness, allows Christ's body to fall to the ground.

SAINT CAESARIUS OF ARLES, SERMON 300.2

Saint Caesarius of Arles, a holy monk and abbot and glory of the church of France, is among the lesser-known Fathers of the Church. Yet, in his time, he exercised enormous influence as the shepherd of a very important region of France.

Caesarius was born in Chalon-sur-Saone, around 470 A.D. He became a monk at a young age, at the famous monastery of Lerins, founded by John Cassian. Because of his exemplary life and his unusual wisdom, he was chosen as abbot of the monastery. His reputation as a holy and wise man extended throughout the region of southern France. One day, around 503 A.D., much to his surprise, he was chosen as bishop of Arles. Caesarius then became famous for his preaching; he knew how to break open the bread of the Word of God in such a way that even the simplest and most uneducated of his flock could understand it.

A delightful story is told about young bishop Caesarius. During his first sermons at the cathedral, when the time came to preach, people began to leave the church. The next time he spoke, Caesarius ordered the doors of the church closed and locked, much to the amazement of the faithful who were unable to leave the premises.

Caesarius would be considered today a progressive, modern bishop. He saw the liturgy as a method of formation for a relevant Christian life, so when he noticed the lack of understanding and poor participation of his people in the worship of the church, he did not hesitate to order the liturgy to be celebrated in the common language of the people.

As a true shepherd, he showed particular care for the poor and the destitute. Like Jesus, he expressed a preference for the marginals of his time: prisoners, pagans, heretics, and public sinners. As a bishop, who was first a monk, he paid particular attention to the development of monastic life in his diocese—particularly to the development of feminine monasticism. Caesarius founded a monastery for nuns in Arles, a foundation considered one of the earliest women's monasteries of France. He wrote the rules for the nuns and saw his own sister Caesaria become the first abbess of the community. Among the provisions of his rule were that all the nuns learned to read and write. He also gave them full autonomy in the selection of their abbess. Caesarius remained faithful to his nuns until the end. He visited them for the last time just a few days before his death. He was seventy-three years when he died, old in age but still young and robust in spirit, eager to reach the Father's house and see him face to face.

— AUGUST 27 —

Saint Poemen the Shepherd

Abba Poemen said, "If a man has sinned and denies it, saying 'I have not sinned,' do not reprimand him; for that will discourage him. Instead say to him, 'Do not lose heart, brother, but in the future be on the guard.' Thus you shall stir his soul to repentance."

ABBA POEMEN, *SAYINGS OF THE DESERT FATHERS*

Our monastic calendar marks today as the commemoration of Poemen the Shepherd. In his time, he was considered one of the great spiritual masters of Egyptian monasticism. Later, he would play an important role in the assembled collection of the *Apothegmata Patrum*, or the *Sayings of the Desert Fathers*. Around 408 A.D., he was forced with many other monks to abandon his abode. Subsequently, he and the others set up their monastic community in the ruins of a pagan temple, where Saint Poemen became the spiritual leader of the group for several years. He was honored among the desert monks for his holiness of life and for the unusual wisdom of his counsels. These bits of wisdom are timeless, as relevant today as they were in his own time. Here are a few for our consideration and nourishment:

> Abba Poemen said one day, "A man may seem to be silent, but if his heart is condemning others he is babbling ceaselessly. There may be another who talks from morning till night and yet he is truly silent; for he says nothing that is not profitable for the soul."

> Abba Poemen said, "If three monks get together, of whom the first fully preserves interior peace, and the second gives thanks to God in time of illness, and the third serves God with a pure mind, these three are equal before God, for they are all doing the same work."

> Abba Poemen said, "Vigilance, self-knowledge and discernment; these are the guides of the soul." He also said, "As the breath which comes out of his nostrils, so does a man need humility and the fear of God."

> Abba Poemen said, "Teach your mouth to say that which you keep in your heart." He also said, "If a monk can overcome two things, he can become free from the world." The brother then asked him what these two things were and he replied: "Bodily comfort and vain-glory."

— AUGUST 28 —

Saint Augustine

In the anguish of my heart I groaned aloud. There is a hidden anguish which is inaudible to men. Yet when a man's heart is so taken up with some particular concern that the hurt inside finds vocal expression, one looks for the reason. And one will say to oneself: perhaps this is what causes his anguish, or perhaps such and such has happened to him. But who can be certain of the cause except God, who hears and sees his anguish? Therefore the psalmist says: In the anguish of my heart I groaned aloud. For if men hear at all, they usually hear only bodily groaning and know nothing of the anguish of the heart from which it issues. Who then knows the cause of man's groaning? All my desire is before you. No, it is not open before other men, for they cannot understand the heart: but before you is all my desire. If your desire lies open to him who is your Father and who sees in secret, he will answer you.

SAINT AUGUSTINE

Today we honor the memory of Saint Augustine, one of the great thinkers of the early Church. After a life immersed in earthly pleasures, he converted to Christianity, thanks to the prayers and tears of his mother, Monica. For almost thirty-four years he was the bishop of Hippo in the North of Africa. He lived in community with his clergy, for whom he wrote a rule. Augustine was controversial during his day, as he is still today. For me, he is a bit too distant from the Eastern Fathers and other Western Fathers, whose writings have influenced me profoundly. Moreover, there are some who see in Augustine's theological arguments the roots of some of our present theological controversies. This being said, I admire greatly the extent of his prolific writing: 113 books and treatises, over 200 letters, and more than 500 sermons. I am particularly fond of his exposition on the Psalms. It is unsurpassable! He speaks the fertile words:

For the desire of your heart is itself your prayer. And if the desire is constant, so is your prayer. The Apostle Paul had a purpose in saying: Pray without ceasing. Are we then ceaselessly to bend our knees, to lie prostrate, or to lift up our hands? Is this what is meant in saying: Pray without ceasing? Even if we admit that we pray in this fashion, I do not believe that we can do so all the time.

Yet there is another, interior kind of prayer without ceasing, namely, the desire of the heart. Whatever else you may be doing, if you but fix your desire on God's Sabbath rest, your prayer will be ceaseless. Therefore, if you wish to pray without ceasing, do not cease the desire.

— AUGUST 29 —

The Jesus Prayer: A Pilgrimage

Lord, Jesus Christ, Son of the living God, have mercy on me a sinner.

THE JESUS PRAYER

For over thirty years now, the Jesus Prayer has been my prayer of pilgrimage. Living in the "here and now," one needs a link that looks towards the eternal. The Jesus Prayer has been that link. The Jesus Prayer is a way of turning aside nonessentials. At the same time, it points us to him, the Eternal One. The prayer, as it weaves quietly into the very fabric of who we are, motivates us to leave behind all encumbrances, all unnecessary human noise, and leads us directly there, to where nothing else is left but Christ and our sinfulness.

The Jesus Prayer is the prayer of the desert, springing from the desire of the early monks to practice a way of unceasing prayer. Far from the multitudes, they found themselves naked in the barrenness of the desert, before the immensity of Him, who was the Focal Point of their aspirations. For these monks, prayer was as much their work as all other occupations. All their daily activities always converged in the Jesus Prayer. The psalms, the Offices, and the Scriptures eventually lead to inner, unceasing prayer: the Jesus Prayer. Through the prayer, the journey towards God was enhanced.

As we embark on this pilgrimage, we must come to terms with the mystery of repentance. One real way to encounter repentance is through the Jesus Prayer. Repentance is not an easy task and is not always easy to talk about. Our world is not geared to the work of repentance. Nor does it grasp its Gospel significance. We live in a world of pretension where we don't really believe ourselves to be sinners. Yet, the Jesus Prayer begins with repentance; it demands repentance. As we enter into this prayer, we begin with the recognition that we are sinners, and thus we pray to repent for the actual sins of our past and present life. Furthermore, we pray that we may be given the grace to repent with our whole being.

Mother Maria, an Orthodox nun whose writings are pure light to the spirit, writes of the mystery of repentance:

> Repentance is an attitude, immensely positive, an attitude forwards, keenly alert, and of love for the Perfect....The call to repentance is the call to leave behind, as achievement, all temporal achievement, good or bad; not to linger in rejoicing or in burying the dead. To leave behind all possession, of matter or of mind, at the every instant of having.

Repentance is the door to the prayer. We need not go far to enter into it. All true prayer begins where we are. Reality is the place of the encounter, the place where God meets us. To start praying, to find God, we don't need to roam around the world. All we need is to enter into ourselves, to cry out in humble repentance, and we shall discover God there, in the midst of it all. The more wholly repentance grasps us and holds us, the more Christ is real. In the way of repentance Christ becomes for us all within all.

The Jesus Prayer is the prayer of the repentant heart who in the desert of life seeks no other companion but Christ alone; but as always, when Christ comes into the human heart, he comes with a whole host of guests as company. As Abba Macarius beautifully puts it: "God is there with the angels, light and life are there, the kingdom and the apostles, the heavenly cities and the treasures of grace: all things are there."

— AUGUST 30 —

Saint Fiacre: Patron of Gardeners

*The garden is the life-breath of this diseased world that
has been so long in sickness: that breath proclaims that a
saving remedy has been sent to heal our mortality.*

SAINT EPHREM, *HYMNS ON PARADISE*

It is hard to believe, but it is indeed the end of August. For a
few months, we have enjoyed the luxury of summertime, all of
its joys and its wonders. But like all good things, it also comes to
an end.

Today we celebrate the feast of Saint Fiacre, the patron saint
of gardeners. As I gaze upon him, well-placed in the center of our
vegetable garden, I think of all the necessary qualities a garden
requires of its gardener. Garden work is a joy, but also very tedious and very hard. It demands our willingness to kneel on the
ground day in and day out. It demands strong knees, strong hands,
and a strong back. The gardener loves to enter into contact with
the soil, to feel the earth. He loves roaming around at all times
through the garden paths, and to be vigilant over what is growing in between the rows. Ah! the gardener keeps so many secrets!

Saint Fiacre, not surprisingly, was a solitary monk. He was
also an Irishman who left the beautiful shores of Ireland for the
cold weather of northern France. Arriving in an area of France
which I know rather well (almost like the palms of my hands),
called *le pays de Brie*, famous for its Carolingian monasteries as
well as for its cheese, he settled near Meaux on a piece of land
given to him by the local bishop. He was very strict about safeguarding his solitude and his monastic enclosure. However, like
all good monks, he was also attentive to the needs of the poor
and misfortunate of the surrounding area. Whenever he could,
he offered help, especially to the sick.

Saint Fiacre died in the obscurity of his hermitage, as he
wished, alone with God. Not so long after, people began arriving
at his sepulcher from all points. Suddenly, everyone knew that a
saint had died in their midst. Miracles were reported over his

tomb. Even the royalty of France came to pray and ask assistance from the holy monk. From France, his fame extended into Belgium and Luxembourg, and pilgrimages continued until the time of the French Revolution.

How Saint Fiacre became the patron of gardeners is an interesting legend. When Fiacre arrived in France and asked the bishop for land for his hermitage, the bishop responded: "You can have as much land as you can trace its contours and demarcations in one day." Saint Fiacre hurried and, without stopping during the full twenty-four hours, was able to trace a significant amount of land, which he later cultivated and around which he placed his monastic enclosure. In the ikonography of Saint Fiacre, the humble monk is always represented as a gardener, with a spade.

— AUGUST 31 —

God Glimpsed in the Garden

A garden is a lovesome thing, God wot!
Rose plot,
Fringed pool,
Fern'd grot—
The veriest school
Of peace; and yet the fool
Contends that God is not—
Not God! in gardens! when the eve is cool?
Nay, but I have a sign;
'Tis very sure God walks in mine.

THOMAS EDWARD BROWN

Summer is quickening toward its conclusion. In the monastery, much of our summer living is intertwined with work in the garden. A good neighbor, a retired gentleman, recently told me, "I didn't appreciate life to the fullest until I started gardening. Life would lose its meaning if I were not engaged in gardening." In his own way, the neighbor was conveying to me what I have often heard repeated by other gardeners: watching life's surprises and its deepest secrets through the prism of one's own garden can be a wondrous occasion, and a thing of pure joy.

Our visitors always question why we have a fenced-in, enclosed garden. One practical reason for the enclosure is to protect it from intrusive animals. Most important, though, the garden fence declares that the space is a sacred and holy one. The visitor may step in to admire it and bask in its energy. Anyone is welcome to enter, and anyone may prolong his or her visit to this sacred realm. All that I usually ask of them is to show reverence and respect for the holy life it encloses.

A monastic garden, within the confines of its rustic simplicity, is a place that recreates the ambiance of Paradise, where both the Lord and his creatures walk together in perfect bliss. It is a garden for all seasons. A garden that renders prodigious gifts to the monastic table: vegetables, fruits, and fragrant herbs, a garden where color, texture, and taste blend together in warm harmony, a garden for meditation, where peace and serenity embrace, a garden for a pensive, reflective walk, a garden that welcomes the guest. It is a garden where the humble monk Saint Fiacre watches over his domain while also remaining its daily inspiration to garden where work is considered a holy occupation, and where God's praises are always sung. A garden, the fruit of prayer and devotion.

A monastic garden's primary purpose is to manifest the glory of God. The magical scent of herbs, the color and the texture of vegetables, and the radiant beauty of flowers never cease to proclaim the wonders of their Creator. A garden's bounty is not only a thing of joy, but also a sign of God's loving providence over all of us, his children.

SEPTEMBER

September Days

The golden rod is yellow,
The corn is turning brown,
The trees in apple orchards
With fruit are bending down;
By all these lovely tokens
September days are here,
With summer's best of weather
And autumn's best of cheer.

HELEN HUNT JACKSON

Last night, as I reflected on another month's natural completion, I thought about the transition that the beginning of
September brings. We know that summer extends itself up to
September 21, but unofficially the summer season ends with Labor Day. Once we reach September 1, certain so-called "summer
activities" wind down, such as vacations and other recreations.

339

The beaches begin to close and young students once again begin their schooling.

During September, we notice how the northern hemisphere begins to tilt progressively away from the sun. As we advance toward the arrival of autumn, the days in our hemisphere begin cooling off, slowly giving us notice that winter is soon to come. September is a month of contrasts. It opens with its warmer, summer-like days, which are gradually replaced by cooler, crisper weather. A chill in the air begins to be felt, and the seasonal progression moves steadily toward winter.

Some important festivals are kept during September: the Nativity of Mary, Saint John Chrysostom, the Holy Cross, Saint Matthew, and Saint Michael. The Orthodox Christians begin today their official liturgical calendar. September, in many ways, is a month of beginnings.

In the monastery, garden work continues at full speed. September is the month of the harvest, and harvesting activities take priority over all other types of labor. The monastic kitchen resembles a busy beehive, with multiple tasks to accomplish: canning and freezing of vegetables, preserving, jam-making, pickling, storing, and a host of other activities. The fragrance that emanates from such preparations seems to permeate the whole monastery. It is a scent fitting for September, a delicious odor that restores our tired bodies and uplifts our spirits.

— SEPTEMBER 2 —

God's Masterwork

Nous sommes l'ouvrage de Dieu: *We are God's work of art.*

EPHESIANS 2:10

Directly and unambiguously, Saint Paul states that we—each and every one of us—are the work of God. If we truly believe this and try to live by the apostle's statement, it means defying all of our preconceived notions about others and, above all, about ourselves. Saint Paul gives us a new way of looking at reality, a reality that now appears to our eyes as transfigured by the light of God and renewed in Christ.

Each element of creation is, therefore, changed and made different. We can no longer "act as usual," as if nothing has happened. We are now in Christ, and each of us is a new creation bearing the image of God. Therefore, we must show utmost respect to one another and to ourselves, because we are all God's handiwork.

This is not always easy to do. We are weak, and we often struggle and fail. We must pray for the sort of faith that strengthens our resolution, so that the grace of God may act in each of us, according to God's wishes. It is said of Saint Seraphim of Sarov that he addressed each person he met with the salutation, "Christ is risen, my joy." He called each and everyone "my joy" because he saw in them the work of God, the image of the invisible God. This is another saint who has so much to teach us.

— SEPTEMBER 3 —

Saint Gregory the Great

He who desires God with his whole spirit certainly already possesses him who he loves.

SAINT GREGORY THE GREAT, GOSPEL HOMILY 30, 1

Today we celebrate the feast of a great Father of the Western Church. Gregory was renowned as the Prefect of Rome before leaving all worldly concerns in order to enter a monastery on the outskirts of the city. He became a monk and a deacon and was eventually chosen as Bishop of Rome due to his wisdom and holiness. His election as pope was the source of personal pain to him, but Gregory accepted it as God's will. He, above all, was a contemplative monk and nothing was more painful than leaving the seclusion of the cloister, where his spirit freely breathed and expanded in the ways of interior prayer.

At the time of his election as pope, the city and its surroundings were beset by plagues, famines, and all sorts of Church and political controversies. Assuming the papacy at such a trying time was an enormous challenge. But Saint Gregory, like Saint Basil of Cesarea and Saint Martin of Tours before him, was a special type of Church pastor who was first formed in the school of monasticism. That formation, perhaps, was the best preparation for assuming such an enormous responsibility.

As pastor of Rome, his main concern was the care of souls and the good of the Church of God. He never forgot, however, that above all things, his initial call was to the monastic life. During his papacy, he surrounded himself by monks and tried, as much as possible, to follow the monastic observances. He remained faithful to prayer and to his great love for *Lectio Divina*. Essentially, he remained a monk his entire life.

Gregory was particularly attached to Saint Benedict, whose Rule he professed in his Roman monastery, and whose life and miracles he described for all of us in his book, *Dialogues*. For this, all of us who live under the inspiration of the Benedictine tradition are eternally grateful. After the Rule, Saint Gregory's writings constitute the most precious documents concerning Saint Benedict and his sister, Saint Scholastica.

Saint Gregory put immense effort into building and expanding the Church of God, not only through his pastoral care but also through his writings. He is often called the "doctor of holy desires," because his writings are a sublime expression of the exact nature of the soul's desire for God. According to Saint Gregory, this desire, when purged of vanity and falsehood, can intensify to such an extent that the soul enters into the possession of God. This desire for God demands of us detachment and purification from all other forms of earthly desire, so that all of our spiritual energies may be unified and directed solely toward God. This desire nurtures prayer, brings inner peace and harmony, and enlightens the soul in the knowledge of the mystery of God.

The Inner Chamber

Whenever you pray, go into your room and shut the door
and pray to your Father who is in secret.

MATTHEW 6:6

The great Saint John Chrysostom once wrote: "Find the door to the inner chamber of your soul, and you will discover the door of the kingdom of God." The task of our exploration is to discover that inner chamber, that intimate place within each of us where God communicates with us. To discover that inner chamber is to discover a place that is personal, mysterious, and elusive. It is a deep place that calls for the company of someone of even greater depth. "Deep calls to deep," as the psalm expresses (Ps 42:7). Mysteriously, God somehow penetrates this inner chamber, which he created and sustains by his power. He chooses to abide with whomever opens the door and welcomes him as a heavenly Guest.

The activity of the soul is then reduced to this: searching for the God within and communing with him who dwells in that secret place. Out of the depths, a soul learns to speak to God. "Out of the depths I cry to you, O LORD" (Ps 130). The challenge of our exploration, therefore, is how to penetrate ever more deeply into our own inner chamber, the place within where God lives, moves, and is free to be himself. When we reach that place, the abyss of our own inner being, and find the ineffable Guest waiting, we shall feel alive and free. The assiduous cultivation of this inner activity, this retreat-into-the-depths, will change our lives forever.

As John of the Cross says: "There is one point where God communicates with us, and that is the center of our own souls."

— SEPTEMBER 5 —

Inner Freedom

Christianity promises to make men free; it never promises to make them independent.

W. R. INGE, *THE PHILOSOPHY OF PLOTINUS*

It is through the grace of God alone, and not by any merit of ours, that we can pursue the path to inner freedom, that is, the glorious liberty of the Gospel. Jesus sees us as we truly are—not as we pretend or wish to be—and still he loves us. Our sinfulness, our passions, our ugliness, our weaknesses, are no obstacles to his love. If Jesus loves us in spite of all our failings then perhaps we too can start accepting ourselves for what we really are, despite our spiritual misery and shortcomings.

Once the grace of God has broken into our lives, we begin to walk the path towards inner freedom by giving ourselves seriously to the practice of humility and simplicity and by abandoning our lives into the hands of a loving Father. Abandonment into God's hands implies complete trust and confidence in his love for each of us. It is in this complete surrender of our personal lives (and all that it implies) into his hands that gradually, as we give up our own independence and take up the yoke of Christ, that we receive from him the gift of inner freedom.

As we struggle daily to walk in the steps of the Gospel, the only true way to inner freedom, we do not give up the practices of humility and simplicity no matter how tedious they may seem at the time. Pushed forward by the burning love that comes from our surrender into God's hands and our complete dependency upon him, we allow our souls to expand into humble acceptance of ourselves and of others. Thus, we slowly achieve the freedom of God's children, which ultimately is a sign of the presence of the Holy Spirit in our lives.

— SEPTEMBER 6 —

Inner Healing

Do you want to be made well?

JOHN 5:6

I am always in awe of this question that Jesus poses in the Gospel passage where he heals the paralytic man by telling him to bathe in the pool of Beth-zatha. Jesus offers healing to the sick man, but he does not force it upon him. Jesus first waits to receive the request from the person who wishes to be healed. In other words, he respects the free will of the person on whom he bestows the gift of healing.

Jesus knows our own need for inner healing, and he is more than willing to grant it. But out of a unique respect for each of us, he waits for our personal requests for healing before he acts. Further, when Jesus addresses us with the question, "Do you want to be made well?" he is asking something more profound. He is asking if we really want to be made well entirely, down to the deepest recesses of our souls. To allow Jesus to heal us is to allow him to encompass our entire being, to have him change within us all that does not conform to God's wishes. Answering his question affirmatively means being totally open to his healing action in all of these ways, so as to allow him to transform the present course of our lives forever.

True inner healing begins when we let the Lord take complete possession of our lives, when we let him act in us as our sole Master. True healing implies also a personal responsibility, that from now on, we will humbly seek God's will in all of life's events, and that we will follow it once it is manifested to us. If we do this, we shall be able to hear the same consoling words Jesus addressed to the paralytic man: "Stand up, take your mat and walk." To which the Gospel adds: "At once the man was made well, and he took up his mat and began to walk."

The Present Moment

Let us strive to make the present moment beautiful.
Saint Francis de Sales

A musician once told me how her life was enriched by the time she spent making music. "These are truly centering moments in my life," she said. Understanding immediately what she meant, I replied, "I know what you mean, but I think that every moment of our lives can be a centering moment. It may not always be a 'peak moment,' as is the moment when you are making music, but certainly each moment can become unique, beautiful, and precious. It can never be duplicated." My friend nodded in agreement.

To live every day fully, to pray deeply, and to love well all depend on our capacity to be totally present in the moment. This is the heart of all cycles of one's spiritual life. Despite constant change, we must make every effort to retain a well-centered inward life, where we become engaged in the unchanging reality within. Pressure may surround us from all sides to run away from the task of remaining "centered" in the moment. Escaping, as we all well know, is easy. Remaining centered is difficult.

In the past, we would speak of "centering" as the "sacrament of the present moment." In truth, we know that we only have today, the present moment, the now; yesterday is gone, and tomorrow is not yet here. This exact moment is holy and uniquely beautiful. Keeping alive the awareness and wonder of the present moment in the continuous flow of time, and throughout all its cycles, enhances our daily lives. We know that the moment will never be recaptured again, but we will keep within us its lovely memory. To live fully and deeply each day is to participate consciously in the mystery and succession of each present moment. The end result will be a positive one, shaped by the wonder, the beauty, and the holiness of each part of the day.

The Nativity of Mary

Your Nativity, O Mother of God, has brought joy to the
universe. For from you has shone forth the Sun of Justice,
Christ our God. He has delivered us from the curse and
blessed us. He has destroyed death to grant us eternal
life.

TROPARION OF THE FEAST

O ur summer celebrations culminate in early September with
the lovely feast of the Nativity of Mary. It marks out this
seasonal transition period, this "in-between" time.

Today's feast originated in the Christian East, where its celebration has the rank of a solemnity. The Nativity of the
Theotokos is one of the twelve major feasts of the Eastern Church.
Today's feast, therefore, is a source of gladness and joy for Christians of both the East and the West.

With her parents Joachim and Ann, we rejoice in the arrival
of Mary into this world, for her birthday announces the proximity of another significant birthday, that of the Son of God. Today's
festival is the one necessary event for the great mystery of the
Incarnation to be accomplished. Mary proceeds forth in time from
the bosom of her mother, Ann, in light, in gentleness, and in peace,
ready to give her assent, her "fiat," to the Almighty One. In due
time, she becomes the Mother of the Son of God. All of creation
and the Church at large keeps this festival holy, rejoicing in the
knowledge that Mary is in our midst and with her, the dawn of
our salvation, the Sun of Justice, is nearer at hand, bringing with
him the gift of redemption to all humanity.

— SEPTEMBER 9 —

The Devout Life

A devout life does bring wealth, but it is the rich simplicity
of being yourself before God.

PARAPHRASE OF 1 TIMOTHY 6:6

A devout lifestyle, the total orientation of one's life toward God, is the basis of deep inner peace and true serenity. Often, we are self-consumed with worry about the state of our business and financial affairs, personal health, success, and emotional fulfillment. We sense that we lack something, that all is not inwardly well with us.

In determining what creates so much anxiety in us, we must undergo a thorough self-examination, looking for the specific roots of our worries. If we are honest enough with ourselves, we shall find that our priorities in life are misplaced. We have perhaps made money, achieved success, found emotional fulfillment, and been blessed by perfect health. In the process, we have let God fall by the wayside.

What we need is to reprioritize our values in life by giving God the first place in our lives, always continuing to seek him out with true simplicity of heart. In following the secret of a devout life, we shall discover the truth of Jesus' promise when he said: "Seek first the Kingdom of God and its justice, and all other things shall be given to you." God alone can free us from our anxieties and fulfill all the cravings of the human heart.

If we seriously pursue the real wealth found in a devout life, we must periodically seek a quiet place and take time to examine where our inner life stands. Taking time daily to pray, in all simplicity, from the depths of our hearts, will be the best proof that God really matters in our lives.

Saint Paul, in his usual wisdom, proposes an excellent program for those seriously considering the possibilities of a devout life:

We have not ceased praying for you and asking that you may be filled with the knowledge of God's will in all spiritual wisdom and understanding, so that you may lead lives worthy of the Lord, fully pleasing to him, as you bear fruit in every good work, and as you grow in the knowledge of God. May you be made strong with all the strength that comes from his glorious power, and may you be prepared to endure everything with patience, while joyfully giving thanks to the Father. (Col 1:9b-12).

— SEPTEMBER 10 —

Pater Noster

Our Father, who art in heaven, hallowed be Thy Name....
OPENING TO THE *PATER NOSTER*

A mong the prayers we learn from early childhood and use in daily life, no other is so much taken for granted as the Our Father. Children pray it at home before going to bed, Christians pray it at the Eucharist and other religious services, and we monks and nuns pray it several times daily in our Offices. But as we pray, do we attentively distill from it all of its richness?

As a prayer taught by the Lord himself, the early Christians loved to say the Our Father. The Fathers of the Church, especially Saint Cyprian of Carthage, left us lofty commentaries on the prayer. In the sixteenth century, the great mystic and saint, Teresa of Ávila, wrote a whole treatise on the richness and depth of the Our Father as an inspiration for contemplation.

As we pray daily the Our Father, we must reflect lovingly on the words used by Christ himself. Can there be a prayer more pleasing to the Father than that uttered by his only-begotten Son? When we pray quietly in the solitude of our hearts, using the formula given to us by the Divine Master, we can be sure that our heavenly Father recognizes the voice, the words, and the sentiments chosen by his own Son during his earthly life. He not only recognizes the words of the prayer, but he recognizes his own Son praying in us as his adopted children, making our humble prayer acceptable and pleasing in his presence.

It is particularly helpful when praying the Our Father to let go of the sense of the individual self and make a conscious effort to be aware that someone else is praying within us: Christ, the Lord, addressing the Father in his own words. Saint Angela of Foligno, a medieval mystic, related to us in her own words the wonders she experienced while praying the Our Father: *As I was saying the Pater, I felt each of the words expanding my heart. I said the words one after another slowly and with profound contrition. And in spite of my tears flowing from a greater knowledge of my faults and unworthiness, I began to feel something of the divine tenderness.*

— SEPTEMBER 11 —

Incense: A Sweet Fragrance for God

Let my prayer be counted as incense before you, and the lifting up of my hands as an evening sacrifice.
PSALM 141:2

In ancient times, the Jewish people offered incense in the Temple as a pledge of their adoration to God. The Christian Church inherited from the Jewish Temple the ancient tradition of offering incense to the divinity. Deeply appreciating the evocative power of incense, the early Church used incense not only during the Divine Liturgy but also during the daily celebration of Lauds in the morning and Vespers in the evening. The sight and smell of incense uplifted the Christian worshiper to the beauty of the Divine Presence. The fragrance emanating from the censer signified, for the Christian, his total participation in the worship of God and became symbolic of the act of prayer itself.

While monasteries still retain the frequent use of incense in their worship, some Western churches have given up this venerable tradition. Indirectly, these churches contribute to the loss of symbolism that has enriched the liturgical experience throughout the ages. Worship planners forget that this sweet-smelling offering is a powerful biblical image of Christ himself: "The golden altar of incense and the ark of the covenant," according to the Letter of the Hebrews.

Eventually I hope, albeit slowly and imperceptibly, the use of incense in liturgy will be rediscovered by a new generation of Christians. They will be inspired by the ancient tradition of using incense as "the fragrance of Christ," a fragrance that calls forth each believer to saturate the world with his love and mystery. One day we can hope the world will be encircled by the perfume of prayer that rises from us as a daily offering to the Father.

— SEPTEMBER 12 —

"And the Name of the Virgin Was Mary"

If you are lashed by the waves of pride, of ambition, of detraction, of envy, look at the star, call on Mary. If anger, or avarice, or the allurements of the flesh have shattered the bark of your soul, look to Mary. In dangers, in straits, in doubts, think of Mary. Have her name always on your lips, in your heart, that you may obtain the help of her prayer.

SAINT BERNARD

These exquisitely poetic words of Saint Bernard are apt for today's prayerful reflection. At one time, the Catholic calendar used to celebrate on this day the feast of the Holy Name of Mary. I have fond memories of this feast, as I do for the ancient feast of the Holy Name of Jesus. A deep spiritual meaning attaches to this honoring of the holy names, for in honoring the names of Jesus and Mary, we are honoring their personhood.

At the beginnings of our lives, each one of us is given a name. The lifelong task thereafter is to become ever more fully the person we are meant to be, to embody the name that we were given. The special mystery of each person is contained in his or her name. Therefore, each time we pronounce someone's name, we are affirming that person's mystery.

When we honor Mary's name, we honor her supreme distinction of being the only woman chosen by God to be the mother of his only Son. When we honor Mary's name, we honor her privileged freedom from the stain of earthly sin, so that she could become a worthy throne for God, the Most High. And, finally, when we honor Mary's name, we honor the depths of her humility that so attracted the eyes of God and made her undistracted in fulfilling God's supreme design for her life.

There is great power in the invocation of the name of Mary, the Theotokos. When we call upon her to help us throughout all the events of our lives, we can be completely sure that she will be there, guiding us on our earthly journey until we reach life's ultimate destination.

— SEPTEMBER 13 —

Saint John Chrysostom

Eloquent preacher, called the "Golden Mouth," such was the beauty of your clear discourses, strong against evil, yet both deep and tender in their persuasion. You were a model for the Christian people, Paul the Apostle you revered devoutly, earnestly striving to become as he did, all things to all men.

VESPERS HYMN OF THE FEAST

One of the loveliest feasts for the September cycle of saints is that of our Father among the saints, John Chrysostom. He was born around 349 A.D., and was appropriately called the "Golden Mouth" because of his eloquent oratory, which he assiduously used to preach the Word of God.

Saint John Chrysostom is one of the great Fathers, a true pillar of the universal Church. He is well revered in our midst, where his ikon holds a special place in our monastic chapel, and his treatises a prominent spot in our modest library. Monks and nuns, and Christians in general, have much to learn from the example and teachings of John Chrysostom. His life was shaped by the Scriptures, especially the Gospels and the writings of Saint Paul, which he commented on with unparalleled wisdom. He also wrote vividly about the practice of charity and the role of almsgiving in the life of a Christian. To this day he continues to remind us, through his writing, to keep the ears of our heart attentive to God's living Word. We shall be blessed indeed if, like John Chrysostom, we learn to shape our lives daily by the teachings of the Scripture.

John Chrysostom died after receiving holy Communion, murmuring slowly, "Glory to God in all things." He died as he lived, passionately immersed in the mystery of God. Today is a good day to remember John Chrysostom and all of our ancient Fathers in the Church. With their exemplary lives and teachings, they have helped preserve intact the treasure of our Christian faith.

— SEPTEMBER 14 —

Triumph of The Holy Cross

O Tree of dazzling beauty,
Adorned by Christ's precious blood,
He chose you as the royal bed
To rest his sacred limbs in death.

HYMN FOR VESPERS

Today is the feast of the Cross, a very special day in every monastery. I wish I could add "in every Christian household," but I fear that the secularized nature of our time attaches no importance to the mystery of today's feast. In the beautiful responsory sung at Matins today, we sing: "The church venerates the glorious day on which the triumphal tree is exalted, on which our Redeemer, breaking the bonds of death, overcame the cunning serpent. Hanging on the Cross, the Father's Word found the way of our salvation."

Today, our attention centers on the strange and wonderful mystery of the Cross. On the day of our baptism, the Sign of the Cross was made over us as we were baptized in the Name of the Father, of the Son, and of the Holy Spirit. The Cross sealed our lives forever. From then on, we belonged to Christ.

Throughout our lives, we are taught to cross ourselves frequently: at the beginning of a new day, at the day's end, before and after our meals, when we pass a church or cemetery. We cross ourselves often during the liturgy and the Offices, when we receive absolution, and when we receive Communion. At the moment of our death, we are anointed with the Sign of the Cross.

When we make the Sign of the Cross, or someone else makes it over us, it is not simply a ritualistic gesture. It is more than that: it is the affirmation of our faith that Christ suffered and died on the Cross for our salvation. This is why one must never cross oneself hurriedly or carelessly. When we do it, we must take our time to do it reverently, for at that moment we are keeping memory of our Lord Jesus Christ's suffering upon the Cross.

When we cross ourselves daily, we must make Saint Paul's words our own: "We glorify the Cross of our Lord Jesus Christ, in whom is our salvation, life, and resurrection, by whom we have been saved and freed." The Cross reminds us also that we are disciples of Christ, and as such are invited to take our crosses daily and follow him. Each day, we carry our own personal crosses, and we do it only in the strength that comes forth from the Cross of Christ.

— SEPTEMBER 15 —

Our Lady of Sorrows

You, his Mother, were there to witness his sufferings, overwhelmed with grief but with a heart that nothing could daunt. Your Son, meanwhile, was hanging on the cross and in his agony uttered deep groans. All torn by the inhuman scourging, and his body all broken with gaping wounds, your Son hung there before your eyes. How often did this sight pierce your heart right through?

VESPERS HYMN OF THE FEAST

S ometimes there is both an inner logic and an apparent contradiction in the liturgy. It seems quite logical that today's feast, dedicated to the sorrows of Mary, should follow yesterday's feast of the Cross, for they are intrinsically united. At the same time, it seems quite a jump in time from the feast of Mary's Nativity, just celebrated last week, to today's feast of her sorrows. The Holy Spirit, I suppose, has his own reasons for inspiring the liturgical calendar in this way.

An ancient monastic custom kept faithfully here is directly related to the mystery of today's feast. On Good Friday, after the solemn liturgy of Christ's Passion, the monks usually retire to their cells for prayer, after which they take a small collation in the refectory. The small collation usually consists of a vegetable soup and a piece of bread, just enough to take us through to the following day. At night, before retiring, we go to the chapel and spend time with Our Lady at the foot of the Cross. In the stark darkness of the chapel, a candle flickers by the ikon of the Descent From the Cross. As we venerate this ikon, we sing the twenty-one stanzas of the *Stabat Mater* in a mournful, Gregorian melody. The stanzas help us recall Mary's loneliness and grief as she wept while receiving the descended body of her Son.

The monks and nuns of the desert, our pioneer fathers and mothers, felt great devotion towards the mystery they called the Compassion of Our Lady. A legendary anecdote from the life of Abba Poemen illustrates the intensity of this devotion.

> It was said that Abba Poemen was seen in one of his frequent ecstasies by fellow brother Abba Isaac. Since the two were close, Abba Isaac felt free to inquire, "Where were you?" Abba Poemen answered in reply, "My thought was with Our Lady, the Mother of God, as she wept by the Cross of the Savior. I wish I could always weep like that."

Abba Poemen knew that the sword of sorrow once foretold by the elder Simeon had plunged deeply into the soul of Mary when she mourned the Passion of her Son. By keeping her company and sharing in her sorrow, Abba Poemen profited from the gift of the redemption brought forth by the Savior. By following his example, we can also experience the grace of such a gift, pleading: *Pray for us, O Queen of Martyrs, for you stood for us by the cross of Jesus.*

Stillness

*The very best and utmost of attainment in life is to remain
still and let God act and speak in thee.*

MEISTER ECKHART

One of the most beautiful and poignant verses of the psalms
tells us simply: "Be still and know that I am God." I often
feel drawn to these words, knowing them to be full of God's
wisdom not only for monks, but for all believers.

The practice of quiet, inward prayer is the best way of attaining the blessed state of tranquil stillness. During prayer, we
open ourselves to God's grace, to the presence of the Holy Spirit
at work within us. At this time, we must make sure to exclude
every distraction that may interfere with our giving total attention to the Divine Presence.

During prayer we open ourselves as we are: naked, poor, and
sinful to his healing presence within us, and remain still. Nothing
is more important at that moment than to preserve a blessed
state of stillness. It is at that point of intense, internal quietude
that we learn to listen, to love, and to abandon ourselves in complete trust into the hands of a loving Father.

Continual Prayer

*You must gather yourself together within your heart and
stand there before the Lord. Pray, and may God grant
you prayer.*

THEOPHAN THE RECLUSE

Many years ago, in the early part of my monastic life, I used
to seek counseling from an older monk. Because of his
saintliness and example, he inspired me and became a true spiritual father. One day I asked him about unceasing prayer, for I
had noticed that he knew its secret. He was always recollected,

imperturbed, constantly engulfed in the "one thing necessary."
When he looked, his gaze was transparent, luminous, and mysterious, as if he was seeing someone beyond us, far, far away.

His response to my question was: "Let the Jesus Prayer be
the first thing in your mind when you wake up, let it stay with
you throughout the entire day, let it be present on your lips when
you are falling asleep at night so that somehow you continue
praying even during the hours of rest.

"Let this short prayer be constant during your daily occupations, be either when you are in church praying the Offices or
when you are busy performing the necessary daily tasks of the
monastery assigned to you by obedience.

"When you find yourself fatigued, distracted, slipping away
from prayer, return to it with renewed strength and resolution. If
you remain steadfast to the task and pray the prayer continually
and lovingly, the Lord will bring you to true union with him."

— SEPTEMBER 18 —

Confidence in God

*Therefore, I tell you, do not worry about your life, what
you will eat or what you will drink, or about your body,
what you will wear. Is not life more than food and the
body more than clothing? Look at the birds of the air.
They neither sow nor reap nor gather into barns, and yet
your heavenly Father feeds them. Are you not of more
value than they?*

MATTHEW 6:25-26

One of the lessons the hermit learns in his desert solitude is
to trust God radically. The hermit, in his utter poverty, has
no one but God to provide for him his basic needs. This absolute
reliance on God, and trust in him alone, becomes his security
and secret joy. For the solitary, to live daily in humble dependence on his heavenly Father, with complete confidence and abandonment, is what liberates him from all fear and anxiety. It leads
him to the path of true inner freedom.

Charles de Foucould, the hermit of the Sahara, wrote a simple prayer in which he expressed this filial confidence and absolute trust in his heavenly Father. It is a prayer for all of us who are called by the Gospel to live in the spirit of trust and complete confidence in God:

Father, I abandon myself into your hands; do with me as you will. Whatever you do, I thank you now. I am ready for all, I accept all, may only your will be done in me and in all your creatures. I desire nothing else, my God. Into your hands, I command my spirit, I give you my soul with all the love of my heart, for I love you, my God, and so need to surrender myself completely into your hands, with confidence beyond all measure, because you are my Father.

— SEPTEMBER 19 —

Birds of the Air

Birds, the free tenants of earth, air, and ocean,
Their forms all symmetry, their motions grace,
In plumage delicate and beautiful,
Thick without burthen, close as fish's scales.

JAMES MONTGOMERY

This afternoon I watched two beautiful little birds playing and amusing themselves in the branches of a tree. It is a very hot day, and obviously they were seeking shelter beneath the shade of the leaves. The trees are wonderfully kind to them. We are used to thinking that birds seek shelter only during winter, because of the cold and snow, but this is not always so.

Watching the bird's simple gracefulness and purity is pure delight. I think of the Gospel text of Matthew: "Look at the birds of the air. They neither sow nor reap nor gather into barns; and yet your heavenly Father feeds them" (6:26). Obviously, the Lord who created them also delights in the work of his hands, in the protection and feeding of them.

I often wonder why it is that the rest of us do not find sheer delight in the simple things of nature. Is it perhaps that we have lost that innate purity of heart that was part of us when we were first created?

When Jesus came to announce the kingdom of God, one of the important messages he left us was "Blessed be the pure of heart, for they shall see God." As I get older I realize that "purity of heart" does not refer only to chastity of body, but also of soul. The purity of heart Jesus speaks of actually goes beyond chastity. It is all-encompassing, the quality of spirit given to the truly humble, which allows them a vision of reality in its innate transparency. In this, they are granted the ability to see themselves exactly as God sees them.

— SEPTEMBER 20 —

Whence Came the Birds:
An American Indian Legend

Bless the Lord, all birds of the air....Bless the Lord, all wild animals and cattle.

BENEDICITE DOMINUM CANTICLE

The following legend, which was first published over one hundred years ago, was found tucked away in a friend's old family Bible. He since passed it on to me.

An Indian story is told about the transformation of leaves into birds. Long years ago, when the world was young, the Great Spirit went about the earth making it beautiful. Wherever his feet touched the ground lovely trees and flowers sprang up. All summer the trees wore their short green dresses. The leaves were very happy and they sang their sweet songs to the breeze as it passed them. One day the wind told them the time would soon come when they would have to fall from the trees and die. This made the leaves feel very sad, but they tried to be bright and do the best they could so as not to make the mother trees unhappy. But at last the time came and they let go of the twigs and branches and fluttered to the ground. They lay perfectly quiet, not able to move except as the wind would lift

them. The Great Spirit saw them and thought that they were
so lovely that he did not want to see them die, but live and be
beautiful forever. So he gave to each bright leaf a pair of wings
and power to fly. Then he called them his "birds." From the red
and brown leaves of the oak came the robins, and yellow birds
from the yellow willow leaves, and from the bright maple leaves
he made the red birds. This is why birds love the trees and always
go to them to build their nests and look for food and shade.

— SEPTEMBER 21 —

Autumn

*The year [is] growing ancient, not yet on summer's death,
nor on the birth of trembling winter....*

WILLIAM SHAKESPEARE, *THE WINTER'S TALE*

Today is officially the first day of autumn. It is also the feast
of Saint Matthew, the apostle tax collector and great evangelist. This morning, at the Office, the Lauds Hymn beautifully
sang his praises:

> While seated at your counting board,
> O Matthew, Christ just bade you come,
> Without a word of all the wealth
> Of grace he had in store for you.
>
> The life the Son of David led,
> The words he spoke, you stored in gold,
> Which, handed down the centuries,
> Have fed and thought the Christian world.

The autumn equinox, occurring today, signals a steady change
in the weather. The autumn mornings are usually clear and bright,
and the evening air is cool and crisp. The labor of the garden is
slowly approaching its completion. Our days are now fully engaged in the work of the harvest. Autumn is a season of contrasts: a quiet, nostalgic, reflective, colorful time. It leaves behind
the pleasures and bustle associated with summer. Autumn as a
season is indeed unique. It stands apart by itself and is full of its

own distinguishable characteristics and beauty. At a certain moment in the season, when the turning of the foliage is at its peak with bright oranges and yellows, reds and browns, we recognize autumn's time of transition. The lushness and excitement of summer begins to fade, and the more contemplative mood of early winter makes its official entrance.

From my innermost being, I sing a canticle of gratitude to our Creator for allowing us to taste his goodness in a season of such exquisite beauty, a season of luscious colors and rich bounties, a season of tremendous joy and great peace.

— SEPTEMBER 22 —

Rhythm of the Seasons

These autumn days are warning us
Of winter sure to be,
When all the leaves have fallen off
From every branch and tree.

These earthly friends are leaving us
Their autumns being past,
And thus the winters of our lives
Will come to us at last.

A SHAKER POEM

As we journey along the pleasant and sometimes unpleasant rhythm of the seasons, we become more and more aware of the immutable wisdom of the seasons and of their Creator. We become more attentive to the question of living in harmony with nature's cycles, of looking deep into the seasons which shape our daily lives. From them, we glean inspiration and inner sustenance.

Ultimately, our lives become fully integrated only when we accept the guidance of God and harmonize with the cycles of nature, the cycles of the heart, the cycles of the liturgy, and the cycles of life and death. In a letter to the Corinthians, Saint Clement of Rome, an early Church Father, exalted God's wisdom in creating the seasons:

By his direction the heavens are in motion, and they are subject to him in peace. Day and night fulfill the course he has established without interfering with each other. The sun, the moon and the choirs of stars revolve in harmony at his command in their appointed paths without deviation. By his will the earth blossoms in the proper seasons and produces abundant food for men and animals and all the living things on it without reluctance and without any violation of what he has arranged....

The seasons, spring, summer, autumn, and winter, follow one another in harmony. The quarters from which the winds blow function in due season without the least deviation. And the everflowing springs, created for our health as well as our enjoyment, unfailingly offer their breasts to sustain human life. The tiniest of living creatures meet together in harmony and peace. The great Creator and Lord of the universe commanded all these things to be established in peace and harmony, in his goodness to all, and in overflowing measure to us who seek refuge in his mercies through our Lord Jesus Christ, to him be glory and majesty for ever and ever. Amen.

— SEPTEMBER 23 —

The Ring of Christ's Presence

Ring out, wild bells, to the wild sky,
Ring in the valiant man and free
The eager heart, the kindlier hand,
Ring out the darkness of the land,
Ring in the Christ that is to be.

ALFRED LORD TENNYSON

A lovely custom is still kept in certain monasteries, especially those in France and Spain. During the celebration of the Eucharist, when the moment of the consecration arrives, the monk or nun who is assigned to ring the bells for that particular week will go to the bell tower and ring one of the large bells slowly— a very solemn moment in the monastic day, reminding monks and nuns of the tremendous event taking place within their midst.

As the bell sounds during the consecration, it announces the good tidings of Jesus descending upon the altar not only to the monastic community, but to those in the surrounding landscape. Everyone in close proximity is made aware that his mystery is being renewed once again. The bell seems to proclaim: "Rejoice, all you creatures! Your Savior comes to you. Open wide your hearts and welcome him."

Bells have a language all their own, and they use it not only to mark the time but to express joy, hope, sorrow, and both good and bad news. When the bell rings at the consecration of the Mass, its sound pierces right through our hearts, heralding the arrival of our Lord and God. Again and again, with every peal the bell repeats: "He is here! Get ready for him."

— SEPTEMBER 24 —

Mater Misericordiae

Hail, Mother of Mercy, Mother of God,
And Mother of us,
Mother of hope and Mother of grace,
Mother, full of holy joy,
O Holy Mary.

HYMN TO MARY

Some Christians, Protestants, and even Catholics think that Catholicism and Orthodoxy in general express too much devotion to Mary. To them, I say that this is false. I am one of those who is greatly attached to the Mother of God. I acknowledge her as being of great importance to my life, because I see her as the one who daily leads me directly to Christ, her Son.

In the center of our chapel, we have life-size ikons of the Deesis. Christ the Pantocrator is in the center, and Our Lady and Saint John the Baptist flank either side. They point Christ out to us, as they also intercede with him on our behalf. That is how I see Our Lady's dual role within our spiritual life. On the one hand, she points us to her Son, and on the other, she makes intercession to him for us.

The ikon of the Incarnation is another example of this. There,

Our Lady holds the Child Jesus to us as she repeats her quiet invitation: "Behold my Son, the Son of the Most High. Do whatever he tells you." True devotion to Mary, the Theotokos, is by necessity centered around Christ. She is passionately attached to Jesus, the Father's Son and her own child. She wishes us to experience an equal passion, and she constantly reminds us that, above all, we must seek and prefer the love of Christ. This love, she proclaims, must be both very real and very personal. Our Lady can only be happy when she sees her children, each one of us, totally bonded with Jesus, her divine Son.

— SEPTEMBER 25 —

Autumnal Beauty

Thrice happy time,
Best portion of the various year, in which
Nature rejoiceth, smiling on her works
Lovely, to full perfection wrought.

AMBROSE PHILLIPS

On this almost perfect autumn day, the leaves are beginning to change their colors. Here on the New York–New England border, the foliage is at its very best. I gaze at the tapestry of beauty around me and delight in the sunlight shining in the trees. The air is crystal clear, and there is nothing finer than breathing it deeply. As I rejoice at the sight of our lovely trees, standing tall in regal colors, I drink deeply the sweetly scented seasonal air. I thank God for the gift of life, for the fact that he brought me here to this place, to this point in time, where I can marvel at the wonders of his creation. It gives complete satisfaction to the heart.

Harvesttime

The feast is such as earth, the general mother,
Pours from her fairest bosom, when she smiles
In the embrace of autumn.

PERCY BYSSHE SHELLEY

S uch a glorious time of year is this! The work of the harvest continues in earnest. Mother Nature, generous as ever, yields fruits, vegetables, and herbs in abundance. Late September is a good time to reap the fruits of our summer work. In the late afternoon, when the sun begins to fade from the fields, I carry large baskets into the garden and immerse myself in harvest work. There are dozens of excellent tomatoes that must be picked and canned before the frost arrives. The same goes for the beans of all sorts, which later I will parboil lightly before placing them in plastic bags and then into the freezer.

Here in the monastery, the work of the harvest is taken seriously, for what we gather now will become our winter's food. Soon, we shall also start the potato harvest, for it must be done before the temperature drops too low at night. When the potatoes are harvested after a hard frost, they tend to change in their taste, and it is more difficult to remove them from the soil.

Harvesttime is also the occasion to remember the Lord's loving mercies, giving thanks for his daily care of us, and for his own immutable method of providing food for all of his children. *Deo gratias.*

— SEPTEMBER 27 —

Eternal Harvest

The sower who planted the seed in rich soil is the man who hears the word and puts it into practice; he is the one who yields a harvest and produces now a hundred-fold, now sixty, now thirty.

PARAPHRASE OF MATTHEW 13:23

The labor of the harvest is intensive and goes on for weeks, taking precedence over all other types of labor in the life of a small monastery such as ours. Other work, including writing, can wait, for the fruits and vegetables must be picked while in their ripest state. Time is of the essence, for as we reach the final days of September we become well aware that we can get an early frost at any time. Throughout my years of gardening and harvesting here, I seem to recall how often the first frost, even if a mild one, arrives on Saint Michael's day. That is only two days from now!

Monastic life is meant to be wholly satisfactory. According to the principle of Saint Benedict, "moderation in all things," the life must be well-tempered, well-ordered, and have ample time for work as well as prayer. The labor of the harvest is indeed intensive, and at times physically exhausting, but it is also spiritually rewarding. I think of the preceding months, of all the work that went into cultivating and caring for our gardens. And here we are today, reaping the fruits of that labor.

In a sense, monastic life should also mirror the work we undertake in the garden. Daily existence in a monastery is a quiet succession of hours, days, months, seasons, and years, in which we are given the time to labor spiritually for the salvation of our souls.

One day, the autumn of our lives shall arrive for each of us. At that point, we will reap from the seeds of our faith. With sincere humility, we must pray daily to the Lord of our harvest. In this way, we will be able to yield a bountiful crop, rendering fruit unto eternal life.

— SEPTEMBER 28 —

A Monastic Industry

Shortly his fortune shall be lifted higher;
True industry doth kindle honor's fire.

ANONYMOUS

The harvest is the time when the farmer must defend and save the fruits of his labor. Today's work in the garden consists in harvesting the varieties of cucumbers and beets sown earlier in the season. With the time of the first frost approaching rapidly, we must save them and turn them into pickles and relishes for the winter. I also gather some onions, dill, and parsley to accompany the pickled cucumbers and beets.

I am very fond of cucumbers, especially the small ones called *"cornichons"* in French. They are expensive when one buys them at the supermarket, as they are probably imported. As I harvest, I recollect that these vegetables are mentioned in the Old Testament, both in the Book of Numbers and in the prophet Isaiah. Apparently, cucumbers were well known and appreciated in antiquity, since they were popular not only in the lands of the Bible, but as far away as India and China.

Preserving vegetables and fruits through canning is an ancient monastic industry. Some monasteries in Europe have become famous because of the preserves, pickles, jellies, and relishes made from the products of their orchards and gardens, and have gone into business selling them internationally. I, however, am content to preserve only enough for our own consumption; the extra I will share with friends at Christmastime. Throughout the week, our kitchen will be overrun with the chores of peeling and slicing the vegetables, sterilizing the jars, pickling the cucumbers and beets in spiced vinegar, and finally sealing and storing our finished product.

Harvesting, freezing, canning, preserving, pickling, and all related activities are part of a monastic life that makes an effort to remain closely connected to the earth. We must work within the cycles of the seasons and cooperate with the Provider of all gifts. These may seem like time-consuming activities, and indeed they are, but they make us grateful to the Creator for providing us with the bounties of the soil. The humble work of our hands is, for us, simply another form of prayer.

— SEPTEMBER 29 —

Saint Michael and the Archangels

Jesus, radiant Light from the Father,
Life and strength of every heart,
In the presence of the angels,
In their praise we would take part.

HYMN OF THE FEAST

As September winds down, we rejoice in celebrating our protectors, the Archangels. From the Old Testament, we learn the names of these three pure Spirits: Michael, Raphael, and Gabriel. They are mentioned frequently in the Scriptures, for the Lord uses them as messengers to his chosen people. As true worshipers of God, they also recall for us God's transcendence and holiness, and of the adoration thus due to him.

As a child, I remember learning in my catechism class the meaning of the Archangels's names, and even today thinking of them evokes an awesome feeling. "Michael" signifies "one who is like God." Gabriel, divinely appointed as the messenger of the Incarnation, means "God is the strong one." Finally, Raphael's name is translated as "God heals."

Two Archangels, Michael and Gabriel, grace our chapel with their presence. Every evening, as I light the oil lamps for Vespers, I commend myself and all those in need to their unfailing protection. I know they watch over us, and keep us sheltered, close to the heart of God. One day, when our final hour arrives and we are called to see God's face, we shall join them in the eternal song of praise: *Holy, Holy, Holy Lord, God of Hosts, heaven and earth are filled with your glory.*

— SEPTEMBER 30 —

— SEPTEMBER 30 —

Mountains

Mountains of the Pyrenees,	*Montagnes Pyrennees,*
You are so loved by us.	*Vous etes nos amours.*
Rich and beautiful hills	*Collines fortunees*
I will love you forever.	*Que j'aimerais toujours.*

CHILDREN'S SONG FROM THE BEARN

As far as I recall, I have always been attracted to mountains. I was once asked by a friend if I would prefer taking a holiday in the mountains or by the beach. Without hesitation, I responded by saying that my first choice would be the mountains. My friend was utterly surprised, for he knew full well how much I love the sea.

Though rationally deciphering our feelings is not always necessary, I have finally come to understand this strange hold the mountains have on me. My ties to the mountains have been lifelong, from my relationship to the French Pyrenees where I have my roots, to my current bond with New York's Catskills and the New England Berkshires.

Spending time in the Pyrenees surrounded by their majestic grandeur has helped me realize the derivation of my powerful inner feelings. If the mountains exercise such power, it is because I am their child: a child of the Pyrenees.

When in the Pyrenees, I never tire of gazing at them. Even at night, I will get up several times to look at them through my window. During those dark hours, they seem so mysterious, so impenetrable. I love the reflection of the moon and the stars shining upon them. They glisten quietly, with great dignity and aristocratic bearing.

It seems as if those mountain peaks and the shimmering stars and moon have known each other well for eons. Their friendship surely goes back a long time, and they are used to each other's company.

When I sing the psalms daily, I am responsive to those passages where the psalmist makes reference to mountains. The same can be said about other biblical passages, either in the Old or New Testament. I feel a sense of exhilaration, a *dilatatio cordis,* that brings me true delight of heart. With the simple mention of the "mountains of the Lord," my entire being is infused with joy.

Mountains, after all, play a special role in the divine plan of Creation. All we need to remember is that the top of Mount Sinai, with all of its sweet and harsh beauty, was where God's glory was manifested to Moses. Later on, Jesus chose the top of Mount Tabor as the place for his glorious Transfiguration. Today, it is from the same mountaintop that the divine light of Christ's Transfiguration continues to shine upon our otherwise dark world.

OCTOBER

Thérèse of Lisieux:
A Vocation to Love

*I have given God nothing else but love: In return, he will
do the same for me.*

SAINT THÉRÈSE, *LAST CONVERSATIONS*

From the Gospel of John we learn that Jesus summarizes all of
his teachings in one word: love. For Jesus, love is all, the one
and only reason for an authentic Christian life: "By this love you
have for one another, everyone will know that you are my disciples." We can call ourselves his disciples, as long as we are
ready to embark on a life of constant loving, as unconditionally
as Jesus did. While the Old Testament places emphasis on worshiping the God of the Law, the New Testament proclaims the
wonders of God's unconditional love for each of us.

The life of Thérèse of Lisieux is an example of true discipleship. Thérèse took Jesus, her Master, at his word, and hence spent her life giving herself totally to the work of love. A few years ago, the renowned French writer Jean Chalon wrote in that impeccable style of his a book called *Thérèse de Lisieux: une vie d'amour* (*Thérèse of Lisieux: A Life of Love*). It has been many years since I last read a book on Saint Thérèse. I recall reading her as a young monk and always loving her, but I was not particularly attracted to her nineteenth-century writing style. For a while I became sort of numb towards *la petite Thérèse*, part of me admiring her and the other not inclined to reread her writings. This all changed the moment Jean Chalon's book fell into my hands. The book allowed me to rediscover Thérèse at a deeper level. The author's masterful narrative of Thérèse's life was illuminating. Gone was the nineteenth-century style that I found in the past a bit too sentimental. Instead, the author explored Thérèse in depth and in contemporary terms. Jean Chalon goes so far as to say that were Thérèse alive today, she would be considered a "marginal person." Her "Little Way" of climbing the mountain of pure love, considered the pinnacle by her mentor John of the Cross, would be considered too radical in these times. Yet, she faithfully adhered to the inspirations of the Holy Spirit, giving herself entirely to the task of loving God and neighbor seriously, continually, and unconditionally.

Jean Chalon mentions several times throughout the book that some Sisters at the Carmel were convinced of Thérèse's attraction towards them, while in fact Thérèse felt the opposite. The sisters never had a hint of this, for Thérèse disguised her own feelings and instead showered them with loving attention. She tried hard and succeeded in pleasing even their smallest wishes.

For Thérèse, all authentic love is expressed in the concrete. Thus, she plunged herself in the ordinary acts of daily living, "to love God and make him loved," as she often said. Moved by divine inspiration, she offered herself as a victim to God's merciful love. With this act of oblation, Thérèse reached the heights of the spiritual life, surrendering in love to a God who is himself pure love. From that moment on, she no longer belonged to herself or anyone else. She became God's possession.

During her final agony, in the midst of excruciating suffering, her Sisters would hear her say: "I don't at all regret having surrendered totally to love." On September 30, 1897, while gazing at her crucifix she uttered her last words: "*Mon Dieu, je vous aime*" ("My God, I love You"). Love summed up her entire short life and, at the end, love was her final act.

— OCTOBER 2 —

The Guardian Angels

May the angels defend us here below
Who walk by faith and not by sight;
Through them bestow on us your gifts
To follow true salvation's light.

O Jesus, joy of angels fair,
Through them direct our steps aright,
That we may also by their care
Rejoice forever in your sight.

HYMN OF THE FEAST

A few years ago the subject of angels was much in vogue. Countless books, some of them bestsellers, were written about angels and people's experience with them. Even a TV series was fashioned exclusively on the theme of good angels.

The name "angel" comes from the Hebrew, meaning "one sent," or "messenger." References to angels abound in both the Old and the New Testaments. The best-known Old Testament passage is the beautiful story of the visit of the three angels to Abraham, often used by ikonographers to depict the ikon of the Holy Trinity. The writings of Saint Justin mention that "a host of good angels was held in the greatest veneration" by the early Christians. These Christians firmly believed that angels were appointed by God to guard them from evil, so they often recommended themselves in prayer to their safekeeping.

Later Fathers, like Saint Basil, wrote that "no one denies that each of the faithful has his own guardian angel." And Saint Augustine followed by thanking God for his guardian angel saying,

"I deem it, O my God, an inestimable benefit that you have granted me an angel as a guide from the moment of my birth to that of my death."

The mystery of angels, at times a bit nebulous, is nevertheless immensely consoling, rooted as it is in the belief that each of us is a child of God and therefore has a heavenly being appointed by him to be our tutor, our guide, and our protector. Our guardian angel also has the unique assignment of being God's particular messenger to each of us. In the Eastern Church, angels are often referred to as "wind" and "fire," images closely connected with the Holy Spirit. Whatever our conception of angels may be, there is no doubt that God entrusted these heavenly spirits with the role of ministering to us and of sheltering us safely beneath the shadow of their wings.

— OCTOBER 3 —

October Weather

O suns and skies and clouds of June,
And flowers of June together,
Ye cannot rival for one hour
October's bright blue weather.

HELEN HUNT JACKSON

With October's arrival, the autumn season expands itself gloriously. October is renowned for its captivating weather: days are typically warm, sun-filled, while the nights turn cool with an exhilarating air that is pure joy to breathe.

October makes us mindful that autumn is a season of contrasts. We no longer have with us summer's exuberance; and hot days are now only a memory. Instead, we are moving toward cooler evenings and the eventual winter cold. We are in a time of transition. Time unravels its mystery in front of our very eyes. October submerges each of us in that almost indefinable, intangible mood: a feeling which presses us to explore further our own mystery, our uniqueness, our humanity in all its depths, in a way that no words can adequately express.

Saint Francis of Assisi:
God's Troubador, Ecologist, Peacemaker

I was a merchant, a man of the world and a sinner: I studied little and read little, save the ledgers of the shop and songs of love and chivalry and ballads and other vanities, until the merciful Lord touched my heart, and gave me the Cross to read. I knew no heretics, I came to know lepers. And then, when the Lord entrusted the friars to me, no one showed me what to do, but the Most High himself revealed to me that I should live according to the holy Gospel.

SAINT FRANCIS, UPON INTRODUCING HIMSELF TO SAINT DOMINIC

Today marks the feast of a saint much loved all around the world: Saint Francis of Assisi. Saint Francis is not a monastic saint, yet his presence is felt very much here in the monastery. His ikon stands in a corner of our chapel, and several shrines are dedicated to him in our gardens and in the barn. Clearly, Saint Francis is a dear friend and much loved.

As the Church of God celebrates one of her beloved saints, I recall fondly some of my own visits to Assisi and La Verna. I especially recall a long retreat I once made in Assisi and the impact that Saint Francis had on me. Saint Francis was foremost a man of the Gospel. Like the first monk, our father Saint Antony, and later our father Saint Benedict who wished his monks to "walk in the ways of the Gospel," Saint Francis embraced the Gospel life ardently. His love for Christ crucified expressed itself in his faithful following of even the smallest Gospel counsels. Saint Francis learned from the Gospel that to become a true disciple of Christ, he was to renounce wealth and security and embrace instead absolute poverty. Ruminating over the words of the Gospel and singing God's praises, Francis wandered across the Italian countryside, never knowing where his next meal would come from, or where he would find rest for the night. He trusted implicitly in God's Providence.

Above all, Saint Francis was a man of peace. Daily he prayed: "Lord, make me an instrument of your peace." Today, Francis, the radical pacifist and peacemaker, encourages us to renounce violence at all cost, at every occasion, and in every form, adhering steadily to the Gospel of peace.

Francis found all strength to follow Jesus through his fidelity to the Gospel. Likewise, we must find strength to face the conflicts and violence of our times in the radical pacifism of the Gospel: "Blessed are the peacemakers, for they shall be called children of God." This is Saint Francis's legacy to all of us.

— OCTOBER 5 —

Sunflowers

The proud giant of the garden race,
Who, madly rushing to the sun's embrace
O'ertops her fellows with aspiring aim,
Demands his wedded love, and bears his name.

WINSTON CHURCHILL

Each moment of the autumn season has its own beauty. During the first days of October, before a hard frost kills much of our garden, it is a lovely sight to behold the last sunflowers of the season. In our rustic garden, they stand tall under a blue, cloudless sky. I gently cut some of them, with some giant zinnias and cosmos, to arrange a bouquet for the chapel. The bright bouquet shall later become a sight to behold.

In the sacristy, as I work to arrange the sunflowers into a large pottery vase, I recall a passage by Caroline Richards, which I had copied into a notebook. In her book *Centering*, she writes:

> It was early fall....sunflowers were in bloom in my garden, their wide orange faces high in the air on spindly stems. It was the season of the harvest, of withering. It was seed time. And there is no air so intoxicating as that season's. I opened my door one early morning and looked out. All the sunflowers were turned toward the rising sun. The sense of outburst in the

air was unmistakable, at the same time a sense of distillation. The seeds had all formed and were about to go their ways from the mother plant. My heart was indescribably full of the simultaneous experience of dying and bearing forth, of levity, of the oracle's message of Decrease and Deliverance, of man's growth through time, and the ultimate release of his perfected powers through "death"— And all, because of those sunflowers.

— OCTOBER 6 —

Saint Bruno: "O Blessed Solitude"

Remote from men, with God he passed his days: Prayer all his business, all his pleasure praise.
"THE HERMIT" BY THOMAS PARNELL (1679–1718)

For those of us who live on the New York–New England border, each autumn day is unique. Today is still and sunny, with a touch of golden balm in the air. The trees show more of their majestic colors as the sunlight is pulled down gently behind the horizon. Soon it will vanish to darkness in the frosty air.

Today the monastic calendar marks the feast of Saint Bruno, founder of the Carthusians. The Roman Martyrology says this about Saint Bruno:

> Bruno was a Canon in Cologne, his native town, and later taught at Reims in a famous school of his time. When he was about fifty years old, he and six companions withdrew to the wilderness of the Grande Chartreuse mountains. There he organized a new form of eremitical life which was to be balanced by certain communitarian structures. Six years later, the Benedictine Pope Urban II, who was a former disciple of his at Reims, called him to Rome. In Italy, he founded a new monastery in Calabria, where he finally died on October 6, 1101.

The stillness and quiet of the season seems appropriate for our celebration of today's saint, for autumn's soothing calm enhances our reflection on this great monastic figure. Looking into the person of Saint Bruno, we discover his emphasis on solitude and silence. These two things were absolute requirements for the monastic life as perceived by him, for it is in silence and solitude that God chooses to communicate intimately with the monk. O *beata solitudo, O sola beatitudo* ("O blessed solitude, O sole blessedness") the sons and daughters of Saint Bruno often repeat, for it is in the deep solitude of the Carthusian cell that they learn the joys and pains of Christian contemplation. Led by Saint Bruno, they appreciate the richness and fullness of their lives in a solitary cell, for it is there that God reveals his face to them daily.

In the *Constitutions* that Saint Bruno wrote for his monks, he rendered utmost praise for the solitary life. For him, in any case, being alone was an inherent fact of life, for we are born alone and die alone. Saint Bruno, however, takes solitude a step further. For him, solitude is meant to be a rich and positive experience, allowing the monk to dig deep into the mystery of his own existence and discover in that stark, existential aloneness the presence of God as the ground of his own being.

Why this emphasis on solitude and silence? Saint Bruno drew his inspiration from the Gospels, concretely, and from the importance that Jesus attached to praying in solitude. It was Jesus' example that motivated Saint Bruno to a life of austere and complete solitude. He knew the adage of the monks of old and totally agreed with them: *Solitude is the home of the saints, and silence is their language.*

— OCTOBER 7 —

Our Lady of the Rosary

Let prayer be the key of the morning and the bolt of the evening.

MATTHEW HENRY

Yesterday's feast brought to mind the necessity of unceasing prayer in the life of the monk. Today's feast, Our Lady of the Rosary, highlights the rosary, a more popular form of prayer. In many ways, it is simpler than the monastic Offices, and yet it is a prayer with a vitality of its own, for it allows us to commune with God by making use of a plain and repetitive formula.

The rosary, similar to the Jesus Prayer, can be prayed under most circumstances, at any time, anywhere. I often say the rosary while driving, while waiting in line, or while weeding the garden. The rosary is also a universal prayer—prayed daily by millions of people all around the world. To avoid distractions, I usually pray each decade of the rosary in a different language. As I say the Hail Marys in various languages, I travel mentally around the world, uniting myself to all people: young and old, poor and rich, sick and healthy, as we all journey together towards God. The rosary, in many ways, is a prayer of the journey, a prayer that provides us Our Lady's assistance while we ponder the events in her Son's life.

As we recite the rosary, it helps to be mindful of the Holy Spirit praying within us. Saint Isaac the Syrian says: "Then the Spirit of God establishes his abode within a person, that person can no longer stop praying, because the Spirit does not cease praying in him or her. If the person sleeps, or keeps vigil, prayer never leaves his or her soul...." If at times we feel discouraged by our distractions while praying the rosary, we can feel confident that the prayer is still pleasing to God, for His own Spirit is praying within us.

— OCTOBER 8 —

Autumn: A Reflective Season

Each moment of the year has its own beauty, a picture which was never seen before and which shall never be seen again.

RALPH WALDO EMERSON

Autumn, in its yearly cycle, never ceases to be a source of inspiration to contemplatives. Its serene, ravishing beauty, though transient, also continues to inspire writers, poets, musicians, and artists of all types.

Autumn at its peak seems to insinuate a sense of infinite realms. The autumn experience is one of such unparalleled beauty that it makes one think of Paradise. The lush tapestry of colors, vivid and fresh as that of a recently finished still life, evokes memories of the past and feeds not only our eyes but our minds and hearts as well.

As we grow older and begin to face the autumn of our own lives, the season becomes more significant to each of us. Quietly, autumn allows us to mirror our past and present experiences in the beauty of the land all around us. As the trees slowly let go of the glory of their leaves, we too are invited to let go of our earthly encumbrances, pressing forward with our spiritual striving. Autumn is a gentle summons, a call to a continual ascension, a moving ahead in our journey toward the mountain top.

Today, the Roman Martyrology keeps the memory of the Elder Simeon. In Jerusalem, after having seen Christ, the light of all nations, Simeon fell asleep in the Lord. This venerable elder, for whom I profess a profound affection, was well-seasoned in years when he received the unsurpassed privilege of seeing his Lord and Savior, a rare gift given to only a few.

— OCTOBER 9 —

Harvest of Herbs

Thy houses and barns would be looked upon,
And all things amended, ere harvest come on;
Things set in order, in quiet and rest,
Shall further thy harvest, and pleasure thee best.

ANCIENT ENGLISH POEM

L ong before summer takes its yearly leave, I begin the careful harvest of our culinary herbs. Some herbs, such as the basil varieties, cannot afford being touched by the frost and must be harvested in late summer. Other herbs, however, are not readily affected by the first frost, unless it is very severe, so they can patiently wait until October for the final harvest. Mid-October, having seen summer's fullness in steady decline, is the propitious time to gather from the bounty of our herb gardens. I say gardens, in the plural, for here in the monastery there are two separate areas where we grow herbs. One of these areas is an exclusive herb garden, where we grow only herbs, culinary and nonculinary. The second area is located in the vegetable garden, and there two small patches are reserved for the cultivation of herbs for the kitchen.

The gathering of herbs, though a delightful activity, demands a substantial amount of time and work. Herbs must always be harvested under the right conditions and in benign weather. Their quality is enhanced when gathered on a warm sunny day when the herbs are totally dried. Usually, I wait until the afternoon to give time for the effects of an early dew to evaporate. Herbs gathered while they are still wet inevitably turn moldy.

Carrying huge baskets and large boxes into the gardens, I begin this afternoon the pleasant task of herb gathering. It seems only yesterday that the herbs were planted and lovingly nurtured; and suddenly, it is time for the *recolte*, as harvest is called in French. As I pensively recall earlier days, I press forward with the work, for as the old French proverb reminds me: *"Recolte rentrée, recolte assurée"* (Harvest gathered, harvest assured).

There was a time when almost every farmer, every monk, received a thorough education in the knowledge of herbs: their cultivation, their harvesting, their careful storage, and, certainly, their proper usage. They learned which herbs were appropriate for kitchen use, and which herbs possessed healing qualities and were therefore reserved for medical purposes. How unfortunate this art has been almost totally lost, and that only a few avid herbalists continue holding on to this wealth of knowledge. I muse on this loss as I cut the parsley, thyme, lemon balm, calendula leaves, chervil, marjoram, chives, savory, tarragon, dill, garlic leaves, hyssop, oregano, sage, sorrel, and all sorts of mint. Some, such as the rosemary and bay plants, are brought inside into the greenhouse to last through another winter. I also bring in some thyme and parsley plants, for fresh usage even on the coldest winter days.

When all the herbs are gathered, I place them to dry in a room located in a northwestern corner. There, they are protected from direct sunlight and are able to retain not only their taste but also their original colors. Once the herbs are sufficiently dried, after a month or two, I shall remove them from their stem, shred them finely with scissors, or pass through the food processor. When this process is completed, I store them in glass jars so as not to loose their aromatic properties. Later on, on a cold winter day, what a treat it shall be to reach for a handful of dried herbs and add them to the just-made evening soup! The mind is renewed at such moments, when the intoxicating aroma from the jar evokes the memory of summer fragrances when herbs were at their best.

— OCTOBER 10 —

Saint Telchilde, Abbess

The monastic life for us [women] is not in essence a battle but a way of love and faith...for only in so glad a love can we make our senses follow after the spirit; hence it may be that women, who love much and intensely, find fulfillment in monastic life.

MOTHER MARIA, *SCEPTRUM REGALE*

As I gaze at the splendor of our area's golden trees, the apple orchards laden with fruit, and the local vineyards with an abundance of pale and purple grapes, I stop for a moment and breathe slowly, deeply. I thank God for the loveliness unfolding before my very eyes, for the transparency of the season. As I continue to gaze at the brilliance of the trees and the superb reflection of the light shining on them, I recall a lovely stanza by Saint John of the Cross:

> Showering a thousand graces
> He came hurriedly through these groves,
> He looked at them
> And in the radiance of his gaze
> He left the woodland robed in beauty.

Today in France, the monastic family keeps the memory of Saint Telchilde, first abbess of Jouarre. She was laid to rest in the famous seventh-century Merovingian crypt, one of the treasures of the Isle de France, where the ancient monastery is located. Saint Telchilde's sarcophagus carries this simple inscription: "Telchilde shined because of her faith. Mother of this monastery, she invites her daughters, wise virgins consecrated to God, to carry their lamps and to join Christ, their eternal Spouse." A stark statement, and an austere reminder of the necessity for constant vigilance in one's daily monastic life.

— OCTOBER 11 —

Autumn Leaves

The leaves fall patiently, nothing remembers or grieves;
the river takes to the sea, the yellow drift of leaves.

SARAH TEASDALE

October in our region of the country is known as the month in which the leaves turn, die, and eventually fall from the trees. The dramatic foliage change is a landmark by which October distinguishes itself from other months.

Here in upstate New York we witness daily the herds of tourists who roam around the countryside, in search of the best vistas. The gentle scenery of our rolling hills and valleys uncover their trees in all their splendor. Lush tapestries of red, orange, brown, green, and golden yellow transport our visitors to other realms and spheres. On a golden, perfect autumn day such as today, the leaves peak and the trees display all their genius: those secret colors that are so well guarded throughout the rest of the year.

Today, while walking to the mailbox to pick up the mail, I reflect on how sad and gloomy October would be without the incomparable tapestries from our friends the trees. I feel a deep sense of gratitude to God for placing me here in this spot, in this region of the country, in this environment, in this hidden corner of his world, where the trees and the entire landscape daily sings his praises in silence, with such rare beauty.

— OCTOBER 12 —

Always in Season

Through everything that lives each has a birth, a purpose
to fulfill. To each an end...and then a new beginning.

GWEN FROSTIC

Through the organic flow of her seasons, Mother Nature unfolds for us her secret, pulsating life rhythm. So, too, as we journey through the liturgical seasons, we see the Church unfold her mystery before our eyes. The liturgy of the Church gradually reveals to us the mystery she holds in secrecy, the "mystery hidden from all ages," Christ, our hope of glory.

Monastic life, in many ways, is precisely an attempt to live out this intimate connection between the seasons of nature and the Spirit. I call them simply the seasons of the heart. For ultimately it is at the point where all seasons meet that we begin to experience the inner fabric of life, as we encounter Christ, the Source and Giver of life.

— OCTOBER 13 —

Simplicity: A Monastic Virtue

Monastic simplicity is the concern with doing ordinary
things quietly and perfectly for the glory of God.

THOMAS MERTON

Contemporary American society places so much emphasis on success, achievement, possessions, and financial security that anything else seems of little value. Few among us would heed the message of evangelical simplicity as lived and taught by the Desert Fathers and Mothers.

Within the monastic world, simplicity is not merely an attitude. It goes well beyond that. Simplicity is a way of life, a cherished virtue very dear to the heart of the monk or nun. I think of simplicity as a limpid mirror in which one can perceive all of reality, clearly reflected in the minutiae of daily events. Above all, simplicity seeks the truth and embraces it. In this living embrace of simplicity and truth, we are given a grace from above to deliberately avoid all that is to the contrary: complexity, falsehood, duplicity, conflict, tension, and all that is harmful and destructive to our very souls. In embracing a life of simplicity, the monk is invited to deliberately leave behind all egocentric attitudes and selfish concerns. Instead, he can begin to respond to the demands of the Gospel that call him to a relationship of fullness with God and all his creation.

— OCTOBER 14 —

Monachos: The Single-Minded One

The monk is a man of one-ness. Simplicity: his very name says it: Monachos: alone, single, simple.

ESTHER DE WAAL

The ancient monastic Fathers always emphasized that the sole reason for which a monk embraced monastic life was to seek God in *simplicitate cordis*, that is, with true simplicity of heart.

The original Greek word for monk is *monachos*, and it defines the monk thoroughly: one who is alone, one in himself, single-minded, and simple. By embracing monastic simplicity as a way of life, the monk receives from God all the goodness and gifts of his wonderful creation. At the same time, he lets go of life's encumbrances and all that is not God-oriented.

The embrace of voluntary simplicity becomes for the monk a transforming experience, for it frees the heart from its endless burdens and expectations, selfish concerns and illusions. It allows him to proceed on his monastic journey with serenity and freedom. Simplicity, in all of life's occasions, reminds the monk that God alone matters, and that through the gratuity of his grace the monk is invited to abide forever in the mystery of his love.

Saint Teresa of Jesus:
The Primacy of Prayer

We need no wings to go in search of God, but have only to find a place where we can be alone, and look upon him present within us.

SAINT TERESA OF JESUS

This afternoon, a cool day with clear skies, I move around the garden, transplanting irises and other perennials in dire need of being subdivided. I like to imagine what they will look like next year, in their new spots in the garden. As I continue to dig, I set aside garden thoughts for a while and think instead about the great mystic, Teresa of Ávila, whose feast we keep today. She is a saint for whom I have a great affinity.

A few decades ago, Saint Teresa was declared a Doctor of the Church, one of the few women saints to have received such acknowledgment. This recognition did not come to her simply because of her charming personality or the influence she exerted, or because of her great work as the reformer of Carmel. No, this recognition on the part of the Church has come about primarily because of her admirable teachings on prayer, on the life of union with God, which she so artfully describes in her writings.

For Saint Teresa, the work of prayer is the beginning and the end of all spiritual life. This is her message to all those who are serious about pursuing a spiritual life. As we read her works, we are encouraged by this *Mater Spiritualium* to embark on an incredible inner journey—an adventure in grace and discovery of the Inner Presence. The realization that a Divine Guest is present within is the catalyst that inspires a dialogue, an ongoing conversation with Him who inhabits us. This dialogue which gradually turns into divine intimacy is prayer. Saint Teresa reminds us that "God grants immense favors to the soul that is generous in her application to prayer." For her, this daily and holy application to prayer is the sure way to God.

— OCTOBER 16 —

Saint Teresa's Secret

*I saw Christ at my side, or, to put it better, I was conscious
of him, for neither with the eyes of the body nor with
those of the soul did I see anything.*

THE LIFE OF SAINT TERESA OF ÁVILA

In her autobiography, Saint Teresa relates her story to us. Mincing no words, she recounts the story of her conversion and
how gradually her life evolved towards one point, one center:
God. She wrote the book reluctantly and under obedient suggestion, not so much to speak about herself, but to tell us about
God, or as she put it in her own words quoting the psalms, "to
sing God's mercies forever."

Saint Teresa had no formal training in the theological sciences. She was, however, a person of great spiritual experience.
What she wished to convey to her Carmelite daughters and all
those who would read her was that unique type of knowledge
that comes from a rich, lived experience. The difference between
her and the trained theologian is that the former teaches about
God in an intellectual, scientific manner, using the mind as a tool
to apprehend God's mysteries. Theologians, in general, never make
reference to their personal experience of God, as the mystics do.
In the theologian, as he or she tries to convey the mystery of
God, there is something lacking, a very real dichotomy between
objective knowledge and experience.

In contrast to theological experts, Teresa speaks of God not
as an intellectual entity but as a living Person with whom she
lives and talks in her daily life. Her knowledge of God derives
from a special bond: the personal, loving relationship that has
been established between her and God. As a woman of her times,
she was not allowed to teach or preach publicly, so she made
recourse to the one medium left to her: writing. She took her pen
and never stopped writing, never stopped singing God's mercies,
until death came to fetch her. Her writings are as popular today
among spiritual people as they were during her time. To all those

who read her, she continues revealing her secret: the incredible joy that comes from living in a personal, loving intimacy with the God that inhabits us all.

— OCTOBER 17 —

Saint Ignatius of Antioch

I am God's wheat and I am ground by the teeth of the wild beasts that I may become pure bread of Christ.

SAINT IGNATIUS OF ANTIOCH

The autumn coloring is slowing down a bit. After the leaves reach their maturity, nothing is left for the season but to begin its slow descent. Until a few days ago I could gaze for long moments at a time at the beauty of our hills, at the cornflower and asters blooming in our meadows, at the trees in their height of their glory—but alas! time moves on, and once again one must prepare for the long quiet of the winter ahead. From now on, much time and energy will be spent on winter preparations.

Today we celebrate the feast of Saint Ignatius of Antioch, one of the jewels of the early Church. He is one of those giant Apostolic Fathers, like Polycarp, Clement of Rome, and Irenaeus of Lyons, who used every possible means to preserve the faith as it was handed down to him by the Apostles. After all, he was a direct successor of Saint Peter in the See of Antioch, and he treasured the faith entrusted to him. He would not compromise the apostolic faith in the face of either the political authorities or the heretics. Around 107 A.D., he was taken prisoner in Syria, where he had lived and preached practically all of his long life. From Syria, he was transferred to Rome in the company of other Christians, and it was there that he was finally put to death, being devoured by wild beasts. He died as he lived, sealing his faith in Jesus Christ with the blood of martyrdom. In the letters he addressed to the Christian communities of his time, he encouraged his fellow Christians to follow his example and not be afraid of those who have the power to kill the body. He also exhorted them to constant prayer and to care for the poor.

I am strongly attached to the Fathers and the saints of the early church. Through their ikons in our chapel, many of them honor us with their presence. Every year, as we relive the events of their lives and keep their glorious memory, it is a source of profound joy to be counted among their numbers, to know oneself a member of Christ's little flock—a flock which, in spite of immense human weakness, is held together by the power of the Holy Spirit and sustained by the example and blood of the martyrs.

— OCTOBER 18 —

Saint Luke

Holy and learned, great Saint Luke, we praise you,
Closely you followed in the steps of Jesus;
As supreme witness to his life and teaching
Shedding your life-blood.

Tender physician, use your gift of healing,
Comfort our weakness with a faith unswerving,
So that rejoicing we may praise forever
God the Almighty.

HYMN OF THE FEAST

Today the calendar marks the feast of Saint Luke, the great evangelist. In Church antiquity his name was interpreted as meaning "lift," also as coming from *lux*, signifying "light." A medieval commentator writes that the application of the word "lift" was very appropriate, for "Luke rose above the enticements of the world, and lifted himself to the supreme love of God." However, the interpretation of the name Luke as "light" is also meaningful, for through his writings he shed light upon the entire cosmos by manifesting Christ, the true light of the world.

Saint Luke was Syrian by birth, a native of Antioch. He was a physician by profession, and according to tradition, he was one of the first seventy-two disciples of the Lord. The same Church tradition assigns him the role of being the author of the third Gospel and of the book of Acts. He was obviously a person of great talent, as shown by his writings and through the high esteem with which he was held by Saint Paul, who lovingly used to refer to Saint Luke as his "dear physician." We owe much to Saint Luke. We would have known little about the birth and childhood of Jesus if it were not for him. It is also reasonable to assume from his Gospel that he knew Our Lady intimately. Tradition also maintains that Saint Luke was a painter, and that the first ikon of the Mother of God was painted by him. Be this as it may, Saint Luke did a great favor for the Church by leaving in his writings a true portrait of Mary.

Something else causes my appreciation of Saint Luke: the parable of the prodigal son. Luke is the only one among the four evangelists to hand down to us this touching story. This incident speaks volumes about Saint Luke, for in doing so, he allows us to get a glimpse into the mystery of God's love and mercy, something so real and yet so beyond our human comprehension. In this parable, we are given a reason for renewed hope, because we are all prodigal children en route, working our way back to our Father's home.

— OCTOBER 19 —

Simplicity As Asceticism

Simplicity means this: to know nothing of guile, and on good works alone to humbly set one's eye.

ANGELUS SILESIUS

A uthentic simplicity implies both detachment and renunciation. The Desert ascetics, desiring to imitate Christ and follow the Gospel to the letter, deliberately withdrew from a society and a church that had been corrupted by power and materialism. In the desert, these *athletae Dei*, or "athletes of God," gave themselves fully to ascetic practices and continual prayer, both of which paved the way that lead to union with God.

Their asceticism was a return to the basic tenet of Gospel simplicity. In contrast to the questions we might ask of ourselves today, they asked themselves instead: How much more can I renounce? What can I do without? How can I learn to love as Christ did, with true compassion and without judging others? and, ultimately, How can I truly love my God?

Seeing all things through the "prism" of simplicity inspired the early ascetics to become living embodiments of the truth emanating from the Gospel. This view is antithetical to the false-hood of the ways of the world. While society, then and now, stressed the accumulation of possessions, the manipulation of others, the glorification of the individual, and the exaltation of the self, the desert ascetics found perfect contentment in the prac-tice of monastic simplicity, humility, and frugality. Such practices freed the human heart and made ample space within for God's love and his Kingdom.

— OCTOBER 20 —
Simplicity Finds a Home in the Daily

Simplicity, letting go of opinions and cravings, is an act of compassion for ourselves. When we let go of yearnings for the future, preoccupation with the past, and strategies to protect the present, there is nowhere left to go but where we are. To connect with the present moment is to begin to appreciate the beauty of simplicity.

JACK KORNFELD AND CHRISTINA FELDMAN

Monastic simplicity is not only a virtue but also a long jour-ney undertaken the moment the monk embraces the mo-nastic state. Simplicity is a pilgrimage, rooted in God, encompass-ing all of the distances contained within our inner landscape. It is the quiet thread that connects all of life's events and occasions along the way.

Monastic simplicity is easily witnessed in the everyday life of the monk. One has only to visit a monastery or hermitage on a weekday and one would find a monk or nun totally involved in such insignificant things as carrying hay to feed the sheep or haul-ing manure from the barn to the garden, peeling potatoes in the kitchen for the evening's meal or weeding out the vegetable patch.

Some of our guests are surprised at how trivial daily monastic life seems to be. Monks and nuns are not always to be found in their choir stalls in a deeply contemplative state, but more often involved in plain manual duties, working with their hands to support themselves like the rest of humankind.

Seeking God daily through the practice of simplicity involves all aspects of the monk's life: prayer, reading, work, silence, solitude, communion with others. Slowly through the grace imparted from above, the monk begins to discover that beneath the simplicity of his daily life lies hidden a great treasure: the realization that it gives unity and purpose to his entire existence. Often, what may appear as contradiction to the worldly eye is precisely a source of richness and unity for the monk. Ultimately, the radiant splendor of monastic simplicity shines forth from the face of Christ, in whom the monk's life is rooted. Simplicity reminds him of his total dependence upon God, and all he receives from above for both his spiritual and bodily sustenance.

An early medieval monk once summarized the monastic mystery in these words: *Our monastic life consists of a humble awareness of God. It is made of utter simplicity and poverty freely accepted; obedience, peace, and joy in the Holy Spirit. Our monastic life teaches us to be silent, to fast, to keep vigils, to pray, to work with our hands, and, above all, to cling to that most excellent way which is love.*

— OCTOBER 21 —

Saint Hilarion

Hilarion being now in the sixty-third year of his age, and finding himself in a large monastery, with a multitude of monks, and crowds of people bringing to him those who were sick or possessed by evil spirits, so the desert was filled all around with people of every sort—he wept daily, and remembered with incredible longing his old manner of life.

SAINT JEROME'S *LIFE OF SAINT HILARION*

The monastic calendar brings us today the occasion to remember Saint Hilarion, a great monastic father and an influential figure in early monasticism. In our kitchen hangs an ikon of him in which Saint Hilarion stands right next to Saint Antony the Great. This is rightly so, for together both became true pillars of the then recently born monastic movement.

Saint Antony, the first monk, left his imprint in Egypt. Saint Hilarion followed the example of Antony and established monastic life in Palestine, his native land. What Antony did for the spread of monasticism in Egypt, Hilarion accomplished for Palestine. Hilarion was born of pagan parents and became a Christian during his early years. Soon after, he made a pilgrimage to the Egyptian desert to meet Antony. What an encounter that must have been!

Saint Hilarion stayed long enough in Egypt to become imbued with the spirit and example of Saint Antony. After his return to Palestine, he continued to correspond with Antony and spared no means to implant in the land of Jesus what he saw and lived in Egypt. His extraordinary holiness attracted innumerable disciples. He continued to teach all of them by the example of his humility and by his continual communion with God. After seeing the monastic life well rooted on Palestinian soil and paying one last visit to his beloved mentor Antony of Egypt, Hilarion retired to a stricter solitude. Unfortunately, he was now too sought-after to be totally left alone by the crowds. Hilarion was eighty-nine years old, according to his biographer Saint Jerome, when he was removed from this earth to the life of heaven. As he was dying, he spoke: "Go forth, my soul, go forth! Why do you hesitate? Almost seventy years you have served Christ, and yet you are afraid of death?"

Death is such a mysterious event, such an unfathomable experience, we must not be surprised that even a great saint such as Hilarion fell prey to its terror and fear. It is part of our human condition to fear the unknown. Saint Hilarion shows us that the fear of death is common to all, even the holiest of Christians; and he also shows us that in accepting God's will, we are able to endure the harsh reality of death with trustful serenity. *In manus tuas Domine, commendo spiritum meum.*

— OCTOBER 22 —

Firewood

Let workman at night bring in wood or a log.
MEDIEVAL SAYING

The first hard frost of the season arrived a few weeks ago—a silent reminder that I must make an inventory of the wood supply for our two stoves. The nights are cooler now, and the warmth emanating from a fireplace becomes more desirable as the days go by.

The firewood has been cut during late spring and early summer, so it could have sufficient time to dry before it gets put to good use during the winter months. The job awaiting me in the next couple of days, or perhaps weeks, is to split the wood to the right size to fit our stoves, then pile it in a dry place in sufficient quantities. I am always amazed at how much wood we use in this small monastery. Late at night before retiring, I refill the stoves with logs in order to prolong the heat until the early hours of the morning. Our three cats—Ebony, Misty, and Fluffy—enjoy sleeping close by the stoves. It is a daily ritual with them.

I am grateful for the firewood available from our property, often the result of a freak storm that ends up knocking down some of our trees. Though Nature gets its own way, nothing really gets really wasted in the monastic scheme, for I know that if the wood does not get used for heating, it will simply decay. Frugality in our daily monastic life is both an art and a gift. Often, it is also the source of small, countless joys, such as the heat and comfort conveyed by wood burning in a humble woodstove.

— OCTOBER 23 —

A Monastery: An Abode of Peace

In peace, there's nothing so becomes a man,
As modest stillness and humility.

WILLIAM SHAKESPEARE

R ecently, a group of children from a local Catholic school offered came to rake the fallen leaves throughout the property. Along with some of their parents, they worked for a few hours and then decided to take a lunch break. The group also visited and played with our pets and farm animals—a rather unusual occurrence for them since, as city children, they haven't had much exposure to farm animals. After the work, the eating, and the playing were done, we all sat down in the garden in a circle, enjoying the blue skies of a perfect October day.

The parents told me that the children wished to ask me some questions. They started by asking about the animals and the gardens. Suddenly, one of them asked, "What is a monastery?" I realized they were so young, and obviously they had never been to a monastery before.

"A monastery," I replied, "is a home of peace, for the people who dwell here seek the God of peace. Do you see that small blue house?" I continued, pointing to the guesthouse. "Well, every year many people come to stay there because they wish to share the life of this place. They come to the monastery in search of inner peace. You see," I told them, "our guests come to the monastery hoping to find in this tranquil setting, something of the peace of God. After all, peace is a great gift from the Lord, a gift given to those who honestly seek and pursue it." A long quiet followed this statement. I hoped that I had planted a small seed in their hearts.

— OCTOBER 24 –

Planting for Spring

For everything there is a season, and a time for every matter under heaven: A time to be born...A time to plant...A time to uproot what has been planted.

ECCLESIASTES 3:1–2

Octber's garden tasks do not concentrate solely on the labor of the harvest. Today, as a gentle breath of soft winds drifts throughout the property, I make myself useful in the garden by planting some bulbs for next spring. The loveliness of today's weather contributes to the task, the rain of the last couple of days has retreated and the sun is shining intensely. Working under a clear-blue sky and feeling the warmth of the sunrays are immensely soothing to one's spirit. I am deeply conscious that as the season progresses, we will not enjoy many more days with weather such as today's.

Every year I add some new bulb species to our gardens, especially tulips, crocus, hyacinths, and some new lilies. The daffodils have multiplied throughout the years, and though now I plant fewer of them, I still go through the task of subdividing and transplanting their bulbs elsewhere in the gardens. I like the fact that they naturalize easily no matter what spot they are planted in. Come spring, each newly planted spot will be embellished by the presence and bright colors of the daffodils.

Working in the garden during these last days of October is indeed an endless source of satisfaction. One season is dying, yet we are already looking ahead by making preparations for next spring. This is the same in our life of communion with God. Though this communion is realized in the present moment, in the daily of our lives, it also looks ahead to the designs God has for each of us, to his promise of eternal life. After the long winter of our lives achieves its completion, we can look forward to the endless spring feast, to the Lord's eternal day.

The Planting of Bulbs Continues

*The human mind may devise many plans, but it is the
purpose of the LORD that will be established.*

PROVERBS 19:21

Today I press forward with the task of planting the remaining bulbs. Recently, someone who has a great feeling of kinship with our gardens and animals sent us several varieties of exquisite Chinese lilies, plus some other bulbs. I delight in these little presents, for next year the lilies shall improve remarkably certain sections of our perennial garden. I am more of an afficionado than a professional gardener. I don't fuss too much about such things as color scheme and other theories that gardeners often discuss. I do pay attention to some basic details, such as the size of the plants, their right location, and consider the final shape of the beds; but I don't go much beyond that.

Today, as I try to build up an already existing herbaceous border close to the garage, I add some tulip and crocus bulbs to enhance the spot. It is a rather shady spot, but the spring flowers will do well there before the foliage from the trees fully develops. It is a seemingly uncomplicated spot, but a very visible one, where a touch of color will convey a certain quality to the setting. When next spring arrives, we shall see if this inner drive that compels me from time to time to improve some uncanny corner of the property was a correct decision or not. Time is always the great revealer....In the meantime, this is another occasion to practice patience and quietly wait until spring for the results of our late fall labors.

Planting bulbs, like other aspects of gardening, is a relatively simple, ordinary task. The experience, however, can be significant, for working with the soil can become an experience of prayer. In all seasons, be it autumn, summer, or spring, as we work our hands into the dirt and enter into direct contact with the soil, one intuitively arrives at the profound discovery of touching the holy.

— OCTOBER 26 —

A Sunset and a Hymn

See the descending sun,
Scatt'ring his beams about him as he sinks,
And gilding heaven above, and seas beneath,
With paint no mortal pencil can express.

GERARD MANLEY HOPKINS

People who live in this area of the country often remark about the unforgettable sunsets at this time of year. One of them, an occasional visitor to the monastery, once said to me, "Those sunsets are part of the territory; they come with the season, they are a gift from the season." I have sometimes noticed cars parked on scenic spots at that precise hour of the day, with a driver watching in delight those last rays from the sun. It is a dramatic experience of day's end, a moment of intense beauty, of privileged stillness, of profound calm and peace.

Watching such sunsets, one gets lost in the richness of the surrounding landscape. Those last sunrays seem to delineate perfectly the undulations in the land, highlighting the brilliance of the trees and the gracious curves of the nearby hills. Suddenly, the whole countryside is at peace. Our bells are pealing, making the call for Vespers. Towards the middle of this Office we shall sing a special hymn to Christ, the Sun that enlightens our darkness. It is a second-century hymn, a hymn of praise to him who is the Giver of light and light himself:

> O gladsome Light of the holy glory of the Immortal Father, heavenly, holy, blessed Jesus Christ. Now that we come to the setting of the sun and behold the light of evening, we praise the Father, Son, and Holy Spirit, God. At all times you are worthy of praise in songs as Son of God, and Giver of Life, the world glorifies you.

I find such comfort in this daily hymn. It never ceases to fill me with an incredible sense of security and peace. All is well, because Christ our Light is there. Evening has come, the sun has set, the shadows of darkness are now scattered over the land, and we can face that darkness confidently, without fear. No longer is there room for gloom or anxiety. Nighttime holds no power over us, for Christ our Savior is there to shed light into our own personal darkness and to dispel the nightly terrors away from our lives.

— OCTOBER 27 —
Inner Healing

Christ came not only to proclaim a message but to use a healing power. He wishes to heal because we have wounds which paralyze genuine love: wounds that make us deaf to his word, blind to what he wants us to see. His healing brings happiness and freedom so that we can carry our burdens and serve more faithfully.

ABBOTT BASIL HUME, *SEARCHING FOR GOD*

Our small guesthouse receives several hundred people a year, all in quest of something. Some come on a spiritual retreat and to share our life of prayer. Others come for physical and mental rest. And there are others, who often come because they are undergoing profound changes in their personal lives, and need time for reflection and clarification.

Recently a man from California came here to spend a few days in quiet and silence. This was his second sojourn at our small monastery. A very well-educated man, he would be considered in our culture to be very successful. I listened attentively as he told his story: "In a few years I made a lot of money, had the most expensive cars, had a great wardrobe, and traveled around the world. I have been almost insane with the idea of making so much money that I never stopped working. I have been working seven days a week, nonstop, for the last couple of years, when suddenly I collapsed. I had a nervous breakdown and was totally distraught. My friends and colleagues couldn't understand what was happening to me. I was crippled, I was wounded, I was in a state of spiritual emergency, and no one, not even a psychiatrist, could figure out what was wrong with me."

The man told me in detail of this experience of being wounded so deeply that he had to be hospitalized. He said, "I was at the point of losing all perception of reality. No one, not even the doctors or counselors, ever figured out what was wrong with me. I eventually came out of it. I was in the process of crawling out of that nightmare when by chance someone introduced me to one of your cookbooks. Then and there I decided I wanted to spend time here. I have never been to a monastery before and never considered the necessity of a spiritual life. But coming here for the first time a few months ago did something to my system that even my stay at the hospital was not able to accomplish. The experience of the life here, the soothing silence, the chant in the chapel, the contact with the animals, all of it slowly started working on me. For the first time I could see I was in the process of finding myself. This is why I have asked to return here. I am not a man of faith. I don't understand it, but I see that you live by it and the difference that it makes in your life." And then he continued: "Slowly I wish to internalize something of what I experience here, and bridge the gap between what I know and live in California, and the truth that I find here. This is my big dilemma, my awesome challenge."

As he spoke of the challenge he faced, I felt the burden of that challenge, trying to find adequate words to comfort him. All I could say was, "Be patient with yourself, be tolerant of yourself and others, do not judge. Let things unfold gradually and if you can, try to trust in God. I know this is a leap of faith for you, for you say you don't know if you believe in God or not. While you are here, look often at the ikon of Christ in the chapel. You don't have to pray or say anything. Just look at him, and let him look at you. Let your gaze remain peacefully fixed on Him. Something will eventually happen. Trust that."

A few weeks after the man returned home to California, he wrote a simple letter saying: "I don't know where this is taking me, but my silent days at the monastery have made such a difference in my life. I have a renewed energy, a desire to live fully. I feel the world is a better a place today, because I discovered there are such islands of peace called "monasteries" where I can retreat and encounter the real. And by the way, I carry with me the ikon of 'Christ, the Merciful One' you gave me before I left the monastery. I look at him frequently, as you suggested, and I feel he is working on me." Needless to say, his letter filled me with a renewed hope.

— OCTOBER 28 —

What a Monastery Means to Others

Often a monastery is built in a secluded place. But this is not simply so that the monks may find peace and quiet there. They come here to undertake the never-ending battle with evil that takes place in prayer. To the visitor, however, the cloister does appear like a haven of peace, far from the world and its troubles.

DOM ANDRÉ LOUF, *THE CISTERCIAN WAY*

A mature woman and frequent guest to our monastery wrote once why she takes yearly retreats at the monastery, and in concrete terms, what a monastery means to her:

The cloister is very different from the outside world. If it were not, those of us who live in the world would not be drawn there. There is in the monastery a pointing of the whole life toward God, a drawing together of every activity into prayer. Again and again each day the monks return to the chapel, the very heart of the monastery, to lift up their hearts to God in silence, in word, and in song throughout the hours bounded by predawn Vigils and evening prayers. These two Offices, Vigils and Vespers, are like jeweled gates through which the monks move the world toward heaven every day of their lives.

— OCTOBER 29 —

Pumpkin Jam

You must boile your frute, whether it be apple, cherie,
peach, damson, peare, mulberie, or codling, in faire water,
and when they boiled inough, put them into a bowle,
and bruse them with a ladle, and when they be cold,
straine them, and put in red wine or claret wine, and so
season it with sugar, cinnamon and ginger.

THOMAS DAWSON, *THE GOOD HUSWIFE'S JEWELL*, 1587

Our homegrown food, as wished by Saint Benedict, allows us in the monastery to live simply, frugally, and healthfully. It is an integral part of the ancient monastic wisdom, a real part of our tradition, that we tend our gardens and grow our own food. Of course, once the vegetables and fruit have ripened, we have to find a way to preserve them for the months ahead. Here, of course, we preserve and freeze the harvest from our garden. We also place it in storage in a cool cellar. And finally, some fruits and vegetables are turned into jams, chutney, and jellies. Today's task is to turn some of our pumpkins into jam. I find it a bit ironic that Halloween is so near—a time when pumpkins will be wastefully used for amusement and decoration—while here at the monastery we are in the hasty process of peeling them to turn them into jams. I am grateful that Michael is here today to help. He is a young student from Vassar doing an internship during the current semester. Michael is much more than a helper, he is a collaborator in multiple monastic tasks.

Our pumpkin recipe for jam is simple. It originally came from France, where pumpkin jam is popular. It has also been enhanced a bit by whatever extra is available: in today's case, apples and pears. I cook the sliced pumpkins in orange juice, add sugar, a vanilla bean, some cinnamon, and the apples and pears, until slowly it turns into a jam. It is a long process, and it can be an arduous job. It always takes two days to complete the task, even when several hands are at work—one day for making the jam and the other for canning and preserving it.

When the jam-making process is completed, the jars are carefully stored on our pantry shelves. Some are destined for Christmas presents, some for sharing with friends and helpers. Michael will take some to school for his daily breakfast and some for his parents. All in all, jam-making in a monastery is a delightful art, part of living in tune with the seasons, part of paying due heed to Saint Benedict's counsel that monks must live and eat from the work of their hands. *May God be glorified in all things!*

— OCTOBER 30 —

This Fruitful Land

That I might bless the Lord
Who conserves all,
Heaven with its countless bright orders,
Land, strand and flood.

A CELTIC POEM BY COLUMCILLE

One of the wholesome pleasures of a late October day is to visit the local fruit orchards, where the apple pickers are slowly ending their seasonal labors and one can still gather and fill a basket of fresh apples from those laden trees. The Hudson Valley is one of the richest agricultural regions of New York state, and is particularly known for its glorious orchards. As one travels up and down the Hudson, all kinds of fruit can be found growing on both sides of the river: peaches, berries, grapes, plums, pears, and apples all thrive there. I often think of the Hudson Valley as the *verger* (orchard) of New York, and compare it to the well-known *verger de la France*: the valley of the Rhone, so famous for its vineyards and orchards.

Throughout all my years here, I have been a strong supporter of the local agriculture, particularly local orchards. They are continually threatened by greedy developers, and I endure immense pain and deep sadness every time I see more orchards or farms turned over to one of them. During the years that I participated in the local farmers' market and sold the vegetables grown in our monastery garden, I would always encourage my fellow farmers to be good stewards of the land—to stand for, protect it, and treat it with great care. Above all, I encouraged them to preserve those havens of green space by keeping it from the hands of developers.

Those orchards provide food for our tables. As a food writer and gardener, I have always been a proponent of buying locally grown produce. The emphasis on local food production and consumption is closely knit to what some environmentally conscious growers call "food security": that is, the principle that encourages people to develop their own local food sources, so as to ease the environmental damages and high costs of transporting produce over long distances. Additionally, there is the security and comfort that comes from knowing that the fruits and vegetables are the products of good soils, often organically grown, and of improved nutritional value. This is the beginning of a good trend in sustainable agriculture; I see this principle being embraced even by local restaurants. Recently, I heard a famous area chef say, "I refuse to buy or cook with apples that are not grown locally. I consider it a cardinal sin to buy an apple from elsewhere but the Hudson Valley." I smiled gently to the chef and, of course, gave him my utmost support.

These final days of October, as the harvest work begins to slow down and we make haste to build our fruit storage for the winter, thoughts of apple pies and tarts often come to my mind. After all, Thanksgiving is not that far away. There is something uniquely American about a homemade pie created from fresh, local, tart apples, the old-fashioned way. The same sense of wonder is felt by the French when an apple *tarte* is presented at the table. I can relate to both, and thus I express endless thanksgiving to the Lord for the joy of tasting and being nourished by the abundances of our locally grown food. *Apple and pear trees, peach and plum trees, all trees, bless the Lord!*

— OCTOBER 31 —

The Desert

*Let us not look upon the world and fancy we have given
up great things. For the whole earth is a very little thing
compared with the whole of heaven.*

SAINT ANTONY THE GREAT

From the very beginning of this small foundation, if one may so call it, monastic life here was intended to be close to that of the early Desert Fathers and Mothers. Life in the desert is a life of solitude. Periodically, I find the need to return to these sources.

Tomorrow, as October ends, the great bulk of my reading will again concentrate on the Apothegmatas and other desert reading. Today, as I walk around the property and feel October's last breezes, I become progressively more and more excited about the prospects of getting reacquainted with those early teachers. In the course of the years I have always found so much nourishment and inspiration in their teachings and in their clear example of Gospel life. As I ponder these thoughts throughout my walk, certain words from the book *Monks and Monasteries of the Egyptian Deserts* resound in my ears and wet my appetite for the days to come: *The desert has provided, from time to time immemorial, a testing ground for the souls of men and women. Go to the desert for food and drink and you will find a barren waste. Go there to listen to the voice of God and you will receive insight, understanding, and wisdom. The desert is silent, apart, different. It conveys a picture, waterless and featureless, yet overwhelming to the senses.*

NOVEMBER

— NOVEMBER 1 —

All Saints

I saw a vast crowd of countless numbers from every nation, standing before the throne.

Vespers Antiphon

A s we leave behind the bright, golden October days and enter into November, the eleventh month of the year, we perceive changes in both weather and duration of daylight. Daylight savings time comes around and, suddenly, we are moved into the cycle of shorter days and longer, darker nights.

November, with its somber days, is often reputed to be one of the gloomiest months of the whole year. It is the time when the brilliant autumnal foliage ends, and the luster of the maples and ashes on the monastic property gradually disappear, leaving only some rugged oak trees with leaves still grasping to their boughs. Later in November, frequent rains and gusty winds will thresh away even the hardiest of the remaining leaves. Nature has its own unmistakable way of telling us that the year's end is quickly approaching.

Just as we enter into our darker, chillier November days, the festival of All Saints arrives as a beam of sunlight into our bleakness. Like many of the great Church solemnities, the feast of All Saints is of great antiquity. There are indications that in the fourth century, some churches commemorated all martyrs on this particular day. Later on, Pope Boniface IV consecrated a church in Rome to the Mother of God and all of the martyrs in the seventh century, and requested that the anniversary of this consecration be observed each year as a feast. A century later, Pope Gregory III dedicated, in Saint Peter's basilica, a chapel to All Saints, and ordered that a festival be observed each November 1, the anniversary of the Chapel's consecration. Thus, the festival was to be observed as the harvest of Christ's Redemption, as a fitting conclusion to the Church year.

The antiphons, hymns, and readings of today's Office carry us to the heavenly Jerusalem, to the throne of the Lamb, around whom the elect worship in jubilant adoration. *Vidi turba magna*: "I see an immense crowd." Vespers' first Antiphon gives us a glimpse of that majestic crowd surrounding the Lamb. Such a glorious gathering is composed of God's friends, who, by the way, are also our own friends and intercessors.

The walls of our tiny chapel are filled with ikons of the Lord, the Mother of God, the Archangels, the Apostles, the Fathers, and monastic saints. To me, they represent "God's family," the *turba magna* of the antiphon. During the liturgical celebrations, oil lamps burn in front of them, as humble homage and as symbol of our silent supplication. Contemplating their presence in our chapel, one comprehends something of that marvelous mystery which is the communion of saints. I consider this to be one of the most consoling mysteries of our Christian faith. "I believe in the communion of saints," we profess in the Creed, and the reality of this mystery should be a source of great joy for all of us.

While on our earthly journey, we can keep no better company than that of the saints. They pray without ceasing for us and they are always ready to come to our rescue. Our great hope is that we shall one day join them, becoming part of that immense *turba magna*, singing with them the eternal Sanctus in the worship of the Trinity.

— NOVEMBER 2 —

All Souls

For since we believe that Jesus died and rose again, even so, through Jesus, God will bring with him those who have died.

1 THESSALONIANS 4:14

Today is one of those gray November days on which cooler temperatures are felt. A deep, misty stillness pervades the property. The splendors of nature's yellows, oranges, reds, greens, and browns have all but vanished from the trees. Winter, though still quite a few weeks away, seems somehow closer.

Today is All Souls' Day, a natural prolongation of yesterday's celebration of All Saints. It is also part of that great mystery of the communion of saints. From the early days of the Church, the faithful were exhorted to pray for our dearly departed. Saint Augustine insisted on the necessity of consecrating one day of the year to commemorating all those who had departed this life. Centuries later, Saint Odilon, the great Abbot of Cluny, requested that all of the Clunician monasteries observe November 2 in remembrance of the faithfully departed. From Cluny, the same custom was extended to the universal Church. Just as yesterday we celebrated the victory of the saints with prayer and song, today we pray for our departed loved ones who we hope have joined with the saints in the vision of God.

In old Europe, the Christians observe today the pious custom of visiting cemeteries where their ancestors are buried, praying with the Church for those "who are gone before us with the sign of faith, and rest in the sleep of peace." Tombs are covered with flowers, and the whole cemetery resembles a radiant, enclosed garden.

Whenever I return to France and visit our family's cemetery

plots, I am reminded of the comforting words of the Preface for today's Mass: "For your faithful, O Lord, life is changed, not taken away, and when the earthly home of our habitation is dissolved, an eternal dwelling is prepared for us in heaven." Our Christian faith is so rich, so positive, so full of hope; and all of it, because of the Resurrection of Jesus.

— NOVEMBER 3 —

The Work of Prayer

Abba Agathon said, "I think there is no labor greater than that of prayer to God. For every time a man wants to pray, his enemies, the demons, want to prevent him, for they know that it is only by turning him from prayer that they can hinder his journey. Whatever good work a man undertakes, if he perseveres in it, he will attain rest. But prayer is warfare to the last breath."

ABBA AGATHON

The desert monks took to heart Abba Agathon's counsel on prayer, and in the solitude of the desert they applied themselves to its continual practice. Prayer was the one constant activity of their days and nights. They chose life in the desert because in their hunger for God they knew the very nature of the desert encouraged contemplative prayer.

For the desert monks every form of prayer came from and resided in the recesses of their hearts. They seldom used long formulas or prayer books as we would today. Instead, they prayerfully read the sacred Scriptures, especially the Gospels and the psalms, and from there they drew short prayers like "Lord, have mercy," which they then repeated again and again until the prayer found a permanent home in the depths of their being.

Attaining unceasing prayer and persevering in this practice was the only good that the monk pursued in the desert. He took to heart the Lord's counsel in the Gospel to "pray without ceasing." To achieve this, the monk endured discipline and struggled with the enemy. And he also prayed for it with tears and great humility, until he was given the gift of constant prayer, a prayer henceforth uttered to God day and night, no longer in words but in pure silence.

— NOVEMBER 4 —

Inner Light

It was revealed to Abba Antony in his desert that there was one who was his equal in the city. He was a doctor by profession, and whatever he had beyond his needs he gave to the poor, and every day he sang the Sanctus with the angels.

SAINT ANTONY THE GREAT

Rereading this episode about the life of Saint Antony is always refreshing. One wonders who is worthy of greater admiration: Saint Antony, the father of monks, who with deep humility recognizes the holiness in another and rejoices in it; or the admirable evangelical witness of this doctor's life, who strove to live by God's word in the midst of the wicked world of his times? Both lives, one lived in the solitude of the desert and the other amid the distractions of the world, spring from the same love for God, have the same purity of intention in God's service, possess the same love for the poor in whom both recognize the person of Christ, and practice the same detachment in giving up what is superfluous in their lives.

Because of this, both Abba Antony in his austere desert solitude and the humble doctor in his noisy city environment are equally pleasing in the sight of the Lord and are given the equal joy of praising God unceasingly, singing daily in the company of the angels the thrice-holy hymn: Holy, Holy, Holy.

— NOVEMBER 5 —

Inner Vigilance

Abba Agathon said, "Man is like a tree, bodily asceticism is the foliage, interior vigilance the fruit. According to that which is written, 'Every tree that bringeth not forth good fruit will be cut down and cast into the fire' (Mt 3:10). It is clear that all our care should be directed towards the fruit, that is to say, guardian of the spirit; but it needs the protection and the embellishment of the foliage, which is bodily asceticism."

ABBA AGATHON

Continual vigilance over one's mind and heart is one of those counsels that the Lord repeated again and again to his disciples. In Matthew 26:41, Jesus tells the disciples, "Stay awake and pray that you may not come into the time of trial," and again in Mark 13:33, he warns them, "Beware, keep alert; for you do not know when the time will come." The Desert Fathers and Mothers, faithful to the Gospel teachings, embraced steadfastly this counsel and developed a whole program to put it into practice.

Inner vigilance, for the desert dwellers, meant continuous, strict scrutiny of one's conscience, an attentive and watchful attitude towards one's thoughts, one's mind, one's feelings, one's obsessions, one's passions, and, especially, one's heart. It was not that they saw all of their thoughts and feelings as necessary evils; but, rather, they saw the need to retrain them and to redirect them solely toward God. Instead of focusing on oneself or other created things, they strove to give their undivided attention to God alone. Their primary goal was to bring their lives into conformity with God's will, with God's design for each of them. And they knew that they could not achieve this without the help of vigilance.

The early monks and nuns made particular efforts to practice this vigilance during "the watches of the night." Nighttime was especially appropriate for prayer and vigil, for "you do not know when the master of the house will come, in the evening or at midnight, or at cockcrow, or at dawn, or else he may find you asleep when he comes suddenly" (Mk 13:35–36). By keeping vigil, the desert dwellers strove to exercise control over their sleep and thus prolong the time given to prayer and the remembrance of God.

By patient perseverance in this task, and helped by divine grace, the desert dwellers were able to keep their minds and hearts free from passions and other encumbrances and thus give themselves totally to the contemplation of their God and Savior.

— NOVEMBER 6 —

The Gospel: Nourishment in the Wilderness

Then Abba Macarius said to the monk Theopemtus, "See how many years I have lived as an ascetic, and am praised by all, and though I am old, the spirit of fornication troubles me." Theopemtus said, "Believe me, Abba, it is the same with me." Abba Macarius went on admitting that other thoughts still warred against him, until he had brought Theopemtus to admit them about himself. Then Abba Macarius asked: "How do you fast?" Theopemtus replied, "Till the ninth hour." Macarius then said: "Practice fasting a little later, meditate on the Gospel and the other Scriptures, and if an alien thought arises within you, never look at it but always look upwards, and the Lord will come at once to your help." When he had given the brother this rule, the old man then returned to his solitude.

ABBA MACARIUS

The Gospel was the daily bread of the desert solitaries. At the beginning of their monastic journey, as we see in the case of Saint Antony the Great, the word of the Gospel was there to encourage them in their resolution to leave all things in order to follow Christ. When assailed by doubts and temptations, the solitaries again and again made recourse to the Gospel to be enlightened and fortified by its teachings. Thus they prepared themselves for the battle. In the Gospel they found their refuge against the enemy and the strength to fight him. This is why Abba Macarius counseled the disciple to go and find in the Gospel the best weapon against the enemy.

For desert solitaries, the Gospel was not just a book; it was the presence of Jesus Christ in the mystery of the Gospel. He alone was the source of their faith and the daily food of their lives. They held fast to his presence in the Gospel, touching in this mystery the hem of his garment as did the woman who suffered from hemorrhages (Mt 9:20–22), knowing that "if I only touch his cloak, I will be made well."

For the monks and nuns of the desert, the Lord Jesus was truly alive in the mystery of the Gospel. The Gospel proclaims the truth, for he said, "I am the truth." The Gospel teaches the way to live, for he said, "I am the way." The Gospel enlightens all those sitting in darkness, for he said, "I am the light of the world." The solitaries held fast to the treasure of the Gospel; for without it, their solitude could not be endured. They knew the journey to be hard, they knew themselves to be poor, weak, and deprived, but they also knew they were not alone, for they were accompanied by he who said, "I am with you always, to the end of the age" (Mt 28:20).

— NOVEMBER 7 —

Holy Weeping

Abba Poemen said this about sins: "He who wishes to purify his faults purifies them with tears, and he who wishes to acquire virtues, acquires them with tears; for weeping is the way the Scriptures and our Fathers give us when they say, "Weep! Truly, there is no other way than this."

ABBE POEMEN

The ancient Fathers used to speak of the gift of tears, and our Lord goes as far as to say "Blessed are you who weep now" (Lk 6:21). What a contrast to our present system of values, where tears are despised as a sign of weakness. The only tears we seem to understand are the tears of self-pity!

There is a great difference, however, between tears of self-pity and tears of compunction. The tears of self-pity are self-oriented, deadly, and consequently lead to nothing except more self-pity. The tears of compunction, on the other hand, are oriented toward God and thus life-giving. Tears of compunction are part of the mystery of repentance to which we all are called.

These tears are born in our innermost hearts, where we keep the memory of God. It is there, when our selfishness, sinfulness, and arrogance are confronted by God's love, compassion, tender mercy, and pity, that we are slowly moved to tears of compunction and repentance. We see that we need to weep and repent daily, because like the tax collector in the Gospels, we are in great need of God's mercy. As such, the water of our tears becomes like the water of baptism, cleansing us from our self-centeredness and harshness of heart. It purifies us from our sinfulness, allowing the Holy Spirit to bestow on us the humility of the tax collector, which is so pleasing to the Lord (see Lk 18:10).

When the Holy Spirit bestows on us this gift of tears, we find out that they are "tears of sweetness and joy," for they liberate us from the heavy burden of selfishness into the embrace of God's love. We experience the fulfillment of the promise: "Blessed are those who mourn, for they shall be comforted" (Mt 5:4).

— NOVEMBER 8 —

The Cost of Discipleship

The brothers praised a monk before Abba Antony. When the monk came to see him, Antony wanted to know how he would bear insults; and seeing that he could not bear them at all, he said to him, "You are like a village magnificently decorated on the outside, but destroyed from within by robbers."

SAINT ANTONY

Nothing is more damaging to the spiritual life than to be taken in by the illusion that we have reached the goal of perfection and are worthy of the admiration of others. This temptation, which can assail any of us at any time, tends to manifest itself in subtle ways, to those who strive for a spiritual life. Especially vulnerable are those who are in positions of authority, those who are leaders and directors of souls, and those who retire to the desert of the monastic life. The enemy of our souls is so disguised so as to make us believe that we are in the midst of wonderful spiritual progress, and are getting closer and closer to attaining the perfect life. Sadly, we fall for this deception.

Saint Antony, however, knows better. Filled with the realism and the wisdom of the Gospels, he knows that true discipleship is tested by adversity, insults, and persecution. He knows that in order to follow Jesus we must take up our cross daily. This is the royal way of the cross, the way of the Divine Master who said, "Blessed are you when people revile and persecute you and utter all kinds of evil against you falsely on my account. Rejoice and be glad, for your reward is great in heaven" (Mt 5:11–12). Saint Antony does not seek to test the perfection of a disciple by the amount of his fasting, the length of his prayers, or the austerity of his lifestyle. Instead, he tests discipleship by the same measure that the Lord does in the Gospel: suffering insults, abuse, and persecution, all accepted in deep humility and without complaint.

No more painful kind of suffering is borne than that which is inflicted personally upon us by others. We can all bear some kind of suffering when it is very general and common to all or unintentionally inflicted. But when it has been deliberately directed at us, our nature rebels against it and against those from whom it comes. This response is perfectly normal on a human level and is inspired by our instinct for self-defense and self-preservation. On a spiritual level, however, this kind of suffering helps us enter into somewhat of an understanding of Christ's Passion. It also has the healing effect of liberating us from the false image we have of ourselves, from our attachment to ego.

In the insults, abuse, and misunderstanding that we receive from others, Saint Antony sees the opportunity for us to see ourselves for what we truly are: poor, imperfect, empty, and naked beings in dire need of God's mercy. The suffering endured through this kind of self-emptying is one that we would never seek for its own sake because it is far too painful. We must accept it on pure faith when it enters into our lives, knowing that God can bring good out of evil.

— NOVEMBER 9 —

Elizabeth of the Trinity

I have only to recollect myself, to go deep within me, to find God there.

ELIZABETH OF THE TRINITY

Today is sunny and mild—what local people call an "Indian summer" day. With a soft wind in the air, I spend part of the day in the garden. There are still some winter vegetables growing there: cabbages, brussels sprouts, turnips, celery, carrots, Swiss chard, spinach, leeks, all sorts of salad greens, and bushels of parsley. Working under a warm sun is an added bonus before the cold weather plunges us into winter harshness.

Today, part of the garden toil encompasses the areas where the frost has already killed the other vegetables. Slowly, I am preparing the garden for winter rest. Later on, in December, when the severe cold makes its appearance and kills the remaining vegetables, the garden will be finally set to rest with only Saint Fiacre in his wooden shrine to watch over it. Before reaching that point, however, I must cover the clean garden beds with compost and sheep manure, as I do every year to properly nurture the soil. Since the day hours are shorter, and dusk descends early, I consciously need to move a bit faster.

Today, our monastic liturgy keeps the memorial of Blessed Elizabeth of the Trinity, the humble Carmelite of Dijon. Blessed Elizabeth is one of the great mystics of the past century, continuing to have an immense impact over those given to the interior life. I remember as a young monk being exposed to her writings and finding them lucid and profound. She entered the Carmel of Dijon as a young woman and spent her remaining years there, growing deeper in personal communion with God. She was totally given over to the Divine Presence within her and oriented all of her inner energies toward continual adoration of the three Divine Persons, whom she called "the beloved guests of my soul." As she lay dying in a humble cell of her Dijon Carmel, on November 9, 1906, she uttered these last words: "I am going to the Light, to Love, to Life."

As it happens, I was able to visit the Dijon Carmel many years ago, before it was moved to its present site at Flavignerot, in the heart of Burgundy. Recently, I revisited the Carmel and prayed with the Carmelites in their new home. I was deeply impressed by the charm and simplicity of the new monastery, which is located in the hills of Burgundy, a good distance from Dijon. A small, makeshift sign saying "Carmel" indicates the hilly, unpaved road leading to the monastery. At the top of the hill, well hidden among surrounding trees, one discovers the new Carmel —small, unassuming, and very silent. In many ways, it is a monastery very much after the wishes of Saint Teresa, who desired her Carmels to be "plain and small, so as not to make too much noise when they fall on the last day." The chapel is of contemporary design and, like the rest of the monastery, of great simplicity. There are no grilles, and the faithful are able to sit right behind the nuns and join into one worshiping community. The altar is at the center, and a tall crucifix behind it. The Blessed Sacrament is at one side, and a statue of Our Lady stands to the left. The nuns sing their daily Offices in French, with frequent pauses after the psalms and readings. All in all, one is left with the impression that this is truly a house of prayer, of silence, and of adoration. The nuns have reproduced the old cell of Elizabeth of the Trinity in a small room attached to the chapel, and there one can admire the place where she lived "alone with him whom one loves, and which is already heaven on earth."

At the Carmel, I had the joy of getting reacquainted with the former prioress, whom I knew from Dijon. She is a remarkable woman, now in her nineties, and the one most responsible for the transfer of the Carmel from the city to the countryside. I mentioned how much Elizabeth of the Trinity would love the deep silence and profound solitude of the new Carmel. She assented with a beautiful smile.

Divine Intimacy

If we seek God, he will show himself to us.

ABBA ARSENIUS

The way to God is an inner journey, inspired in the deepest recesses of our being by the Holy Spirit. This journey takes into account the place of both the mind and the heart in our spiritual life. Synchronizing our minds and our hearts allows us to unite these two aspects of our being into one in our search for God. If we seek God daily, with our mind and heart prayerfully attuned as one, we will receive eventually the gift of an inner light that will show the Lord's presence in our innermost being. The eyes of our mind and heart will become clearer, purified, and ready to gaze on the light that shines from God's countenance, as it once did on the three apostles on Mount Tabor during the Lord's glorious Transfiguration.

Once the Lord bestows the mysterious light of his presence on us, we must do everything on our part to keep him with us. As Abba Arsenius advises, we need to apply ourselves constantly to the remembrance of God, not only during times of prayer, but throughout all of the day's activities. If we show undying devotion to God at all times and keep our inner eyes fixed on his presence, we can be sure that he will remain faithful to his promise: *I am with you always, to the end of the age* (Mt 28:20).

Martin of Tours: Monk and Shepherd

Filled with joy, Martin was welcomed by Abraham. Martin left this life a poor and lowly man, and entered heaven rich in God's favor.

ANTIPHON OF THE FEAST

Today, we celebrate the feast of a truly monastic saint: Martin of Tours. Here in this monastery, his feast is like a ray of sunlight shimmering through an otherwise gray and obscure November day. Saint Martin is one of those monastic fathers whose life and example have had a great influence over my own life. Most people think of him foremost as Bishop of Tours, forgetting that before anything else, he was a monk through and through.

Sometime after becoming a Christian, Martin was inspired by the life of the father of monks, Saint Antony. Fired up by his example, he retired with his disciples to the solitude of Liguge, near Poitiers, where his friend, Saint Hillary, served as bishop. In Liguge, he founded a monastery that still exists today.

When Martin arrived at Liguge in 361 A.D., he and his disciples began to immediately emulate the life and example of the monks in the Egyptian desert. The Liguge monastic solitude was precisely what his spirit was seeking. During those years of intense prayer and deep silence, Martin became conscious of the strong workings of the Holy Spirit within him. He felt that he was being prepared for a greater role in the Church of God.

Saint Martin can be considered one of the great founders and promoters of the monastic life in France. He founded not only the monastery of Liguge but also that of Marmoutiers, near Tours, where he resided after being made bishop of the town. Throughout all of his activities as the prelate of Tours, he remained strongly attached to his monastic calling and made every effort to continue living as a monk.

As the pastor of Tours, Martin showed remarkable sensitivity toward all—a fact attributed to his monastic formation. His biographer, Sulpicious Severus, wrote: "We have seen numbers of Martin's noble young monks made bishops....For what city or church would there be that would not desire to have its priests from among those in the monastery of Martin?" The biographer goes on to express the quality of Martin's pastoral care: "He displayed such marvelous patience in the endurance of injuries, that even when he was chief priest, he allowed himself to be wronged by the lowest clerics with impunity, nor did he either remove them from office on account of such conduct or repel them from a place in his affection."

Martin died in 397 A.D., surrounded by his monks and faithful, filled with immense desire to meet God. Because of his extraordinary holiness, Martin became the first person to be canonized who was not a martyr. Up to that time, only those who had shed blood for their faith were recognized as saints. Both France and the monastic movement owe much to Saint Martin; so it is not surprising to see how many thousands of churches dedicated to Saint Martin are scattered throughout the French landscape.

— NOVEMBER 12 —

Spiritual Guidance

As a servant, who is near his master, is always under fear, being so close to him, and he does nothing without his master's order, so also should we place our thoughts under our master, Christ, who knows our hearts. We should open them to him and we ought to place hope and trust in him, saying: "He is my glory; he is my Father; he is my riches."

PSEUDO-MACARIUS

One of the first demands that the elders of the desert placed on their young disciples who sought their counsel was the renunciation of the way of thinking as previously practiced in the world. In order to achieve mastery over one's thoughts and put on the new man in Christ, it was necessary to first renounce the old man, one's former way of thinking.

The chief work of the desert elders was to provide assistance in the arduous preparation of mind and heart required of those beginning the slow ascent toward communion with God. Under the guidance of the elder, the young disciple was taught to deal with the discomfort of accepting the limitations of one's mind, and of living with those limitations. In the desert, one had to daily face one's own darkness, ignorance, and inability to reach the truth by a purely intellectual path.

The elder labored patiently with the disciple, slowly opening his soul, his mind, and his heart to the light of grace and truth which is Christ. In order to be illuminated by the light of truth, the disciple had to learn to let go of his former way of thinking, which was motivated primarily by self-interest, presumption of knowledge, and, ultimately, pride.

Guided by the elder, the disciple learned gradually to accept his ignorance in the ways of the spiritual path, and how much in need he was of the intense discipline of retraining the mind. This meant dying daily, always ready to sacrifice one's thoughts. Unhampered by self-concern, one could then freely surrender the whole of the mind and heart to the sweet yoke of Christ.

Humility of mind and heart, and all the hardships it entails, was the essential requirement demanded of the sincere disciple. The disciple accepted the elder's teaching, pressing forward in the hope of one day reaching the blessedness of continual communion with God, the one true source of richness and glory.

— NOVEMBER 13 —
Closeness to Christ

Abba Paul said: "Keep close to Jesus."
ABBA PAUL THE GREAT

Those of us who work with farm animals or have charge of livestock know the importance of the bonding attachment that exists between the mother and her newborn. Every spring, when our ewes give birth to their young lambs, I never cease to marvel at the sight of this phenomenon. It is nature itself that programs the mother ewe to welcome her little lamb and give it all the care it needs, from cleaning its body to allowing it to nurse at her udder. This maternal instinct, which is present in most mammals, evokes a special kind of close response on the part of the young animal toward its mother. I see this strong bond also present in two of our monastery dogs, who happen to be mother and daughter. Though the young female is already eighteen months old, she remains deeply attached to her mother. They are absolutely inseparable, and though we know it is purely instinctual, their tender and faithful love for each other is something to be admired.

The imagery of this particular type of closeness, such as the bonding attachment that exists in both humans and animals, comes readily to my mind when I reflect on this apothegmata. Though quite short, this wise saying is extremely dense in meaning. I am attracted to it in particular because the Lord himself makes use of this sort of imagery to express his tender love for us and the kind of closeness he would like to have with each of us (Lk 13:34). We must not be afraid, therefore, to seek to grow into this type of closeness and intimacy with Jesus. In fact, we must go further: we must make it the central goal of our lives.

Jesus, the Son of God, loves each of us in such a measure that he became human in order to forge the closest possible relationship with us. He wanted to love us and be close to us not only as God but also as man. If the reality of Jesus as God evokes an image of father and mother, the reality of Jesus as man evokes an image of friend and lover. In his great love for us, and in his desire to remain close to us, Jesus makes it possible to be each of these things for us.

All we need to do is to come to him in faith and draw near to his loving presence. Through the eyes of faith, we can see Jesus daily in the mystery of the ikon, in the presence of our neighbor, and in the splendor of his creation. We can hear him in the holy Gospels. We can partake of him in holy Communion. And we can touch and embrace him during prayer, where we are welcomed into his arms, enveloped by all of his love.

Discernment

Abba Macarius said, "If you want to live in peace, go to the interior desert, to Petra, and therefore you will be at peace." And so he found peace.

ABBA MACARIUS

A bba Moses faced the kind of conflict that often came upon those who retired to the wilderness for the sake of God. The monks went into the desert to seek what they called *hesychia*, that is, a kind of inner peace that made unceasing prayer possible. They worked diligently, and were solicitous to preserve the solitude that safeguarded their inner quiet. Yet, no matter how careful they were, they were often interrupted by the brethren who came to consult them. This was particularly true of the elders, whose experience and wisdom the young monks often sought.

These fervent elders were torn between the two occupations. Their main desire was for quiet and uninterrupted prayer; but they also knew that, for the Christian, love of God and love of neighbor are not separated. They realized that Saint Antony, the first monk and father of all monks, taught that "our life and our death are with our neighbor. If we gain our brother, we have gained God." Abba Antony was also known to have said that "he never recalled having preferred his own good to the welfare of the least of the brethren." There was no selfishness or self-centeredness on their part, and they tried to live the practice of charity at all costs, even when such charity was abused by others. For monks like Abba Moses, who was extremely sensitive and kind towards his brethren, the conflict between an inner calling to complete quiet and the social calling to the practice of charity could not easily be resolved. With true humility, he opens himself to Abba Macarius, expresses his conflict, and seeks advice, knowing full well that Abba Macarius was filled with the Holy Spirit.

Abba Macarius offers him a solution of great simplicity. He

does not discourage Abba Moses from serving the brethren, but discerning that he is called to greater quiet and prayer, invites him to go further into the interior of the desert. It is here that he will be less hampered by the visits of the other monks. Therefore, he will avoid offending or hurting anyone, while at the same time obtain the quality of peace and quiet he needs to apply himself to the practice of unceasing prayer.

— NOVEMBER 15 —

Stability

A brother came to the desert of Scetis to visit Abba Moses and asked him for a word. The old man said to him, "Go, sit in your cell, and your cell will teach you everything."

ABBA MOSES

How difficult it is in the twenty-first century to conceive of staying put in one place for an indefinite period of time. For most of us, this would be totally unacceptable. "How could we ever relinquish our freedom of mobility?" we ask. "How could we forfeit our desire to see new things and explore new places?"

Yet Abba Moses, with the rest of the Desert Fathers and Mothers, tells us precisely to stay within the boundaries of one place. He knows that in order to truly explore the territories of the inner journey, the discipline of stability is absolutely essential. He knows that if God cannot be found in the solitude of his own heart, within his very self, he cannot be found anywhere. The Gospel teaching, which says "The kingdom of God is within you," is paramount. Under the guidance of the Holy Spirit, the desert elders pursue an inner life with God that is truly free and self-directed, while they control their thoughts and passions, watching continuously over the dispositions of their hearts.

For desert monks, the desire to leave one's solitude and seek distractions, even ones of a spiritual nature, was a true temptation. This is why when the disciple asks for a word of wisdom, the old Abba sees the disciple's inquiry as an excuse for leaving his cell and thus reprimands him. He tells him to give up the illusion of finding wisdom on the outside; he must return to his cell and stay there, for "your cell will teach you everything."

Stability and perseverance in one's cell, in spite of the daily temptation brought by boredom, was essential to the life of the desert monk. It was there, and no place else, that he was able to do battle with himself, his passions, and the forces of evil. It was also there that he would come to the true discovery of himself and learn to renounce the false illusions of his former self. In his desert cell, he would learn to renounce one of our supreme worldly values, that of mobility. But in renouncing it for the sake of God, and by humble perseverance in his seclusion, he came to obtain from the Lord the gift of peace and inner freedom.

We may not all be able to retire to the seclusion of the desert, nor even be called to the solitary cell of a monastery; but we can let go of the many temptations that encumber our spiritual lives. We can establish stability in the solitude of our hearts and, with the aid of the Holy Spirit, preserve the advice of another wise Abba: "Sit in your cell and always be mindful of God" (Abba John the Dwarf).

— NOVEMBER 16 —

Saint Gertrude

Your desire is your prayer: If your desire is an unceasing one, your prayer is also unceasing.

SAINT AUGUSTINE

Saint Gertrude, a thirteenth-century Benedictine nun, was born in Germany around 1259. She was still a young girl when her parents placed her in the monastery where she would spend the rest of her life. As a young novice, she received a thorough monastic and intellectual formation. She was deeply attracted to the Rule of Saint Benedict, under which she made her monastic profession.

Early in her monastic life, she was favored with mystical graces that radically changed her spiritual life. In the light of these graces,

Gertrude suddenly discovered her emptiness and poverty, and began to seriously apply herself to prayer. Her desire for God continued to grow in proportion to her intensified prayer. The desires of her heart rested in God alone and in her increasing knowledge of him. In prayer, she realized that God alone is Light, Truth, and Love. In one of her writings she addresses the Lord with these words: "It is not sufficient to me to know your name. I wish with all my strength to know you completely, to love you not only in a sweetly fashion but also with wisdom. I desire to attach myself to you inseparably, so that I may begin to live, not in myself, but in you alone."

Saint Gertrude died as she lived, filled with the desire to enter into the eternal possession of him whom she so passionately loved during her earthly pilgrimage. The prayer for her feast sums it up: *Saint Gertrude, whose young eager heart the Godhead blessed as ark and shrine, help us to sing the mystery of Christ's delight within the soul.*

— NOVEMBER 17 —

How to Please God

Someone asked Abba Antony, "What must one do in order to please God?" The old man replied, "Pay attention to what I tell you: Whoever you may be, always have God before your eyes; whatever you do, do it according to the testimony of the holy Scriptures; in whatever place you live, do not easily leave it. Keep these three precepts and you will be saved."

ABBA ANTONY

When Saint Antony is asked by a disciple what he ought to do to please God, the Abba first counsels the disciple to keep the remembrance of God always before him. God is the one absolute; there is no compromising this truth. Following in the footsteps of the prophets, Apostles, and martyrs, the desert Christian is called to devote all spiritual energies to the "one thing necessary" of the Gospels: the continuous, undivided, loving attention to God. Abba Antony knows that to approach God and keep the memory of him in our hearts is to live a life of continual prayer. Through prayer, we preserve a loving tie to God, as we humbly ask him to reveal his face to us. With the psalmist we pray daily: "O God, you are my God, I seek you, my soul thirsts for you; my flesh faints for you….So I have looked upon you in the sanctuary, beholding your power and glory" (Ps 63:1-2).

Second, Abba Antony says, whatever you do, do it always in conformity with the teachings of the sacred Scriptures. For Saint Antony, there was no room in the desert for subjectivism and esoteric teachings. They were Christian monks, and the revealed Word of God, particularly the Gospels, was the objective norm to which they tried to conform their lives. It is interesting to note that the early desert monks and nuns did not have what was later called a "Rule." Rather, they looked directly to the Scriptures, to the monastic tradition, and to the wisdom of the elders for direction and daily inspiration. Later, in the fifth century, we see Saint Benedict reaffirming this principle for his monks as he counsels them in the Rule to "take the Gospel as a guide as we tread the path that the Lord has cleared for us."

Third, Abba Antony reiterates the discipline heard in the solitude of the desert: "Whatever place you choose as your dwelling, stay put there. Don't give in to the temptation to move from place to place." The abbas and ammas knew from experience that it was a very natural temptation for the desert solitary to want to move on and look for some sort of escape in another setting. To them, as it is for us today, the pastures always seem greener on the other side of the fence. Against this obvious temptation, the Desert Fathers and Mothers would counsel one another in the words of Abba Macarius: "Sit in your cell and weep for your sins." Much later, Saint Benedict would also emphasize the same point to his monks. He required them to surrender independence and mobility by taking a vow of stability to the monastery of their profession. Only through stability could the monk persevere in the practice of virtue, and thus achieve *hesychia*, that is, harmony, security, repose, and inner peace.

Simplicity

Simplicity is an enduring habit within a soul that has grown impervious to evil thoughts.

JOHN CLIMACUS

Part of the Gospel message is an invitation to the Christian disciple to choose true simplicity of heart, mind, and life. Jesus was born, lived, and died in great simplicity, and the task of the disciple is to follow in the footsteps of the Master. True assent to the Gospel, as we witness in the lives of the Desert Fathers, implies a rejection of worldly complexity. For them, Christian life was a call to radical simplicity.

Human existence, as we experience it daily, is the very essence of complexity. We find this complexity impregnated in the core of our being, where we are most ourselves. It is also invariably present in almost every event of our lives. Often, we find ourselves unable to handle its weight, tensions, and potential seeds of destruction. To this complexity, which deeply affects our state of mind, the desert monk or nun juxtaposes the fundamental Gospel message of radical simplicity. By following the example of Jesus' simplicity, the desert solitary is able to raise himself above the conflict brought about by complexity. The Gospel becomes a liberating force against the values of a complex world.

We ordinary Christians are called to strive for what may be called a simplicity of the intellect, by the complete surrendering of our minds and thoughts to truth. Filled with humility, we begin to do this by acknowledging the limitations of our own minds and by renouncing all of our intellectual illusions. Nothing is more dangerous to a true spiritual life than an attitude of intellectual vanity and self-importance. Once we have renounced our self-interest, and acknowledged our capacity to know and understand nothing, we can then become capable of pursuing the truth. For then, we are given the grace to discover that truth is the Lord who says, "I am the way, and the truth" (Jn 14:6) and he prays to his Father that we may "be rooted and consecrated in this truth" (Jn 17:17-19).

— NOVEMBER 19 —
Listening Silence

Arsenius, "Flee, be silent, pray always, for these are the source of sinlessness."

ABBA ARSENIUS

I f we take our spiritual life seriously, and apply ourselves stead- fastly to the practice of prayer, we know that silence must become an integral part of it. A life of prayer and interior recollection presupposes a high degree of silence, both interior and exterior.

Abba Arsenius learned this lesson from the Lord himself, and he not only practiced it but also taught it to his disciples. For Arsenius, this silence was not deadened or muted. It was something more. Through it, he cultivated the difficult art of listening to God, to his Word, in all events and manifestations in life. Listening to God also implied listening to all of those whom the Lord sent to him. Thus, he developed what one would call today a "listening silence," that is, he possessed an inner disposition by which both his silence and his listening were transformed into continual prayer.

— NOVEMBER 20 —
Love of Silence

The friend of silence draws near to God, and by secretly conversing with him is enlightened by God.

JOHN CLIMACUS, *THE LADDER OF DIVINE ASCENT*

T he desert monk, from the beginning of his monastic life, is taught the love of silence; but the silence of the desert is not exactly what we think it is: emptiness and death, or simply the absence of sound and noise. No, it is something much deeper.

The monk in the desert is taught to cultivate silence or, in the words of Abba John Climacus, to become "the friend of silence" in order to draw nearer to God. By learning to be silent, not only in words and speech but also in mind and thought, the monk becomes receptive to the Word of God that is spoken in the depths of his heart. There, in his inner being, he hears the Word and engages himself in a loving dialogue with God, which is the experience of true prayer. In prayer, he becomes enlightened by God's presence and totally absorbed by the mystery of his love. The desert elders never ceased to encourage and stimulate in the disciple the love of silence, for they knew that it would ultimately lead to the silence of love.

— NOVEMBER 21—

Presentation of Our Lady

It is easier to depict the sun with its light and its heat than to tell the story of Mary in its splendor.

JACOB OF SERUG

In the Eastern Church, today's feast marks the entrance into Advent, the time of preparation for the festival of Christ's Nativity. During one of the long Offices, we hear the first allusions to Christmas:

> Christ is born; glorify him!
> Christ comes from heaven; go forth to meet him!
> Christ comes down to earth; exalt his name!
> Sing to the Lord, all the earth!
> Praise him with joy and gladness, O people,
> For he has been glorified!

Today we honor Mary, the handmaiden of God, who as a small child is brought to live in the Temple. Mary is separated for a while from her parents, set apart, and offered in gratitude to God. For Mary, this is a time of preparation for her future role. From now on, her entire life will be spent in intimacy with God.

She, who today is carried into the temple, will in time become God's living temple, carrying God's Son, the Savior, within her womb. As the entire Church pays homage today to the humble Mother of God, we can use for our reflection the beautiful words of an early Christian author, Jacob of Serug:

> Our Lord descending to earth beheld all women; he chose one for himself who among them all was pleasing. He found humility and holiness in her, and limpid impulses and a soul desirous of divinity. And a pure heart and every reckoning of perfection, because of this he chose her, the pure and most fair one. He descended from his place and dwelt within the glorious one among women, because there was not a companion comparable to her in the world.

— NOVEMBER 22 —

True Solitude

Said the Abbess Matrona: "Many people living secluded lives on the mountain have perished by living like people in the world. It is better to live in a crowd and want to live a solitary life than to live a solitary life but all the time be longing for company."

AMMA MATRONA

"For where your treasure is, there will be your heart also," says the Lord (Mt 6:21). Speaking to the desert dwellers, Amma Matrona reminds them of this Gospel saying. With deep intuition and insight, she sees that many so-called solitaries do not have their minds and hearts set on the Lord and his designs for them but on the seductions of the world, in the vain flattery of crowds, in the pleasures of worldly company. This is opposite to the purpose for which they have come to live in the desert.

With candor, Amma Matrona confronts those who think of themselves as true spiritual people simply because they live in solitude or are dressed in the monastic habit, while all along their minds and hearts are elsewhere. To them, she admonishes: "It is better to live in a crowd and to wish to live a solitary life." The desert itself does not create solitaries any more than a habit makes a monk. It is the attitude of one's mind and heart alone that does it. Amma Matrona, with true desert wisdom, reminds us all that we can be true solitaries, true contemplatives, no matter where we may be. We must simply work to train our desires and make space for God within our hearts.

— NOVEMBER 23 —

The Desert Is Beautiful

"The desert is beautiful," the Little Prince said. And that was true.

One sits down on a desert sand dune, sees nothing, hears nothing. Yet through the silence something throbs, and gleams.... "What makes the desert beautiful," said the Little Prince, "is that somewhere it hides a well."

ANTOINE DE SAINT EXUPERY, *THE LITTLE PRINCE*

The renowned French writer, Antoine de Saint Exupery, expresses the wisdom of the desert in these beautiful contemporary words. Christian monastic life is a hidden well, which had its humble beginnings in the Egyptian desert. The first monks deliberately chose the desert wilderness as their abode to pursue an unhindered life of close union with God.

However, one thing we can all learn from these same desert monks is that "desert" does not always need to be a geographical place. In their deep realism, the Desert Fathers would tell us today that God, above all, must be sought and found in the innermost space of our hearts. All that really matters is our inner attitude.

— NOVEMBER 24 —

True Joy

Amma Syncletica said, "In the beginning there are a great many battles and a good deal of suffering for those who are advancing towards God, and afterwards, ineffable joy. It is like those who wish to light a fire; at first they are choked by the smoke and cry, and by this means obtain what they seek as it is said: "Our God is a consuming fire" (Heb 12:29). So too must we also kindle the divine fire in ourselves, through tears and hard work.

AMMA SYNCLETICA

Amma Syncletica, with the realism and stark wisdom she inherited from her experience in the desert, knows quite well that pursuit of the Christian spiritual life always contains some amount of suffering and grief. In the first place, there are the conflicts and battles that one must undergo with the old self in order to put on the new one: for we know, in our Lord's words, that "the kingdom of heaven has suffered violence" (Mt 11:12).

Second, the experience of suffering has the healing effect of teaching us acceptance of our weaknesses; henceforth, it leads us to greater humility of spirit. Every grief, every form of suffering, conceals the presence of grace. In God's own mysterious design, he does not allow us to be immune from suffering and pain any more than he allowed Jesus, his Son, to be immune from them. But, if like Jesus we humbly accept God's will and submit to his desires for us, we shall also experience the triumph and power of his grace.

Per crucem ad lucem (through the Cross to the light) was the motto of many of the ancient saints. The humble acceptance of our daily crosses, found in the pains and tribulations of life, brings with it the presence of infused joy from God, which no one can take away. "Through tears and hard work," says Amma Syncletica, "we kindle the divine fire in ourselves." This fire is the Holy Spirit, the same Spirit who pours his love into our hearts and makes us experience the joy of being children of God.

— NOVEMBER 25 —

Thanksgiving

Come, ye thankful people, come;
Raise the song of harvest home.
All is safely gathered in
Ere the winter's storm begin.
God, our Maker, doth provide
For our wants to be supplied;
Come to God's own temple, come,
Raise the song of harvest home.

HENRY ALFORD (1810–1871)

Toward the end of November, farmers and gardeners begin to complete their fall work. Our animals seek shelter in a warm barn, woodpiles are assembled near the monastery building, hay is stored in the barn, and the last vegetables are harvested from the garden. Another full cycle arrives at its completion, and all of us move on to the annual celebration of Thanksgiving.

On Thanksgiving day, we sing in the monastery the *Te Deum*, in its solemn tone, at the conclusion of the morning Office. The *Te Deum* is our prayer of praise and gratitude to the Lord for the miracle of a good harvest. Thanksgiving provides us the opportunity to thank God not only for the miracle of the harvest, but also for all the blessings and small miracles of everyday life accorded to us throughout the entire year. With Thanksgiving, we reach the peak of our fall celebration. After today, we begin to feel autumn's steady decline as it merges with the rapidly arriving winter. Very soon, Advent shall be knocking upon the door, and we must begin to prepare our hearts for the Lord's coming. Today, our Thanksgiving prayer is expressed in the words of the early Christians:

Father, creator of heaven and earth, you have beautified the sky with a crown of stars and illuminated it with the sun and the moon. You have also adorned the earth with its fruits to be of service and use to humankind. You have willed that all your people should rejoice in the bright shining of the sun and moon and be nourished by the fruits of the soil. Grant, we beseech you, to send us rains in abundance and to bless the earth with rich harvest and great fertility. We ask this of your goodness through your only-begotten Son, Jesus Christ our Lord. Amen.

— NOVEMBER 26 —

A Desert Message

"Do these three things and you will be saved: Be always joyful, pray without ceasing, and give thanks in all things."

ABBA BENJAMIN

This saying, full of Gospel simplicity, almost seems to have come straight out of the letters of Saint Paul, which were often read in the desert. In Philippians 3:1, Saint Paul tells his disciples to rejoice in the Lord at all times. For Saint Paul, as for Abba Benjamin, joy is a sign of the presence of the Holy Spirit in the soul. Many centuries later, Saint John Vianney would affirm the same thing by saying, "It is always spring in the soul united with God."

The joyful experience of the newness of life that we all feel during the course of spring is only a pale symbol of the joy experienced by the soul united with God. The latter is much deeper and more permanent, for again, in the words of Saint Paul, "We have peace with God through our Lord Jesus Christ, through whom we have obtained access to this grace in which we stand; and we boast in our hope of sharing the glory of God" (Rom 5:2). The desert monks and nuns were conspicuous in their joy — a clear sign that they had attained their soul's desire of union with the Lord. This union brought all of the powers and affections of their souls to experience the richness and harmony of constant joy.

In 1 Thessalonians 5:17, to the "rejoice always," Saint Paul adds, "Pray without ceasing, give thanks in all circumstances."

Abba Benjamin and Saint Paul say nothing new but exhort the disciple to heed the Lord's own words: "To pray always and not to lose heart" (Lk 18:1). All Christians, in desert landscapes or otherwise, are called to fellowship with God. According the Gospel, prayer is the medium whereby they enter into communion with God who is Father, Son, and Holy Spirit.

Abba Benjamin, in his final moments, seeing everything in its true light and proportion, left a simple but deep testament to his disciples. It is simple because it is short in words; deep because it contains all the wisdom of his long struggle in the desert. His last legacy is as timely for us Christians today as it was for his disciples, and earlier for Saint Paul and his followers. We are called to the joy of constant prayer and union with God, aware of the gift of His love for us. Abiding and abounding in grateful thanksgiving, we know full well that "this is what God expects us to do in Christ Jesus" (1 Thess 5:18).

— NOVEMBER 27 —

The Miraculous Medal

This is the symbol of the graces that are showered upon persons who ask for them.

OUR LADY TO SAINT CATHERINE LABOURE

In the center of Paris, on a discreet, quaint street named the *Rue du Bac*, there exists a small chapel which somehow seems to be the spiritual heart of the French capital. The importance of the Chapel of the *Rue du Bac* goes back to the night of November 27, 1830.

The Chapel of the *Rue du Bac* is part of the Mother-house of the Daughters of Charity, founded earlier by Saint Vincent de Paul and Saint Louise de Marillac. In that chapel, back in 1830, the sisters attended daily Mass, prayed the rosary, and performed their other devotions. This humble chapel was to be privileged by a special heavenly visitation.

Among the members of the community was a young novice named Catherine Laboure, who left her native province of Burgundy and came to Paris with the sole desire to be of service to God and to the poor. Catherine arrived at the Motherhouse in late April, 1830, full of enthusiasm. As a young woman, filled with great love, she turned over all her love to both God and his Mother. Since the days of her childhood, Catherine would ask her guardian angel to help her to see the Blessed Virgin during her earthly life.

On the night of November 27, 1830, all of the sisters were asleep and the whole house was immersed in deep silence. Suddenly, Sister Catherine heard someone call her name three times. She was startled by the call, for who would summon her in the middle of the night? She pulled open the door of her cell, and she saw a young child bathed in brilliant light, standing before her. The child spoke to her and said: "Come to the chapel. The Blessed Virgin is waiting for you." Noticing her surprise, the child added, "Do not be afraid. It is half-past eleven and everyone is asleep. Come, follow me." Sister Catherine followed the child to the chapel in a hurry, and when they arrived, he opened the doors for her.

Inside the chapel, Sister Catherine was surprised by a most beautiful vision. A lady descended from on high and sat upon a chair on the Gospel side of the chapel. The child messenger uttered to Sister Catherine: "Here is the Blessed Virgin." Sister Catherine couldn't believe her eyes. Here was the Mother of God next to her, and as she knelt down, she could rest her hands on Our Lady's knees. Her heart warmed up and her soul was filled with joy. As she looked to Our Lady, she heard her voice proclaim: "The times are difficult and France will undergo many trials. Calamities will upset the world. But God desires to entrust a mission to you." Deeply moved by the transient vision, Sister Catherine returned to the quiet of her cell.

Our Lady made several more visitations to Sister Catherine, and promised her that many graces shall be showered upon those who come to pray by the altar in the humble chapel. During one of the visions, Our Lady appeared inside of what seemed like an oval medallion, around which was printed: "O Mary, conceived without sin, pray for us who have recourse to thee.

Our Lady instructed Sister Catherine, saying: "Have a medal

struck after this model. All persons who wear it shall receive many graces from God, especially if they wear it around their necks. There will be graces in abundance for those who wear the medal with confidence."

For me, personally, wearing the Miraculous Medal since childhood has been a great privilege and a source of grace. It is a symbol of the protection of the Mother of God in our lives, and of the many favors received through her intercession. Whenever in Paris, I have the joy of attending Mass and praying often at the Chapel of the *Rue du Bac*, since I usually lodge a short distance from it. The experience is always moving: seeing thousands of people, pilgrims from all over the word, looking to receive the shower of Mary's promised graces. They worship with confidence, laying down at her feet all of their pains, joys, struggles, and sufferings. There is a unique feeling in that chapel that inspires so much devotional prayer and profound conversion. Our Lady's watchful protection and compassion for all of her children is nearly palpable. She awaits each of us, just as she did for Catherine on that blessed evening in 1830.

— NOVEMBER 28 —

The Desert Today

The desert is the place where faith is enthroned. It is the ark of virtue, the sanctuary of charity, the deposit of justice. The desert is above all the place par excellence for prayer, because it was there that Christ chose to pray.

SAINT EUCHER OF LYON

The call to the desert, though rare, is one of timeless appeal. It is well known that Christian monasticism originated in the deserts of Egypt and Palestine. What is less known is that today, as we speak, monastic life continues to flourish in the deserts of ancient Egypt, in continuity with the rich tradition received from the past. Currently, there is a strong monastic revival taking place in the desert, a spiritual resurgence, partly due to the charismatic influence of a leader named Matthew the Poor.

Matthew the Poor, like Saint Antony before him, heeded the call of Christ when he said: "Go and sell your possessions, give it to the poor, and then come, follow me." Matthew the Poor did just this, giving up his business and friends, houses and cars, and withdrew into the wilderness of the old Saint Macarius monastery. In the desert monastery, he found the spot where he best felt to be alone with God, even though it cost him much suffering. This is how he relates his experience:

> I went to the monastery with a great fear. I wondered how I could fill this heart of mine in the desert, alone, because I am a man fond of human social contact. I enjoyed the company of women, of my sisters and family. I love music and used to attend concerts in Alexandria almost every week. How could my heart be filled in lonely isolation? But God kept his promise to me. When I retreated to the desert, God gave me mountains of celestial sympathy. Instead of symphony concerts, I heard heavenly music.

Matthew the Poor not unlike the ancient desert fathers that preceded him, authenticates the desert experience and its necessity for beholding God's undistorted image. The powerful example of his desert life for the last fifty years continues to have great impact on young Christians in the Coptic community. Many students spend their vacation in retreat at the desert monastery; others join for periods of time to pray and work with monks. A considerable number of them, after completing their studies, join the monastery permanently. The present-day community at Saint Macarius consists of several doctors, lawyers, teachers, pharmacists, and engineers who have left behind all worldly things in quest for intimate communion with God in the solitude and silence of the desert.

The significance of this contemporary desert father is not surprising, for to reach the blessed state of communion with God is the final goal of all Christian life. As Saint John of the Cross affirms, "A soul united with God does more for the good of the Church and the salvation of souls than any other work."

— NOVEMBER 29 —

Servant of God: Dorothy Day (1897–1980)

Thank God for retroactive prayer! Saint Paul said that he did not judge himself, nor must we judge ourselves. We can turn to Our Lord Jesus, who has already repaired the greater evil that ever happened or could ever happen, and trust that he will make up for our faults, for our neglects, for our failures in love.

DOROTHY DAY, *LOAVES AND FISHES*

R ecently, we received the wonderful news that our dear friend Dorothy Day has been officially declared "Servant of God." This is largely thanks to the petition, labor, and devotion of Cardinal John O'Connor, who professed great admiration for Dorothy and her work.

Now that the two are together in heaven, I imagine them engaged in deep conversation while becoming one in the worship of the Triune God. Right after Dorothy died, I wrote to friends of the monastery the following letter. It was meant to convey, in all monastic simplicity, our deep feelings for her and the very particular relationship we shared.

In the early evening of November 29, Dorothy Day died peacefully in the Lord at the Maryhouse Catholic Worker House on New York's Lower East Side. The association between Dorothy Day and Our Lady of the Resurrection goes back many years, to the humble beginnings of this monastery, and has remained close ever since. Because of our intimate bond, I feel somehow compelled to remember her in a special way.

The first time I met Dorothy remains fresh in my mind, as though it were yesterday. She was addressing a group of Franciscans on the subject of peace. A friar got up and asked her, "It is fine to be a pacifist when you are not attacked, but what do you do when you are attacked?" She responded, "Our Lord tells us that when we are stricken on one cheek, we must show the other as well." Everyone present laughed, finding such a naive answer incredible. But she was in deadly earnest. She took the Gospel at its word, and the answer to every question for her lay there. Indeed, this first impression of Dorothy has never altered over the years I knew her. People often said that she was either "a fool or a saint." Only God can answer that.

When we first settled in Barrytown, only five miles from the Catholic Worker farm in Tivoli, the farm provided us both food and help. There was a continual exchange between Tivoli and Barrytown. Both Dorothy and other Catholic Workers came for retreats at our small monastery. Many times we shared lunch or an evening meal. At the table with Dorothy were Helene Iswolsky, Deane Mowrer, and Emily Coleman, the goddaughter of Jaques and Raissa Maritain.

In 1975, when Helene Iswolsky was dying in Cold Spring, Dorothy came to stay with us for about six weeks and helped to care for Helene in a loving way. It was a beautiful sight to see their love for one another, their close friendship. Whenever Dorothy entered the room, Helene's eyes would light up. Dorothy used to say, "Helene and I are true sisters." Dorothy spent many hours and days praying at Helene's bed with both us and Marguerite Tjader. In fact, it was Helene's death that allowed us to have Dorothy stay during Christmas of 1975. On December 26, after the Byzantine funeral, Dorothy and a small group of friends accompanied Helene to her resting place in Tivoli.

During her last visit with us, Dorothy took a chain from her neck which contained a reliquary of Saint Anthony. She told me she'd had it for many years and that every time a Catholic Worker was sick, she'd leave it with them. "Now I want you to have it, for I don't know what will happen to it when I die," she said. She was detached from everything. Today, this relic is among others in the sanctuary of our Chapel. During Christmas 1975, she also gave us some of her paperback books, which she had inscribed. In *Loaves and Fishes* she wrote: "Pray for me that I learn to see Christ in all who come to us. Alas, for my failures in charity." In *Pilgrimages* she wrote: "For Brother Victor, on whose prayers we depend for stability on our pilgrimage. Love and gratitude. In *The Long Loneliness* she wrote: "From a humble intruder into the library of Our Lady of the Resurrection." These books, as well as other memories, remain a treasure in our hearts.

In her last letter to us, she stressed how similar she found the monastic life to the ideals of the Catholic Worker. "Remain small, poor, and simple," she often said to me. Her funeral was attended by multitudes of people. It was a symbol of the impact her life had upon others. For all of those who loved her, we know we have an advocate in heaven. *Requiescat in pace.*

— NOVEMBER 30 —

Advent

"See the Lord coming from afar; his splendor fills the earth."

ANTIPHON OF THE FIRST SUNDAY OF ADVENT

Once again, we arrive at the threshold of Advent and are invited by the Church to enter into the mystery that Advent represents. During these quiet four weeks that precede Christmas, the Church asks us to think, live, and pray in the spirit of Advent. But what is the mystery of Advent all about? Advent is that unique and privileged time of preparation for the great event commemorated at Christmas: the Incarnation of the Son of God and his humble appearance among us as a tiny child. Jesus is commonly announced by the prophets of old in the words of the Liturgy as "he who would one day come from afar and save his people, filling the whole earth with the splendor of his light and glory."

Advent helps us relive this mystery. Jesus, as we know, has already come; but Advent helps us to realize that he comes again, anew, each day, to each one of us. Furthermore, he promises to return at the end of time, when he will gather all of us into the eternal embrace of the Father.

Today, we keep the memory of the Apostle Andrew, "the first called." He was the one who initially encountered the Lord and then brought the good tidings to his older brother, Peter, with the words: "We have found the Messiah" (Jn 1:41). As we enter the quiet days of Advent, we can ask Saint Andrew to inspire us and give us the incentive to strive in word and deed in our own search for the Messiah.